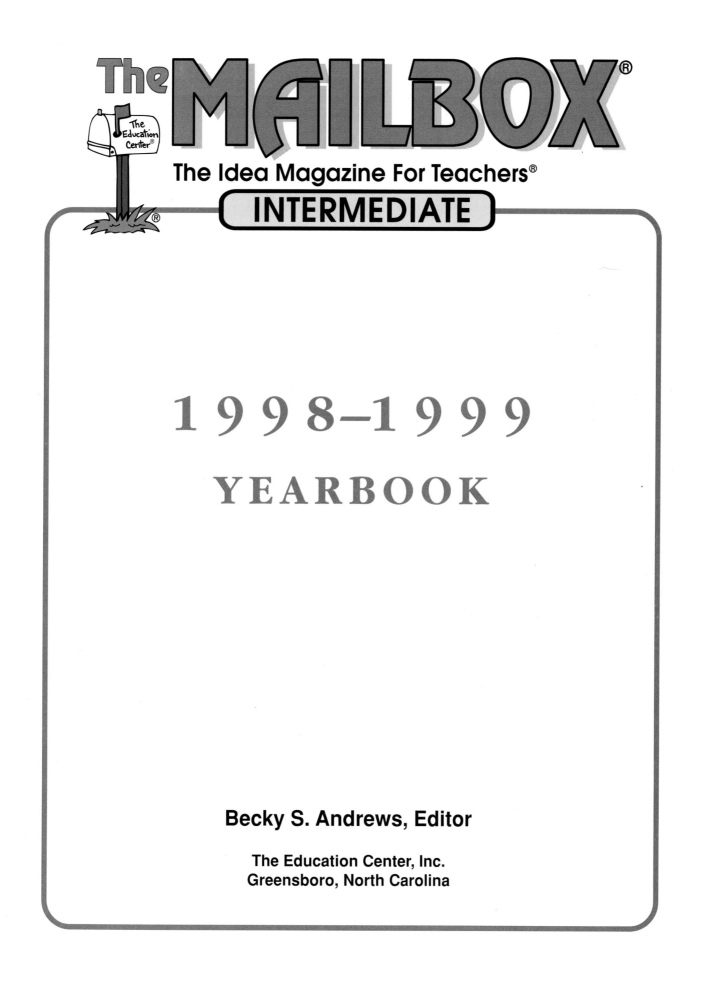

The MAILBOX®

The Idea Magazine For Teachers®

INTERMEDIATE

1998–1999

YEARBOOK

Becky S. Andrews, Editor

The Education Center, Inc.
Greensboro, North Carolina

The Mailbox® 1998–1999 Intermediate Yearbook

Editor In Chief: Margaret Michel
Magazine Director: Karen P. Shelton
Editorial Administrative Director: Stephen Levy
Senior Editor: Becky S. Andrews
Associate Editor: Peggy W. Hambright
Contributing Editors: Irving P. Crump, Rusty Fischer, Thad H. McLaurin, Cindy Mondello
Copy Editors: Karen Brewer Grossman, Karen L. Huffman, Tracy Johnson, Scott Lyons, Debbie Shoffner, Gina Sutphin
Staff Artists: Cathy Spangler Bruce, Pam Crane, Teresa R. Davidson, Nick Greenwood, Clevell Harris, Susan Hodnett, Sheila Krill, Rob Mayworth, Kimberly Richard, Rebecca Saunders, Barry Slate, Donna K. Teal, Jennifer L. Tipton
Editorial Assistants: Terrie Head, Laura Slaughter, Wendy Svartz, Karen White
Librarian: Elizabeth A. Findley

ISBN 1-56234-296-7
ISSN 1088-5552

Printed in the United States of America.

The Education Center, Inc.
P.O. Box 9753
Greensboro, NC 27429-0753

Look for *The Mailbox*® 1999–2000 Intermediate Yearbook in the summer of 2000. The Education Center, Inc., is the publisher of *The Mailbox*®, *Teacher's Helper*®, *The Mailbox*® BOOKBAG®, *Learning*®, and *The Mailbox*® *Teacher* magazines, as well as other fine products. Look for these wherever quality teacher materials are sold, or call 1-800-714-7991.

Contents

TEACHER RESOURCE IDEAS

Color Me Organized!

Ideas To Help Students Become Better Organized

Have lost papers, cluttered desks, and missed assignments got you singing the "My students are so disorganized" blues? Then change your tune with these terrific ideas from our readers on how to help intermediate kids become better organized.

Organizing Student Supplies

School Supply Labels

Get students organized before the new school year even begins! Every summer I send home a letter to the parents of my new students. The letter includes a list of supplies the child will need for the upcoming school year. I also enclose several sheets on which I've typed (with the help of my computer's word-processing program) the student's name in different sizes and fonts. I ask that the parent affix these labels to all of the student's school supplies before the child brings them to school. With this simple idea, my students don't come to school with supplies they won't need or without necessary items. Plus I've eliminated the problem of lost pencils, assignment pads, and glue sticks! *Janice Barger—Gr. 5 Gifted, Moon Lake Elementary, New Port Richey, FL*

EXTRA DESK

The Storage Desk

One obstacle to organization is a cluttered desk. But what does a student do when he has more supplies than storage space? Solve this problem by arranging student desks in groups of four. Place an extra empty desk at the end of each arrangement as shown. Encourage students to use this desk as an overflow area for supplies that don't fit in their own desks. Bye-bye, clutter! *Phyllis Ellett—Grs. 3–4 Multiage, Earl Hanson Elementary, Rock Island, IL*

Have Binder, Will Travel!

A three-ring binder = an organizational lifesaver? It does in my class! Each of my students has a two-inch binder that holds these items:

- a pocket folder (labeled "Home Folder") for storing notes to parents and completed homework
- an assignment notebook
- a spiral notebook
- notebook paper
- a pencil case containing two pencils, a red pen, and a highlighter

No matter where my students are, they're always prepared. Have binder, will travel! *Pat Murray—Grs. 3–4, St. Rita of Cascia School, Aurora, IL*

Organizing Handouts And Graded Papers

Color-Coded Handouts

"Where do I put this?" Yes, it's the desperate call of the disorganized student! At the start of the new school year, display a poster as shown. Throughout the year, copy all handouts on paper that coordinates with the poster's color code (for example, duplicate all math sheets on green paper, all language handouts on blue paper, etc.). When a student receives a handout, he'll know to file it in his notebook with other papers of that color. Toward the end of the school year, start duplicating all handouts on white paper (with the appropriate subject noted at the top) to get students ready for the increased responsibilities of the next grade level. *Liane Kabatoff— Gr. 5, Lochearn School, Rocky Mountain House, Alberta, Canada*

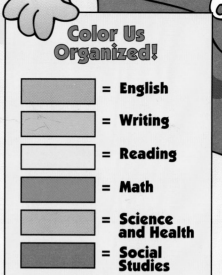

Color Us Organized!

	= **English**
	= **Writing**
	= **Reading**
	= **Math**
	= **Science and Health**
	= **Social Studies**

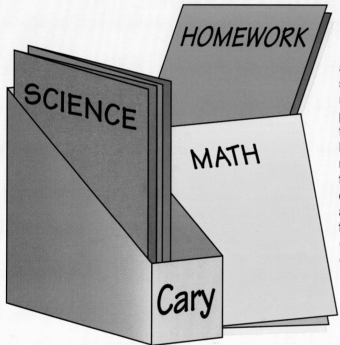

SCIENCE

HOMEWORK

MATH

Cary

Flashy Folders

Looking for a plan that will help students organize handouts and graded papers in a flash? For each subject, provide every student with a different-colored folder (one with brads), coordinating the folder colors with those of your textbooks. Also provide a folder for homework. Have each student label each folder with its subject; then have her store her folders in a labeled magazine box that is kept on a bookshelf in the classroom. Before distributing handouts to students, hole-punch them so students can file them in the appropriate folders. At the end of the day, have students take any folders out of their desks and return them to their magazine boxes. Send the homework folders home. Organized students in a flash! *Michelle R. Pratt— Gr. 4, James Morris School, Morris, CT and Melaine Brown— Gr. 6, Western Middle School, Elon College, NC*

Assignment Folders With A Twist

Looking for a way to organize each student's graded assignments? Try this system that also involves students in valuable critical thinking about their work. Label an assignment folder for each child; then place seven colorful sheets of paper in each folder, labeled as follows:

- Best Work
- Assignment That Allowed Personal Expression
- Most Difficult Assignment
- Most Enjoyable Assignment
- Least Difficult Assignment
- Most Creative Assignment
- Assignment That Taught Me The Most

Give each child another folder to keep in his desk for storing graded work. Every few weeks have each student choose a paper from his desk folder to put behind each of the labeled sheets in his assignment folder, replacing older papers as desired. This system teaches students to keep up with graded work and critically evaluate their assignments. Plus it's a great tool for parent/teacher conferences. *Linda Flores, Melanie Haynes, and Sandra Tilford—Gr. 6, Southwest RV Elementary, Washburn, MO*

BEST WORK

MOST DIFFICULT ASSIGNMENT

Accordion File To The Rescue!

Most of my students keep a separate folder for each subject. Invariably, a more disorganized child brings the wrong folder to class, leaving the correct one in her homeroom. Or she frequently files a paper in the wrong folder. To help, I ask the child's parents to purchase a letter-sized accordion file with about eight to ten sections. I label each section with a different subject, in the order of the student's class schedule. Now the child can store all of her papers in one convenient place, with only *one* file to keep up with. Even some of my organized students have started using this tip! *Terry Castoria—Gr. 5, Frank Defino Central School, Marlboro, NJ*

Graded-Papers Notebook

Dreaming of a way to keep graded work from becoming an organizational nightmare? Each of my students has a binder notebook with a labeled divider for each subject. In the front of each subject section, the student keeps a table of contents page (see the illustration). I hole-punch three holes in all graded papers before distributing them. Each student places her papers in the correct sections of her notebook. She then lists each assignment and its grade in the appropriate table of contents. When it's time to study for a test, the student has all of her graded work at her fingertips. She also has a list of her grades, so there's never a surprise when report-card time rolls around. Each student takes her notebook home—along with a parent signature form—each Friday for parents to see. *Shannon Hillis—Gr. 5, La Maddalena American School, Italy*

Clean Out Your Folder!

How can you keep students' desks from becoming the black hole of old papers? At the beginning of the school year, give each child a pocket folder for each subject. Have the student label each folder with his name and decorate it with illustrations for that subject. As you work on a particular unit, direct students to file all unit handouts in their appropriate subject folder. At the conclusion of each unit, have a clean-out-your-folder session during which students organize and staple together their papers for that topic. Send the papers home so students can start the next unit with empty folders. *Maddy Smith—Grs. 3–5, St. Joseph School, Louisville, KY*

Subject:	Math	
#	Assignment Name	Grade
1	Fraction Action Sheet	B+
2	p. 32, 1–15	A

Saving Papers For Quizzes

To motivate my students to stay organized, I give each child a special folder for each new unit. All papers and assignments for that unit are kept in the folder. At the end of the unit, each student is allowed to use the papers in his folder as a reference during the final test. If a student has carefully filed papers in his folder, he earns this special advantage during testing. Motivation made simple! *Phyllis Ellett—Grs. 3–4 Multiage, Earl Hanson Elementary, Rock Island, IL*

Homework Organization Ideas

Homework Calendar

Instead of assigning homework at the end of each day, I assign it on Monday for the entire week. To help my students plan ahead and complete their assignments by Friday's due date, I created a weekly homework calendar. I attached bulletin-board border around a colorful sheet of poster board. Then I divided the board into four labeled sections as shown. Finally I laminated the calendar. On Mondays I use an overhead marker to write each day's homework assignments on the board. Each student copies the assignments onto his own duplicated calendar (made to resemble the larger one). If a student has been absent, he can easily check the homework calendar when he returns to class. On Friday afternoons, I simply wipe the board clean so it's ready for Monday. *Bonnie Gibson—Gr. 5, Kyrene Monte Vista School, Tempe, AZ*

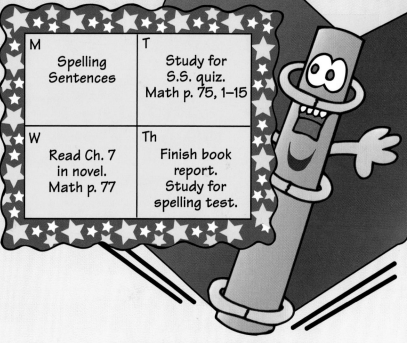

M	T
Spelling Sentences	Study for S.S. quiz. Math p. 75, 1–15
W	**Th**
Read Ch. 7 in novel. Math p. 77	Finish book report. Study for spelling test.

Homework Folder

Do your students have difficulty keeping track of homework? At the beginning of the school year, give each student a pocket folder labeled "Homework." Also give the student two labels: "To Do" and "Done." Have the student affix the "To Do" label to the left pocket and the other label to the right pocket. At the end of the day, have each child deposit assignments that need to be completed in the left pocket of his folder. At home, the student places completed homework in the right pocket. No more homework headaches! *Lisa Carlson, Bear Path Elementary, Hamden, CT*

The "Due Today" Board

With a simple display, I give my more forgetful students the extra help they need to remember assignments. Near my homework assignment chart, I mount a small bulletin board titled "Due Today." Each morning I staple an extra copy of a homework assignment that is due that day to the board. Students can refer to this display whenever they need a reminder of work that is due. *Nancy Hatalsky—Gr. 4, Hiller Elementary, Madison Heights, MI*

Cereal-Box Homework Caddies

Having a place to deposit assignments can really help the disorganized student stay on top of his work. Have each student bring an empty cereal box to school. Help students cut their boxes as shown; then provide glue and colorful paper so students can cover the boxes. Assign each child a number to write on the front of his box. Then staple the boxes together side by side. Each morning have students deposit homework assignments in their cereal-box caddies. As you check the boxes each morning, you'll notice in a snap, crackle, and pop who's come to school unprepared! *Jennifer Kendt—Grs. 4–5, Ohio School, North Tonawanda, NY*

Friday Folders

Does getting notes home to parents seem like a Herculean task? It is to some students! Help them out with this easy organizational system. Label a file folder for each child; then have her title the folder "Friday Folder" and decorate its cover with markers or crayons. Each week fill the folders with weekly progress reports, news and notes, lunch menus, and other information that parents need. Send the folders home each Friday to be signed and returned on Monday. *Maddy Smith—Grs. 3–5, St. Joseph School, Louisville, KY*

No Lockers? No Problem!

Without individual lockers or a coatroom, the storage area in our classroom (which included a shelved rack and a few coat hooks) always seemed to be littered with fallen backpacks, lunchboxes, and coats. To help organize our belongings, I brought coat hangers from home. Now students keep their coats on hangers hanging from the shelved rack. They put their backpacks on the coat hooks, and their hats, gloves, and lunches on the shelf. No more tripping over lunchboxes and backpacks! *Phyllis Ellett—Grs. 3–4 Multiage, Earl Hanson Elementary, Rock Island, IL*

Personal Helper

To help a child who's having difficulty with organization, I ask a classmate to be his personal helper. The helper reminds the child of classwork assigned while he was out of the room for a pull-out activity. He also makes sure that his charge has packed all necessary books and assignments in his bookbag at the end of the day. After about six weeks, the disorganized student usually no longer needs help. I thank the helper with an inexpensive gift. *Vera Stillman, Menlo Park School, Edison, NJ*

Pam Crane

Check It Off!

Opening Period
- [ ] Lunch count
- [ ] Turn in money or notes
- [ ] Hand in homework
- [ ] Fill out homework book
- [ ] Put up homework sticker
- [ ] Complete morning work on board

Closing Period
- [ ] Put books for homework in bookbag
- [ ] Check to see if I have homework book
- [ ] Do class job
- [ ] Clean desk and surrounding area
- [ ] Check in/out library books
- [ ]

Daily Checklist

Do you live and die by your "To Do" list? To help my students learn to use this handy organizational tool, I attach a checklist to each child's desk with clear adhesive paper. (Use the reproducible on page 11 to create a checklist for your class.) The list reminds students of all the tasks they must do during our class's "Opening Period" and "Closing Period" each day. During each of these times, each student must go down the checklist and put an imaginary check next to each completed task on the list. The responsibility for remembering these daily tasks is now on the shoulders of my students, not mine. *Loraine Moore—Gr. 4, Pearl Preparatory School, El Monte, CA*

Check It Off!

Opening Period

Closing Period

☐ ☐ ☐ ☐ ☐ ☐ ☐   ☐ ☐ ☐ ☐ ☐ ☐

©The Education Center, Inc. • THE MAILBOX® • Intermediate • Aug/Sept 1998

Check It Off!

Opening Period

Closing Period

☐ ☐ ☐ ☐ ☐ ☐ ☐   ☐ ☐ ☐ ☐ ☐ ☐

©The Education Center, Inc. • THE MAILBOX® • Intermediate • Aug/Sept 1998

Note To The Teacher: Use with "Daily Checklist" on page 10. Before duplicating, fill in the two checklists with the tasks you want students to complete at the start and close of each day.

Different As Night And Day

Ideas For Meeting The Needs Of A Diverse Class

If you're like most teachers, your class is a marvelously mixed bag. With that variety comes the challenge of reaching students with a wide range of special needs and abilities. Meet the needs of your diverse class with these bright ideas for teaching kids who are as different as night and day!

Class Treasure Chest

Teachers aren't the only ones who can be daunted by a diverse class. Often students focus on their differences while ignoring their commonalities. To highlight similarities, cover an old study carrel or project board with colorful paper. Label the carrel "Treasure Chest"; then set it up on a table. Challenge each student to bring in an item related to a current unit and place it in the Treasure Chest. For example, during an oceans unit have students bring in seashells, postcards from coastal sites, and other items collected from trips to the shore. Discuss with students the similarities in their treasures and ocean experiences. Build collections for other units, pointing out the common experiences illustrated by each collection. The more students see how much they're alike, the easier it will be for them to appreciate their differences! *Phyllis Ellett— Grs. 3–4 Multiage, Earl Hanson Elementary, Rock Island, IL*

Book Clubs To The Rescue!

"I'm planning a unit on space, but some of my students can't read the books I have on that topic!" Sound familiar? Solve this problem with the help of book clubs. Use the bonus points collected with your students' orders to purchase different levels of reading material for the units you teach. (Also check with teachers in grade levels above and below yours to see if you can order appropriate books from their book clubs.) With this idea, you'll soon have multileveled book collections on the topics you teach. *Cheryl Radley, Lake Norman Elementary, Mooresville, NC*

Take-Home Study Guide

Help lower-achieving students find success with this simple study technique. After you've finished a lesson and made an assignment, briefly meet one-on-one with each underachieving child. Ask the student to restate in his own words the steps needed to complete the assignment. As the child talks, transcribe his instructions onto paper, pointing out any corrections and drawing illustrations as needed. Have the student take the paper home to use as a study guide (and to provide his parent with an easy-to-read explanation of the assignment). Use the same paper for the entire week so the student can see how each day's lesson builds on the previous one. *Cara N. Duffy— Gr. 5, Sweetser Elementary, Sweetser, IN*

Partner Up!

Here's a simple way to make sure even your most disorganized students don't miss important information. Divide the class into pairs, placing each student who struggles with organizational skills with a capable classmate. Write the following responsibilities on the board and discuss them with the class:

- Check my partner's assignment pad at the end of the day. Initial the sheet to verify that it is correct.
- Make my partner aware of assignments or announcements he may have missed if absent from the class for any reason.

At the end of several weeks, hold a "Partner Powwow" during which students share about the partnering experience. Then assign new pairs and let the partnerships begin! *Faye K. Wells, Marion City Elementary, Buena Vista, GA*

Good job, Sunny!

Beg And Borrow

If several of your students are working below grade level, send out an SOS to friends who are primary grade teachers! Beg or borrow manipulatives, games, workbooks, and other appropriate items to use with your less able students. You may find your colleague is willing to swap her materials for higher-level ones for her more capable students. *Teresa Williams—Gr. 4, Silver Creek School, Hope, British Columbia, Canada*

Desk Clusters

Turn your students' desks into a handy teaching tool! Cluster most of your desks in groups of two, three, or four. Assign students to clusters with others who are working on similar material. Keep a couple of single desks for students who need time to work alone. During certain periods of the day, allow students to move to different desk clusters to get help from classmates while you teach small groups. With this plan, students have easy access to their peers without interrupting your instructional sessions. *Phyllis Ellett—Grs. 3–4 Multiage, Earl Hanson Elementary, Rock Island, IL*

May I borrow this board game?

1 2 3 4 5 6 7 8 9 10 NUMBER TREK

Pam Crane

Let's Do Lunch!

Get to know the students whose needs you're trying to meet with this deliciously simple idea! Duplicate a calendar page for the upcoming month. Mount the calendar on a small poster labeled "Let's Do Lunch!" Write one to three students' names in each school day's box. Then use the calendar to invite students to lunch privately with you on their scheduled day. As you learn more about each other, it will be easier for you and your students to work together to meet their special needs. *Lisa Groenendyk—Gr. 4, Pella Christian Grade School, Pella, IA*

Bulletin-Board Centers

Want to work with students needing extra help, but don't know what to do with the rest of the class? Turn your bulletin boards into activity centers that provide plenty of independent work for your more capable students. Post brainteasers, math challenges, writing ideas, or out-of-the-ordinary research topics on your bulletin boards. Direct students to head to the bulletin boards during those times when you need to work uninterruptedly with small groups. *Lisa Groenendyk—Gr. 4*

Spotting Our Strengths

Shine the spotlight on your students' strengths with a bright display! Have each student cut out a large circle from construction paper and label the top of it with his name. Laminate the circles and post them on a bulletin board titled "Spotting Our Strengths!" When a student becomes aware of a classmate's strength, have him use a wipe-off marker to write a short sentence about it on that child's spot. After everyone's spot has been filled, wipe the circles clean and start over. Not only will your students become aware of each other's strengths, but they'll also discover whom to ask for help with class projects or assignments! *adapted from an idea by Faye K. Wells, Marion City Elementary, Buena Vista, GA*

Week:_____
Goal:_____
_____
Mon.
Tues.
Wed.
Thurs.
Fri.

Personal Goals Booklet

Challenge students to set their own weekly learning goals with this easy-to-manage activity. Give each student one copy of the chart shown for every week in the grading period. Have the student staple his copies between two sheets of construction paper; then have him decorate the front cover of the resulting booklet. Every Monday have the student write a personal goal at the top of a booklet page. Before each day's dismissal, have the child write a sentence on his chart describing how he did on his goal. On Friday provide time for students to share their progress on their goals. *adapted from an idea by Debbie Erickson, Waterloo Elementary, Waterloo, WI*

Reinforcement Folders

Meeting the individual needs of your students is just a folder away with this easy idea! Label a file folder for each student; then place the folders in a file box. Each day place a couple of reproducible activities—ones that provide reinforcement of a needed skill and can be completed independently—in each child's folder. When a student completes an activity, have him put it back in his folder for you to evaluate later. *Elaine Kaplan—Grs. 3 & 4, Laurel Plains School, New City, NY*

Tutor Time

Wishing you could clone yourself so you could reach every student who needs one-on-one help? When there doesn't seem to be enough of you to go around, periodically schedule a "tutor time" session. During this period, pair each struggling student with a capable classmate who can "reteach" the skill to him. Everyone wins with this activity: the tutor reinforces her own skills by helping a classmate, while the previously confused child gets the help he needs. *Kirsten Sasaki—Gr. 6, Copiague Middle School, Long Island, NY*

Give 'Em Options!

Time to assign a book report or another big project? Instead of giving everyone the same assignment, offer students options so they can find a way to complete the assignment within their abilities. Duplicate a list of five to ten project options, making sure to include activities that accommodate the students' different learning styles and talents. Your students will experience greater success—plus you won't have to face the drudgery of grading 30 identical projects! *Phyllis Ellett—Grs. 3–4 Multiage, Earl Hanson Elementary, Rock Island, IL*

Partner Up!

Here's a simple way to make sure even your most disorganized students don't miss important information. Divide the class into pairs, placing each student who struggles with organizational skills with a capable classmate. Write the following responsibilities on the board and discuss them with the class:

- Check my partner's assignment pad at the end of the day. Initial the sheet to verify that it is correct.
- Make my partner aware of assignments or announcements he may have missed if absent from the class for any reason.

At the end of several weeks, hold a "Partner Powwow" during which students share about the partnering experience. Then assign new pairs and let the partnerships begin! *Faye K. Wells, Marion City Elementary, Buena Vista, GA*

Beg And Borrow

If several of your students are working below grade level, send out an SOS to friends who are primary grade teachers! Beg or borrow manipulatives, games, workbooks, and other appropriate items to use with your less able students. You may find your colleague is willing to swap her materials for higher-level ones for her more capable students. *Teresa Williams—Gr. 4, Silver Creek School, Hope, British Columbia, Canada*

Desk Clusters

Turn your students' desks into a handy teaching tool! Cluster most of your desks in groups of two, three, or four. Assign students to clusters with others who are working on similar material. Keep a couple of single desks for students who need time to work alone. During certain periods of the day, allow students to move to different desk clusters to get help from classmates while you teach small groups. With this plan, students have easy access to their peers without interrupting your instructional sessions. *Phyllis Ellett—Grs. 3–4 Multiage, Earl Hanson Elementary, Rock Island, IL*

Pam Crane

Let's Do Lunch!

Get to know the students whose needs you're trying to meet with this deliciously simple idea! Duplicate a calendar page for the upcoming month. Mount the calendar on a small poster labeled "Let's Do Lunch!" Write one to three students' names in each school day's box. Then use the calendar to invite students to lunch privately with you on their scheduled day. As you learn more about each other, it will be easier for you and your students to work together to meet their special needs. *Lisa Groenendyk—Gr. 4, Pella Christian Grade School, Pella, IA*

Bulletin-Board Centers

Want to work with students needing extra help, but don't know what to do with the rest of the class? Turn your bulletin boards into activity centers that provide plenty of independent work for your more capable students. Post brainteasers, math challenges, writing ideas, or out-of-the-ordinary research topics on your bulletin boards. Direct students to head to the bulletin boards during those times when you need to work uninterruptedly with small groups. *Lisa Groenendyk—Gr. 4*

Spotting Our Strengths

Shine the spotlight on your students' strengths with a bright display! Have each student cut out a large circle from construction paper and label the top of it with his name. Laminate the circles and post them on a bulletin board titled "Spotting Our Strengths!" When a student becomes aware of a classmate's strength, have him use a wipe-off marker to write a short sentence about it on that child's spot. After everyone's spot has been filled, wipe the circles clean and start over. Not only will your students become aware of each other's strengths, but they'll also discover whom to ask for help with class projects or assignments! *adapted from an idea by Faye K. Wells, Marion City Elementary, Buena Vista, GA*

STACEY

Stacey is a great editor!

Week:_____ Goal:_____ _____
Mon.
Tues.
Wed.
Thurs.
Fri.

Personal Goals Booklet

Challenge students to set their own weekly learning goals with this easy-to-manage activity. Give each student one copy of the chart shown for every week in the grading period. Have the student staple his copies between two sheets of construction paper; then have him decorate the front cover of the resulting booklet. Every Monday have the student write a personal goal at the top of a booklet page. Before each day's dismissal, have the child write a sentence on his chart describing how he did on his goal. On Friday provide time for students to share their progress on their goals. *adapted from an idea by Debbie Erickson, Waterloo Elementary, Waterloo, WI*

Reinforcement Folders

Meeting the individual needs of your students is just a folder away with this easy idea! Label a file folder for each student; then place the folders in a file box. Each day place a couple of reproducible activities—ones that provide reinforcement of a needed skill and can be completed independently—in each child's folder. When a student completes an activity, have him put it back in his folder for you to evaluate later. *Elaine Kaplan—Grs. 3 & 4, Laurel Plains School, New City, NY*

Tutor Time

Wishing you could clone yourself so you could reach every student who needs one-on-one help? When there doesn't seem to be enough of you to go around, periodically schedule a "tutor time" session. During this period, pair each struggling student with a capable classmate who can "reteach" the skill to him. Everyone wins with this activity: the tutor reinforces her own skills by helping a classmate, while the previously confused child gets the help he needs. *Kirsten Sasaki—Gr. 6, Copiague Middle School, Long Island, NY*

Hope I helped clear up your confusion, Starry!

Thanks, Moon!

Give 'Em Options!

Time to assign a book report or another big project? Instead of giving everyone the same assignment, offer students options so they can find a way to complete the assignment within their abilities. Duplicate a list of five to ten project options, making sure to include activities that accommodate the students' different learning styles and talents. Your students will experience greater success—plus you won't have to face the drudgery of grading 30 identical projects! *Phyllis Ellett—Grs. 3–4 Multiage, Earl Hanson Elementary, Rock Island, IL*

Beating The Test-Taking Blues

Do standardized tests have your kids singing the test-taking blues? Help students deal with testing stress and anxiety with the following teacher-tested tips from our readers. Then say "Bye-bye!" to those ol' test-taking blues!

Basketball Review

Have a ball preparing for standardized testing with this fun review game! Set up an over-the-door Nerf® basketball goal in your classroom. Divide students into two teams. Label two containers with each team's name; then have each student write his name on a slip of paper and place it in the appropriate container.

To play, pull out one name from Team One's container and ask that player a review question. If he answers correctly, let the student try to shoot the Nerf® ball into the basket for two points. If he answers incorrectly or misses the shot, no points are scored. Keep playing until each student plays or all questions are asked. The team with the most points wins. *Libby L. Davis—Gr. 4, Wateree Elementary, Lugoff, SC*

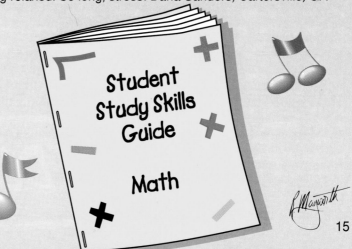

Confidence Boosters

To boost your students' confidence before a test, surprise them with the following treats. Give each student a sparkling new pencil that has a positive message written on it, such as "I'm proud of you!" or "You can do it!" Attach to each pencil a homework coupon that the student can use in place of one future homework assignment. *Lori Brandman—Gr. 5, Shallowford Falls Elementary, Marietta, GA*

Because of all your hard work and effort during testing, you can redeem this coupon in place of a future homework assignment.

YOU CAN DO IT

The Stress Chain

Help students say "So long!" to test stress with this super tip. A few days before the test, give each student two ten-inch strips of colorful construction paper. On each strip, have the student write a worry that she has about the upcoming test. Use tape to link all of the students' strips together to make a large paper chain. Hang the chain outside your classroom door. Then announce to students that the chain is holding all of their stress outside so that they can enter the room on test day feeling relaxed. So long, stress! *Dana Sanders, Cartersville, GA*

Study Skills Guide

Tame your students' anxiety about standardized testing with this activity. Develop a brief study skills guide that contains advice about reading directions and looking for key words in each area to be tested (for example, math words and phrases, such as *product, sum, remainder, in all, find the total,* and *find the difference*). Give each student a copy of the guide; then review it daily the week before the test. With this simple tip, students are sure to enter testing situations better prepared and more confident. *Vera Stillman, Edison, NJ*

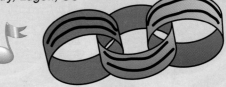

Student Study Skills Guide

Math

Breakfast Of Champions

A hungry stomach makes for a long and difficult test. Be sure your students are fueled up on test day with a variety of breakfast foods. Work with your school cafeteria manager or parents to provide a quick and convenient breakfast that can be served right in the classroom each morning of standardized testing. For example, one morning serve banana-bread squares and milk. The next morning serve juice and breakfast bars. Once your students are fueled up, they'll be ready to hit the test-taking road! *Debbie Erickson—Multi-age, Waterloo Elementary, Waterloo, WI*

Brain Food

Try giving your students a little brain food to motivate them, generate strong thinking skills, and squelch any growling tummies. Ask parent volunteers to donate the following items:

1 box of Cheerios®
1 box of lowfat granola cereal
1 box of Chex® cereal (wheat, corn, or rice)
1 jar of peanuts
1 box of raisins
1 bag of mini chocolate chips
small cups (two for each student)
napkins
juice

Mix together the cereals, peanuts, raisins, and chocolate chips in a large bowl or container. Give each student a cupful of brain food, a napkin, and a cup of juice. This easy-to-make, nutritious snack will help ease stress as well as prepare students for the test.

For another tasty treat, place a few sugar-free candies in a baby-food jar for each student. Label the jars "Test Vitamins" and give to the students before the test. Caution each student not to eat all of her vitamins before the test, but to save some to boost her thinking cells after the brain-draining test. *Adapted from an idea by Heidi Tschetter—Grs. 3–4, Leota Christian School, Leota, MN*

I can feel my brain getting stronger!

Buddy-Boosting Name Tents

Before standardized testing, give each child in your class a boost of self-confidence with this great idea. Pair up your students. Instruct one student to tell his partner the positive qualities and talents he admires about her. After a few minutes, have the partners switch roles. Next give each student a 6" x 8" piece of tagboard and markers or crayons. Instruct him to fold his tagboard in half lengthwise, then write his partner's first name on one side of the resulting tent. Next have the student write words and phrases and/or draw illustrations that symbolize the good qualities he shared earlier about his partner. During testing have each student display his name tent on the corner of his desk as a reminder of the special person he is. *Debbie Erickson—Multi-age*

Athletic   Smart
DUNCAN
Kind   Creative

BULLETIN BOARDS

Bulletin Boards ....

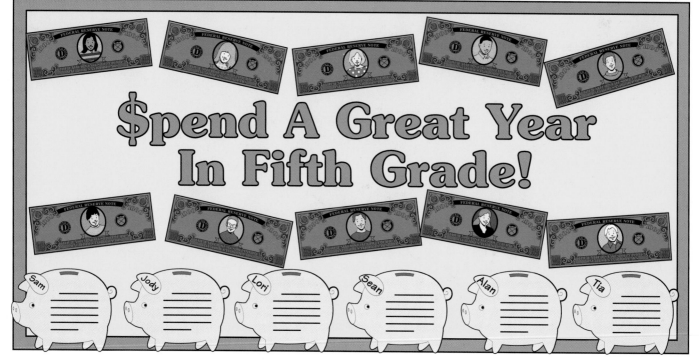

Let your new students know they can bank on a great year! For each child, duplicate the bill pattern on page 30 on green paper. Cut out the center oval; then tape a photo of the new student behind it and post as shown. Add a border of pink paper piggy banks (pattern on page 30) on which students have written paragraphs describing their hopes for the school year or how they'd spend $1,000.

Karen Maresca—Gr. 6, St. Vincent de Paul School, Stirling, NJ

Set aside a spot to share everyone's good news with this idea! Label and display a six-inch paper circle for each student as shown. Encourage students to share their good news—awards, newspaper clippings, birth announcements, photos, etc.—by stapling them onto their spots. Periodically remove old spots and replace them with new ones.

Pat Twohey—Gr. 4, Old County Road School, Smithfield, RI

Look Out! Great Year Ahead!

S.S. Libby
S.S. Eric
S.S. Diana
S.S. Dustin
S.S. Carla
S.S. Ramona
S.S. Trey
S.S. Paolo
S.S. Robert
S.S. Akila
S.S. Jason

Post a lighthouse on a background of light and dark blue paper as shown. Add beams of light with yellow chalk. Have each student fold up and glue down the bottom inch or two of a white paper triangle. After labeling and coloring the boat's bottom as shown, have the student draw a vertical line on the sail and label it with words to describe himself. Have students use the words later in descriptive paragraphs about themselves.

adapted from an idea by Colleen Dabney—Grs. 6–7, Williamsburg Christian Academy, Williamsburg, VA

Brush up self-esteem with this group good-work display! Post simple easel, paintbrush, and palette cutouts as shown. Each week display papers selected by members of one student group. Accent each paper with a cut-out paint splotch labeled with the student's name. On Monday feature a different group's work on the display. Also use this idea to showcase honor roll students, your school's extracurricular activities, or other items of interest.

adapted from an idea by Libby Stanley and
   Dayna Sullivan
Browning Springs Middle School
Madisonville, KY

"Easel-ly" Our Best!

Bulletin Boards ....

Count the importance of Halloween safety with this eye-catching display. Enlarge the pattern on page 31 for several students to color. Have each student create a mock treat bucket from orange and black paper. Then have him use a fine-tipped black marker to write a safety tip (such as "Get parents to inspect candy before you eat it") on the bucket. Display the buckets as shown.

"Tie-mely" expressions of thanks are what this board is all about! Send a note home requesting donations of old ties. Have students work together to create the turkey, stuffing newspaper behind a piece of burlap, felt, or paper for the body. Arrange the ties and display students' writings about thankfulness or Thanksgiving as shown.

Marilyn Davison—Grs. 4–5, River Oaks School, Monroe, LA

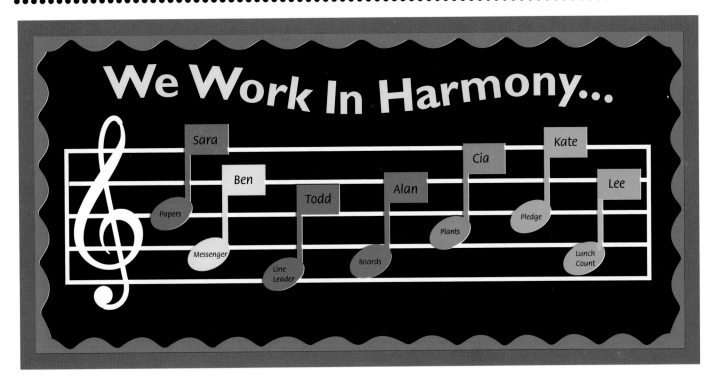

Harmonious helping abounds with this class helpers board! Use chalk to draw a music staff and clef sign on black background paper. Label a note cutout with each job. Laminate the notes; then assign jobs by writing students' names on them with a wipe-off marker. Each week allow new helpers to rearrange the notes' placement. A different melody will always be playing!

Rebecca R. Amsel—Gr. 4, Yeshiva Shaarei Tzion, Piscataway, NJ

Celebrate National Children's Book Week with this bulletin board that alerts students to prepare for book talks. Mount a paper telephone on the board as shown. Use a black marker to add the phone's details and draw the transmission lines. Give each child a pager pattern from page 31 to decorate with his name and the title and author of the book he's just read. Post several pagers on the board. Explain that students whose pagers have been posted have one week to prepare a brief book talk and a written summary. As students present their book talks, remove the pagers from the board, tape them to the tops of their summaries, and reposition them around the perimeter of the board. Change the pagers on the board each week until everyone has had a turn.

Rusty Fischer
Cocoa Beach, FL

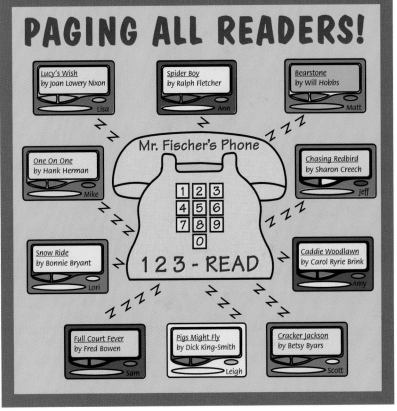

Bulletin Boards ....

Deck the halls with this student-made display that sharpens research skills! Give each student an unlined index card. Have the student choose a country's flag to research; then have him illustrate the flag on his card. Arrange the flags in the shape of a holiday tree. Have students add shiny foil stars to the background for a finishing touch.

Julia Alarie—Gr. 6, Essex Middle School, Essex, VT

It's the Hanukkah season—a perfect time to promote teamwork with this bright display! Have students trace their hands on bright blue and white paper. After cutting out the tracings, have students outline the cutouts in glitter and arrange them to make a giant menorah as shown. Add cut-out flames; then glow with pride at the shining results of your group effort!

Michelle Kasmiske—Gr. 4, Monroe Elementary, Janesville, WI

Get It Together This Year
By Using

T	E	A	M	W	O	R	K
Trying your best.	Each person accepting responsibility.	Always staying on task.	Managing your time.	Willingness to cooperate.	Organizing your time and work.	Reaching the goals set.	Keeping the noise level low.

Welcome the new year with a display that encourages teamwork! Duplicate eight copies of page 32. Write a letter from the word *TEAMWORK* on each pattern; then cut out the patterns and distribute one to each of eight groups. Have each group create a cut-out head, tape it to the pattern, and then color the pattern. Display the projects as shown. Add steps for accomplishing teamwork—each beginning with one of the word's letters—as handy reminders.

Patty Hamilton, Harbor Creek Youth Service, Erie, PA

If students are motivated to do their best, chalk it up to this easy display! First prepare a supply of seasonal cutouts, such as mittens for January, hearts for February, etc. Cover a bulletin board with black paper. Then let students use white chalk to decorate the board with phrases that describe their best work. Each time a student receives an exemplary grade, let him write his name and grade on a cutout and add it to the display as shown. When there's no more room for cutouts, celebrate with a class party. Then prepare a new set of cutouts and start again!

Teresa DeWeese—Gr. 5
James Lewis Elementary
Blue Springs, MO

Chalk It Up To Excellence!

Great A+ WOW!
Fantastic! Beautiful!
Creative! Way to go!
Magnificent!
Great! Good thinking!

Bulletin Boards ....

Pour on the Valentine's Day spirit with this heartfelt display! Staple a large heart cutout as shown on the board. Duplicate the heart patterns on page 33 onto pink paper (one heart per child). Have each student choose a favorite assignment and staple it onto red construction paper; then have him fill out his heart pattern with reasons for his choice. Display the hearts with your students' papers.

Lisa LeFiles, Eastbrook Elementary, Winter Park, FL

Tip your hat to great books with this reading motivation display! Have students read fiction books independently; then have each child complete a copy of the book-review form on page 33. Next have each student create the hat she mentioned on her form using scrap paper and other art materials. Post the hats and forms on a bulletin board that will cause more than a few heads to turn!

Colleen Dabney—Grs. 6–7, Williamsburg Christian Academy, Williamsburg, VA

Even non-Irish eyes are sure to smile at this nifty science display! In March provide time for students to research the human eye. Then have each child label a cut-out shamrock with a fact about the eye. Post the cutouts with photos of your smiling students as shown. Vary this idea by having students find facts about Ireland or any of the human body's five senses.

Melissa A. McMullen—Gr. 5, Saint Patrick School, Newry, PA

Help starstruck students sharpen their letter-writing skills with an out-of-this-world display! Ask your media specialist for reference books that list the addresses of popular entertainers, sports teams, and other famous folks. Select several addresses; then write each one on an envelope to post on a board that is decorated as shown. Encourage each student to choose an address and write a letter. If desired, provide stamped envelopes in which students can mail their letters.

Colleen Dabney—Grs. 6–7, Williamsburg Christian Academy, Williamsburg, VA

Bulletin Boards ....

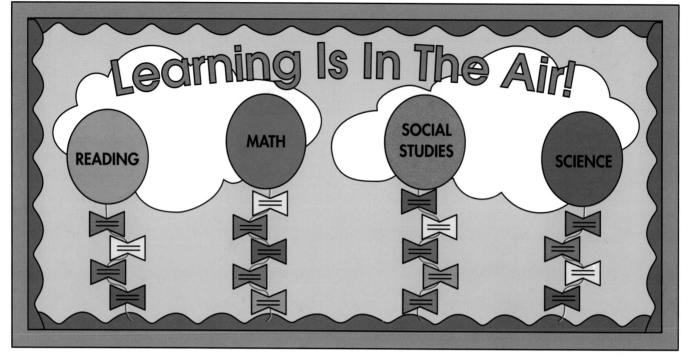

Help students find real-life applications of what they've learned with this high-flyin' idea! Display four balloon cutouts as shown. Tape a length of yarn to each cutout. When a student comes across a newspaper or magazine article, a television news report, or another item related to a topic recently studied (for example, a vocabulary word or a mixed numeral), have him describe the item on a small cut-out bow. Then have him tape the bow to the appropriate balloon's string.

Miriam Krauss—Grs. 4 & 5, Beth Jacob Day School, Brooklyn, NY

Let the fun shine with this sunshiny poetry display! Purchase a class supply of bright yellow picnic plates (or spray-paint white paper ones). Have each child trace around her hands several times on yellow paper; then have her cut out the tracings and glue them around the rim of a plate to create a sun. Finally have her write a poem about having fun in the springtime sun and glue it in the center of the plate. Better grab those sunglasses!

Heidi Graves—Gr. 4
Wateree Elementary
Lugoff, SC

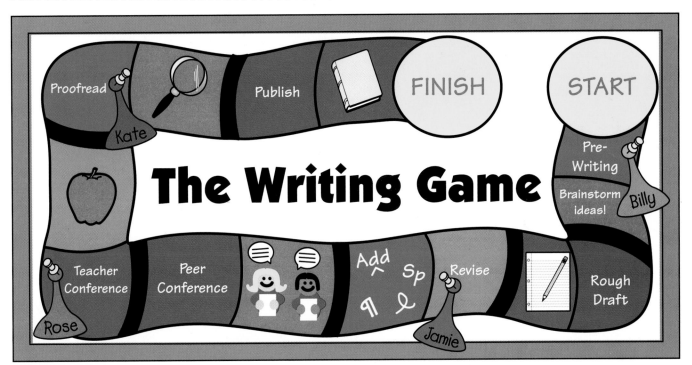

Keep track of students' progress on writing projects with this fun display! Draw and label a simple game-board on a paper-covered board as shown. Also duplicate, cut out, and label a game pawn (pattern on page 34) for each student. As a child works on a writing piece, have her pin her pawn to the display to show where she is in the writing process. Point out to students that, just like in a board game, a writer may have to move her pawn back a few spaces as she works.

Kimberly Feldman—Gr. 6, Salt Brook Elementary, New Providence, NJ

Fishin' for a way to hook your students on math? Give each child a copy of the pattern on page 34. Have him write a math problem on his fish with a fine-tipped black marker; then have him color and cut out his fish, and staple it on the board. Next have each student write his problem's answer on a cut-out bubble. Scatter the bubbles around the display; then challenge students to match each fish with its bubble.

Sora Miriam Zucker—Gr. 5, Beth Jacob Day School, Brooklyn, NY

Bulletin Boards ....

Reflect on a super year with this sunny display! Duplicate a class supply of page 35 on construction paper. Have each student cut out his pattern and label its frames with favorite school year memories. Then have him stick a white file-folder label (cut in half) to the left lens and label it with his name. On the right lens, have him tape a small drawing of himself. Use the display again in August with the title "Reflections Of Last Year's Class."

Traci Baker—Gr. 4, Brassfield Elementary, Bixby, OK

Re-create the excitement of Times Square with this "apple-lutely" terrific countdown display! Write your current grade level on a cut-out apple and the grade to which your students will graduate on a star cutout. Next label a strip of bulletin-board paper as shown. Staple the strip and star to the board. Then attach the apple at the strip's top with a pushpin. Have students add curly streamers and colorful confetti as a finishing touch. Each day let a student lower the apple one space. Five...four...three...two...one...school's out!

Dana Stone Sanders
Kingston Elementary
Cartersville, GA

Top tropical trees with tons of trivia during your next rain forest unit! Staple seven paper trunks labeled as shown to the board. Copy a large supply of leaves on green paper for students to cut out and place in a basket near the display. During the unit, have students label the leaves with facts they've learned and staple them atop the appropriate trunks. *(For more rain forest ideas, see pages 164–171.)*

Simone Lepine—Gr. 5, Gillette Road Middle School, North Syracuse, NY

Encourage summer reading with this delightful deep-sea display! Enlarge, color, and cut out the octopus pattern on page 36, cutting slits where indicated. Have each student write a brief review of a favorite book on an index card. Place eight cards in the octopus's arms (changing them weekly). Have each student list his classmates' recommendations on a copy of the form on page 36. Then add to the display students' drawings of scenes from the books.

Diane Hasler—Gr. 5, North Daviess Intermediate, Plainville, IN

Patterns
Use with the bulletin board on page 18.

FEDERAL RESERVE NOTE

THE FEDERAL RESERVE

D

THE UNITED STATES OF AMERICA
ONE THOUSAND DOLLARS

Patterns

Use with the bulletin boards on pages 20 and 21.

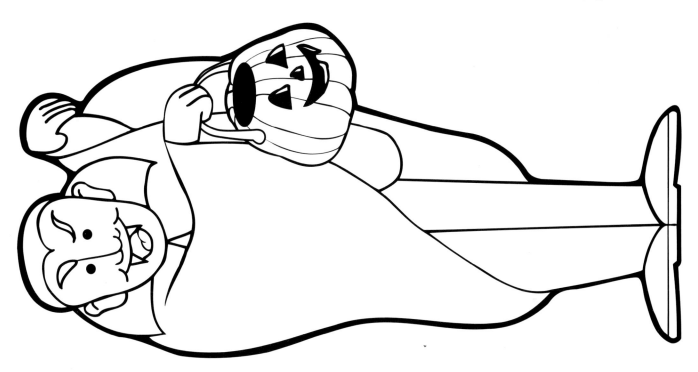

Pattern

Use with the bulletin board on page 23.

Name:

I can tell that I poured my heart into this assignment because _____

_____

_____

_____

_____

_____

_____

_____

I can tell that I poured my heart into this assignment because _____

Name:

_____

_____

_____

_____

_____

_____

_____

_____

©The Education Center, Inc. • *THE MAILBOX®* • *Intermediate* • Feb/Mar 1999

Hats Off To A Great Book!

Name: _____

Book: _____

Author: _____

Summary of plot: _____

_____

Character I take my hat off to (most admire): _____

Hat that best represents this person: _____

Reason for choosing this hat: _____

I take my hat off to this book because _____

©The Education Center, Inc. • *THE MAILBOX®* • *Intermediate* • Feb/Mar 1999

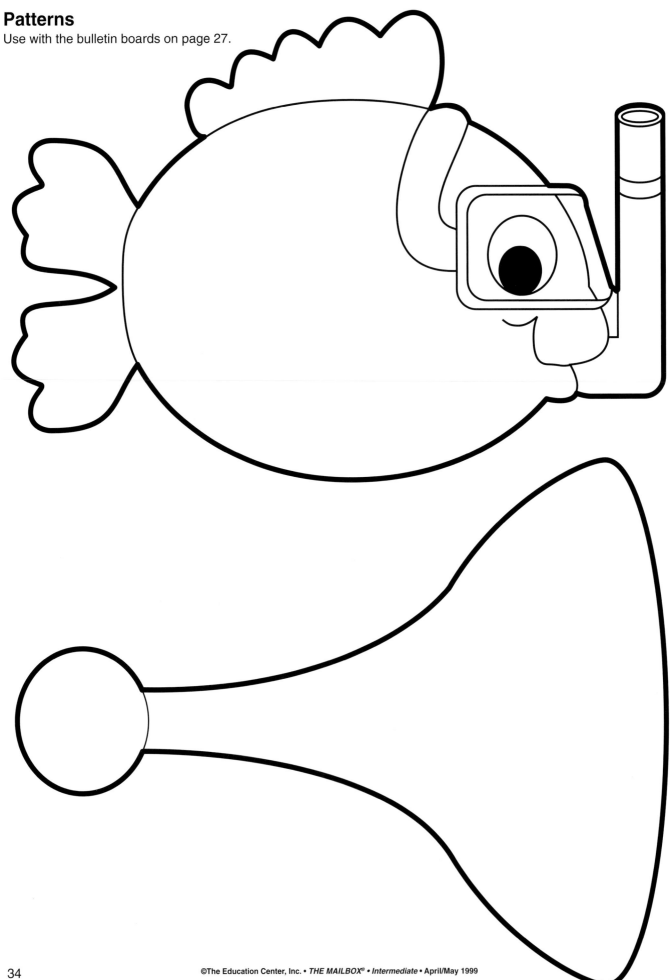

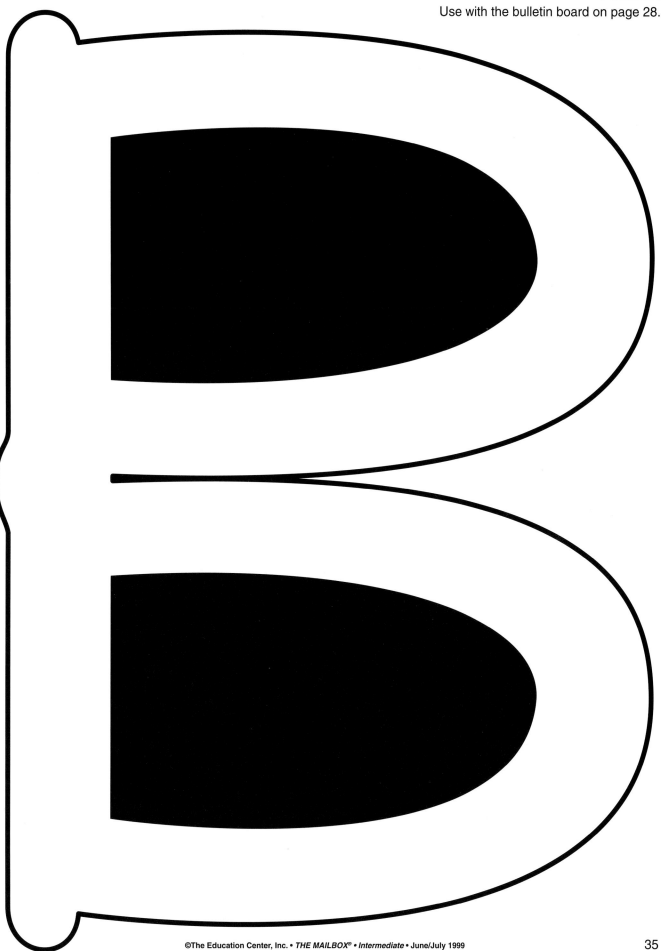

Pattern And Form

Use with the bulletin board on page 29.

Wrap Your Arms Around These Good Books!

This booklist belongs to

_____

Ten books recommended by my classmates that I'd like to read:

1. _____
2. _____
3. _____
4. _____
5. _____
6. _____
7. _____
8. _____
9. _____
10. _____

Other Great Books To Grab!
- *The Castle In The Attic* by Elizabeth Winthrop
- *The Ballad Of Lucy Whipple* by Karen Cushman
- *The View From Saturday* by E. L. Konigsburg
- *There's A Boy In The Girls' Bathroom* by Louis Sachar
- *Knights Of The Kitchen Table* by Jon Scieszka
- *Turn Homeward, Hannalee* by Patricia Beatty
- *Ella Enchanted* by Gail Carson Levine
- *Redwall* by Brian Jacques
- *The Wolves Of Willoughby Chase* by Joan Aiken
- *Poppy* by Avi
- *The Missing 'Gator Of Gumbo Limbo: An Ecological Mystery* by Jean Craighead George
- *Trouble River* by Betsy Byars

ART ACROSS THE CURRICULUM

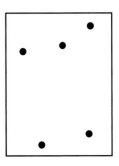

Materials for each student:
1 classified newspaper section, cut to 9" x 12"
tissue paper in different colors
small container of liquid starch
1 wide paintbrush
scrap paper
1 black crayon

Steps:

1. Tear the tissue paper into medium-sized pieces.
2. Paint the newspaper with liquid starch.
3. Lay one piece of tissue paper at a time on the starch-covered newspaper. Cover the tissue paper with a coat of starch.
4. Repeat Step 3 with the remaining tissue paper, overlapping the pieces. Leave the outer edges of the newspaper uncovered.
5. Let the paper dry overnight.
6. The next day choose an action verb from the chart paper. On a scrap piece of paper, draw a stick figure doing that action by connecting just five dots (see the illustrations). Use one dot for the head and the other four dots for the hands and feet. Remember to draw lines for the elbows and knees.
7. Draw your action figure on the dried paper with black crayon.
8. Label your work with the action verb.

Step 6

Language Arts: Action-Verb Figures

Follow up a lesson on action verbs with this two-day project that all but screams with action! Have students brainstorm action verbs for you to list on chart paper. Direct each student to use the materials and steps at the right to illustrate one of the words. Then watch as your classroom literally comes to life!

Science: 3-D Habitats

Complement a study of animal habitats with a crowd-pleasing project that's textured and three-dimensional. If desired have each student write a poem to attach to his artwork before displaying it.

Materials for each student:
1 sheet of white construction paper
several white paper towels
glue
colored markers or tempera paint and a paintbrush
pencil

Steps:

1. With the pencil, draw a picture on the white paper of an animal in its habitat.
2. Fill in the picture with paper-towel pieces that have been torn, cut, twisted, or braided.
3. Glue the paper-towel pieces in place.
4. Color the picture with markers or paint.

Math: More Than Mirror Images

Combine symmetry with a review of geometric shapes and patterns for an eye-catching project that can't be missed!

Materials for each student:
two 9" x 12" sheets of aluminum foil
one 9" x 12" piece of poster board
two 9" x 12" sheets of colorful construction paper
scissors

glue
1 small index card
clear tape
hole puncher
length of string

Steps:
1. Glue the aluminum foil to both sides of the poster board.
2. Cut one sheet of construction paper in half on the diagonal.
3. Cut a repeating pattern of geometric shapes along the center edge of one half of the construction paper. Flip over the cut-out pieces as shown.
4. Glue Section A on one side of the poster board as shown. Glue the cut-out pieces in place to create a mirror image.
5. Repeat Steps 2–4 with the second sheet of construction paper, gluing the cutouts on the other side of the poster board.
6. Describe one repeating pattern on one side of the index card and the other pattern on the flip side.
7. Tape the index card to the bottom edge of your artwork so that the descriptions match the patterns.
8. Punch a hole at the top of your creation and tie the string through it for hanging.

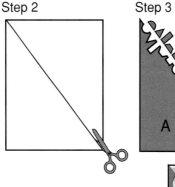

Step 2

Step 3

A

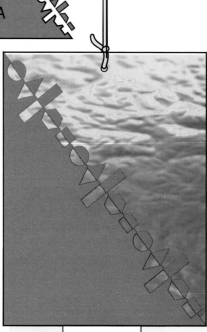

Social Studies: Hopi Pueblos

Celebrate Native American Day (the last Friday in September) with chalk rubbings that creatively depict the homes of Hopi Indians.

Materials for each student:
two 12" x 18" sheets of white construction paper
scissors
5 pieces of chalk: black, brown, orange, yellow, blue
3 tissues

(Color brown.)
(Color orange.)
(Color yellow.)

Steps:
1. Cut one sheet of construction paper into three stencils as shown.
2. Color one stencil with brown chalk, one with orange chalk, and one with yellow chalk.
3. Match the straight edge of the brown stencil with the top edge of the remaining sheet of construction paper. Use a tissue to rub the brown chalk downward toward the bottom edge of the white paper. Discard the brown stencil.
4. Place the orange stencil a few inches below the top edge of the paper. Rub downward with a clean tissue in the same way as before. Discard the orange stencil.
5. Place the yellow stencil a few inches below the top of the orange rubbings and rub to the bottom edge of the paper. Discard the yellow stencil.
6. Use the blue chalk to color the sky. Use the black chalk to add ladders and other details.

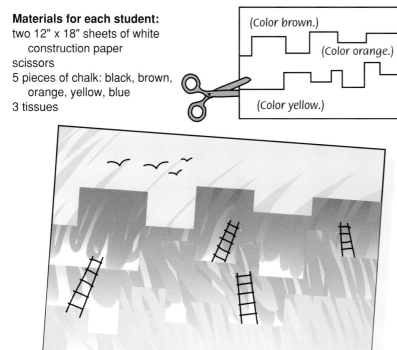

Joan M. Macey—Grs. 4–5
Benjamin Franklin School
Binghamton, NY

39

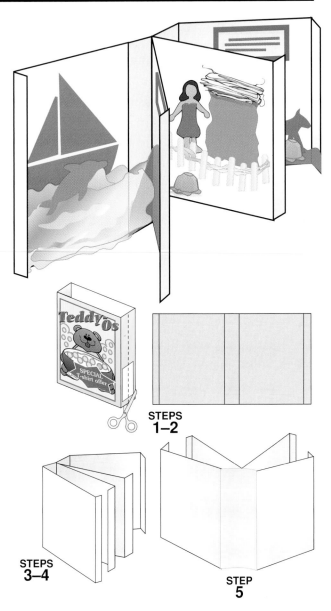

STEPS 1–2

STEPS 3–4

STEP 5

Language Arts: Cereal-Box Diorama

Showcase a book report for National Children's Book Week or anytime with this unique cereal-box diorama. For another can't-be-beaten box project, see "Haunted-House Book Reports" on page 266.

Materials: 2 same-size cereal boxes, scissors, clear tape, glue, 4 sheets of 12" x 24" white construction paper, 6" x 12 1/2" strip of white construction paper, construction-paper scraps in different colors, colored markers, various other art materials

Steps:

1. Cut off the tops and bottoms of both boxes.
2. Vertically cut down the center of one side of each box. Open both boxes so they lie flat.
3. Cover both sides of each box with white construction paper.
4. Refold the boxes and stand them side by side. Tape the boxes together at the spine.
5. Cover the spine with the white paper strip, trimming it to fit if necessary. Glue the strip in place so that it completely covers the taped area.
6. Use construction-paper scraps, glue, and other art materials to create three 3-D scenes from the book (each scene covering two facing panels). Glue short descriptions of the scenes to the panels.
7. Use a marker to write the book's title and author on the spine.
8. Attach a brief summary of the book on the back cover; then illustrate the front cover.

Julie Boyington
Oklahoma City, OK

Science: Camouflage Art

Conclude a study of animal adaptations with an art project that will impress Mother Nature herself! Cut a colorful outdoor scene from an old magazine. Next trace and cut out a butterfly from white paper. Color the butterfly to match the colors in the magazine picture. Then glue the picture and butterfly to a 9" x 12" sheet of construction paper that's also similar in color. Display the project on a bulletin board. Keen eyes won't miss this great work of art, no matter how well it's camouflaged!

Jennifer Balogh-Joiner—Gr. 4
Franklin Elementary
Franklin, NJ

Math: Leaf Tessellations

Integrate math and art by changing a geometric shape into a lively leaf that tessellates!

Materials: scissors, 12" x 18" sheet of white construction paper, tape, pencil, 4" tagboard square, crayons

Steps:

1. Lightly color the tagboard square. This will help you remember to keep the colored side up as you work.
2. Using curved cuts, carefully cut a section from the top of the square as shown.
3. Slide the cut-out section to the bottom of the square. (Do not flip it!) Match the edges; then tape them securely.
4. Cut a section from the right side of the square as shown.
5. Slide the cut-out section to the left side of the square. (Do not flip it!) Match the edges; then tape them securely.
6. Place the tile (leaf) in the center of the white paper; then trace it with a pencil.
7. Slide the tile (up, down, right, or left) and match its edge with the tracing. Make another tracing.
8. Continue sliding and tracing until you cover your paper with shapes.
9. Draw details on each shape, making sure to add the same details to each shape. Color the shapes to complete the project.

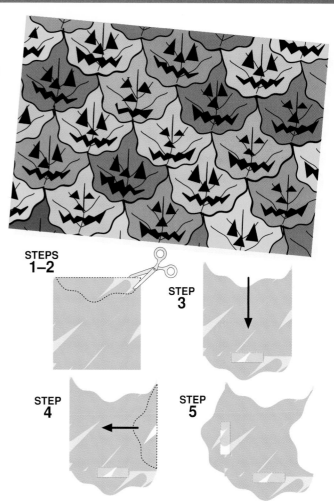

STEPS 1–2

STEP 3

STEP 4

STEP 5

Social Studies: Cave Paintings

Prehistoric artists created pictures from materials found around them. Using pieces of sharp rock, they etched lines that became bison, deer, horses, ibex, and cattle on the walls and ceilings of caves. Using minerals found in the Earth, they often filled in their outlines with red, yellow, brown, black, and sometimes white. At other times they simply outlined their drawings in black. Help students appreciate the art of prehistoric people by having them create their own versions of cave art.

Materials: 9" x 11" sheet of medium-grade sandpaper; pencil; red, yellow, brown, black, and white chalk; 11" x 13" sheet of black construction paper; glue

Steps:

1. Use a pencil to sketch the outline of a bison, a deer, a horse, an ibex, or a cow on the sandpaper.
2. Fill in the outline with colored chalk, blending colors and creating areas of light and dark color.
3. Trace the outline with black chalk.
4. Add simple details as desired; then mount the drawing on black construction paper.

Michelle M. McAuliffe and Marsha W. Black
Greensburg, IN

ART

ACROSS THE CURRICULUM

Writing: **Patriotic Poetry**

Use vivid images evoked by events from the American Revolution—or any other historical period—to get students excited about poetry writing. Have each student write a free-verse poem about the Revolution. Next direct the student to use watercolors to paint a colorful background on a 12" x 18" sheet of white construction paper. As her paper dries, have the student cut silhouette shapes—such as soldiers, fences, cannons, or ships—from black construction paper. Instruct her to glue the silhouettes to her background; then have her use a fine-tipped black pen to copy her poem in the remaining space as shown. Display the completed projects on a classroom bulletin board or in your school's media center.

Debbie Patrick—Gr. 5
Park Forest Elementary
State College, PA

Bombs burst in the early morning sky.
The air filled with billowing smoke.
The meadows were enveloped in fire
As the bombs whistled through the air.
The soldiers never quit.
Determined to win,
They kept on fighting for independence.

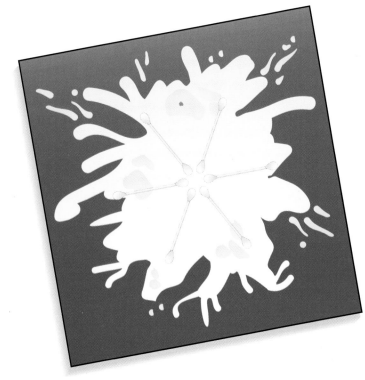

Science: **Full-Blown Snowflakes**

Help students anticipate the first snowfall of the season—and reinforce an important fact about snow—with snowflake designs they can *blow* into shape! Display the dainty snowflakes to make a winter wonderland right in your classroom!

Materials for each student:
a 12-inch square of blue construction paper
6 Q-tips® swabs
glue
drinking straw
small cup filled with equal parts (about 1 tablespoon each) of white tempera paint and water

Steps:
1. Glue the Q-tips® onto the blue paper to make a six-pointed star (to represent a snowflake's six sides). Be sure to leave a space in the center of your paper.
2. Pour the paint mixture into the center space.
3. Use the straw to blow the paint between the Q-tips®, creating a snowflake's shape.
4. Allow the paint to dry.

Carrie L. Ohlms—Gr. 5, Hawthorn Elementary, St. Peters, MO

Math: The "Geome-Tree"

Get set for a geometrically merry Christmas with this holiday tree made from simple geometric figures. Mount a very large, green paper triangle on a bulletin board or wall. Add a brown rectangle for its trunk. Then supply students with compasses, protractors, rulers, scissors, glue, and a variety of art materials for making geometric-shaped ornaments to decorate this class tree. For example, have students use a circle to make a wreath or an angel's head, or use a cone to make an angel's body. Encourage students who are really into the holiday spirit to shape squares, rectangles, or rhombuses into gifts to go under the tree!

Nancy Terrell—Grs. 4–12 Special Education
Jacksonville, FL

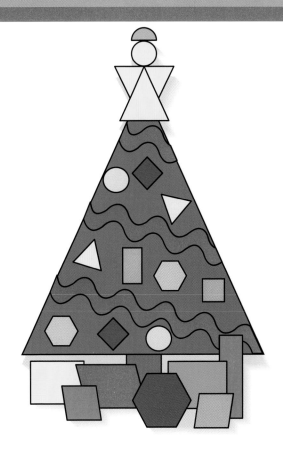

Social Studies: Artificial Stained Glass

Take students back in time with a two-day project that's sure to help them appreciate art from the Middle Ages. Plus you'll wind up with beautiful stained-glass decorations that are just right for the holiday season!

Materials for each student:
1 simple pattern or stencil (commercial or student drawn)
1 transparency
black glue (from a craft store)
7 oz. plastic cups, one for each color of "paint" to be made
white glue
red, blue, green, and yellow food coloring
Q-tips® swabs, one for each plastic cup
optional: one 9" x 12" sheet of black construction paper, scissors, stapler, hole puncher, one 18-inch length of yarn

Steps:
1. Place the transparency over the pattern, centering the design in the middle of the transparency.
2. Use the black glue to trace the pattern onto the transparency. Allow the glue to dry overnight.
3. The next day pour white glue into the plastic cups—one cup for each different color to be made. Add drops of food coloring to each cup of glue, stirring the mixture with a Q-tips® swab. Mix different colors as needed to create the desired hues.
4. Use the Q-tips® swab to spread the colored glue between the spaces of the black outline.
5. Allow the glue to dry overnight.
6. To display, frame the design within a border of black construction paper. Or cut out the design and hang it with yarn threaded through a hole punched at its top.

Abel made a glider to fly to his wife.

Literature: From Novels To Picture Books

Imagine a favorite children's novel transformed into a picture book! That's exactly what happens with this art project that helps students review a recently read book. After reading a novel together, have students brainstorm a sequential list of scenes from the book. Assign each student a different scene to sketch on white paper. After the student completes his sketch, have him use a black Sharpie® marker to outline the scene and write a sentence about it. (Direct the student to place extra paper under his scene to absorb ink that might bleed through.) Then have him paint his scene with watercolors. After the scenes have been painted, laminate them to enhance the colors and add durability. Bind the completed pages together with a large metal ring, or use a bookbinding machine and plastic spirals. What a winning way to review a novel and add student-made books to your classroom library!

Phyllis Hart Pettit—Gr. 4
North Chatham School, Pittsboro, NC

Social Studies: Eagle Mosaic

Add a touch of art to a study of our government, the American Revolution, or national symbols with this patriotic mosaic. Post a color photograph of a bald eagle—our national bird—in a prominent place in your classroom. Then give each student (or small group) the materials listed to create a stunning 3-D project.

Materials for each student:
1 sturdy box lid or piece of cardboard
pencil
a supply of dried great northern beans, black beans,
    yellow split peas, chickpeas
glue
watercolors
paintbrush

Steps:
1. Turn the box lid so that its sides form a frame around the lid's interior.
2. Study the eagle photograph; then sketch the eagle's outline on the inside of the lid.
3. Arrange the beans and peas inside the outline to match the eagle's coloring.
4. Glue the beans and peas in place a small amount at a time.
5. After the glue has dried, paint the background around the eagle with watercolors.

Math: Number-Pattern Puzzlers

Turn your students into math sleuths by having them create dot-to-dot puzzles that are solved by completing number patterns! Supply each child with the materials listed and guide her through the steps below.

Materials for each student:
2 sheets of white duplicating paper
pencil
black marker
tape
colored pencils
optional: glue
optional: yarn

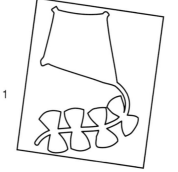

Step 1

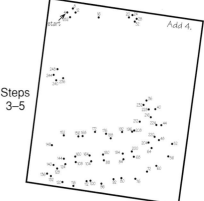

Steps
3–5

Steps:

1. With a pencil, draw a very simple picture of an object on one sheet of white paper. Go over your drawing with a black marker.
2. Tape the drawing to your desktop. Then tape the other piece of white paper over it.
3. Decide on a number pattern to use. Write the name of the pattern at the top of the top sheet of paper.
4. With a pencil, draw a dot somewhere on the picture's outline. Label it with the first number in your pattern and the word "Start" as shown.
5. Make another dot beside the Start dot. Label it with the next number in the pattern. Continue drawing and labeling dots so that when they are connected in the proper sequence, the original picture will appear. Avoid drawing dots so close together that the original picture can easily be seen without connecting them.
6. Remove the dot-to-dot picture from your desktop; then give it to a classmate to solve. Tell him to connect the last dot in the pattern with the Start dot to complete the picture.
7. If the resulting picture does not look like the original, check the numbers in your puzzle. If necessary make corrections; then have the classmate work the puzzle again.
8. When the completed puzzle is returned to you, color it with colored pencils. Glue yarn to the picture's outline if desired.

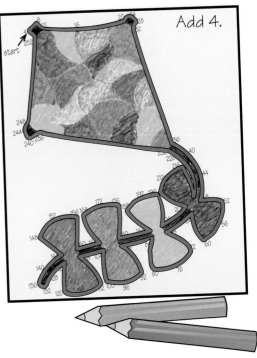

Science: Outer-Space Resists

Crayons can resist this art technique, but your students sure won't be able to! While studying the solar system, ask each child to draw stars, planets, and other heavenly bodies on a sheet of paper. Next ask the student to color his picture heavily with crayons, pressing firmly and filling in the drawing completely. Then have him cover his drawing with black watercolor paint. The resulting picture will look like it's been beamed straight from space! Use this irresistibly simple idea when studying the ocean too.

Sandi Norton—Gr. 4
Valley Springs Elementary
Valley Springs, AR

45

ART ACROSS THE CURRICULUM

Language Arts: Raindrop Rhymes

Grab your umbrellas—and get ready for this downpour of poetry! Review with students that a *couplet* is a two-line stanza that rhymes. Have each student write his own couplet about something getting caught (or being left outside) in a rain shower. Then have him cut out shapes, including one large object, from assorted colors of tissue paper to create a scene that illustrates his couplet. Have the student use a fine-tipped black marker to add details to his cutouts and copy his couplet onto the largest cutout. Next have him fold in half a 24-inch-long sheet of waxed paper. Direct him to open the paper, arrange his cutouts on the lower half, and then fold the upper half down to sand- wich his scene between the two layers. Use a warm iron (set on the lowest setting) to press the waxed paper sheets together until they're sealed. Have the student use a pencil to draw a large raindrop shape around his scene; then have him cut out the shape and punch a hole in the top. After the student has tied yarn through the hole, suspend the project from your classroom ceiling.

Red bird, red bird, you're all alone.
Why, oh why, don't you fly home?

Science: Hurricane Spirals

This unique art project is just what you need to help students understand the counter-clockwise, swirling pattern of hurricanes. First demonstrate the steps at the right, using the resulting design to point out the locations of the eye, the eye wall, and the rainbands. Then put the supplies and directions in a center so that one student at a time can create a satellite shot of her own hurricane! *(Don't miss the severe storms unit on pages 158–163!)*

Materials:
record player with a turntable
1 large Styrofoam® plate per child
various colors of tempera paint
1 paintbrush for each color of paint
scissors
9" x 12" sheet of blue construction paper per child
glue
crayons or markers

Steps:
1. Center the plate over the record holder's knob on the turntable. Push down gently on the plate until the knob makes a hole and holds the plate in place.
2. Dip a paintbrush into one color of paint. Spin the turntable by hand. (Or operate the turntable at 33 1/3 speed.)
3. Touch the paintbrush near the center of the plate. Keeping the turn- table spinning, slowly move the paintbrush in a straight line toward you and the plate's outer edge, creating a spiral pattern.
4. Repeat Steps 2–3, each time using a different color of paint and starting the paintbrush at a different distance away from the center of the plate.
5. Allow the paint to dry. Trim away the plate's rim and glue onto blue paper. Add "Hurricane [your name]" to the paper with a crayon or marker.

Gail Peckumn
Jefferson, IA

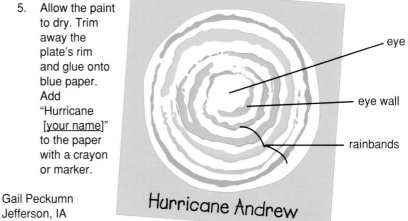

eye

eye wall

rainbands

Hurricane Andrew

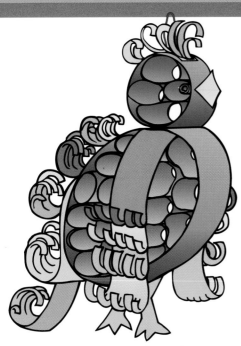

Social Studies:
Tropical-Bird Sculpture

Culminate a study of the rain forest or animal habitats with a three-dimensional art project that will turn your classroom into a tropical aviary!

Materials for each bird:
12" x 18" sheets of construction paper (assorted colors), cut into 3" x 18" strips
stapler
ruler
scissors
glue
18" length of yarn
pencil

To make the head:
1. Staple the ends of one paper strip together to make a small oval.
2. Fill this oval (the head) with about four strips, each rolled into a circle. Staple each circle to the oval and, if desired, to the other circles near it.

To make the body:
1. Staple the ends of two strips together to make a longer strip; then staple the ends of this long strip together to make a large oval.
2. Fill this oval (the body) with rolled and stapled strips as in Step 2 above. Then staple the head to the body.

To make the wings:
1. Staple four strips together on one end. Trim about three inches from the length of the bottom strip, four inches from the strip above it, five inches from the next strip, and six inches from the top strip.
2. Make three-inch cuts lengthwise into the trimmed end of each strip. Curl the end of each strip by rolling it on a pencil.
3. Repeat Steps 1 and 2 for the second wing. Then staple the wings to the bird's sides as shown.

To make the tail:
1. Follow the directions for the wings (Steps 1–2), using six strips instead of four.
2. Staple the tail to the bird's back as shown.

To complete the bird (using scraps from the steps above):
1. Make two head plumes as the wings were made, using two short strips for one and four short, narrow strips for the other. Staple the plumes to the top of the head.
2. Make a mouth by cutting a square, folding it in half to form a triangle, and gluing it to the front of the head along the opened fold.
3. Make the eyes by rolling a short strip into a small circle and gluing it inside a circle at the front of the head.
4. Cut out two legs and feet and glue them to the bottom of the bird's body.
5. Loop the yarn and staple it to the top of the bird's head for hanging.

Bernadine Peterson—Gr. 4, Dodgeland School District, Pardeeville, WI

Math: Fraction Friend

This is one art project that lets students get by with a little help from their friends! Give each student a supply of one-inch squares of colorful construction paper. Have the student arrange the squares on a 12" x 18" sheet of light-colored paper to create the shape of a boy or girl; then have her glue the squares in place with a glue stick. Next have the student use crayons or markers to write her friend's name on the paper and add details, such as facial features, hair, buttons, etc.

Next have the student count the total number of squares she used to make her friend and record that number on her paper; then have her list all the colors she used. Next to each color, have her write the fraction that compares the number of squares of this color to the total number of squares. For example, 8/54 of Fran is brown. Direct the student to check her work by adding the fractions together to see if they equal one whole. Follow up by having each student reduce her pal's fractions to lowest terms or use them in problems for a classmate to solve.

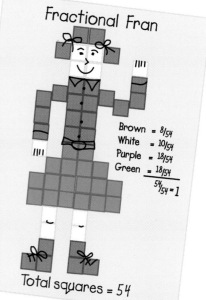

Fractional Fran

Brown = 8/54
White = 10/54
Purple = 18/54
Green = 18/54
—————
54/54 = 1

Total squares = 54

47

ART

ACROSS THE CURRICULUM

Science: Bushy Bromeliads

Turn your classroom into a lush green rain forest—and enhance the thematic unit that begins on page 164—with easy-to-make tropical plants. *Bromeliads* are a group of about 2,000 plant species found mostly in the rain forests of Central and South America. The leaves of this plant form a tank that holds up to ten gallons of water and becomes home sweet home to many animals.

Materials for each student: three 6" x 9" sheets of green bulletin-board paper, pencil, clear tape, scissors, paper scraps in various colors, glue

Steps:
1. Starting at the short end, roll one green sheet into a tube, stopping about two inches from the end. *(Hint: Wrap the paper around a pencil to get started.)*
2. Place the short end of another green sheet on the unrolled part of the first sheet. Roll these sheets together as before. Repeat with the third sheet.
3. Tape the resulting tube at one end.
4. Flatten the untaped end of the tube. With an adult's help, cut halfway down the tube.
5. Flatten the tube again. Have an adult help you cut halfway down two more times, making one cut to the right of the original cut and another to the left.
6. Find the center of the leaves and pull up *gently* so that the bromeliad grows right before your eyes!
7. Glue small cutouts of rain forest animals and water pools to the leaves.

Simone Lepine—Gr. 5
Gillette Road Middle School
North Syracuse, NY

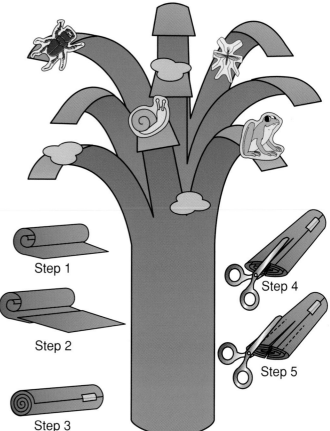

Step 1

Step 2

Step 3

Step 4

Step 5

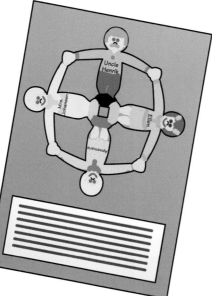

Literature: Paper-Dolls Project

Book characters and fun go hand in hand with this project that takes paper-doll cutting to a higher level! Give each student a white paper square to fold in half diagonally and then in half again. Next direct the student to draw a doll figure on the folded paper as shown, being sure to draw the hands and feet all the way to the folds. Then have him cut out the doll, open up the paper, and use fine-tipped markers to add names and details to the resulting four characters. To complete the project, have the student glue the dolls and a book summary on a sheet of colorful construction paper. What a doll of a project!

LANGUAGE ARTS UNITS

Calling All

Solving The Mystery Of Reading Comprehension

Looking for a way to turn your students into readers who can solve the mystery of reading comprehension? Investigate no further than the following creative activities and reproducibles!

by Simone Lepine

At The Scene Of The Crime

Skill: Setting a purpose for reading

Good reading comprehension is much like a good investigation! A detective first analyzes what she knows and what she wants to find out. Likewise, a good reader has a basic idea of what she is about to read and what she hopes to discover or learn. Whether students are reading a novel, studying the Civil War, or learning about climate or fractions, setting a purpose before reading establishes a foundation on which they can build understanding. Help your students set a purpose for reading any type of material with the reproducible on page 53.

The Focus Of The Investigation

Skill: Comprehension during independent reading

Do you have students who often read an entire chapter in a book—and still have no clue as to what happened? Try the following activities to help students increase comprehension when reading on their own.

Exhibit A: Independent Reading Of Individual Books

Here's an easy way to guarantee that students put some thought behind what they read independently. Give each student several small sticky notes. Have the student read the selection one time. Then have the student read the selection a second time to look for certain evidence—depending on your objectives. When they find the evidence, they are to tag it with sticky notes. For example:

- If students are reading for pleasure, have them tag areas that they particularly enjoyed.
- If you're studying a figure of speech, such as alliteration, have students tag examples of it.
- If students are reading in a subject area, have them tag certain vocabulary words or concepts.

When the student is finished reading, have him write about each piece of tagged evidence in his own detective notebook (a spiral notebook or pad). Use these notebooks during class discussions or when you have conferences with students about their reading.

Exhibit B: Independent Reading Of Class Materials

When orally reading a novel or textbook together in class, you can guide students with questions and reflective comments. But keeping some students focused is more difficult when they have to read these materials independently. Use the reproducible on page 54 to guide students to become independent readers. Make a copy of page 54 and program it with page and paragraph numbers, plus questions to which you want students to respond; then duplicate a class set. Have students read the selection one time. Then have them go back and read the selection again, stopping at certain pages to investigate questions. When students have finished reading, have them share their answers in groups.

Reading Detectives!

Skill: Using context clues

Who says cloze activities have to be boring? They aren't anymore with this game that "clozes" the case on reading comprehension! Select an excerpt from a novel or textbook chapter you are studying. Delete an even number of words from the passage; then list the words and a few extras on the board or on a transparency. Also make a transparency of the excerpt for easy checking. To play the game:

1. Divide students into pairs. Give each pair a die, and one index card for each missing word.
2. Have each pair copy the words on the cards—one word per card.
3. Have each pair shuffle its cards and divide them equally. Then give each pair a copy of the passage.
4. Have each pair read the passage and try to determine the word that goes in the first blank.
5. The student who thinks one of his cards fits that blank lays it on the passage.
6. When every pair has chosen its card, reveal the answer by writing it on your transparency.
7. If the student who placed the card is correct, he rolls the die and notes the number showing as his score.
8. Play continues until all the words needed to complete the passage have been used. The player with the highest score at the end of the game wins.

Picking The Summary Out Of A Lineup

Skill: Summarizing

This cooperative group activity is a great way to sharpen students' summarizing skills. Duplicate four short stories of about the same length. Write a brief summary of each one, without including its title, characters' names, or author. On a single page, write all four summaries. Make a copy of that page for each group of four students. Then cut each page apart and paper-clip the four summaries together. Next:

1. Divide students into groups of four and assign each student one of the four stories to read.
2. After reading his story, have the student write a brief summary of it.
3. When all four students in each group have written their summaries, give them your summaries. Make sure each student has the summary of a story that he *did not* read.
4. Have each student read the summary that you gave him.
5. Next have each student read aloud to his group the summary that he wrote. Each group member listens and decides if the student-written summary matches the teacher-written summary that he has.
6. The student who thinks his teacher summary matches his student summary then reads it aloud, and the group decides if it is indeed a match. The matches are then paper-clipped together.

When the groups are all finished, review the correct answers. Discuss how the summaries they wrote were similar to and different from the ones you wrote.

Taking Basic Drill Sheets Down To The Station

Skill: Varied reading comprehension skills

Do you have more comprehension drill sheets than you'll ever be able to use? Make a reusable, self-teaching reading station with those sheets. Follow these steps:

1. Make two copies of each skill sheet.
2. Fill in the answers on one sheet, adding comments to help students understand any of them.
3. Glue the sheets back-to-back on a piece of construction paper.
4. Number the sheets; then laminate them.
5. Supply the station with wipe-off markers.
6. Post a reminder for students to clean each sheet before returning it to the station.

To motivate students, display a chart that lists the sheet numbers and skills. Have students keep track of the activities they complete.

Interrogating The Suspect

Skill: Vocabulary development

Review the vocabulary from a unit or novel with this game any gumshoe would love! Write each word on an index card. Make enough cards for half of your students. Then make another set of cards with the words' definitions. To play:

1. Divide students into two teams: detectives and suspects.
2. Give a vocabulary card to each detective; give a definition card to each suspect.
3. While the suspects remain seated, the detectives "interrogate" them, trying to find the matching definitions for their words.
4. When a detective has identified her suspect, she "arrests" him (escorts him back to her desk).
5. When all the detectives have identified their suspects (or determined that a suspect has been mistakenly apprehended by another detective), have each pair share its word and definition.
6. Ask the class to determine if each word and definition match.

After every pair has shared, collect the cards, shuffle them, and have the detectives and suspects switch roles.

Classified Information

Skill: Making inferences

Haven't a clue about how to teach inferencing skills? Turn to the classified ads! Lots of information is squeezed into a small space, and much of the reader's understanding depends on making inferences. Cut out ten classified ads that lend themselves to making inferences. Enlarge each ad and glue it onto a sheet of construction paper. Number the sheets and post them along your classroom's walls. As a warm-up activity, share the ad shown and ask students to make inferences about the family who placed the ad. Then divide the class into small groups. Instruct each group to visit and read each ad and make an inference about it. Have a recorder in each group write down the inference. When all the groups are finished, discuss each ad and have the groups share their inferences.

Garage Sale Tons of toddler toys & clothing, rowing machine (brand-new condition), hamster cage (with bedding & food), 100s of 8-track tapes & vinyl records...and much, much more! Sat., Dec. 5, 8:00 A.M.–4:00 P.M.; 508 Spruce St.

The Crime? Writing In Books!

Skill: Locating information

Students will feel downright criminal with this activity! Provide each student with a blank, half-page transparency and a wipe-off marker. Ask each student to bring in an old sock from home. When you're reading a page of text in which you want students to locate information, instruct each child to place his transparency on the page and circle the answer with his marker. Students will love tracking down the answers just so they can "write in their books"! When finished, have students remove the transparencies and clean them with their socks.

Investigative Book Report

Skill: Summarizing a plot

Close the case on plot summaries with the reproducible on page 55. Explain to students that recognizing the plot of a story is like solving a crime: you focus on the facts and events that are important to understanding what happened. Before assigning the page, complete the page with students using a well-known story, such as *Cinderella*.

MARY LESTER

Be A Reading Detective!

Reading is a lot like detective work! Detectives face a lot of questions when they begin a case. By using what they already know—plus what they learn while investigating—detectives can solve a mystery! Become a reading detective with your next reading assignment. Before you begin to read, fill in the information on the clipboards. When you finish reading, see how many of the things that you thought you knew were correct. How many of your questions can you answer now that you've finished reading?

Reading Detective Notes

What I already know:

Reading Detective Notes

Questions I want to answer:

Bonus Box: Begin your own investigation of a famous person whom you would like to know more about. On a sheet of paper, list everything you already know about the person. Then list what you would like to find out. Now investigate, write your findings, and close the case on this mystery!

©The Education Center, Inc. • *THE MAILBOX® • Intermediate • Dec/Jan 1998–99*

Note To The Teacher: See "At The Scene Of The Crime" on page 50. Use this reproducible with any reading assignment: a textbook selection, a novel chapter, a basal story, etc.

Investigate Reading

A good detective asks questions and looks for answers while investigating a mystery. A good reader does the same thing, whether he or she is reading a story, a novel, or a chapter from a textbook.

Below are some questions that you will need to stop and investigate while you're reading. As a reminder, place a piece of scrap paper at each page where you should stop. Listen to your teacher's directions for what you are to do once you have completed this activity.

Investigative File

Stop on page _____, paragraph _____.

Investigate this: _____

_____

Findings: _____

_____

_____

_____

_____

_____

_____

_____

Investigative File

Stop on page _____, paragraph _____.

Investigate this: _____

_____

_____

Findings: _____

_____

_____

_____

_____

_____

_____

Investigative File

Stop on page _____, paragraph _____.

Investigate this: _____

_____

Findings: _____

_____

_____

_____

_____

_____

_____

Investigative File

Stop on page _____, paragraph _____.

Investigate this: _____

_____

_____

Findings: _____

_____

_____

_____

_____

_____

Note To The Teacher: See "Exhibit B…" on page 50 for information on using this activity.

Book 'Em!

Close the case on the book or story you just read by creating detective files! Tell about the plot of your book or story by filling in the blanks of the files. Then cut out the four files, stack them in order, and staple where shown. If you need more room for writing, just make your own files and add them to the report.

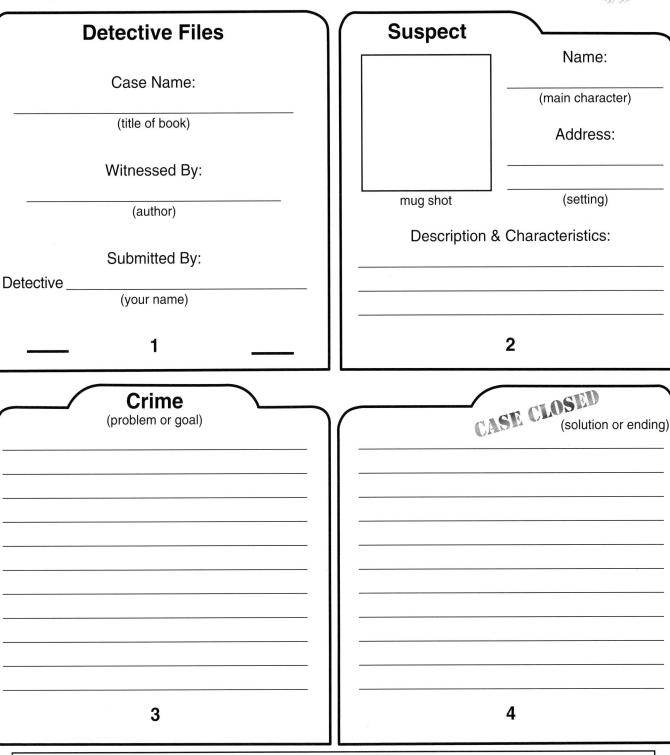

Detective Files

Case Name:

_____
(title of book)

Witnessed By:

_____
(author)

Submitted By:

Detective _____
(your name)

____   **1**   ____

Suspect

[mug shot box]

mug shot

Name:

_____
(main character)

Address:

_____
(setting)

Description & Characteristics:

_____

_____

_____

2

Crime
(problem or goal)

_____

_____

_____

_____

_____

_____

_____

_____

3

CASE CLOSED (solution or ending)

_____

_____

_____

_____

_____

_____

_____

_____

4

Bonus Box: Choose a famous historical figure or someone in the news today. Create a detective file about that person's life, achievements, successes, and failures.

©The Education Center, Inc. • THE MAILBOX® • Intermediate • Dec/Jan 1998–99

Note To The Teacher: Use with "Investigative Book Report" on page 52. Provide students with scissors and a stapler. Have the student draw a picture of the main character for page 2's mug shot above.

Step Right Up To Writing Essays

Take a giant step toward better student essays with the following "shoe-fire" activities and reproducibles— all guaranteed to bring students to their feet!

with ideas by Terry Healy

A Footnote On Essays

An *essay* is a short composition that has one main idea. It may require some research and often contains the writer's personal opinions. A person writing an essay should pick a topic that interests her, she already knows something about, and she has a strong opinion about. There are three basic types of essays:

- *Informational essay:* presents important facts about a subject or teaches a new skill. It's like a report, but is shorter and not as detailed.
- *Persuasive essay:* presents the author's opinion, backed up by believable supporting details. The author tries to convince a reader to agree with his point of view.
- *Personal essay:* shares the writer's thoughts about a fun or serious subject related to his personal life. The goal is to entertain readers or express feelings about a subject.

Using This Unit

The first six activities in this unit are on basic essay-writing skills that pertain to writing any type of essay. You'll also find a list of terrific Internet connections to use when teaching about essay writing. The unit concludes with creative ideas that provide practice on writing each of the three different types of essays.

Essay-Writing Skills

A "Shoe" Fit

Skill: Choosing a topic

Help students learn how to choose an essay topic that's a "shoe" fit with this activity. In advance write each of these topics on two slips of paper: Sports, Friends, Buildings, Food, Clothes, Music, Animals, School, Books, Careers, Family, Movies, Transportation, Computers, Television. Place the slips in a shoebox. After reviewing the three types of essays (see above), explain to students that sometimes a writer chooses a topic that's too broad or too narrow. Write "Holidays" on the board. Ask if this topic is too broad, too narrow, or a good fit for an essay *(too broad)*. Then write "Christmas Sugar Cookies" on the board and repeat the question *(too narrow)*. Finally web the broad topic "Holidays" with the class. Based on the web, help students identify topics that would be good fits for an essay.

Next have each child draw a slip from the shoebox and web its topic on her paper. After the web is complete, have the student remove one shoe and trace her socked foot on colorful paper. Then have her cut out the tracing and label it with three to five good essay topics from her web. Collect these cutouts; then place a small sticker beside each topic that is a good fit for an essay. Post the cutouts on a large piece of bulletin-board paper titled "Topics That Are A 'Shoe' Fit!" Have students refer to this poster whenever they need an essay topic.

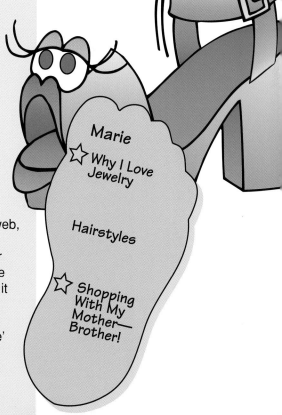

Marie
☆ Why I Love Jewelry

Hairstyles

☆ Shopping With My Mother— Brother!

Don't Forget The Details!

Skill: Developing details

An essay without details is like a television show without color—pretty dull! To help students get the hang of coloring their essays with details, write the following questions on the board: "Who? What? Where? When? How?" Also list the five senses—*touch, taste, hearing, sight,* and *smell*—and the following topics:

- The day you first met your best friend
- Your first day in this class
- When you finally overcame a big fear
- The day you got your pet
- The last time you ate ice cream
- The time you won a hard-fought game

Ask each student to select one of the topics; then have him list details from that experience to answer the five questions on the board. Encourage students to also include sensory details in their answers.

Next give each student a white paper plate. Have the student write his topic in the center of the plate with a marker. Then have him surround his topic with at least five descriptive sentences about it—each written with a different color of fine-tipped marker. After students share their sentences, post the plates on a bulletin board titled "Color Your Essay With Details!"

The Day I Got My Pet.

Pam Crane

A Step Above The Rest

Skill: Planning an essay

Writing an essay that's a step above the rest is a cinch when you've got a good plan! The reproducible on page 61 features a step-by-step outline for planning an essay. Give each student a copy of the page. Go over the outline with your class. Then assign the first essay (for ideas on specific essays to write, see pages 59–60). Duplicate extra copies of the reproducible to have on hand for planning essays throughout your unit.

See Ya At The Top!

Skill: Writing an introductory paragraph

A good writer knows to top off a great essay with an attention-grabbing introduction! Help students learn how to write good introductory paragraphs with this group activity. Collect four or five brief essays or letters to the editors from several popular children's magazines. (Ask your media specialist for help.) Clip a large index card onto each essay to conceal its introductory paragraph; then give one essay to each student group.

Next review with students these guidelines for writing a good introductory paragraph:

- Include a few sentences that tell your point of view, give a reason for the reader to read the essay, and tell the reader the purpose of the essay.
- Grab the reader's attention by opening with a question, a quotation, or a unique statement.

Distribute one essay to each group. Have the group read its essay together, then collaborate to write a four- or five-sentence introduction for it. After each group has finished, let students remove the index cards and compare their introductions to the original ones. Discuss students' reactions and insights as a class. If time allows, let groups put the index cards back on the original essays; then have them swap essays and repeat the exercise.

A Title Match
Skill: Choosing a title

Coming up with a good title for an essay is often difficult for students. Join forces to craft great essay titles with this fun activity. After you've assigned an essay and students have completed the reproducible essay planner on page 61 (see "A Step Above The Rest" on page 57), divide your class into groups. Instruct each group to review its members' planners and suggest titles for each essay. Remind students that a good title not only fits the essay but also grabs the reader's attention. Direct each student to write three of the titles suggested by his group on a Post-it® Brand note, leaving room beneath each title as shown. Then have him attach the note to his planner. Collect the planners and mount them on a bulletin board. Ask students to vote on their favorite title for each planner by drawing a tally mark beneath it on the note. After two days of voting, return each child's planner to him with its note. Then have students start working on their rough drafts. Teamwork + titles = a perfect match for everyone's essay!

Making An Essay Shine!
Skill: Editing a rough draft

Once a rough draft has been written, it's time to polish it up. And the reproducible checklist on page 62 is just the tool for the job! First display a list of proofreading symbols you want students to use when editing their work. After each child has written her essay's rough draft, give her a copy of page 62. Have the student list the names of two other people who will edit her rough draft besides herself (you may wish to stipulate that you be one of the three editors). Then instruct her to complete the page as directed. After the third edit has been completed, have the essay and checklist returned to its original owner so she can begin revisions. After this great polish job, be ready for a finished essay that simply shines!

The Internet Connection

Take a look at these terrific Web sites that feature kids' writings, including examples of essays *(current as of 4/98):*

*   **http://www.kidpub.org:** KidPub, an outstanding publishing site, features student-written work (stories, essays, poems, etc.) that your kids can read, review, and critique. Plus you can hook up your class with key pals to discuss writing ideas and peer-edit each other's work.

*   **http://www.cyberkids.com:** Enjoy *Cyberkids,* a quarterly on-line magazine by kids and for kids. Offering fiction, art, and news articles, this site also includes the "Launchpad" that lists other good children's sites.

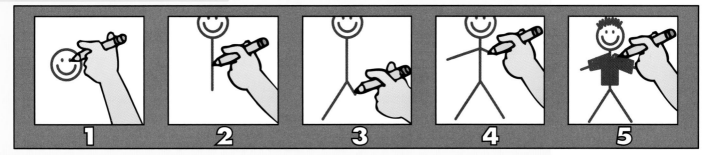

Storyboard Sequencing

Sequencing skills are often put to the test when writing an informational essay. Make sequencing a snap with the help of simple storyboards. Take a series of photographs that show a co-worker or student completing each of the following simple multistep tasks:

- wrapping a gift
- cutting out a paper snowflake
- sharpening a pencil
- tying a shoe
- drawing a stick person on a piece of paper

After the pictures are developed, mount each task's photos in sequence on a strip of poster board. Give a storyboard to each small group of students. Have each child (or each group working collaboratively) write a short informational essay to teach the skill displayed on his group's storyboard. Display the finished essays on a bulletin board with the storyboards. Or place the storyboards in a center for students to work with during free time. The next time a student must write an informational essay, suggest that he draw out a simple storyboard first—before he begins writing—to help organize his thoughts in the proper sequence.

Up Close And Personal

Provide practically painless practice in writing informational essays with this interviewing activity! Ask another teacher in your school (either one on your grade level or of a younger class) to have her class help with this project. Brainstorm with your students a list of interview questions that will help them get to know another child in your partner class. Encourage students to be creative in forming their questions since they will be using the information gathered to write interesting essays. Pare the list down to no more than ten questions, avoiding those that require only a yes/no answer. Provide each of your students with a duplicated copy of the questions.

Next pair each of your kids with a child in your partner class. Have your student interview his partner using the interview questions. After the interviews are over, direct each of your students to use his partner's answers to write an informational essay about his buddy. Bind the finished essays in a book to share with your partner class during a special Up Close And Personal party.

Steppin' Out In Style!

Watch out, Nike®! There will be a new group of shoe designers on the loose after this persuasive-essay activity! Divide your class into small groups. Give each group a large piece of art paper with instructions to design and color the ultimate new shoe for next year's market. After all designs are complete, have each team write a persuasive letter to the CEO of the Feet First Shoe Company. In this letter, have the group convince the executive that its shoe is sure to be the next best-seller. Remind each group to provide facts and details to support its assertion that its shoe is the best. Post the final drafts of the letters with their matching shoe designs on a bulletin board titled "Steppin' Out In Style!"

hidden money pouch

comb pocket

glow-in-the-dark shoestrings

super gripper tread

Time To Take Action!

Call students to action with this real-life writing assignment. Ask, "How would you make this school or community a better place?" Have students brainstorm while you list their ideas on the board; then select one problem as a class and develop a solution. Next display a transparency of the form shown. Explain to students that "Reason" means to list a reason or fact that will persuade someone to use your solution. Using transition words like *First* and *Also* helps the essay flow smoothly from one paragraph to another. Work together to fill out the form. Point out that students could now easily take the information on the form and write a persuasive essay about the problem. (You may want to complete this step with your class.)

For homework, provide each student with a blank copy of the form. Challenge each child to choose a different problem, fill out the form, and then use the form to write a persuasive essay. If appropriate, share completed essays with school or community officials.

Problem: _____

Possible solution: _____

Reason: First _____

Reason: Secondly _____

Reason: Also _____

Conclusion: _____

Writing A Personal Essay

Oh, Bother!

For a personal-writing exercise that's no bother to do, try this kid-pleasin' idea! Brainstorm with students a list of pet peeves that *really* bother them. Then have each student choose one item and write a personal essay expressing his thoughts and feelings about the annoyance. Extend this activity on an upbeat note by having each student write another brief essay called "Learning To Live With My Pet Peeve."

For a math extension, list the topics of the students' essays on the board; then poll the class to find out who else is also annoyed by each pet peeve. Have students graph the class results.

Walking In Your Shoes

Need a topic for a personal essay? Look no farther than your feet! With students, brainstorm a list of personal-essay topics related to shoes on the board. Some suggestions follow:

- My Most Favorite Shoes
- How Shoes Are Like People
- The Day I Got Cold Feet!
- Shoes I'd Like To Fill Someday
- My Time In The Footlights
- Thinking On My Feet

For homework ask each child to bring a shoe (or a picture of a shoe) to class. Also have the student describe in a brief paragraph a shoe-related topic on which he'd like to write a personal essay.

The next day have each student share his shoe and paragraph with the class. Provide time for you and the student's classmates to give feedback on his topic. Does it appear to be a comfortable fit for a personal essay, or does it need to be "resized"? After this sharing period, have each child write a personal essay about his topic. Display the essays and shoes on a table in your classroom or media center.

Name _____

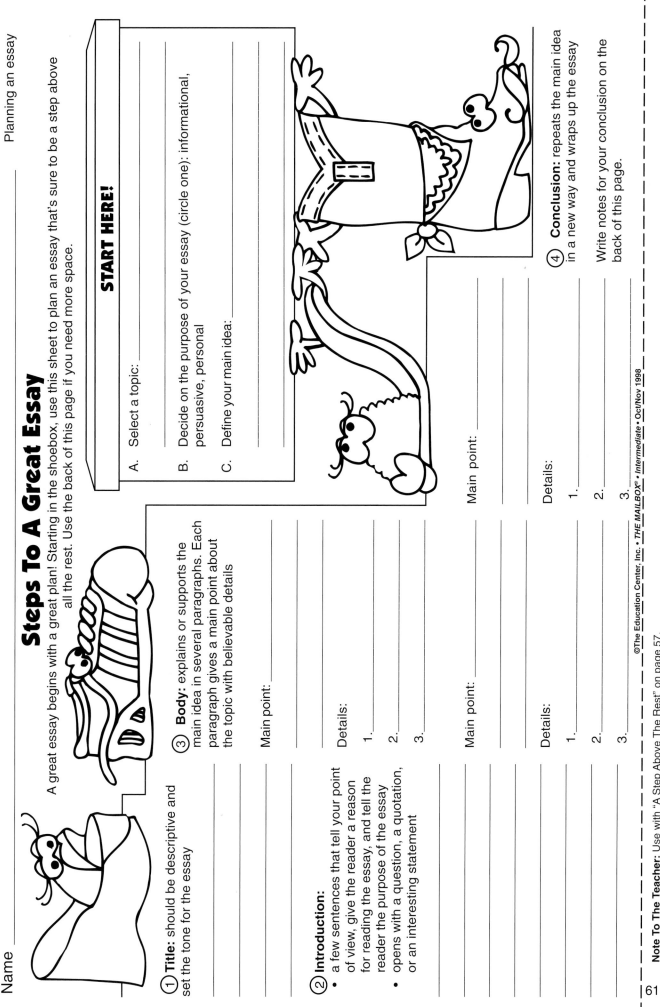

Name _____

Steps To A Great Essay

A great essay begins with a great plan! Starting in the shoebox, use this sheet to plan an essay that's sure to be a step above all the rest. Use the back of this page if you need more space.

START HERE!

A. Select a topic: _____

B. Decide on the purpose of your essay (circle one): informational, persuasive, personal

C. Define your main idea: _____
_____

① **Title:** should be descriptive and set the tone for the essay
_____

② **Introduction:**
- a few sentences that tell your point of view, give the reader a reason for reading the essay, and tell the reader the purpose of the essay
- opens with a question, a quotation, or an interesting statement

_____
_____
_____
_____
_____
_____

③ **Body:** explains or supports the main idea in several paragraphs. Each paragraph gives a main point about the topic with believable details

Main point: _____
_____

Details:
1. _____
2. _____
3. _____

Main point: _____
_____

Details:
1. _____
2. _____
3. _____

Main point: _____
_____

Details:
1. _____
2. _____
3. _____

④ **Conclusion:** repeats the main idea in a new way and wraps up the essay

Write notes for your conclusion on the back of this page.

©The Education Center, Inc. • THE MAILBOX® • Intermediate • Oct/Nov 1998

Note To The Teacher: Use with "A Step Above The Rest" on page 57.

61

Polishing Up A Rough Draft

You want your essay to really shine, right? Then start with polishing up your rough draft! First fill in the names of your second and third editors below. Then edit your draft according to the questions. After you edit for a question, check it off in the column labeled "1st edit." When you're finished, pass your essay and this checklist to the Second Editor. When your checklist and essay are returned, use the checklist and comments to help you write a final essay that really shines!

Second Editor: _____   Third Editor: _____

Questions	1st edit	2nd edit	3rd edit
1. Is the purpose of the essay clear and followed throughout the essay? Comments:			
2. Is the introduction interesting? Does it open with a question, a unique statement, or a quotation? Comments:			
3. Is the essay written in an organized and logical way? Comments:			
4. Are there at least three related main points to support the topic? Comments:			
5. Does the author include believable details to support the main points? Comments:			
6. Does the conclusion restate the main idea in a different way? Comments:			
7. Is the title descriptive, and does it do a good job of setting the tone of the essay? Comments:			
8. Does the author use the rules of good capitalization, punctuation, spelling, and grammar? Comments:			

©The Education Center, Inc. • THE MAILBOX® • Intermediate • Oct/Nov 1998

Note To The Teacher: Use with "Making An Essay Shine!" on page 58.

Servin' Up Sentence Skills

If the order of the day is stronger sentence skills, then serve up this full-course collection of creative activities and reproducibles!

by Lori Sammartino

Sentence Sponge Slam
Skill: Four kinds of sentences

Help students soak up plenty of sentence practice with this wet 'n' wild game! Draw and label a 4 x 3 grid on the chalkboard as shown. Divide your students into teams. Have each team select a recorder. Begin by having a student toss a damp sponge at the grid. Erase the sentence type hit by the sponge; then signal each team to think of a sentence to match the type just erased. As soon as the recorder copies the sentence, have her stand. When all recorders are standing, have them share their sentences in turn. Give one point to each team that has written a correct sentence. Award an extra point to the team whose recorder was first to stand (if that team's sentence was correct). Play additional rounds by choosing different students to toss the sponge and act as recorders. If the sponge hits a space already erased, allow the student to toss it again. The game ends when the entire grid has been erased. Declare the team with the most points the winner.

interrogative	declarative	exclamatory	imperative
imperative	interrogative	declarative	exclamatory
declarative	exclamatory	imperative	interrogative

Snapshot Sentences
Skill: Four kinds of sentences

Create a bulletin board about the four sentence types in a snap! Give each student a copy of page 66 to complete as directed. Also provide students with scissors, glue, and discarded magazines. Display the resulting snapshots on a board titled "Snapshot Sentences." Next have each student read his four sentences aloud and challenge classmates to pick out his snapshot. Or program the back of each snapshot and its set of sentences with matching numerals. Post the sentence sets and snapshots in scrambled order on the bulletin board; then challenge students to match them.

Sentence Roundup
Skill: Subjects, predicates, sentence building

You'll search a long time before finding a sentence-building game that's as much fun as this one! Inflate three balloons. Label one balloon "subject," one "predicate," and the third "sentence." Seat the class in a circle; then give each balloon to a different student. At your signal, have students pass the balloons to their left until you say "Stop." Direct the student holding the "subject" balloon to give an example of a subject. Ask the child holding the "predicate" balloon to give an example of a predicate. Then have the student holding the "sentence" balloon use both examples in a complete sentence. To vary the game, play music as your signals to start and stop passing the balloons.

subject

predicate

sentence

simple subjects	simple predicates
owl	gave
groceries	worried
pizza	cried
shamrocks	eat
wallet	follow
policemen	taught
triangle	dropped
snowflakes	lost
visitors	quits
walnut	speaks
valentine	slept
desk	starve
bodyguard	performs
banjo	understands
apples	grow
pumpkin	shivered
milkshake	recorded
computer	listen
wood	trimmed
handyman	blew
glider	injured
lamp	writes
geese	builds
farmer	annoys
notebook	charged
lighthouse	cooked
library	kept
steaks	took
magazine	held
waterfall	dropped

It's So Simple!
Skill: Simple subjects and predicates

Introduce your students to simple subjects and predicates with this simple relay game! In advance, program a stack of subject and predicate cards using the word lists shown on the left. Save a few blank cards for later. Then divide students into two teams and have them stand in two single-file lines. Show one card to the first two players; then hand the card to the first player who correctly identifies the word as a subject or a predicate. Direct these two players to then move to the ends of their lines. If both players answer correctly at the same time, give one player the word card and the other a blank card. Declare the team holding the most cards at the end of the game the winner.

A Large Order Of Silly Sentences
Skill: Sentence building, alliteration

Serve up a large order of sentence building—sprinkled with a dash of silliness—by playing this creative-thinking game! Divide your students into groups of four or five; then have each team select a recorder. Start the game by announcing a simple subject, such as *cats*. Then challenge each group to make up a sentence using that subject with other words that begin with its first letter (for example, *Clever cats claw clean couches*). Direct all group members to stand as soon as their recorder has written the team's sentence. After each recorder has read her team's sentence, award one point for each word that begins with the designated letter. Award a bonus point to the group that stood first. Declare the group with the most points at the end of the game the winner.

Pleasant people paint pretty pictures.
Clever cats claw clean couches.
Dirty dogs draw diamonds in the dirt.

Dinner And Dessert
Skill: Compound predicates

Help students gain a better understanding of compound predicates with this quick activity. Have the class suggest a list of places as you write them on the board. Next ask your students to think of at least two activities that can be done at each place (for example, you can *purchase a ticket* or *pick up your luggage* at an airport). Record these activities on the board beside their matching places. Then pair your students and assign each pair a different place. Direct each twosome to write a sentence that includes a compound predicate and incorporates both of the activities suggested for its place (for example, *At the airport Mary picked up her luggage and purchased a ticket for her next trip*). Then have students share their sentences with the class. Extend this activity to a writing lesson on transitional words. Have each student write a story about a busy day. In the story, have the student include any five places listed on the board, two sentences with compound predicates, and several transitional words, such as *first, next, later,* etc.

Sweet Or Sour?
Skill: Compound sentences, antonyms

Compound sentences can be a mouthful if you don't know how to write them correctly! To help your class serve up compound sentences with confidence, have students brainstorm a list of antonym pairs, such as *sweet—sour* and *hot—cold*. List students' responses on the board. Next have each child fold an 8 1/2" x 11" sheet of white paper in half lengthwise. Assign each student an antonym pair; then have her use these words in a compound sentence that joins two or more simple sentences with a conjunction and a comma. Have the student copy her sentence along the bottom of her paper and then illustrate each antonym in one of the sections above. Bind students' completed papers into a class book titled "Now Serving: Compound Sentences And Antonyms."

Some people think lemons are sweet, but they're actually sour!

Can It!
Skill: Subject-verb agreement

Help students understand the importance of subject-verb agreement with this fun game. In advance, prepare a set of simple-subject and simple-predicate cards (or use the cards prepared for "It's So Simple!" on page 64). Label an empty frosting container "Simple Subjects" and another "Simple Predicates"; then place the appropriate cards inside each container.

Divide students into two teams. Direct the first player on Team One to draw one card from each can; then have her read the cards aloud, starting with the subject card. Next have her state whether the subject and verb agree. If they don't, have the student tell how they can be changed so that they do agree. *(The subject and predicate don't have to make sense together as long as they agree in person and number. For example, "Apples quits" does not agree, but changing the words to either "Apple quits" or "Apples quit" does.)* Give the player one point for correctly identifying whether or not the subject and verb agree. Award a bonus point for correctly changing the subject or verb to make the words agree. The team with the most points at the end of the game wins.

Sentence Scramble
Skill: Subject-verb agreement

It's everyone to his corner with this fun interactive game that sharpens subject-verb agreement skills! Before playing, remind students of this important rule: compound subjects (like *the dog and the cat*) are plural when joined by *and,* and are used with a plural verb (like *were splashing in the puddle*).

To prepare:
1. Label four large signs "Simple Subjects," "Compound Subjects," "Simple Predicates," and "Compound Predicates." Post each sign in a different corner of your classroom.
2. Program a set of index cards with the simple subjects and predicates listed on page 64, or use the cards already prepared for "It's So Simple!" Add cards listing the compound subjects and predicates found below. Be sure to prepare an equal number of subject and predicate cards, and that each student will get one card.

To play:
1. Give each child a card. Have him decide if it is labeled with a simple subject, compound subject, simple predicate, or compound predicate. Then have him stand in the appropriate corner of the room.
2. Beginning at one corner, have each child read aloud his card. Direct his classmates to determine if he's in the correct corner. If not, have him move to the correct corner.
3. Instruct this child to choose a partner from another corner who can help him build a complete sentence. (Allow students to add articles like *the, an,* and *a* if necessary.) For example, a child with either a simple or compound subject card would choose a child from one of the verb corners. Allow silly sentences to be formed, as long as the subject and verb agree.
4. After the pair shares its sentence, collect their cards and have them return to their seats. Repeat Steps 2–4 until everyone is seated.

compound subjects	compound predicates
the sun and the moon	are sniffling and sneezing
my socks and shoes	is howling and yowling
the lions and the tigers	were polished and scrubbed
her burger and fries	is hammered and pounded
the kitten, duck, and frog	are laughing and crying
math, science, and spelling	is whining and pouting
Mary, Bob, and I	were barking and hissing
a doctor, a lawyer, and a teacher	is slipping and sliding
ice cream, cake, and cookies	is skipping and hopping

Snapshot Sentences

Directions:

1. Find an interesting magazine picture. Cut it out and glue it in the box below.
2. At the bottom of this page, write an example of each kind of sentence. Write each sentence so it can be used as a clue to identify your "snapshot."
3. Cut along the dotted line below to divide this page into two sections. Then cut out the snapshot and give it to your teacher.
4. Keep the bottom section to read as clues to your classmates.

Glue your snapshot here.

- -

(Cut here.)

Declarative: _____

_____

Imperative: _____

_____

Interrogative: _____

_____

Exclamatory: _____

_____

Bonus Box: On another sheet of paper, write four sentences about last weekend. Be sure you include an example of each of the four sentence types above.

©The Education Center, Inc. • THE MAILBOX® • Intermediate • Feb/Mar 1999

Note To The Teacher: Use with "Snapshot Sentences" on page 63. Provide students with scissors, glue, and discarded magazines.

What's On My Plate?

Read the sentence part on each plate. If the sentence part is a subject, color the plate blue.
If it is a predicate, color the plate red.

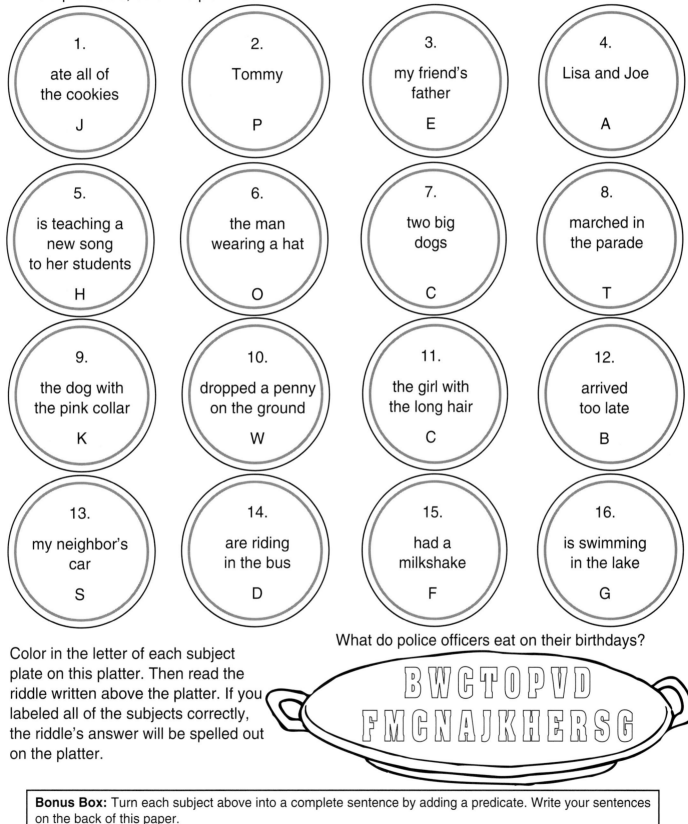

1. ate all of the cookies J

2. Tommy P

3. my friend's father E

4. Lisa and Joe A

5. is teaching a new song to her students H

6. the man wearing a hat O

7. two big dogs C

8. marched in the parade T

9. the dog with the pink collar K

10. dropped a penny on the ground W

11. the girl with the long hair C

12. arrived too late B

13. my neighbor's car S

14. are riding in the bus D

15. had a milkshake F

16. is swimming in the lake G

Color in the letter of each subject plate on this platter. Then read the riddle written above the platter. If you labeled all of the subjects correctly, the riddle's answer will be spelled out on the platter.

What do police officers eat on their birthdays?

B W C T O P V D
F M C N A J K H E R S G

Bonus Box: Turn each subject above into a complete sentence by adding a predicate. Write your sentences on the back of this paper.

Dinner At The Diner

Mel has a new special on tonight's menu. Now he must change the sign in front of the diner to let everyone know. Help Mel by reading each sentence. If a sentence contains a compound subject, write its letter on the box at the left. If it contains a compound predicate, write its letter on the box at the right. Then follow the steps below to find out tonight's special.

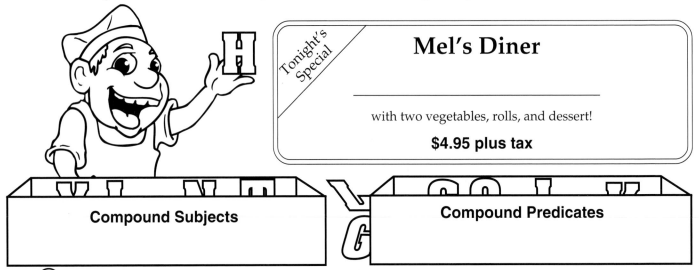

Tonight's Special

Mel's Diner

_____

with two vegetables, rolls, and dessert!

$4.95 plus tax

Compound Subjects

Compound Predicates

(L) The cat and the dog fought over the food scraps.

(N) Tiny ants marched across the floor, climbed the cabinets, and crawled on the counter.

(S) Lions, tigers, and bears are at the zoo.

(C) Four cars turned off the street and followed the truck into the gas station.

(K) A beautiful rainbow stretched across the sky and soon disappeared.

(I) Mr. Edwards and Mr. Bowman are brothers.

(P) Mrs. Bray's nieces and nephews are visiting her.

(C) Bill looked at the clock and realized he would be late for his appointment.

(R) The new table and chairs looked so pretty in the dining room.

(E) Amy finished her math homework, studied for her science test, and practiced her spelling words.

(I) The neighbor's cat ran up the tree and wouldn't come down.

(W) Hot dogs and hamburgers are easy to grill.

(U) Brad, Angie, and Todd like to play volleyball on Saturdays.

(H) Sarah shopped at the mall and visited the ice-cream shop with her aunt.

When you're finished: If you correctly identified the compound subjects and predicates, one box above is now labeled with letters that spell tonight's special. On the back of this sheet or a piece of scrap paper, try to unscramble the letters on each box. When you think you know tonight's special, write it on Mel's sign.

Bonus Box: If you had a diner, what special would you offer tonight? Write a one-paragraph description of this delicious meal on the back of this sheet.

Brushin' Up Punctuation Skills!

Brush up students' punctuation skills anytime during the year with the following favorites from our readers.

Sentence Strip Punctuation
Skill: Using quotation marks

Climb the ladder of punctuation success with this nifty hands-on activity! To prepare, label several sentence strips with sentences that are missing quotation and other punctuation marks. Also write these sentences on an overhead transparency. Next cut ten small squares from index cards and label each with a punctuation mark listed below. Make a set of these cards for each group in your class; then store each group's set in its own plastic zippered bag.

To play, give each small group one programmed sentence strip and a set of punctuation marks. Have students in each group work together to read their sentence and then place the correct punctuation marks directly on the strip. After the groups are finished, have each team leader read aloud his group's sentence with its punctuation marks as you insert the marks on the transparency. When all of the groups have shared, give a new sentence strip to each team and have students repeat the activity. *(For a similar activity, see "Rearrange Me!" on page 71.)*

Lisa Carlson—Gr. 4, Bear Path Elementary, Hamden, CT

Why don't you ask Mom, Lee?

Punctuation marks per set:
period
question mark
exclamation mark
comma *(two)*
colon
semicolon
quotation marks *(one card for each pair)*
apostrophe *(draw a line under it to distinguish it from a comma)*

PUNCTUATION
Super Glossy

Questions For The Teacher
Skill: Punctuating questions, spelling

Give your students the inside scoop on one of the most interesting people they know—you!—with this fun punctuation activity. Have each student write three to seven questions to you on a sheet of paper. Collect the papers; then announce that you will read aloud and answer each question *if* it has been capitalized and punctuated correctly, and includes no spelling errors. If a sentence doesn't meet these criteria, it will be skipped over. Then read aloud each correct question and answer it. Not only will students get some great practice punctuating sentences, but they'll also get the skinny on you!

Carol Hopkins—Grs. 4 & 5, Margaret Collins Elementary, Pinole, CA

Clever Conversations
Skill: Punctuating dialogue

A picture's not only worth a thousand words—it's also a terrific tool to help students punctuate dialogue! Cut out magazine pictures (one for every pair of students) that depict at least two people engaged in an activity. After reviewing the rules for punctuating dialogue, divide the class into pairs; then give each pair a picture. Have each twosome write a conversation between the people in its picture that includes at least one example of each of the following: a direct quote at the beginning of a sentence, a direct quote at the end of a sentence, and a divided quotation. Discuss how students can use the facial expressions, setting, and activity the people seem to be engaged in to help them determine the content of the conversation. Have each pair mount its conversation and picture on a large sheet of construction paper. Display the projects on a bulletin board titled "Can We Talk?" Follow up this activity with the reproducible on page 72.

Terry Castoria—Gr. 5, Defino Central School, Marlboro, NJ

Activities To Review Punctuation Skills

Review the punctuation skills you need to reinforce with the following three pages of activities!

Punctuation With A Personal Touch

If you're tired of boring punctuation worksheets, think about how your class feels! Instead of duplicating pages from a workbook, create your own with sentences that star your students. Write unpunctuated sentences about your students' birthdays, the school science fair, someone's new baby brother, or the holiday that's just around the bend. After students have completed several of these fun reproducibles, challenge each child to write a paragraph about himself, leaving out the necessary punctuation. Then have the student and a classmate swap papers and correct each other's paragraphs. Bye-bye, boredom!

Rebecca Amsel—Gr. 4, Yeshiva Shaarei Tzion, Lakewood, NJ

BINGO

B	I	N	G	O
5	!	34	49	70
18	19	40	58	•
?	30	FREE SPACE	50	60
,	24	43	" "	,
7	33	:	46	72

Punctuation Bingo

Turn a standard bingo game into powerful punctuation practice with this easy idea! Cut small square markers from construction paper; then label each with a period, a pair of quotation marks, an exclamation point, a question mark, or another punctuation mark you want students to practice. Also write a list of unpunctuated sentences on a transparency.

To play, give a supply of markers and a regular bingo card to each student. As you call out a number to cover, display a sentence on the overhead and write the letter-number combination called (such as *B-10*) beside it. Challenge each student to cover that number on his board (if he has it) with a marker that is labeled with a punctuation mark needed in the sentence. When a child gets "Bingo!", read aloud each sentence that he used. As each sentence is read, have the student name the punctuation mark he used to cover that space (for example, "I covered that space with a question mark."). Award a small treat to the winning student; then continue play to discover the next winner.

Cathy Ogg—Gr. 4, Happy Valley Elementary, Johnson City, TN

Punctuation Posters

Punctuation a work of art? It can be with this review activity that's disguised as an art project. Give each student a copy of page 73, scissors, colored pencils or fine-tipped markers, glue, and a 12" x 18" sheet of white construction paper. Have the student follow the directions on page 73 to create a miniposter of important punctuation rules. Set aside time for students to share their posters before displaying the projects on a bulletin board titled "Punctuation With Pizzazz!" If desired, give each student two copies of page 73 to create a larger poster that reviews more punctuation rules.

Mark: semicolon

Rule: Use a semicolon to join the independent clauses of a compound senten together when you a comma and a c

Mark: quotation marks

Rule: Put quotation marks before and after the names of articles in magazines and newspapers.

| " | Today | must | be | Monday | ! | " | she | sighed | . |

Rearrange Me!

When it's time to review punctuation skills, it's time to play "Rearrange Me!" Write sentences that contain a variety of punctuation marks (including semicolons, colons, parentheses, quotation marks, and apostrophes) on sentence strips. Cut apart each strip—making sure to cut each punctuation mark as a separate piece—and store the pieces in an envelope. Divide students into groups of four or five; then give each group an envelope. Challenge each group to reassemble its sentence, making sure that all punctuation marks are positioned correctly. Award a bonus point or small treat to the first team that correctly reconstructs its sentence. As students' skills progress, repeat the activity with more difficult sentences.

Julie Gartner—Gr. 6, Virginia Lake School, Palatine, IL

Dear Devon

Devon's Mailbox

Pen Pal Punctuation Day

Passing notes in class? You bet, when you hold a special Pen Pal Punctuation Day! For morning work, have each student decorate a file folder as a personal "mailbox." After the mailboxes are completed, have each student draw a classmate's name out of a container of name slips. Then have him write his pen pal a brief letter that includes no punctuation and deliver it to her mailbox. After all the mail is delivered, have each student edit his pen pal's letter and then return it to be checked. How's that for a special delivery of letter-perfect punctuation practice?

Samantha Klein—Grs. 4–6
Jamison Elementary, Jamison, PA

Roll A Punctuation Mark

Roll out the fun with this punctuation game for two players. First prepare two lists of ten unpunctuated sentences each. Be sure each list requires the same number of punctuation marks and is labeled with the number of missing punctuation marks (see the illustration). Then duplicate the lists so that you have one copy of each for every pair of students.

Divide students into pairs. Give one student in each pair a copy of List A sentences; give the other student a copy of List B sentences. Also give each twosome a die. Display a chart like the one shown. To play, one student rolls the die; then he adds the corresponding punctuation mark where needed to one of his sentences. If the student rolls a six, he may choose to add any punctuation mark he wants. The winner is the first player to correctly punctuate all of his sentences. Adapt the game by changing the chart to include different punctuation marks.

Kelly A. Lu, Berlyn School, Ontario, CA

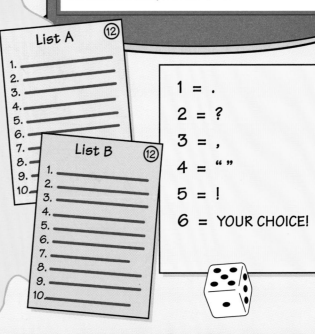

List A ⑫
1.
2.
3.
4.
5.
6.
7.
8.
9.
10.

List B ⑫
1.
2.
3.
4.
5.
6.
7.
8.
9.
10.

1 = .
2 = ?
3 = ,
4 = " "
5 = !
6 = YOUR CHOICE!

71

You Ought To Be In The Comics!

Below are four cartoons that include some pretty famous people from the past. First draw yourself in each cartoon and answer the question(s) in the speech bubble. On another sheet of paper, re-write each cartoon as a conversation between you and the famous person. Don't forget to use quotation marks and other punctuation marks correctly.

Name ____________________ Punctuation project

Pulling Together A Punctuation Poster

Need to brush up your punctuation skills? Follow these directions to pull together a punctuation masterpiece!

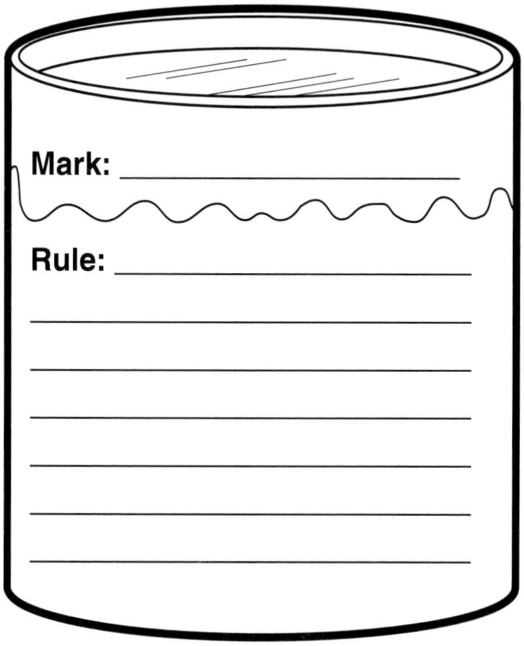

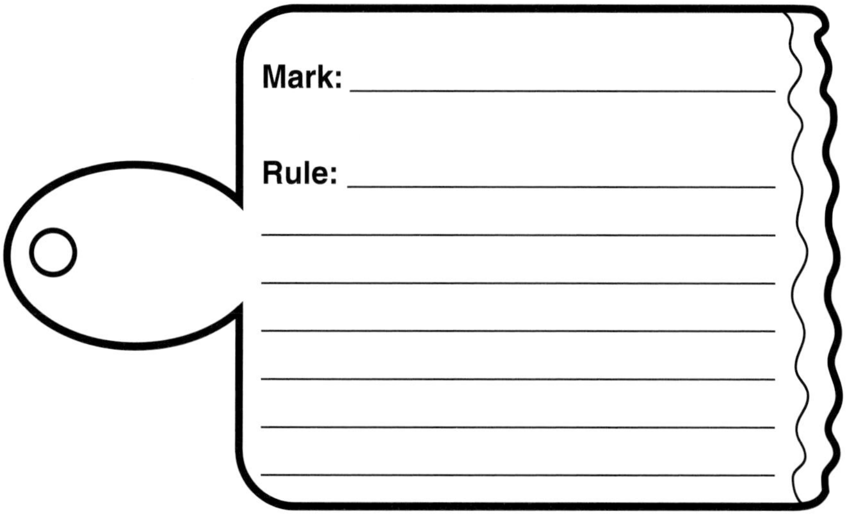

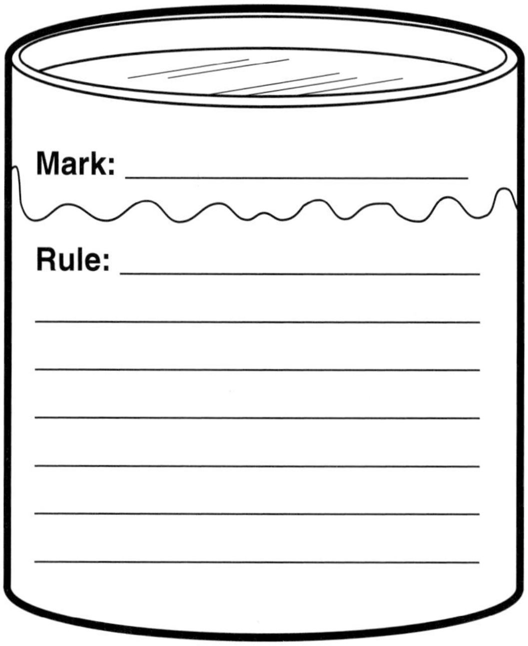

Punctuation Marks

apostrophe	hyphen
colon	parentheses
comma	period
dash	question mark
ellipsis	quotation marks
exclamation point	semicolon

1. Choose four of the punctuation marks listed. Write the name of each on a pattern below. Then write one punctuation rule about the mark on the lines.
2. Lightly color the patterns; then cut them out.
3. On scrap paper, write a sentence that illustrates each of your rules.
4. Arrange the patterns on a sheet of construction paper to make an attractive poster. Leave room to write each of your sample sentences.
5. Glue the patterns to your poster. Add your sample sentences. Also add a title and other illustrations.

Mark:
Rule:

Mark:
Rule:

Mark:
Rule:

Mark:
Rule:

Note To The Teacher: Use with "Punctuation Posters" on page 70.

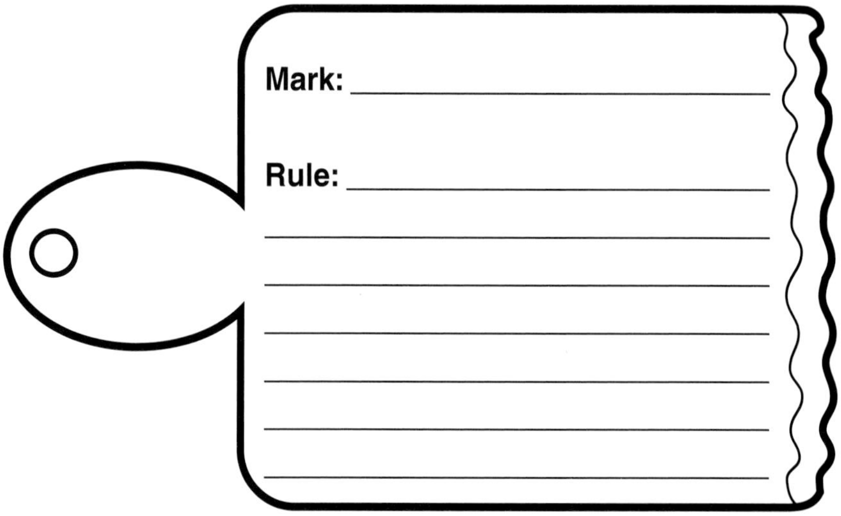

The Rematch

The Brushin' Up Paint Company guys are taking a break from their work by reading a favorite book. It's called *The Hare And The Tortoise: A Rematch*. According to this book, who wins the second run of this classic race? To find out, follow the directions in the box.

Make each **correct** sentence into a tortoise.
Make each **incorrect** sentence into a hare.
Then rewrite the sentence correctly on
the back of this page.

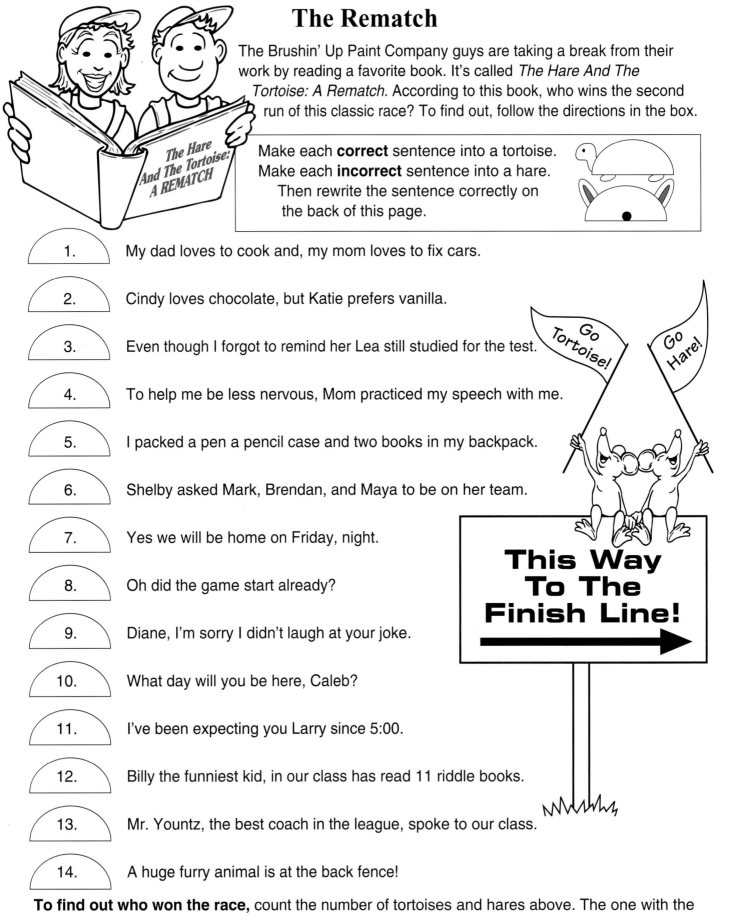

1. My dad loves to cook and, my mom loves to fix cars.

2. Cindy loves chocolate, but Katie prefers vanilla.

3. Even though I forgot to remind her Lea still studied for the test.

4. To help me be less nervous, Mom practiced my speech with me.

5. I packed a pen a pencil case and two books in my backpack.

6. Shelby asked Mark, Brendan, and Maya to be on her team.

7. Yes we will be home on Friday, night.

8. Oh did the game start already?

9. Diane, I'm sorry I didn't laugh at your joke.

10. What day will you be here, Caleb?

11. I've been expecting you Larry since 5:00.

12. Billy the funniest kid, in our class has read 11 riddle books.

13. Mr. Yountz, the best coach in the league, spoke to our class.

14. A huge furry animal is at the back fence!

To find out who won the race, count the number of tortoises and hares above. The one with the greater number is the winner.

Dear Favorite Character,
A Class Bookmaking Project For The End Of The Year

Reminisce about the memorable book characters students have met throughout the school year with this letter-perfect project!

idea by Barbara Parker—Gr. 6, Fredericktown Intermediate School, Fredericktown, OH

Day 1: Brainstorming And Assigning Characters

Launch this project by having students discuss the novels the class has read during the year. List these titles on the board. Then have students name the main characters in each book. List these characters beside their titles. Next direct each student to write on his paper the names of the three characters to whom he'd most like to write a letter (in order of preference). Collect the papers. Before the next class, assign each student a character. Be sure that no two students get the same character.

Day 2: Planning The Letters

Set the stage for writing by sharing *The Jolly Postman: Or Other People's Letters* by Janet and Allan Ahlberg (Little, Brown And Company; 1986). Discuss with students the unique format of this book (writings penned by one book character to another, tucked inside open-pocket envelopes). Also discuss the different forms of writing contained in the envelopes: a friendly letter, a postcard, an invitation, an advertisement, a legal notice, etc. List these formats on the board; then have each student choose one for the piece he'll write to his character.

Day 3: Writing The Letters

Direct each student to write his rough draft (in the format he has selected), edit his letter, and make any necessary revisions. Then have him copy his letter in its final form and add colorful illustrations to it.

Day 4: Making The Envelopes

To prepare for this step, allow students to study the Ahlbergs' book to see how its envelopes were designed, marked, and illustrated. Then give each student scissors, glue, markers, and a copy of page 76 to complete as directed.

Day 5: Completing And Sharing The Book

Conclude this project by having each student tuck his letter into his envelope, folding it if necessary. Collect the envelopes. Remove each letter before positioning its envelope so that the opening is at the top. Then punch two holes in the envelope's left side and reinsert the letter, refolding it if necessary to make sure it doesn't block the holes. Sandwich the envelopes between two oaktag covers that have also been hole-punched. Thread lengths of yarn through the holes to bind the pages together. Write "[your name]'s Students: Or Other People's Letters" on the front cover. Allow students to sign out this letter-perfect book to share with family members.

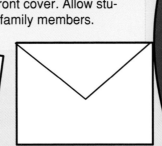

Dear Favorite Character,

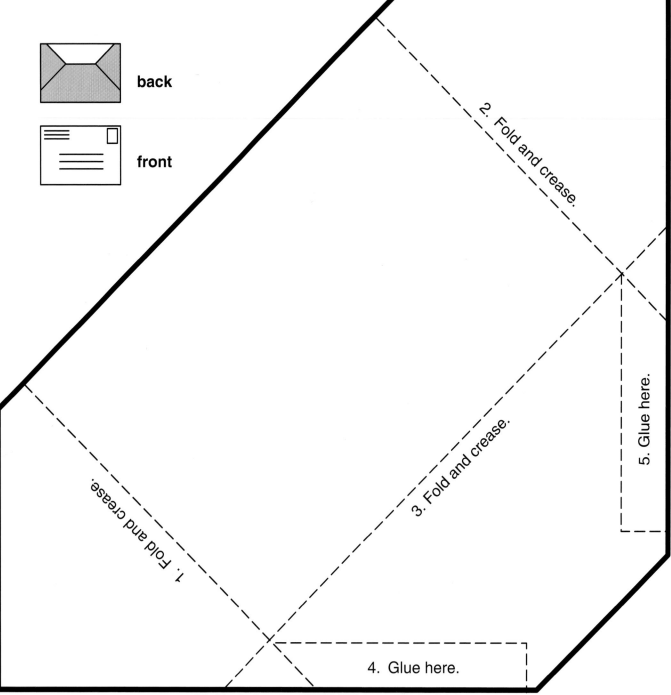

How to make your envelope:

1. Cut out the pattern along the bold lines.
2. Fold in and crease dotted lines 1–3.
3. Open the folds.
4. Spread glue in spaces 4 and 5.
5. Refold at lines 1 and 2; then refold line 3. Press to help the glue hold.
6. Turn the envelope over so it is faceup.
7. Label and illustrate your envelope to make it look real. Don't forget the stamp!

Pattern

back

front

2. Fold and crease.

3. Fold and crease.

5. Glue here.

1. Fold and crease.

4. Glue here.

Making The Writing-In-Math Connection

Eager to integrate writing and math, but unsure about how to make the connection? Plug in to the following creative ideas and reproducibles to electrify your students' skills in two of the three *R*s!

by Peggy W. Hambright

Why Write In Math?

According to the new math standards released by the National Council of Teachers of Mathematics (NCTM), students are now expected to *communicate* their understanding of math concepts. In order to know whether students can communicate their understanding, they are being asked to explain concepts in their own words. Writing allows students to clarify their thinking and summarize what they're learning. Save yourself some planning time and strengthen two important skills at once by having students practice writing while doing math. The easy ideas that follow will help you make the connection with ease!

Daily Math Journals

Skill: Problem solving, expository writing

Keep 'ritin' and 'rithmetic skills sharp with the help of daily math journals. Each Monday have students follow the steps shown to make simple flip books. Following each day's math lesson, write a prompt (a problem to solve and explain) on the board. Have each student copy the prompt onto the corresponding journal page and write his response (see the example). Each Friday collect the books to assess students' understanding.

Directions:

Step 1: Stack three sheets of paper so that the top edges are 1/2-inch apart.

Step 2: Fold over the top half to form six layers.

Step 3: Staple the book at each side near the top of the fold.

Step 4: Label the top flap "[your name]'s Math Journal" and illustrate it.

Step 5: Label the space on each remaining flap with a different day and date.

Step 6: Copy the day's prompt from the board in the space above the date. Then solve and explain the problem.

Step 1:

Step 2:

Steps 3–5:

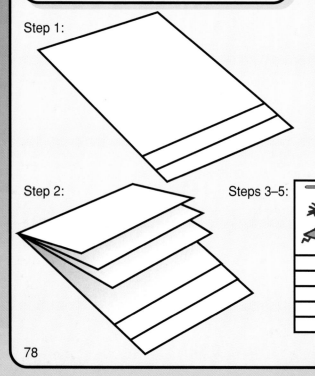

Erin's Math Journal

Monday, Sept. 14
Tuesday, Sept. 15
Wednesday, Sept. 16
Thursday, Sept. 17
Friday, Sept. 18

Step 6:

Problem: Draw an acute angle, a right angle, and an obtuse angle. Explain how they are different.
Solution: A right angle measures exactly 90°. An acute angle measures less than 90°. An obtuse angle measures more than 90°.

90°

Less Than 90°
Acute Angle

Right Angle

More Than 90°
Obtuse Angle

Friday, Sept. 18

"Math-Maginations"

Skill: Finding perimeter and area, descriptive writing

Pull out all the stops—and the pattern blocks—for this fun-filled math lesson that doubles as a descriptive-writing exercise! Give each student a zippered bag of pattern blocks (minus the white and orange pieces), a sheet of drawing paper, colored pencils, and the directions below.

1. Construct a shape—such as an animal or an object—with the pattern blocks on your drawing paper. Trace the blocks; then color the drawing.
2. On a sheet of lined paper, record the number of blocks of each kind you used to make your shape.
3. Use the side of a green triangle as one unit to find your shape's perimeter. Record it on the lined paper.
4. Use the area of a green triangle as one unit to find your shape's area. Record it on the lined paper.
5. On the lined paper, write a descriptive paragraph about your shape. Tell what it is, its name, its color, the kinds of blocks you used, its size (perimeter and area), and what it can and cannot do, along with any other important characteristics.
6. Edit your paragraph; then copy it in the extra space on your drawing.

Display students' papers in the classroom. For additional ways students can incorporate math with descriptive writing, see the list below.

P = 48
A = 66

Writing Math

Describe:
- yourself using math sentences and math terms.
- a geometric design you made by drawing line segments on poster board.
- a geometric design you created by overlapping the tracings of circles or polygons.
- a shape you created from tangram pieces (described from top to bottom or side to side).
- any symmetrical shape.
- a design you created by connecting ordered pairs of numbers on a grid.
- any shape without naming it.
- how well your group worked together to solve an assigned problem.

Same Or Different?

Skill: Finding attributes of polygons, classificatory writing

Many math topics lend themselves to classificatory writing. Draw a Venn diagram on the board. Label the left circle "Square" and the right circle "Rectangle." Have students compare and contrast the two polygons as you record their comments in the appropriate spaces of the diagram. Next direct each student to describe the similarities of squares and rectangles in one paragraph and their differences in another. Then give each student a copy of the pattern at the bottom of page 84 to use for comparing and contrasting one of the topics on the right. Display students' cut-out patterns on a bulletin board titled "We've Got A Yen For A Venn!"

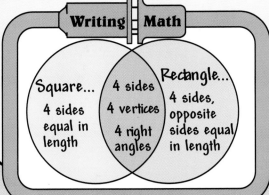

Writing Math

Square...
4 sides
equal in
length

4 sides
4 vertices
4 right
angles

Rectangle...
4 sides,
opposite
sides equal
in length

Writing Math

Compare And Contrast:
- an English ruler and a metric ruler
- any two different periods in a place-value chart, such as ten thousands and ten millions
- any fraction with its equivalent decimal, such as 3/4 and 0.75
- any two sets of multiples
- an acute angle and an obtuse angle
- a bar graph and a line graph
- two inverse operations, such as multiplication and division, or addition and subtraction
- using mental math instead of a calculator
- a line and a ray

As Easy As 1, 2, 3!
Skill: Reviewing math concepts, expository writing

Expository writing is as easy to integrate into the math curriculum as 1, 2, 3! Try one of the following activities:

- Pair students; then give each pair colored markers and a sheet of white poster board. Have the pair create a math game that's correlated to another subject, writing directions on the gameboard or on an index card clipped to the board. Allow students to trade and play their games.

- Duplicate the reproducible on page 83 for each student to complete as directed. Then follow up by having students make flow charts of favorite "arithmetricks," such as the one shown, or other simple math problems. Give each student a sheet of white poster board, colored markers, scissors, a hole puncher, and yarn. Direct him to create his flow chart by labeling and connecting poster-board pieces (shaped according to the legend on the reproducible) with yarn as shown. Display the flow charts. For additional ideas on expository math writing, see the list below.

START

Think of a number.

Add 10.

Multiply by 4.

Add 200.

Divide by 4.

Subtract the original number.

Did you get 60?

Yes? Great! Try another number.

No? Check your work.

Writing · Math

Write directions for:
- dividing a Geoboard to show fractional parts of a whole.
- drawing the missing part of a symmetrical design.
- creating a bar graph that shows favorite Saturday-morning TV shows.
- solving a problem with the working-backwards strategy.
- setting up a table that shows the total wheels on 16 bicycles and 7 tricycles.
- making change from a particular bill for a certain amount of purchases.
- doubling or tripling a recipe's ingredients for a party.
- measuring the dimensions of a box.

Do It My Way!
Skill: Problem solving, persuasive writing

There's more than one way to solve most problems. Challenge pairs of students to think of a problem that could be solved in different ways (for example, acting out the problem instead of drawing a picture). Direct one student to use biased wording to write a persuasive paragraph favoring one method while her partner writes about the other. Remind students to support each reason they provide with a logical explanation or an example. Finally instruct each pair to fold a large sheet of construction paper in half vertically. Have one student in the pair glue her paragraph and an illustration on the top half of the paper, while her partner does the same on the bottom half. Display the projects on a bulletin board titled "I'd Do It My Way!"

Writing · Math

Persuade a partner to:
- find the cost of three packs of gum using mental math instead of a calculator or paper and pencil.
- find the weight of three new pencils using metric instead of English measurement.
- find the number of feet from her desk to the nearest trash can using estimation instead of an exact measurement.
- find the length of an object using a nonstandard unit, such as a paper clip, rather than a standard unit, such as an inch.
- agree that your favorite team should be in first place. Use statistics to support your opinion.

Once Upon A Math Time...

Skill: Checking understanding, narrative writing

Want to make sure your students understand new math concepts? Turn them into math storytellers! Pick a picture book that complements a math unit the class is currently studying (see the books suggested below or ask your media specialist for help). After sharing the book, give each student a copy of the story-planning guide on page 84 to complete as directed. Then combine the students' completed stories into a class book. At the end of math class each day, share several of the stories aloud. Talk about a great ending!

Writing — Math

PICTURE BOOKS TO CONNECT MATH AND NARRATIVE WRITING

Addition And Subtraction
Elevator Magic by Stuart J. Murphy; HarperCollins Publishers, Inc.; 1997
Ten Sly Piranhas: A Counting Story In Reverse (A Tale Of Wickedness—And Worse!) by William Wise, Dial Books For Young Readers, 1993

Multiplication
Anno's Mysterious Multiplying Jar by Mitsumasa Anno, Philomel Books, 1983
Bunches And Bunches Of Bunnies by Louise Mathews, Scholastic Inc., 1991
How Many Feet? How Many Tails? A Book Of Math Riddles by Marilyn Burns, Scholastic Inc., 1996
One Grain Of Rice: A Mathematical Folktale by Demi, Scholastic Inc., 1997
One Hundred Hungry Ants by Elinor J. Pinczes, Houghton Mifflin Company, 1993
Too Many Kangaroo Things To Do! by Stuart J. Murphy, HarperCollins Children's Books, 1996

Division
A Remainder Of One by Elinor J. Pinczes, Houghton Mifflin Company, 1995
The Doorbell Rang by Pat Hutchins, Mulberry Books, 1989

Large Numbers
The King's Chessboard by David Birch, Puffin Books, 1993

Fractions
Gator Pie by Louise Mathews, Sundance Publishing, 1995

Measurement
Counting On Frank by Rod Clement, Gareth Stevens Inc., 1991
How Big Is A Foot? by Rolf Myller; Dell Publishing Company, Inc.; 1991
Jim And The Beanstalk by Raymond Briggs, Sandcastle Books, 1989
Spaghetti And Meatballs For All! by Marilyn Burns, Scholastic Inc., 1997
The Librarian Who Measured The Earth by Kathryn Lasky; Little, Brown And Company; 1994 (a biography, but still a good one to share with students)
Twelve Snails To One Lizard: A Tale Of Mischief And Measurement by Susan Hightower, Simon & Schuster Books For Young Readers, 1997

Geometry
Grandfather Tang's Story: A Tale Told With Tangrams by Ann Tompert, Crown Books For Young Readers, 1990
Sam Johnson And The Blue Ribbon Quilt by Lisa C. Ernst, Mulberry Books, 1992
The Greedy Triangle by Marilyn Burns, Scholastic Inc., 1995

Money
Alexander, Who Used To Be Rich Last Sunday by Judith Viorst, Aladdin Paperbacks, 1987
Pigs Will Be Pigs: Fun With Math And Money by Amy Axelrod, Aladdin Paperbacks, 1997

Patterns
Anno's Magic Seeds by Mitsumasa Anno, Philomel Books, 1994

Data Collection, Graphing, Probability, Statistics
The Best Vacation Ever by Stuart J. Murphy; HarperCollins Publishers, Inc.; 1997

Miscellaneous
Alice In Pastaland: A Math Adventure by Alexandra Wright; Charlesbridge Publishing, Inc.; 1997
Math Curse by Jon Scieszka, Viking Children's Books, 1995

Make The Math And Writing Connection!

Want to make a positive connection every time you must write in math? Then get some practice with math writing by completing ____ of the following activities. Color the outlet when you complete its activity.

Write clues to help a classmate guess a given number.

Write clues to help a classmate solve a logic-grid problem.

Read or listen to a fairy tale; then write five math word problems related to the tale.

Write about a day during which you could use no math at all.

Look at a magazine picture; then write a math word problem related to the picture.

In writing, explain a shortcut for solving a math problem. For example, to explain how to subtract by adding, you might write: "In the problem 107 – 85, 107 is 7 more than 100, and 85 is 15 less than 100. Since 7 + 15 = 22, then 107 – 85 = 22."

Write a letter to an absent classmate explaining what the day's math class was about.

Write a phrase to help others remember a math concept. For example, use "Dad, Mom, Sister, Brother" to help someone remember these long-division steps: Divide, Multiply, Subtract, Bring Down.

Study a chart, map, or graph; then write at least five questions a classmate could answer by using it.

Write a math riddle to share with the class.

Write an explanation of how to solve the last problem in tonight's math homework.

Write an "If…then" problem for a classmate to solve. For example: If Brett eats four pieces of pizza each week for a year, then how many pieces will he eat in ten years?

Make a Word Bank for a current math unit; then write a story using as many words from the bank as possible.

Write a math word problem your teacher could include on the class's next math test.

©The Education Center, Inc. • THE MAILBOX® • Intermediate • Aug/Sept 1998

Goin' With The Flow!

Graphic organizers, such as flow charts, can help you solve math problems. Study the flow chart below. It explains how to subtract 756 from 1,642. Follow its steps to help you solve the problem.

Next write the steps explaining how to subtract 2,408 from 5,117 on the lines provided. Use the flow chart as a guide. Be as specific with your steps as you can.

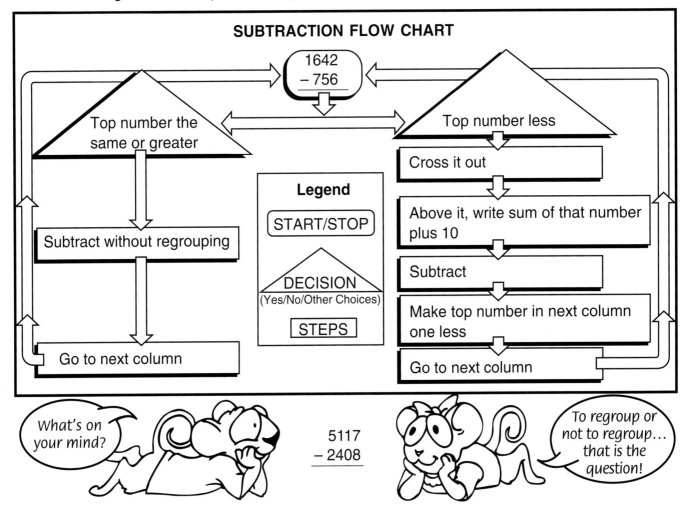

SUBTRACTION FLOW CHART

1642
− 756

Top number the same or greater

Top number less

Cross it out

Above it, write sum of that number plus 10

Subtract without regrouping

Subtract

Make top number in next column one less

Go to next column

Go to next column

Legend

START/STOP

DECISION
(Yes/No/Other Choices)

STEPS

What's on your mind?

5117
− 2408

To regroup or not to regroup... that is the question!

_____
_____
_____
_____
_____
_____
_____

Bonus Box: Write a different subtraction problem on another sheet of paper. Ask a classmate to write the steps that explain how to solve it. Then check his or her work.

©The Education Center, Inc. • THE MAILBOX® • Intermediate • Aug/Sept 1998 • Key p. 308

A Math Story From Scratch

The yummiest foods can come from mixing together just the right combination of ingredients. Likewise, coming up with just the right mixture of story elements is what makes a great story. Use the recipe card to plan your own made-from-scratch story that includes a concept you're studying in math. Then write and illustrate your story on another sheet of paper.

Title: _____

Setting: _____

Main character: _____
Other characters: _____
Main character's goal: _____
_____
Math concept in my story: _____
_____
Plot (problem/conflict): _____
_____
Event 1: _____
Event 2: _____
Event 3: _____
_____
Climax: _____
_____
Resolution: _____
_____

©The Education Center, Inc. • THE MAILBOX® • Intermediate • Aug/Sept 1998

Note To The Teacher: Use with "Once Upon A Math Time…" on page 81.

Pattern Use with "Same Or Different?" on page 79.

Writing | Math

_____   How   _____
                  They're Alike

Isn't Math "Moo-velous"?

Looking for greener pastures and fresher ideas for math-skills practice? Then "moo-ve" your herd of students toward the following activities on measurement, multiplication, problem solving, and more!

Making Numbers Make Sense
Skill: Number-sense concepts

Steer your students to a greater grasp of number sense with this long-range journaling activity. Ask each student to bring in a 100-page spiral notebook. Have him write the numeral 1 at the top of the first page, the numeral 2 at the top of the second page, and so on until he reaches the numeral 100. Using the form in the illustration as a guide, help students complete their first journal page together. Then, throughout the year, assign two or three successive numbers each week until students' journals are completed. Don't be surprised if this practice leads your more creative students to play around with some advanced math concepts! *Phyllis Ellett—Grs. 3 & 4, Earl Hanson Elementary, Rock Island, IL*

1
Roman-numeral form:
Prime or composite?
Factors:
Multiples:
Real-life use of the number:
Simple addition sentence with this number as the sum:
Complex addition sentence with this number as the sum:
Subtraction sentence with this number as the difference:
Multiplication sentence using this number:
Division sentence using this number:
Fraction form:
Decimal form:

Do-Si-Do Multiplication
Skill: Multiplication steps

Hoof it up while students "moo-ve" through this reel that reviews the steps of multiplication! Begin by writing a multiplication problem on the board. Have several students form two facing lines, with the number of students per line corresponding to the place values of the two numbers to be multiplied. For example, if multiplying a three-digit number by a two-digit number, one line should have three students and the other line two. As the students in line perform the motions below, ask the other class members to clap their hands in a steady tempo while saying:

Ones times ones do-si-do. *(The two students representing the ones digits do-si-do.)*
Ones times tens do-si-do. *(The two students representing these positions do-si-do.)*
Ones times hundreds do-si-do. *(The two students representing these positions do-si-do, continuing in this manner for larger numbers until the ones have do-si-doed with all other place-value numbers in order.)*
Put a place holder down below. *(Students turn around once in place, then point to the spot where the place holder should go.)*

Repeat these lines for the tens place *(tens times ones do-si-do, tens times tens do-si-do, etc.)*. To conclude, shout, *"Now add!"* Students are sure to love the movement of this "moo-velous" multiplication hoedown! *Julie A. Rowan-Wolford— Gr. 5, Romney Elementary, Romney, WV*

Hundreds-Chart Multiplication
Skill: Basic multiplication facts

Don't get stampeded when students have difficulty mastering their multiplication facts. Instead, give them some hands-on practice that's "udder-ly" fantastic! Give each group of students a copy of the hundreds-chart pattern on page 88 and a supply of colored markers. Point out how this chart differs from the standard hundreds chart *(it begins at 100 and counts backward to 1)*. Assign each group a different multiplication table to cover on its chart as shown. Then have the group write a paragraph describing the pattern that emerges. Later on, use the hundreds charts to have students cover prime and composite factors of assigned numbers. *Patricia A. Shaw—Gr. 5, Blain Elementary, Blain, PA*

100	90	80	70	60	50	40	30	20	10
99	89	79	69	59	49	39	29	19	9
98	88	78	68	58	48	38	28	18	8
97	87	77	67	57	47	37	27	17	7
		76	66	56	46	36	26	16	6
	85	75	65	55	45	35	25	15	5
84		54	44	34	24	14	4		
		63	53	43	33	23	13	3	
82	72	62	52	42	32	22	12	2	
81	71	61	51	41	31	21	11	1	

Sports-Stats Trackers
Skill: Computation skills

If you or your students are sports fans, milk that passion for all the math practice it's worth! As a class, follow the progress of a professional (or college or local high school) sports team, a student's soccer team, or even *your* own bowling scores! Begin by setting up a chart to keep track of weekly statistics as shown. The first week, provide students with calculators and the data they need (such as scores for each game). Guide students through all the computations. On successive weeks, provide less and less guidance. Not only will students get the computation practice they need in a real-life situation, but they'll love cheering someone on from week to week! *James R. Lowry—Gr. 4, Webster Elementary, Pemberville, OH*

WEEK NUMBER	NUMBER OF GAMES	GAME 1	GAME 2	GAME 3	TOTAL PINS FOR THE WEEK	TOTAL PINS FOR THE YEAR	AVERAGE FOR THE YEAR
1	3	177	149	184	510	510	170
2	6	137	180	166	483	993	165
		193	167	172			

Soap-Bubble Math
Skill: Linear measurement

Beef up your next lesson on linear measurement with a hands-on activity that bubbles with fun! Mix together 2 cups of Joy® dishwashing liquid, 100–120 drops of glycerin, and 2 gallons of water in a large dishpan. Give each student a straw and a plastic cup filled with 1/2 cup of the bubble solution. Have him pour most of the solution on his desktop, spreading it so there are no dry spots to cause bubbles to break. Next have him dip his straw in the cup of solution, angle it in the puddle on his desk, and blow gently until a dome-shaped bubble appears. While students practice blowing bubbles, place plastic rulers (cm or standard) in the remaining solution in the dishpan. Show students how to insert a wet ruler into a bubble's dome and measure its height. Have students complete this step. Then have each student blow a bubble, pop it, and measure the resulting soap ring to find the bubble's diameter. To extend the activity, combine students' measurements; then have students graph the average height of a bubble's dome and the average diameter of a popped bubble. *Lucille G. Gluck—Gr. 5, Oak Street School, Lakewood, NJ*

Polygon Perimeter Posters
Skill: Polygons, finding perimeter

Corral your students for a rousing geometry review with this measurement activity. Write clues such as the following on the chalkboard:
- the side of a pyramid
- a sailboat's sail
- a yield sign
- a slice of pie or pizza
- a Doritos® chip

Ask students to guess the shape these clues suggest *(a triangle)*. Next divide students into groups. Direct each group to draw and cut out one of the objects above from construction paper. Then have the group glue the object on construction paper. Finally have the group measure and record the object's perimeter on the miniposter. Display the posters on a classroom wall or bulletin board titled "What's The Shape?" Use this activity to review the perimeter of other polygons—and for finding the circumference of circles too!

Slice Of Pizza

Perimeter = 36 cm

Name _____ Problem solving

Down On Farmer Phil's Farm

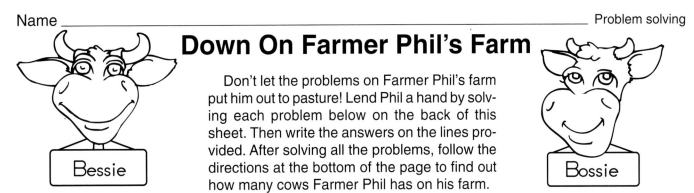

Don't let the problems on Farmer Phil's farm put him out to pasture! Lend Phil a hand by solving each problem below on the back of this sheet. Then write the answers on the lines provided. After solving all the problems, follow the directions at the bottom of the page to find out how many cows Farmer Phil has on his farm.

Bessie

Bossie

1. On clear mornings Farmer Phil walks to the south pasture. This pasture is one mile from his farmhouse. If his stride measures four feet, how many strides will it take him to reach the pasture? _____

2. During Farmer Phil's walk to the south pasture, he counts the number of animals that he sees (such as rabbits and birds). During the first five minutes, he sees seven animals. During the next five-minute periods, he sees four animals, then five animals, and two animals. At this rate, for how many minutes will he walk before he sees no animals at all? _____

3. Dairy farmers in Farmer Phil's state were asked, "Do you raise Holsteins, Jerseys, or both?" Of the 100 farmers who answered the question, 85 raised Holsteins, 75 raised Jerseys, and 60 raised both. How many farmers raised only Holsteins? _____ How many farmers raised only Jerseys? _____

4. Farmer Phil and his wife, Fannie, just bought new tables and stools for their farmhouse. Altogether the furniture has 14 legs. How many four-legged tables and three-legged stools did the couple buy?_____

5. Farmer Phil has two old dogs named Rosco and Ray. The product of their ages is 150. The sum of their ages is 25. What is the difference in their ages? _____

6. Farmer Phil is planning to add a new 100-foot section to the fence around the north pasture. How many posts will he need if he wants them to be ten feet apart? _____

7. Fannie and Phil take in stray dogs and chickens. One morning they counted a total of 10 heads and 34 legs. How many dogs and chickens do they have? _____

8. Bessie, Bossie, Mabel, and Matilda are Farmer Phil's favorite cows. He wants to get special gifts for them. Matilda doesn't like it when flies land on her head. Bessie and Mabel get skittish when they hear tinkling noises. Mabel also doesn't like to be brushed. Make a ✓ or an ✗ in the grid to help you find which cow gets which gift.

	Bell	Hat	Brush	Harness
Bessie				
Bossie				
Mabel				
Matilda				

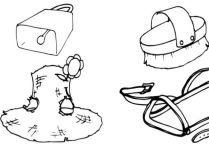

Now add 150 to the sum of the answers for problems 2–7 to find out how many cows Farmer Phil has on his farm. _____ **cows**

Bonus Box: On another sheet of paper, write a story about an emergency Farmer Phil has with one of his favorite cows.

©The Education Center, Inc. • THE MAILBOX® • Intermediate • Oct/Nov 1998 • Key p. 308

Milk-Cap Toss

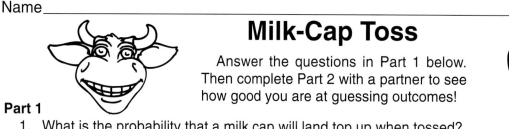

Answer the questions in Part 1 below.
Then complete Part 2 with a partner to see
how good you are at guessing outcomes!

Part 1

1. What is the probability that a milk cap will land top up when tossed? _____ Why? _____
   _____

2. If you toss the cap 50 times, how many times do you think it will land top up? _____ Why?
   _____

Part 2

1. To play Round 1, toss the cap 50 times. Have your partner use tally marks in the chart to record how the cap lands each time.

	Round 1	Total	Round 2	Total
Top Up				
Top Down				

2. To play Round 2, switch places with your partner and repeat Step 1.

3. Does the data in your chart support the prediction you made in Part 1 (#2)? _____ Why or why not?
   _____
   _____

Bonus Box: Use the totals from your two rounds to find the average number of times the milk cap landed up and the average number of times it landed down. Use the back of this sheet to show your work.

©The Education Center, Inc. • *THE MAILBOX®* • *Intermediate* • Oct/Nov 1998 • Key p. 308

- -

Note To The Teacher: Make one copy of this page for each pair of students. Give each pair of students a clean cap from a milk jug.

Pattern

Use with "Hundreds-Chart
Multiplication" on page 85.

100	90	80	70	60	50	40	30	20	10
99	89	79	69	59	49	39	29	19	9
98	88	78	68	58	48	38	28	18	8
97	87	77	67	57	47	37	27	17	7
96	86	76	66	56	46	36	26	16	6
95	85	75	65	55	45	35	25	15	5
94	84	74	64	54	44	34	24	14	4
93	83	73	63	53	43	33	23	13	3
92	82	72	62	52	42	32	22	12	2
91	81	71	61	51	41	31	21	11	1

©The Education Center, Inc. • *THE MAILBOX®* • *Intermediate* • Oct/Nov 1998

SCORING BIG WITH FRACTIONS AND DECIMALS

When students come up against fractions and decimals, they need a game plan that's loaded with can't-be-beat offensive and defensive strategies. As their coach, prepare them to take on these challenging opponents with the following creative ideas and reproducibles!

by Marsha Schmus

FIRST-HALF ACTION: FRACTIONS

GOING FOR ONE!
Skill: Identifying fractions

Tip off the unit with this hands-on activity on identifying fractions. Place 15 color tiles or paper squares—five blue, two red, three yellow, and five green—in a paper lunch bag. List the four colors in separate columns on the board; then select five students to help with the activity. Have four students take turns drawing one tile at a time from the bag while the other student tallies the tiles on the board by color. After the bag has been emptied, help students understand that the separate drawings represent the different parts of a *whole*, or the total contents of the bag. For example, since two of the 15 tiles are red, they represent 2/15 of the bag's total tiles. As students identify the fractional parts by color, record the parts on the board as addends equaling one whole as shown. Repeat this activity several times, each time varying the number of tiles per color. Then place the materials in a free-time center for extra practice.

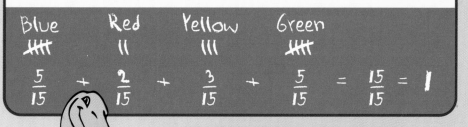

Blue	Red	Yellow	Green
‖‖‖	‖	‖‖	‖‖‖

$$\frac{5}{15} + \frac{2}{15} + \frac{3}{15} + \frac{5}{15} = \frac{15}{15} = 1$$

BOWLING FOR FRACTIONS
Skill: Adding fractions

Looking for a winning way to practice addition of fractions? Take a shot at this super small-group game! Gather a small ball and an inexpensive set of plastic bowling pins (or use ten empty paper-towel tubes instead). Label each pin with a different fraction, using like or unlike fractions depending on students' abilities. Set up the pins; then have one student start by rolling the ball toward the pins. Have her add together the fractions from the knocked-down pins. Direct the other group members to check her sum. If correct, the player scores her sum for that frame. If the player adds incorrectly, she doesn't score. At the end of ten frames, have students total their scores to determine the winner. If desired, reprogram the pins to reinforce other important skills, such as adding decimals.

MYSTERY FRACTION OF THE DAY
Skill: Number sense

How can riddles rev up fraction skills? You'll soon see with this easy idea! Program large index cards with the following fractions (one fraction per card): 3/4, 9/10, 5/6, 8/12, 6/12, 3/8, 5/10, 2/3, 1/3, 1/4. Display the cards in your classroom. Each day write a different fraction riddle—such as those suggested below—on the board. Ask students to select the correct answer from the fraction cards. Challenge each student who solves the riddle to write another riddle for one or more of the other fractions displayed. With this idea, you'll always have a fresh supply of fraction riddles on hand!

- My numerator and denominator are both divisible by 3. I am equal to 1/2. What fraction am I? *(6/12)*

- My numerator is between 7 and 11. My denominator is less than 14 and is divisible by 3. What fraction am I? *(8/12)*

- My numerator is less than 5. My denominator is a multiple of 2 that's greater than 6. I am less than 1/2. What fraction am I? *(3/8)*

- My numerator is the smallest odd number. My denominator is the next largest odd number. I am less than 1/2. What fraction am I? *(1/3)*

- Both my numerator and denominator are divisible by 2. I am less than 2/3 and greater than 1/3. What fraction am I? *(6/12)*

- My denominator is a two-digit number divisible by 5. I am greater than 2/3. My numerator is a one-digit number divisible by 3. What fraction am I? *(9/10)*

FULL-COURT GRAPHIN'
Skill: Identifying fractions, graphing

Provide your students with a perfect shot at learning more about one another—*and* about fractions—with this kid-pleasin' activity! Direct each student to choose a different topic—such as students who Rollerblade®, students who watch [name of TV show], or students who have home computers—and interview his classmates. Meanwhile, mount bulletin-board paper on a board or wall. Draw a graph on the paper as shown, labeling it with your number of students. Have each student write his interview topic on a sentence strip and post it on the graph's horizontal axis. Then assist students with compiling and plotting their data on the graph. Discuss the graph's information with students in terms of fractions: 2/25 of the students live in apartments, 5/25 watch game shows, etc. Follow up by having students write the graph's fractions in order from greatest to least.

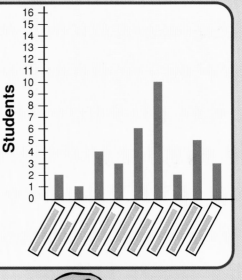

FRACTION-ACTION BINGO
Skill: Fraction concepts

Coaches know that practice is the key to improving any skill. Use the familiar game of bingo to strengthen students' understanding of several fraction concepts. Give each student scissors and a copy of page 92. Review the sheet's directions with students; then give them time to program and cut out their gameboards. Next distribute dried beans for students to use as markers. Read aloud one clue at a time from the list below until a student calls, "Bingo!" To play additional games, suggest that students trade gameboards.

Clues:

- the fraction equivalent to 1 *(18/18)*
- the picture that shows 3/4 ( )
- the fraction equivalent to 4/6 *(2/3)*
- a mixed number *(1 2/3)*
- an improper fraction *(9/7)*
- the picture that shows tenths ( )
- the fraction equivalent to 1/2 *(10/20)*
- the picture that shows 2/8 of a set ( )
- the fraction with 11 as its numerator *(11/23)*
- the sum of these fractions is 1 *(3/8 + 5/8)*
- 3/5 is lowest terms for this fraction *(12/20)*
- 1/5 is lowest terms for this fraction *(2/10)*
- this fraction is lowest terms for 14/28 *(1/2)*
- this fraction is lowest terms for 4/12 *(1/3)*
- the least common denominator of 1/12 and 1/24 *(24)*
- the difference between these fractions is 5/7 *(7/7 – 2/7)*
- the least common denominator of 1/3 and 1/4 *(12)*
- the picture that shows unequal parts ( )
- the difference between 7/11 and 5/11 *(2/11)*
- the fraction equivalent to 6/14 *(3/7)*
- the whole number equivalent of 20/5 *(4)*
- the whole number for 12/6 *(2)*
- 4/7 is the sum of these fractions *(3/7 + 1/7)*
- the picture that shows fourths ( )

LCD RECIPES
Skill: Finding the lowest common denominator

Evaluating players' strengths and weaknesses is part of a coach's job. Quickly assess students' abilities for finding lowest common denominators with this easy task. Clip recipes from old newspapers and magazines; then give each student one recipe. Challenge the student to rewrite his recipe's ingredients so that all the fractions have common denominators. What a simple exercise for finding out exactly how much each student knows!

MIXING IT UP
Skill: Sequencing decimal numbers

Order up some terrific decimal practice with this beat-the-clock game! Write 30 decimal numbers on index cards, one number per card. Place any five cards on your chalkboard tray, arranging them so they're not in sequential order. Select one student to rearrange the cards from least to greatest as you time her. When she completes this task, record her time; then have the rest of the class check her arrangement. If she has ordered the cards correctly, announce her time as her score. If she has ordered them incorrectly, add ten seconds to her time to determine her score. Continue play by replacing the cards with five different ones and calling up another student. After everyone has had a turn, declare the student with the lowest score the winner.

SIZE 'EM UP!
Skill: Rounding decimals

Help students size up their decimal skills with this rounding activity! Draw a number line on the board as shown. Use the number line to review how to round several decimals to 0 or 1; then erase it. Next ask each student to write a one- or two-digit decimal number that is less than 1 on the board. Have each student use the key (see the illustration) to draw a shape around his decimal. Then point to the decimals with squares around them. Have students help you order them from least to greatest. In the same manner, have students order the decimals with triangles around them. Use this activity and a number line divided into sixteenths to help students round fractions to 0 or 1!

```
|----|----|----|----|----|----|----|----|----|----|
0   0.1  0.2  0.3  0.4  0.5  0.6  0.7  0.8  0.9   1
```

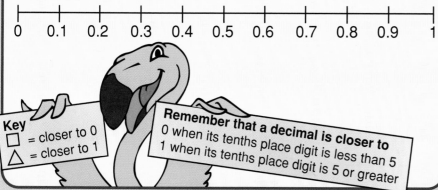

Key
□ = closer to 0
△ = closer to 1

Remember that a decimal is closer to
0 when its tenths place digit is less than 5
1 when its tenths place digit is 5 or greater

SLAM-DUNKING DECIMALS
Skill: Decimal concepts

Watch decimal skills soar as high as Michael Jordan with this multipurpose activity! Make a transparency of a 10 x 10 grid; then use wipe-off markers to color a design on the grid as shown (or draw the grid on the chalkboard and use colored chalk). Have students tell you the decimal numbers that represent the colors on the grid (for example, .04 of the grid is black). Next ask the class to add all the decimal numbers together to see that they equal one whole. Afterward direct students to compare one color's decimal value with another and/or perform specific calculations, such as finding the sum of the decimal values of any three colors or the difference between the decimal values of any two colors. Lastly have students order the decimal values of the colors from greatest to least or least to greatest. To follow up this activity, reach for the reproducible activity on page 95!

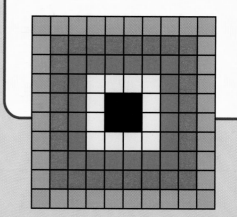

FRACTION-ACTION BINGO

Directions: Choose any 16 items from the box below. Write or draw each item in a different square on the gameboard at the bottom of the page. Then cut out the gameboard. Listen to the clues that your teacher gives you; then cover the square on the gameboard that matches a clue. When you've covered four squares in a row—horizontally, diagonally, or vertically—call out, "Bingo!"

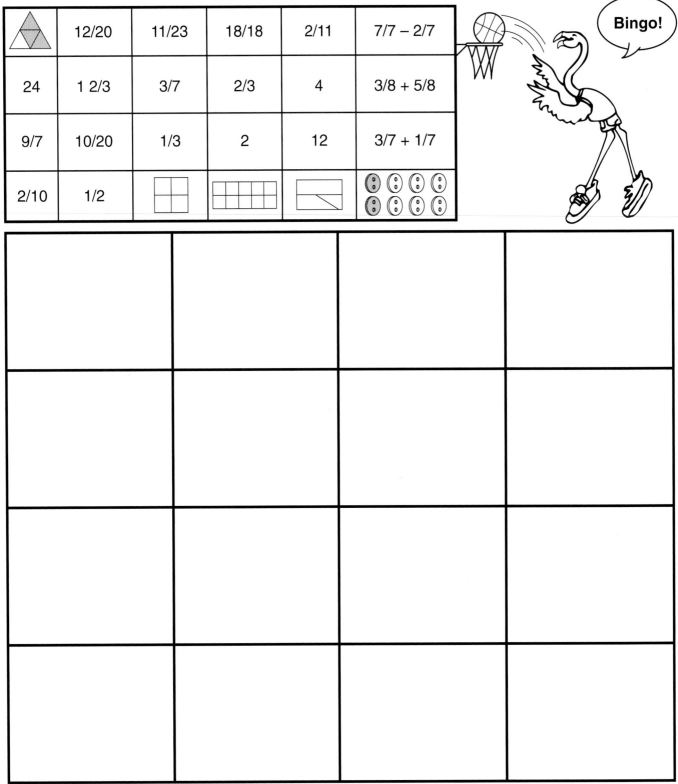

©The Education Center, Inc. • THE MAILBOX® • Intermediate • Dec/Jan 1998–99

92   **Note To The Teacher:** Use with "Fraction-Action Bingo" on page 90.

GOING ONE-ON-ONE!
A Game For Four Players

Getting ready to play:
1. Cut out the box below. Glue it to tagboard; then cut the cards apart. Also cut out the key.
2. Shuffle the cards. Deal the same number of cards to each player.
3. If you have a fraction card and a decimal card that are equivalent, lay them faceup on the table. Use the key to check.

Playing the game (follow these steps when it's your turn):
1. Ask any player for a card you need to make a match. If you have a fraction card, ask for its matching decimal card ("Do you have a decimal card that matches 1/5?"). If you have a decimal card, ask for its matching fraction card ("Do you have a fraction card that matches .33?").
2. If the player doesn't have a matching card, he or she says, "No match."
3. If the player has the card you want, he or she gives it to you. Check the match with the key. If it's correct, lay it faceup on the table. If the cards don't match, the player must give one of his matching pairs to the player on his left.

When all cards have been matched, count your matches. The player with the most matches wins.

Key		
Fraction		**Decimal**
1/3, 2/6	=	.33
1/2, 2/4, 3/6	=	.50
2/3, 4/6	=	.67
1/4, 2/8	=	.25
1/5, 2/10	=	.20
3/4, 6/8	=	.75
5/5	=	1.0

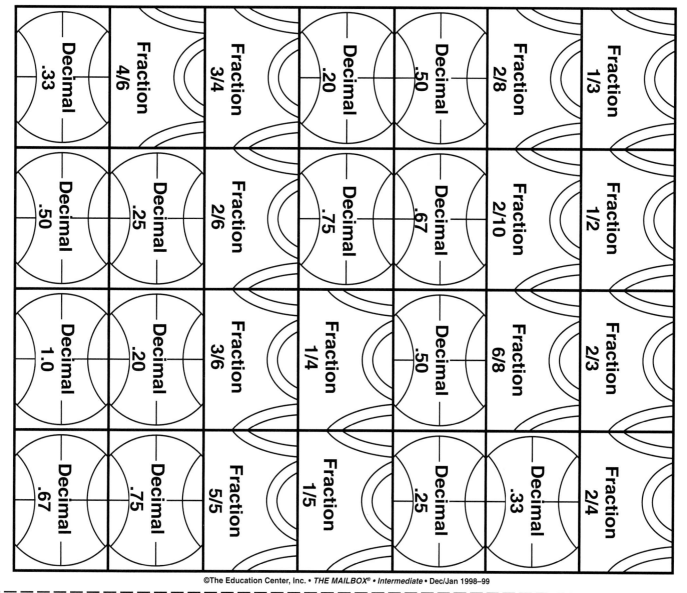

Note To The Teacher: Give scissors, a sheet of tagboard, glue, and one copy of this page to each group of four students.

TIC-TAC-TOE FRACTIONS

Practice games are good for sharpening players' skills. Strengthen your ability to find equivalent fractions with this tic-tac-toe game. All you need is a partner, a die, and a winning effort!

Code:

⚀ = 1/4   ⚂ = 1/3   ⚁ = 1/2   ⚃ = 1/8   ⚄ = 3/4   ⚅ = 2/3

Directions for two players:

1. Roll the die. The player with the higher roll becomes player 1.
2. Player 1 rolls the die and uses the code above to find the equivalent fraction on gameboard 1. If he or she finds a correct fraction, player 1 writes his or her initials in that block.
3. Player 2 rolls and repeats step 2.
4. Play continues until one player initials three blocks in a row—vertically, horizontally, or diagonally—to get the win. Record the winner's name on the line below the gameboard.
5. Repeat steps 1–4 for the three remaining gameboards.

Gameboard 1

$\frac{3}{6}$	$\frac{2}{16}$	$\frac{3}{24}$
$\frac{2}{6}$	$\frac{3}{12}$	$\frac{4}{6}$
$\frac{6}{9}$	$\frac{5}{10}$	$\frac{9}{12}$

Winner: _____

Gameboard 2

$\frac{6}{8}$	$\frac{2}{8}$	$\frac{8}{12}$
$\frac{3}{9}$	$\frac{4}{32}$	$\frac{4}{16}$
$\frac{4}{12}$	$\frac{4}{8}$	$\frac{6}{12}$

Winner: _____

$\frac{1}{2}$

$\frac{8}{16}$

Gameboard 3

$\frac{5}{20}$	$\frac{6}{18}$	$\frac{7}{14}$
$\frac{12}{18}$	$\frac{4}{6}$	$\frac{9}{18}$
$\frac{4}{32}$	$\frac{6}{8}$	$\frac{3}{24}$

Winner: _____

Gameboard 4

$\frac{5}{40}$	$\frac{12}{16}$	$\frac{10}{15}$
$\frac{2}{4}$	$\frac{2}{8}$	$\frac{8}{12}$
$\frac{6}{12}$	$\frac{4}{16}$	$\frac{9}{27}$

Winner: _____

Note To The Teacher: Give a die, an enlarged copy of the answer key on page 308 (if desired), and a copy of this sheet to each pair of students.

GOING ONE-ON-ONE!
A Game For Four Players

Getting ready to play:
1. Cut out the box below. Glue it to tagboard; then cut the cards apart. Also cut out the key.
2. Shuffle the cards. Deal the same number of cards to each player.
3. If you have a fraction card and a decimal card that are equivalent, lay them faceup on the table. Use the key to check.

Playing the game (follow these steps when it's your turn):
1. Ask any player for a card you need to make a match. If you have a fraction card, ask for its matching decimal card ("Do you have a decimal card that matches 1/5?"). If you have a decimal card, ask for its matching fraction card ("Do you have a fraction card that matches .33?").
2. If the player doesn't have a matching card, he or she says, "No match."
3. If the player has the card you want, he or she gives it to you. Check the match with the key. If it's correct, lay it faceup on the table. If the cards don't match, the player must give one of his matching pairs to the player on his left.

When all cards have been matched, count your matches. The player with the most matches wins.

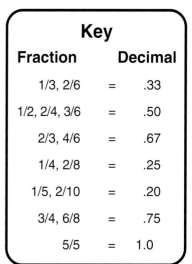

Key		
Fraction		**Decimal**
1/3, 2/6	=	.33
1/2, 2/4, 3/6	=	.50
2/3, 4/6	=	.67
1/4, 2/8	=	.25
1/5, 2/10	=	.20
3/4, 6/8	=	.75
5/5	=	1.0

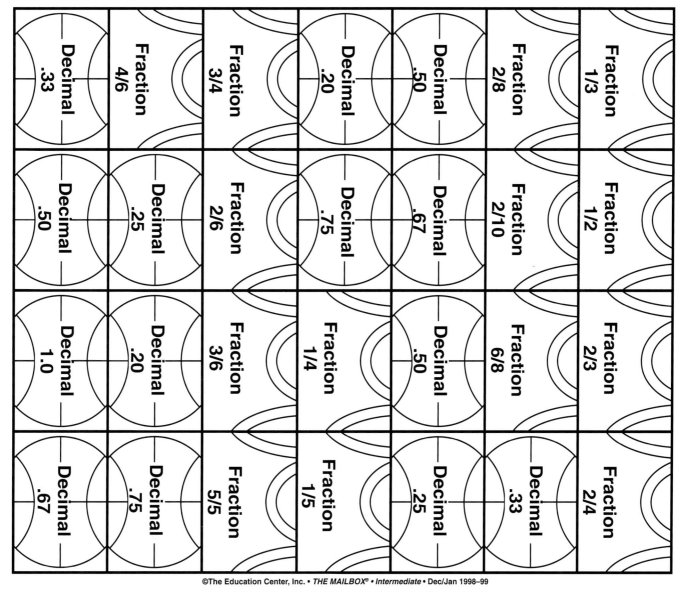

Decimal .33	Fraction 4/6	Fraction 3/4	Decimal .20	Decimal .50	Fraction 2/8	Fraction 1/3
Decimal .50	Decimal .25	Fraction 2/6	Decimal .75	Decimal .67	Fraction 2/10	Fraction 1/2
Decimal 1.0	Decimal .20	Fraction 3/6	Fraction 1/4	Decimal .50	Fraction 6/8	Fraction 2/3
Decimal .67	Decimal .75	Fraction 5/5	Fraction 1/5	Decimal .25	Decimal .33	Fraction 2/4

Note To The Teacher: Give scissors, a sheet of tagboard, glue, and one copy of this page to each group of four students.

TIC-TAC-TOE FRACTIONS

Practice games are good for sharpening players' skills. Strengthen your ability to find equivalent fractions with this tic-tac-toe game. All you need is a partner, a die, and a winning effort!

Code:

$\boxed{\cdot} = 1/4$ $\boxed{\because} = 1/3$ $\boxed{\cdot\,\cdot} = 1/2$ $\boxed{::} = 1/8$ $\boxed{:\cdot:} = 3/4$ $\boxed{:::} = 2/3$

Directions for two players:

1. Roll the die. The player with the higher roll becomes player 1.
2. Player 1 rolls the die and uses the code above to find the equivalent fraction on gameboard 1. If he or she finds a correct fraction, player 1 writes his or her initials in that block.
3. Player 2 rolls and repeats step 2.
4. Play continues until one player initials three blocks in a row—vertically, horizontally, or diagonally—to get the win. Record the winner's name on the line below the gameboard.
5. Repeat steps 1–4 for the three remaining gameboards.

Gameboard 1

$\dfrac{3}{6}$	$\dfrac{2}{16}$	$\dfrac{3}{24}$
$\dfrac{2}{6}$	$\dfrac{3}{12}$	$\dfrac{4}{6}$
$\dfrac{6}{9}$	$\dfrac{5}{10}$	$\dfrac{9}{12}$

Winner: _____

Gameboard 2

$\dfrac{6}{8}$	$\dfrac{2}{8}$	$\dfrac{8}{12}$
$\dfrac{3}{9}$	$\dfrac{4}{32}$	$\dfrac{4}{16}$
$\dfrac{4}{12}$	$\dfrac{4}{8}$	$\dfrac{6}{12}$

Winner: _____

$\dfrac{1}{2}$

$\dfrac{8}{16}$

FRACTIONS

Gameboard 3

$\dfrac{5}{20}$	$\dfrac{6}{18}$	$\dfrac{7}{14}$
$\dfrac{12}{18}$	$\dfrac{4}{6}$	$\dfrac{9}{18}$
$\dfrac{4}{32}$	$\dfrac{6}{8}$	$\dfrac{3}{24}$

Winner: _____

Gameboard 4

$\dfrac{5}{40}$	$\dfrac{12}{16}$	$\dfrac{10}{15}$
$\dfrac{2}{4}$	$\dfrac{2}{8}$	$\dfrac{8}{12}$
$\dfrac{6}{12}$	$\dfrac{4}{16}$	$\dfrac{9}{27}$

Winner: _____

Note To The Teacher: Give a die, an enlarged copy of the answer key on page 308 (if desired), and a copy of this sheet to each pair of students.

PUTTING NEW MOVES ON DECIMALS

During a basketball game, players guard each other and try to keep opponents from scoring. You can guard against confusion about decimal numbers with the help of this activity. Just follow the directions below, and you'll come out a winner!

Code:
R = red
Bl = blue
G = green
B = black
W = white

G	G	W	R	B	B	R	W	G	G
G	G	W	R	B	B	R	W	G	G
W	W	R	B	B	B	B	R	W	W
W	R	B	Bl	B	B	Bl	B	R	W
R	B	B	B	B	B	B	B	B	R
B	Bl	B	Bl	B	B	Bl	B	Bl	B
R	B	B	B	B	B	B	B	B	R
W	R	R	R	B	B	R	R	R	W
G	W	W	R	B	B	R	W	W	G
G	G	W	R	B	B	R	W	G	G

Directions:

1. Color the squares in the grid above according to the code. Don't color the squares marked with a *W*.

2. Record the number of squares for each color as a decimal number.

   R = _____   Bl = _____   G = _____   B = _____   W = _____

3. Find the sum of the decimals in step 2.

   _____ + _____ + _____ + _____ + _____ = _____

   Explain the importance of this sum. _____

   _____

4. Calculate the sum or difference of each problem below. Use the back of this page to work the problems if you need more space.

   R + Bl = _____   G + B = _____   R + G + W = _____

   Bl + B = _____   B – W = _____   R – G = _____

   (B + Bl + G) – (R + W) = _____

5. Use <, >, or = to compare the following:

   B _____ R   R _____ W   G _____ W   G _____ Bl   W _____ Bl

   Bonus Box: On the back of this page, order the decimal numbers in step 2 from greatest to least.

©The Education Center, Inc. • THE MAILBOX® • Intermediate • Dec/Jan 1998–99 • Key p. 308

Divide And Conquer!

Creative Activities To Strengthen Students' Division Skills

Does the mere mention of long division cause a collective moan to rise from your class? If so, include the following fun-filled games and reproducibles in your math plans. They're sure to help students conquer the division blues!

by Irving P. Crump

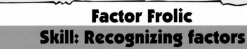

I've got a factor of 18.

Just A Faster Way To Subtract
Skill: Understanding division

Yep, that's what division is—a shortcut for subtraction! Help students understand this concept with a simple calculator activity. Provide each student with a calculator. Then write a division problem, such as $59 \div 7$, on the board. Remind the class that to divide 59 by 7 means to find out how many whole groups of 7 are in 59. One way to do that is by subtracting.

Direct each student to enter $59 - 7 =$ in his calculator and note the display *(52)*. This represents one group of 7. Next tell students to press the = key again and note the display *(45)*. Two groups of 7 have now been subtracted from 59. Have students continue to press the = key (and count the number of times they press it) until 3 is displayed. Students should count eight whole groups of 7 subtracted from 59, with 3 left over. Repeat these same steps with other dividends and divisors. (This would be a perfect time to review the calculator's *constant function*. To repeat an operation without reentering it, such as *subtract 7,* simply continue to press the = key the number of times that you want to perform the operation.)

Factor Frolic
Skill: Recognizing factors

Factors are numbers that multiply to give a product. So a factor of a number divides that number without a remainder—an important concept to grasp when doing long division. Provide practice with recognizing factors by playing this mental-math game. Give each student five index cards. Direct her to write a number from 2 to 10 on each card, without repeating a number (example: 2, 3, 6, 7, and 10). Have each student lay her cards faceup on her desk. Tell students that the object of this game is to determine factors of numbers that you call out. Here's how to play:

1. Call out any two-digit number, such as 20.
2. Each student checks her cards to see whether she has a factor of 20.
3. If a student has a card with a factor of 20, she holds it up so that you can check it.
4. If she is correct, she turns that card over. If not, she places the card back faceup on her desk.
5. Although a student may have more than one factor of the number you call, she can hold up only one card at a time. For example, if a student has cards with 2, 3, 6, 7, and 10, she may hold up either the 2 or the 10, since each is a factor of 20.

Continue play until a student wins by being the first to turn over all of her cards. Then have students swap cards and begin a new game. For a variation, allow students to hold up more than one card at a time. In the example above, the student could hold up the 2 and the 10 since they are both factors of 20. For more fun with factors, see the reproducible on page 98.

Stand Up And Divide
Skill: Long-division steps

Why does division often unnerve intermediate kids? Maybe it's because they must know their multiplication facts in order to have a good grasp of division—plus they must have good subtraction skills. Help students get the hang of the long-division process with this fun game. Gather 36 index cards; then divide them equally into two 18-card sets. In each set, label one card 0, one 9, and two cards each with the digits 1–8. Divide the class into two teams, and distribute a set of cards to each team. Have a dealer deal his team's cards. Some players will have two cards, but make sure that no player has duplicates. Write a division problem, like the one shown, on the chalkboard. To play, follow these steps:

1. Say, "Divide," to Team 1. Each student on that team mentally divides 51 by 8 *(6)*.
2. Each student on Team 1 who has a 6 card stands and shows it to you to be checked.
3. After you check the cards, award each correct response a point.
4. Appoint one of the 6-card holders to go to the board and write 6 in the quotient.
5. Next say, "Multiply," to Team 2. Each student mentally multiplies 6 times 8 *(48)*.
6. Each student on Team 2 who has a 4 or an 8 card (for the product 48) stands and shows it to you to be checked.
7. After you check the cards, award each correct response a point.
8. Appoint one of the 4- or 8-card holders to go to the board and write 48 in its position.
9. Next say, "Subtract," to Team 1. Each student on Team 1 mentally subtracts 48 from 51 *(3)*.
10. Each student on Team 1 who has a 3 card stands and shows it to you to be checked.
11. After you check the cards, award each correct response a point.
12. Appoint a 3-card holder to go to the board and write 3 in its position. Also tell that player to bring down the 8 from the dividend's ones place.
13. Begin the cycle again by saying, "Divide," to Team 2. Each student mentally divides 38 by 8.

Continue the steps of the game until the problem is solved. Then erase the problem and write another one on the board. The team with the most points at the end of the game wins.

Right On Target!
Skill: Division and multiplication

More practice with long division is in store with this game of chance. First, remove the cards ace through 10 of two suits from a deck of playing cards. Shuffle these 20 cards; then have a volunteer draw four. Write the values of the four cards on the chalkboard (ace = 1; ten = 0). Next, have each student arrange the digits to make a four-digit number and write it on his paper. Direct students to divide their numbers by 2. Then instruct students to check their work by multiplying (quotient x divisor + remainder = dividend). Instruct students to put down their pencils when they are finished.

When every student has checked his work and is satisfied with his answer, call out a target number—any digit from 0 to 9. Tell students that if the target digit
- is in the ones place of the quotient, score 5 points;
- is in the tens place of the quotient, score 10 points;
- is in the hundreds place of the quotient, score 15 points;
- is in the thousands place of the quotient, score 20 points;
- matches the remainder, score 50 points.

After teaching this game to the entire class, provide each pair of students with a copy of page 100. Each pair also needs 20 playing cards, so you'll need a deck of cards for every four students.

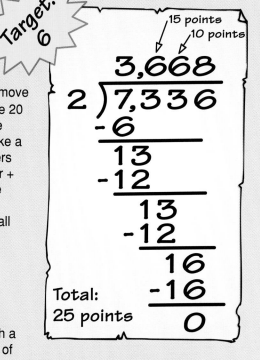

Factor Face-off

How well do you know the factors of numbers? Find out by challenging a friend to a game of Factor Face-off!

Materials: 2 different-colored pencils, a die, a calculator

How to play:

1. Each player rolls the die. The player with the higher roll is Player 1.
2. Player 1 rolls the die and writes the number showing in the first blank of Game 1, Round 1. Player 1 rolls the die again and writes the number showing in the second blank.
3. Player 1 studies Game 1's factors and then circles each one that is a factor of his two-digit number.
4. If necessary, Player 2 checks Player 1's circled factors with the calculator. If Player 1 has circled an incorrect factor, Player 2 marks through it.
5. Player 2 repeats steps 2–4, with Player 1 checking. Player 2 cannot circle a factor that is already circled or marked out.
6. Play continues for four rounds. The winner of the game is the player who correctly circles more factors.
7. Special rule for Game 4: Add 2 to each roll of the die.*
8. Special rule for Game 5: Add 3 to each roll of the die.**

Player 1:	**F A C T O R S**					Player 2:
Rounds 1.___ ___ 2.___ ___ 3.___ ___ 4.___ ___	**Game 1** 2 3 5 6 11 4 9 8 7					Rounds 1.___ ___ 2.___ ___ 3.___ ___ 4.___ ___
Rounds 1.___ ___ 2.___ ___ 3.___ ___ 4.___ ___	**Game 2** 2 3 5 7 4 6 8 12 13 9 11					Rounds 1.___ ___ 2.___ ___ 3.___ ___ 4.___ ___
Rounds 1.___ ___ 2.___ ___ 3.___ ___ 4.___ ___	**Game 3** 2 3 4 5 9 8 13 7 6 15 11 14 12					Rounds 1.___ ___ 2.___ ___ 3.___ ___ 4.___ ___
Rounds 1.___ ___ 2.___ ___ 3.___ ___ 4.___ ___	***Game 4** 7 6 3 2 8 5 9 4 11 14 13 15 18 12 16					Rounds 1.___ ___ 2.___ ___ 3.___ ___ 4.___ ___
Rounds 1.___ ___ 2.___ ___ 3.___ ___ 4.___ ___	****Game 5** 2 6 16 11 3 7 9 13 12 4 5 8 18 15 14					Rounds 1.___ ___ 2.___ ___ 3.___ ___ 4.___ ___

Note To The Teacher: Use with "Factor Frolic" on page 96. Provide each pair of students with two different-colored pencils, a die, and a calculator.

Remainder Relay

Go to battle with a friend as you divide by the divisors 6, 7, 8, and 9!

Materials: 4 index cards (numbered 6–9)   pencils and paper   1 calculator
9 playing cards (ace–9)   2 different-colored markers

Directions: The object of the game is to circle four numbers in a row in the grid—down, across, or diagonally. First, mix up the nine playing cards and stack them facedown. Mix up the four index cards and stack them facedown. To play:

1. Player 1 turns over the top three playing cards.
2. Player 1 makes any three-digit number with the three numbers showing (ace = 1) and writes it on his paper.
3. Player 1 turns over the top index card.
4. Player 1 divides his three-digit number by the number on the index card.
5. Player 2 checks Player 1's work with the calculator (quotient x divisor + remainder = dividend).

6. If Player 1 is correct, he chooses a number in the grid that matches his remainder and circles it with his marker. If he is incorrect, he does not circle a number.
7. Player 1 then mixes up each set of cards and stacks each set facedown.
8. Player 2 repeats steps 1–7, with Player 1 checking.
9. Continue play until a player circles four numbers in a row with his marker.

7	0	2	1	8	2	0	3	4
4	3	5	7	6	1	7	5	8
6	2	6	8	2	5	3	1	6
3	5	4	5	1	4	8	7	2
4	7	1	8	0	6	1	3	5
1	0	3	6	2	5	4	0	8
6	7	2	8	0	7	2	3	5
2	4	6	1	4	3	8	4	0
8	7	0	3	5	6	0	1	7

Right On Target!

With a little luck, maybe you can hit the target!

Materials: 20 playing cards, including 2 each of ace–10 (ace = 1; 10 = 0); pencils and paper; calculator

To play each round:

1. Shuffle the cards. Stack them facedown.
2. Player 1: Turn over the first four cards. Arrange them to form a four-digit number. Write it on your paper.
3. Player 2: Turn over the next four cards. Arrange them to form a four-digit number. Write it on your paper.
4. Divide your four-digit number by 2—the divisor for the first round. See the example below.
5. After dividing, check each other's work with the calculator. Remember that quotient x divisor + remainder = dividend. If your answer is incorrect, rework the problem.
6. Player 1 or Player 2: Turn over the next card in the deck—the target number. Write its value in the target space for Round 1.

To score:

If your quotient has the target number
- in the ones place, score 5 points;
- in the tens place, score 10 points;
- in the hundreds place, score 15 points;
- in the thousands place, score 20 points;
- as its remainder, score 50 points.

At the end of the game, add your total score. Write it in your box on the scorecard.

Example: A player draws 8, 10, ace, and 5. Then the player writes 5,108 and divides:

```
      2,554 r.0
2)5,108
   -4
    11
   -10
    10
   -10
    08
    -8
     0
```

If the target is 5, the player scores:
10 points for 5 in the tens place
+15 points for 5 in the hundreds place
25 points in all

Rounds			Player 1	Player 2
1	divide by **2**	target		
2	divide by **5**	target		
3	divide by **7**	target		
4	divide by **3**	target		
5	divide by **6**	target		
6	divide by **8**	target		
7	divide by **9**	target		
8	divide by **4**	target		
9	divide by **2**	target		
10	divide by **5**	target		
11	divide by **7**	target		
12	divide by **8**	target		
13	divide by **9**	target		
14	divide by **3**	target		
		Totals		

Terrific Tools For Teaching MATH

Math Activities Using Manipulatives

Just as a builder uses a variety of helpful tools to create a product, you can use a variety of creative tools to help you teach math skills, too! Take a look at some of our readers' clever ideas using easy-to-make, easy-to-use manipulatives.

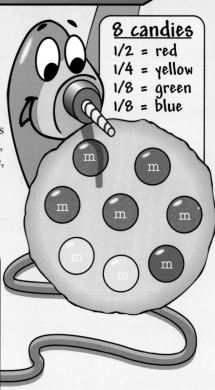

8 candies
1/2 = red
1/4 = yellow
1/8 = green
1/8 = blue

A Mouthwatering Manipulative

Here's an idea that melts in your mouth *and* is a great addition to your fractions unit. Prepare a batch of cookies decorated with M&M's® candies, putting a random number of candies and colors on the top of each one. Give each student a cookie and direct him to count the number of its candies, thus determining the denominator for his set. Then have him write a fraction to show the part of the set represented by each color. Also have students figure out whose cookie has the greatest fraction of each color, find common denominators, order and reduce fractions, and add fractions to equal one whole. When all the work is done, have the most fun of all by eating your tasty manipulatives!

Denise Coleman—Gr. 5, St. Mary School, Menomonee Falls, WI

Quick And Easy Tangrams

Tangrams are one of the best math tools around because they provide plenty of hands-on experiences—and kids love them! However, funds to buy such items are often limited. To save money, make tangrams from sheets of foam purchased in a craft store. These colorful foam sheets cost less than 50¢ each, and you can make two sets of tangrams from each one. If pieces of a tangram set are lost, they're easy to replace—just trace and cut out new ones!

Rochelle Chenoweth, Elkins Middle School, Elkins, WV

Easy-To-Store Meter Stick

Do you dread giving out rulers and seeing them whirl around the classroom like 25 miniature helicopters? Here's a simple solution! Purchase a roll of calculator or cash-register tape. Tear off a piece equal in length to your outstretched arms for each student. Next provide each student with a centimeter ruler. Direct her to align her ruler with the end of the paper strip and near the top edge. Then have her mark and number a short line for each centimeter. At every tenth mark, have the student draw a long vertical line to show decimeters. (Demonstrate on a piece of tape attached to your chalkboard.) When each student has marked 100 centimeters, she'll have her very own portable meter stick. These rulers can be either rolled up and secured with paper clips, or folded accordion-style and stored in math books. Laminate the rulers, and they'll last all year long.

Sherwin Washburn—Gr. 4, Cliffside Elementary, Cliffside, NC

1st necklace
(Use 24 Froot Loops®)
$1/4$ = pink
$1/3$ = orange
$1/12$ = green
$1/3$ = yellow

2nd necklace
(Use 30 Froot Loops®)
$1/3$ = green
$1/5$ = yellow
$1/6$ = orange
$3/10$ = pink

3rd necklace
(Use 40 Froot Loops®)
$1/5$ = green & yellow
$1/20$ = pink
$1/10$ = orange
$1/40$ = green
$1/10$ = pink
$1/40$ = yellow
$1/10$ = orange
$1/40$ = yellow
$1/10$ = pink
$1/40$ = green
$1/20$ = orange
$1/5$ = green & yellow

Looping The Loops

Introduce finding a fraction of a whole number with this "cereal-ously" fun lesson! The day before the lesson, fill a plastic bag for each student with Froot Loops® cereal pieces (ten of each color), plus a 24-inch length of string.

On the day of the lesson, provide each student with a premade bag; then write the directions for making the first necklace as shown on an overhead. Have each student string a necklace with the correct number of each color of Froot Loops® cereal pieces. Offer hints as you move about the room and check each necklace. After students have completed the first necklace, have each child take it apart and follow the directions shown to begin the second one. After checking it, have each student make the third necklace to tie around his neck. Check the necklaces against ones you've already made. Then congratulate everyone for a job well done!

Becky Webb—Gr. 6, Hamilton, OH

A Perfect Ten

This fun game reinforces decimal place value and addition of decimals. Before play begins, hold up a domino horizontally. Point out that any domino (except the doubles) can be read in four different ways (see the illustration). Add that the double-blank domino equals 0.0. Draw the examples shown on the board and discuss them.

Next divide students into groups of four, and provide each group with a set of double-six dominoes (a set of dominoes that only goes up to double-six). Also provide each student with a copy of page 104. Have a student in each group turn the 28 dominoes facedown in the middle of his group and mix them up. The object of the game is to see which player can get a sum equal to ten, or closest to ten without going over it. An important rule to remember: during the game each player must reject one domino, which means he cannot include it in his total. He does this by placing it facedown in a discard pile. To begin play, each student chooses one domino, decides a decimal value for it, and writes that decimal on his score sheet. He then places that domino facedown in the discard pile. Each player then chooses a second domino, decides a decimal value for it, and writes the decimal on his score sheet. The player then adds the first two decimals and records the sum. Each player keeps a running total until the end of the game. Play continues until each player has drawn seven dominoes—remembering to reject one. The player with a final total closest to ten without going over it is the winner. Continue until students have played four games or time runs out.

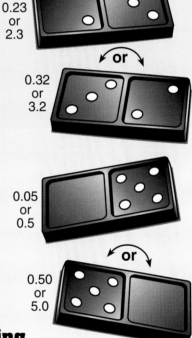

0.23
or
2.3

or

0.32
or
3.2

0.05
or
0.5

or

0.50
or
5.0

Geometric Terms On A Shoestring

Use this hands-on visual to help students understand some abstract geometry terms a little better. Provide each student with a 16- to 20-inch shoelace, two adhesive labels, and scissors. First instruct each student to tie three knots in his shoelace: one in the middle, plus one about five inches from either side of the middle one. Next direct each student to trace and cut out four arrowheads from the adhesive labels and attach them— sticky sides together—to each end of the shoelace as shown. Then tell students to hold their shoelaces out straight. Ask these questions:

- What does the shoestring represent? *(a line)*
- What do the arrows at each end of the string mean? *(that the line extends infinitely in each direction)*
- What do the three knots represent? *(points on the line)*
- What does the distance between any two knots represent? *(a line segment)*
- What does the length from any knot to an arrow represent? *(a ray)*

With the help of these simple shoestring models, students will get a jump on geometry in no time!

Susan White—Gr. 5, Cranston-Johnston Catholic Regional School, Warwick, RI

Candy Heart Division

Want to put a little heart into your division lessons? Then grab a bag of candy hearts to teach your students that they cannot divide by 0. Give each student eight hearts. First direct her to divide 8 by 2, resulting in 4 groups of 2 hearts each. Then have each student divide 8 by 3 to make 2 whole groups of 3 hearts each, plus 2/3 of a group, for an answer of 2 2/3. Then tell students to divide 8 by 0 by making groups of 0 hearts. Students will quickly see that they can make an infinite number of groups of 0—but never use any of the 8 hearts. They'll then see that division by 0 is "undefined." Next have each student promise never to divide by 0, and celebrate this pact by eating the candy hearts!

Debbie Lee—Math; Christian Heritage Schools, Inc.; San Antonio, TX

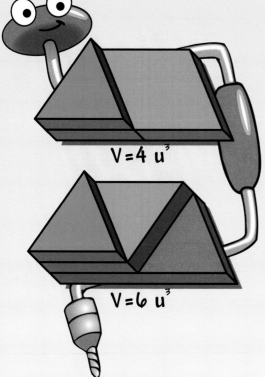

$V = 4 \ u^3$

$V = 6 \ u^3$

Pattern-Block Mysteries

Spatial thinking is important in three-dimensional geometry. Give students a better understanding of the concept using pattern blocks. Provide each pair of students with the following pattern blocks: one hexagon, two trapezoids, three rhombuses, and three equilateral triangles. As pairs of students examine the relationships among the different blocks, ask them:

- How is the trapezoid related to the hexagon? *(It's 1/2 of the hexagon.)*
- How many equilateral triangles equal a rhombus? *(2)* A trapezoid? *(3)* A hexagon? *(6)*
- How many trapezoids equal the hexagon? *(2)*
- How many rhombuses equal the hexagon? *(3)*

Next hold up a green equilateral triangle and tell students that it represents *1 cubic unit*. Then ask students, "How many cubic units is the rhombus?" *(2)* Have students place two triangles on top of the rhombus as proof. Next ask how many cubic units the trapezoid is. *(3)* The hexagon? *(6)* Have students stack the pattern blocks to discover each relationship. Next have each pair of students make a stack of three pattern blocks: a trapezoid on the bottom, then a rhombus, then a triangle. Ask students to determine the volume of this figure. *(6 cubic units)*

Pretzel Geometry

Help students better understand some basic geometry concepts with the following activity. Provide each student with about 20–25 pretzel sticks and a sheet of waxed paper. Next give each child a large spoonful of canned frosting. Also provide each small group of students with a bag of alphabet macaroni. Direct students to use the pretzel sticks and macaroni—connecting any angles with frosting as shown—to make and label the following:

- line segment AB
- line CD
- ray AB
- a plane with points QRST
- right angle BCD
- a 140° obtuse angle—NOP
- a 45° acute angle—STU
- ray CD
- line segment FG

After you check the figures, invite students to eat their pretzel projects!

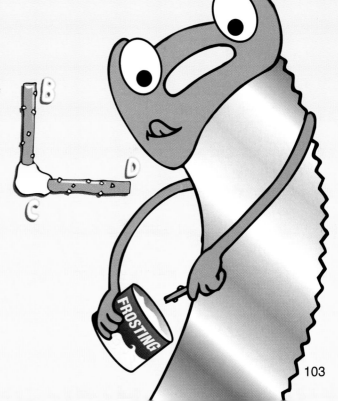

Phyllis DeFilipps—Gr. 5
Holley Intermediate School, Holley, NY

103

A Perfect Ten

Can you score a perfect ten? Play this dominoes game with three of your friends. The object of the game is to see who can reach a score of ten—or closest to ten—without going over it. Remember to keep decimal points lined up when adding. Each domino (except the doubles) can be written in four different ways. Check out these examples:

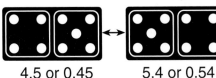  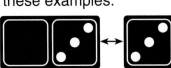 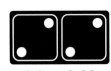

| 4.5 or 0.45 | 5.4 or 0.54 | 0.3 or 0.03 | 3.0 or 0.30 | 2.2 or 0.22 |

Your teacher will explain the directions for playing this game.

Game 1	
Domino #1	
Domino #2	
sum	
Domino #3	
sum	
Domino #4	
sum	
Domino #5	
sum	
Domino #6	
total	

Game 2	
Domino #1	
Domino #2	
sum	
Domino #3	
sum	
Domino #4	
sum	
Domino #5	
sum	
Domino #6	
total	

Game 3	
Domino #1	
Domino #2	
sum	
Domino #3	
sum	
Domino #4	
sum	
Domino #5	
sum	
Domino #6	
total	

Game 4	
Domino #1	
Domino #2	
sum	
Domino #3	
sum	
Domino #4	
sum	
Domino #5	
sum	
Domino #6	
total	

Note To The Teacher: See "A Perfect Ten" on page 102 for information on how to use this reproducible.

Pattern Puzzles

Can you line up the colored blocks to make the patterns described below? First color and cut out the seven blocks at the bottom of this page. Choose the colors of blocks needed to complete a pattern; then read and follow its clue(s). Place the blocks in the blank boxes, moving them around until you make the pattern. Once you have the pattern, draw and color it on another sheet of paper.

 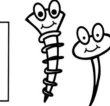

Use these blocks: **Make this pattern:**

1. 1 red, 1 green, 1 blue.......................... It doesn't have a red beginning or end.
2. 1 red, 1 green, 1 blue.......................... The red block is the second block from the green one.
3. 1 green, 2 blues................................. The pattern is symmetrical.

Use these blocks: **Make this pattern:**

4. 2 greens, 1 red, 1 blue......................Both ends of the pattern are the same color.

5. 2 greens, 2 blues..............................The pattern is a repeating one.

6. 2 reds, 1 green, 1 blue......................The blue block does not touch a red one.

7. 2 greens, 1 red, 1 blue......................The blue block doesn't touch the red one.
   The green blocks touch each other.

8. 2 reds, 1 yellow, 1 green...................The green block touches the yellow one.
   The yellow block is between the red ones.

9. 2 reds, 1 blue, 1 yellow.....................The blue block is not between the red ones.
   The yellow block is between the red ones.

10. 1 red, 1 blue, 1 green, 1 yellow.........The green block is the third block from the yellow one.
    The red block doesn't touch the yellow one.

11. 1 red, 1 blue, 1 green, 1 yellow.........The red block is between the blue and the green blocks.
    The green block doesn't touch the red one.

12. 1 red, 1 blue, 1 green, 1 yellow.........The yellow block is between the green and red blocks.
    The red block is between the green and blue ones.

red	blue	green	yellow	red	blue	green

MATH ON THE GO!

Teaching Everyday Math Skills That Students Will Use For A Lifetime

Balancing a checkbook, comparing prices, planning a vacation—what do all these everyday activities have in common? If you answered "doing math," you're absolutely right! Use the following creative projects and reproducibles to help students better understand some of the answers to the common math class question, "When will I *ever* use this?"

by Beth Gress

Numbers All Around
Skill: Number concepts

Whether they realize it or not, kids see examples of math and numbers all around them. Highlight some of these numbers with this simple bulletin-board idea. First use a computer and a variety of fonts to print the following headings on colorful paper (one heading per sheet): *Number Expressions, Fractions, Decimals, Percents, Negative Numbers, Averages, Rates, Rankings, Ranges,* and *Prices.* Next glue each heading to the top of a piece of poster board. Title a bulletin board "Numbers All Around" and attach the ten sheets to the board. Challenge each student to search in newspapers, magazines, advertisements, coupons, photos, and junk mail to find examples of each number concept. Then have him cut out each example and glue it onto the appropriate poster.

Each day choose an example from the bulletin board. Then have students answer the following questions about it in their journals:

- Where do you think this number probably appeared?
- Express this number in some other form.
- Explain this number in such a way that a creature from outer space could understand it.
- Draw a simple illustration that explains the number.
- List three occupations that may use this kind of number.

Whee! A Shopping Spree!
Skill: Addition, estimation

Everyone dreams of winning big in the lottery. Bring that dream to life with this fun activity. Several days before the activity, begin gathering a variety of catalogs. Ask students to bring their favorites from home, and include some of your own as well as the newspaper's classified ads. Be sure to include ads that feature high-ticket items, such as cars, boats, and furniture.

After the catalogs have been collected, ask students, "What would you buy if you won the lottery? Where would you go?" Then invite your students to go on an imaginary spending spree with their lottery winnings! Divide the class into groups of three or four. Give each group several catalogs, a pair of scissors, and some glue; also give each student a large sheet of construction paper. Tell students that they have each won $25,000. Instruct each child to create a wish list of items that he would like to buy, listing the items and their prices on a sheet of notebook paper. Caution students not to go over their lottery winnings of $25,000. Next direct each student to make a collage of his items on the construction paper, listing the price of each item beside its cut-out picture. Finally have each student tape his wish list to one side of his poster. Display these colorful posters on a bulletin board titled "Shopping Spree!" with a border of play money.

For additional math skills reinforcement, have each student

- use a calculator to determine the sales tax on his items (such as 6% or 8%)
- order his items from least to most expensive
- compare his total to the other students' totals in his group
- find the average cost of his items

Check It Out!
Skill: Math writing, addition, subtraction

Help your students stretch their imaginations—and their dollars—while practicing real-life consumer skills. Photocopy pages 109 and 110 back-to-back and provide each student with a copy. (Tell students *not* to write on their copies.) In addition, make transparencies of the two pages to demonstrate this lesson. First discuss with students definitions of such banking terms as *transaction, deposit, withdrawal, debit, credit,* and *balance.* Then read the story below, while demonstrating on the transparencies how to fill out a deposit ticket, complete a checkbook transaction register, and write checks.

Last Friday night, I baby-sat for my neighbor's kids and was paid with a check for $10.50. On Saturday I took seven boxes of stuff to my aunt's house for her garage sale. I helped her all day and made $67.50 in cash. My aunt gave me a $10 bill for helping out! On Sunday I was lazy! After church, I watched TV, read books, and played video games all afternoon. Then I did my homework after supper. On Monday after school, I mowed the lawn and helped Dad clean out the attic. He rewarded me with a $20 bill. Wow! On Tuesday after school, I rushed to the bank to deposit my stash of cash. *(Stop here to demonstrate how to fill out the deposit ticket and transaction register.)*

On Wednesday afternoon I went shopping with Mom at J-Mart. I bought a sweatshirt, a paperback book, and a CD. I wrote a check for $36.64. *(Stop here and demonstrate how to write check #1 and fill in the transaction register.)*

The next day I went to The Timeshop and bought a watch that I've wanted for months. That put me back another $29.95! *(Stop here and demonstrate how to write check #2 and complete the register.)*

Friday night I invited some friends over for a party. I wrote a check for $23.12 to Pizza Planet. Wow, what a week! *(Demonstrate how to write check #3, complete the register, and balance the account.)*

Now direct students to make up their own money stories—like the one above—describing how they might earn and spend money. Have students follow the directions on their copies of pages 109 and 110 for writing their stories and completing the checking account activities.

NUMBER	DATE	DESCRIPTION OF TRANSACTION	PAYMENT/ DEBIT	DEPOSIT/ CREDIT	BALANCE
	6/1	Deposit		$108 00	$20 00 / +108 / 128 00
1	6/2	J-Mart	36 64		-36 64 / 41 64
2	6/3	The Timeshop	29 95		-29 95 / 61 41
3	6/4	Pizza Planet	23 12		-23 12 / 38 29

How About A Credit Card?
Skill: Computing interest

How many students would jump at the chance to have their very own credit cards? But do they know what it means to have to pay for credit card purchases…with interest added? Provide each student with a copy of page 111. Work the first few steps together on the chalkboard (or on a transparency of the page) until students grasp the basic steps. Then allow students to work in pairs and use calculators to complete the activity. Discuss with students the variables that can affect how much a charged item may end up costing in the long run, such as the interest rates and the amount of the monthly payment that is made. After checking the activity with students, assign the Bonus Box to be completed as classwork.

Savvy Shoppers
Skill: Using a calculator

For kids (as well as adults!), nearly anything to do with food provides a motivating incentive. Obtain a class set of grocery ad circulars from your local grocery store. Divide students into pairs. Then give each pair a circular and a calculator. Encourage students to work together to solve the following problems:

1. List three different items whose total comes closest to $10.00 without going over.
2. Which single item has the largest discount?
3. Find two items priced as a pair. What is the price of one item?
4. Find an item that is now 50% less than its original price.
5. Find an item priced by the pound. Find the cost of a two-ounce serving.
6. Choose five items and find their total cost.
7. Find the sales tax on the total of the five items in #6. Use 6%.
8. Choose appropriate items to plan a meal for four. What is the total cost of the items?

Room For Improvement
Skill: Scale drawing, perimeter and area

Most kids' rooms have room for improvement—besides picking clothes up off the floor! Give students a taste for interior design by having them plan scale models of their dream rooms. For homework, have each student measure and record the sizes of the major items in his room, such as the bed, closet, desk, chair, rug, toy box, nightstand, table, etc. Remind students to measure both the length *and* width of each item. In class the next day, provide each student with two sheets of 1/2-inch graph paper, scissors, and glue. Then follow these steps:

1. Discuss the concept of *scale drawing*. Tell students that with this particular scale drawing, 1/2 inch on the graph paper equals one actual foot. Demonstrate how a 3' x 6' bed equals a 1 1/2" x 3" rectangle on the graph paper.
2. Have each student plan and then draw the items he wants in his room on a sheet of graph paper. (Tell students not to worry at this point about placement, but just to draw the items.) Review with students what the term "bird's-eye view" means.
3. Have the student label each item, then color it with colored pencils.
4. Have each student cut out all the items.
5. Next direct each student to arrange his items on his second sheet of graph paper. Students may move the items around to form any arrangement they desire. If necessary, an item may be omitted or a new one drawn. Also remind students to include the placement of windows, closets, and doors.
6. When finished, have each student glue each item onto the graph paper.

Follow up this activity with questions such as:
- How many square feet is your room?
- About how many square yards of carpet would your bedroom need? (Remember: 1 square yard = 9 square feet.)
- What is the perimeter of your room?
- How large is each closet?
- How far is it from your bed to the entry?

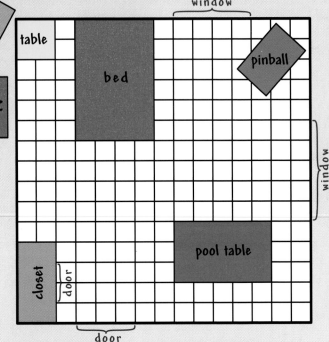

What I Wish I Could Do On My Summer Vacation
Skill: Budgeting, using a calculator

Spark your students' taste for adventure as they plan their own summer vacations. Ask students to bring to class any travel brochures that they may have at home. Divide students into pairs. Then provide each pair with a road map of the United States and a copy of the planning sheet on page 112. Explain to students that they get to plan a five-day excursion to the destination of their choice. Then discuss the following guidelines:
- The trip must have an itinerary detailing daily plans.
- Travel must be planned by mileage and by the time required to travel those miles.
- Use an estimate of 50 miles of travel each hour and an estimate of $1.00 per 25 miles traveled.
- Include visits to at least four points of interest during the trip. These places may be located along the route or at the destination. Use a variety of tourism and travel information sources, including the Internet.
- Include an itemized daily expense estimate for meals, entertainment, lodging, and any miscellaneous expenses.
- Present the trip to the class in a creative way.

Celebrate the conclusion of this fun project by holding a bon voyage party, complete with punch, cake, and other tasty treats.

Going To The Bank!

Stretch your imagination—and your dollars—with this math money activity! On another sheet of paper, write a money story like the one your teacher read to you. Follow these guidelines:

1. Begin by describing at least three ways you've earned money. Make up each amount, but be realistic. You should be paid in cash at least once and by check at least twice.
2. Complete the deposit ticket based on your earnings.

deposit ticket

name		DEPOSIT TICKET		
address		CASH		
	CHECKS	#		
		#		
Date_____		#		
_____		Total Deposit		
signature				

SCHOLAR DOLLARS
$ 0123456789   school math money deposit   0123456789 $

3. Enter the above deposit in your checkbook register at the bottom of this page. You already have a balance of $20.00 in your checking account.
4. Plan three ways to spend your money and describe them in your story. Remember: you can't spend more money than you have!
5. On the other side of this sheet, write a check for each expense that you described in Step 4.
6. Enter each withdrawal (check) in the register below.
7. Balance your checkbook.

checkbook register

RECORD ALL CHARGES THAT AFFECT YOUR ACCOUNT

NUMBER	DATE	DESCRIPTION OF TRANSACTION	PAYMENT/ DEBIT		DEPOSIT/ CREDIT		BALANCE $ 20	00
			$		$			

Note To The Teacher: Photocopy pages 109 and 110 back-to-back. See "Check It Out!" on page 107 for more information on using these reproducibles.

Going To The Bank!

name_____   #001
address_____
_____
                                     Date_____
Pay To The
Order Of _____ $ [   ]
                                          SCHOLAR
                                          DOLLARS

SCHOLAR DOLLARS CLASSROOM CHECK

On-The-Go
Bank

MEMO_____   Signature_____

---

name_____   #002
address_____
_____
                                     Date_____
Pay To The
Order Of _____ $ [   ]
                                          SCHOLAR
                                          DOLLARS

SCHOLAR DOLLARS CLASSROOM CHECK

On-The-Go
Bank

MEMO_____   Signature_____

---

name_____   #003
address_____
_____
                                     Date_____
Pay To The
Order Of _____ $ [   ]
                                          SCHOLAR
                                          DOLLARS

SCHOLAR DOLLARS CLASSROOM CHECK

On-The-Go
Bank

MEMO_____   Signature_____

Going For A Credit Card!

How would you like your very own credit card? Sounds great, huh? But have you ever wondered why businesses want you to have credit cards? Because you pay them extra money for the use of their cards. This extra money is called *interest.* The higher the interest rate and the lower the amount you pay each month, the more extra money (besides the cost of the items you charged) you'll have to pay.

And just how much can that be? Use a calculator to complete the chart below. This credit card charges 10% interest per year. Follow these steps:

1. Suppose you charge an item that costs $100. See *new balance* in the chart.
2. You make payment #1 of $15.00.
3. Subtract $15.00 from $100.00 to get a *balance* of $85.00.
4. Use a calculator to determine the *interest* on that balance: $85.00 x 10% = $8.50 per year.
5. Divide $8.50 by 12 to find the interest for one month: 0.7083333. Round 0.7083333 up to the next cent: $0.71.
6. Add the interest to the balance to get the *new balance*: $85.71.
7. Now make your next payment: repeat Steps 2–6.
8. Continue making payments until your balance equals 0.
9. Add the total amount of the payments you made. What was your total payment for this $100 item?

monthly payment	amount	balance	interest	new balance
	——	——	——	$100.00
1	$15.00	$85.00	$0.71	$85.71
2	$15.00			
3	$15.00			
4	$15.00			
5	$15.00			
6	$15.00			
7	$_____			
	_____ = total payment			

Bonus Box: Use the same procedure above to find the total payment on a $100 charge if you pay $10 per month and the interest rate is 20%. Show your work on the back of this sheet.

Note To The Teacher: Use with "How About A Credit Card?" on page 107.

Going On A Vacation!

or bust!

Use this sheet to plan your five-day vacation.

Day 1

Travel: Depart from _____ and arrive at _____ at _____ (time).
mileage (about 50 miles per hour): _____ mileage costs (about $1.00 per 25 miles): _____
Meals: breakfast: _____ lunch: _____ dinner: _____
Entertainment: _____
_____
Lodging: _____ **Miscellaneous expenses:** _____

Day 2

Travel: Depart from _____ and arrive at _____ at _____ (time).
mileage (about 50 miles per hour): _____ mileage costs (about $1.00 per 25 miles): _____
Meals: breakfast: _____ lunch: _____ dinner: _____
Entertainment: _____
_____
Lodging: _____ **Miscellaneous expenses:** _____

Day 3

Travel: Depart from _____ and arrive at _____ at _____ (time).
mileage (about 50 miles per hour): _____ mileage costs (about $1.00 per 25 miles): _____
Meals: breakfast: _____ lunch: _____ dinner: _____
Entertainment: _____
_____
Lodging: _____ **Miscellaneous expenses:** _____

Day 4

Travel: Depart from _____ and arrive at _____ at _____ (time).
mileage (about 50 miles per hour): _____ mileage costs (about $1.00 per 25 miles): _____
Meals: breakfast: _____ lunch: _____ dinner: _____
Entertainment: _____
_____
Lodging: _____ **Miscellaneous expenses:** _____

Day 5

Travel: Depart from _____ and arrive at _____ at _____ (time).
mileage (about 50 miles per hour): _____ mileage costs (about $1.00 per 25 miles): _____
Meals: breakfast: _____ lunch: _____ dinner: _____
Entertainment: _____
_____
Lodging: _____ **Miscellaneous expenses:** _____

©The Education Center, Inc. • THE MAILBOX® • Intermediate • June/July 1999

112   **Note To The Teacher:** See "What I Wish I Could Do On My Summer Vacation" on page 108 for information on how to use this reproducible.

Social Studies Units

TRAVELING TRAVELOGS

Take your class on a grand tour of the globe—without having to leave the classroom—with this exciting geography project!

by Patricia Altmann

What Is A Traveling Travelog?

In this project, each student will make a travelog consisting of a journal and a scrapbook. The *journal* is sent to an out-of-town friend, who is asked to complete information about his or her city, state, or country. This person is also asked to send the student a postcard from his or her city, then forward the journal to another friend. The journal will be returned to the student after it has traveled to six different locations. The *scrapbook* is kept in the classroom to display postcards and to record data on the locations the journal visits. After all the traveling journals are returned to your students, complete the activities below for some "geo-rific" practice with important skills.

Activities To Do After The Journals Are Returned

- Using a U.S. and/or world map and its mileage scale, estimate the distance your travelog traveled. Then find the latitude and longitude of each location in your travelog.
- Write a first-person narrative from the viewpoint of your journal about its journey.
- Choose one place your journal visited that you would like to visit one day. Write a short paragraph explaining your choice.
- Make a travel brochure about one of the places your journal visited.
- Create a mural, collage, or pop-up book showing all of the locations your journal visited.

Getting Ready

The first step is to have each student make his travelog journal and scrapbook.

Materials For Each Student:
1 copy of pages 115, 116, and 118; 2 copies of page 117; 4 sheets of construction paper in various colors; 1 recent student photograph; 1 envelope; stapler; glue; crayons

Making The Travelog Journal:
1. Have each student complete page 115.
2. Have the student color his copy of page 116 and glue his photograph where indicated.
3. Have the student staple together page 115, page 116, and the two copies of page 117 (in that order).
4. Have the student address an envelope with an out-of-town friend's address, write the school's return address on the envelope, and then place his travelog journal inside.
5. Mail each student's journal.

Making The Travelog Scrapbook:
1. Have the student staple the four sheets of construction paper together.
2. Instruct the student to glue the top half of page 118 to the first page of the scrapbook. Then have him glue the bottom half of page 118 onto the next page. Have the student glue the postcards he receives on both sides of the remaining pages.
3. When a student's travelog journal returns, instruct him to use the information in each entry to complete his Travelog Scrapbook Data Sheet.

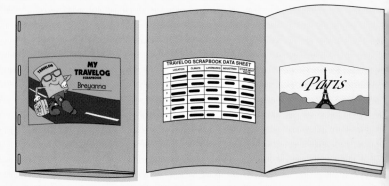

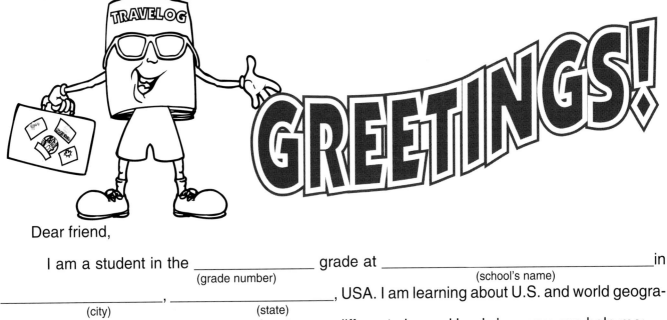

Dear friend,

I am a student in the _____ grade at _____ in
                (grade number)   (school's name)

_____, _____, USA. I am learning about U.S. and world geogra-
     (city)   (state)

phy. With your help I can learn more about many different places. Here's how you can help me:

1. Complete one journal entry in my attached Travelog Journal by writing about the city in which you live.

2. Send a postcard from your city addressed to me at the school address below.

3. Send my Travelog Journal on to a friend or relative who lives in a different region of the United States or another country.

I will be keeping track of my journal's journeys back here in the classroom. I've created a scrapbook for the postcards that I'll receive from around the country and the world. I will also record in my scrapbook data on each location my journal visits.

Thank you for helping me with this fun project. Don't forget to send me a postcard and forward my journal to a friend. If you are the last person to receive my journal or if it is close to the due date below, please return my Travelog Journal to the address below along with your postcard.

Send postcard to

_____
(student's name)

_____
(teacher's name)

_____
(school's name)

_____
(school's address)

_____
(city, state, zip code)

Sincerely,

_____
(student's name)

VERY IMPORTANT

This Travelog Journal is due back to the address at the left by

_____.
(date)

Note To The Teacher: Use with "Getting Ready" on page 114.

Travelog Journal Entry
Date: _____

Name: _____ Location: _____

Climate: _____
_____

Landmarks: _____
_____
_____

Industries: _____
_____

Other neat facts: _____
_____
_____

Travelog Journal Entry
Date: _____

Name: _____ Location: _____

Climate: _____
_____

Landmarks: _____
_____
_____

Industries: _____
_____

Other neat facts: _____
_____
_____

Travelog Journal Entry
Date: _____

Name: _____ Location: _____

Climate: _____
_____

Landmarks: _____
_____
_____

Industries: _____
_____

Other neat facts: _____
_____
_____

Note To The Teacher: Use with "Getting Ready" on page 114.

MY TRAVELOG
SCRAPBOOK

_____
(student's name)

TRAVELOG SCRAPBOOK DATA SHEET

	Location	Climate	Landmarks	Industries	Other Neat Facts
1					
2					
3					
4					
5					
6					

Note To The Teacher: Use the two forms above with "Getting Ready" on page 114.

Voyage To The Colonies

All aboard for the American colonies! Set sail with this easy-to-do simulation that whips writing, research, math, and critical-thinking skills into shipshape condition!

from an idea by Kristina Sipe—Gr. 5, Santa Sophia Academy, Spring Valley, CA

1 Preparing To Weigh Anchor:

Launch this project by gathering reference materials and books about the first colonists. Make two copies of the cards on page 121. Cut the cards apart and put them in a bag. Also duplicate page 120 for each student.

Begin by discussing your students' thoughts and questions about what life was like in the Old World in the 1700s. Why do students think some people wanted to move to the New World? Would life be better there? How? What things would be needed on such a long journey? How did colonists probably feel about making such an important decision? Next invite each student to become a passenger on a ship that's heading to the New World, *The [your school's name]*. Have each student draw a card from the bag to determine his identity on this exciting voyage. Point out that the cards list males (except the "Stowaway" card) because, during that time period, the man tended to be the family member with a trade or occupation.

2 Setting Sail:

Head out to sea by giving each student a copy of page 120, which lists the steps in this project. Discuss the sheet together and how it is organized by *legs*. After pointing out the location of the reference materials, have students start working on the first leg/assignment of their trip.

3 On The Open Seas:

Sail on as students continue working on the assignments listed on page 120. As ship captain, periodically announce an unusual experience for students to include in their stories (for example, a storm throwing the ship off course or an unscheduled stop at a Caribbean island). Also suggest that students have different passengers/classmates interact in their stories (for example, one passenger buying or trading goods with another). As stories are completed, put them in a three-ring binder. Read a different completed story at the beginning of each day's social-studies lesson.

4 Arriving In The Colonies:

Before students make land (Leg 4), spend time reviewing the colonies' different geographic regions. Also design a *manifest* page for the binder that lists each passenger's name and occupation, with room for each passenger's signature. Have students organize their stories in the binder according to the manifest. Then place the book in your school's media center for others to enjoy.

5 Side Excursions:

Extend this project by sending students on the following side trips:
- Chart the ship's course from the Old World to the colonies on a map.
- Set up a log of itemized travel expenses.
- Survey the passengers to determine the geographic regions in which they settled. Graph the results.

Fourth-grade teachers:
Use this activity with students while studying the colonization of your state!

Comin' To America

Why would someone want to come to America from his or her homeland? What would it have been like to travel for many months on a ship across the ocean? What things would people need to take with them on such a journey? Answer these questions and more as you pretend to be a passenger on a ship headed to America!

Directions:

1. Pretend you are the passenger described on your card. Give this person and each of his family members a name.
2. Write a story to tell about each leg of the trip. You can write your stories in the form of a personal narrative, a journal entry, a letter, a mystery, or a humorous tale.
3. Use reference materials and other books to add facts to your stories to make them more believable.
4. Edit your stories; then write your final copies as neatly as you can.
5. As you complete each story, color its trunk. Give the story to your teacher to put into a class book.
6. When you have completed all your stories, sign your name on the ship's *manifest* (the table-of-contents page) in the class book.

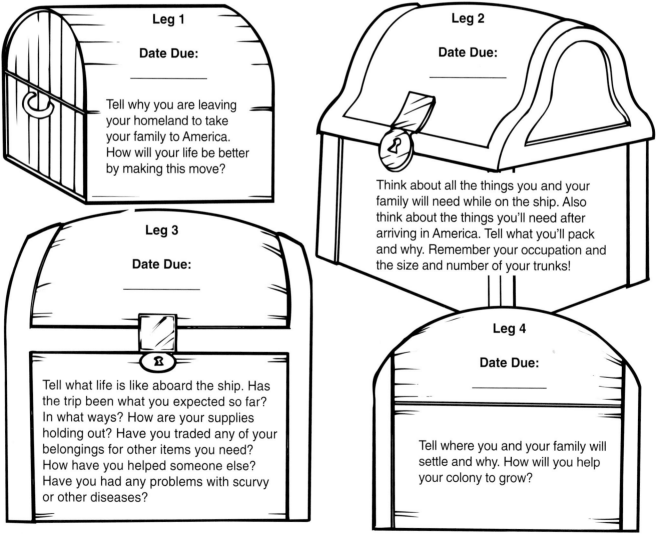

Leg 1

Date Due:

_____

Tell why you are leaving your homeland to take your family to America. How will your life be better by making this move?

Leg 2

Date Due:

_____

Think about all the things you and your family will need while on the ship. Also think about the things you'll need after arriving in America. Tell what you'll pack and why. Remember your occupation and the size and number of your trunks!

Leg 3

Date Due:

_____

Tell what life is like aboard the ship. Has the trip been what you expected so far? In what ways? How are your supplies holding out? Have you traded any of your belongings for other items you need? How have you helped someone else? Have you had any problems with scurvy or other diseases?

Leg 4

Date Due:

_____

Tell where you and your family will settle and why. How will you help your colony to grow?

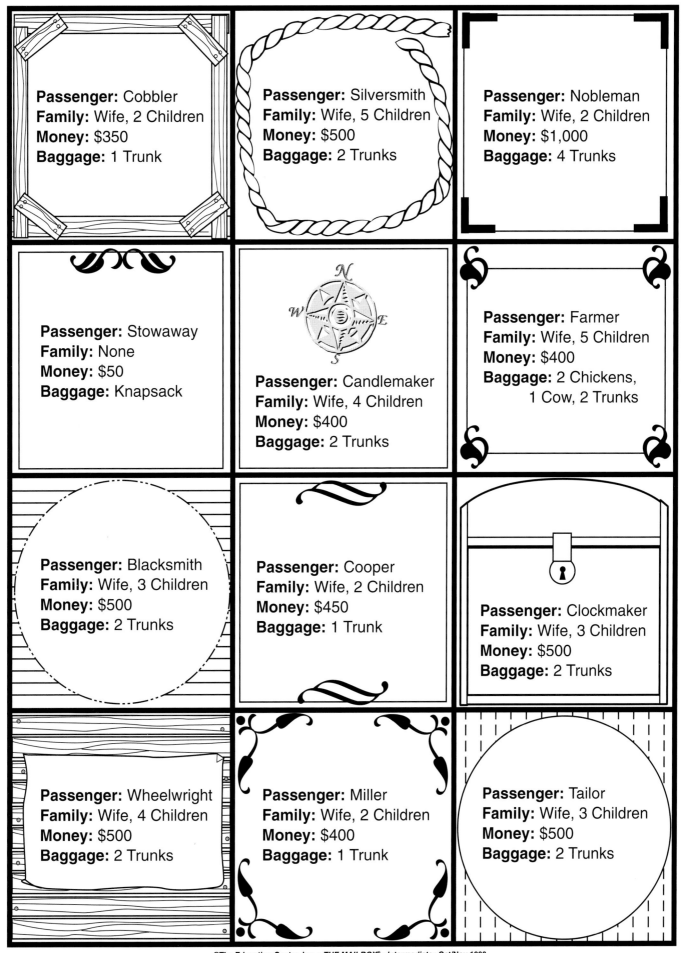

Passenger: Cobbler
Family: Wife, 2 Children
Money: $350
Baggage: 1 Trunk

Passenger: Silversmith
Family: Wife, 5 Children
Money: $500
Baggage: 2 Trunks

Passenger: Nobleman
Family: Wife, 2 Children
Money: $1,000
Baggage: 4 Trunks

Passenger: Stowaway
Family: None
Money: $50
Baggage: Knapsack

Passenger: Candlemaker
Family: Wife, 4 Children
Money: $400
Baggage: 2 Trunks

Passenger: Farmer
Family: Wife, 5 Children
Money: $400
Baggage: 2 Chickens,
1 Cow, 2 Trunks

Passenger: Blacksmith
Family: Wife, 3 Children
Money: $500
Baggage: 2 Trunks

Passenger: Cooper
Family: Wife, 2 Children
Money: $450
Baggage: 1 Trunk

Passenger: Clockmaker
Family: Wife, 3 Children
Money: $500
Baggage: 2 Trunks

Passenger: Wheelwright
Family: Wife, 4 Children
Money: $500
Baggage: 2 Trunks

Passenger: Miller
Family: Wife, 2 Children
Money: $400
Baggage: 1 Trunk

Passenger: Tailor
Family: Wife, 3 Children
Money: $500
Baggage: 2 Trunks

Globe-trottin' It!

Creative Ideas For Studying Other Countries

From one hemisphere to another, a curious globe-trotter will find hundreds of countries filled with intriguing people, exotic places, and amazing cultures. Make the study of another land an unforgettable adventure with the following creative ideas and reproducibles—all designed to be used with any country on the globe.

ideas by Hellen Harvey

"Geogra-Tree" Bulletin Board

Skill: Research skills

Bring a paper tree—and your students' research skills—to life with this colorful display! Draw, color, and label a large tree cutout; then mount it on a bulletin board. Have each child cut a leaf shape from light green paper and program it like the one illustrated. Next direct the student to research the country of her ancestors and fill in the information on her leaf. (If a student is unable to identify the country of her ancestors, allow her to research any nation that interests her. Have her change the top two lines on the leaf to read "[student] would love to visit [country].") After she fills in her leaf, have the student decorate an unlined index card to represent her country's flag. Tape the completed flag to its leaf; then staple the project to the tree. Use the information on the leaves to spark many interesting discussions or as informative five-minute fillers!

in _____ student's name _____ 's roots are _____ country _____.
People there speak _____ language _____.
People there eat _____ popular food _____.
Claim to fame: _____ amazing/unique fact _____.

Help Wanted!

Skill: Drawing conclusions, narrative writing

Have students investigate the relationships between a country's economy and the jobs available to its people with this thought-provoking activity. First review with students what they've learned about the natural resources, climate, agriculture, and manufacturing of the country you're studying. Based on this information, what jobs might be most abundant in this land? For example, forestry and forest products provide 40% of Finland's exports, so jobs in forestry, woodworking, and paper-manufacturing industries would probably be plentiful there. Next have each student pretend that she has found herself without money in the country you're studying. Instruct her to write a narrative in which she explains her situation, lists five jobs she applies for and her qualifications for them, and tells about the job she finally gets. After the student shares her story with the class, challenge her to explain why the job she wound up getting is likely to be available in that country.

122

"Geo-Bingo"

Skill: Research skills, categorizing

Whether you're studying one country or several countries at a time, this version of bingo is guaranteed to generate lots of learning! A few days before the game, list the categories shown on a sheet of chart paper. Give each student three index cards. Assign a category to each child; then have him find three facts about the country being studied that relate to his category. Direct him to write his category and one fact on each index card. Collect and shuffle the cards; then number them sequentially. When you're ready to play, follow these steps:

1. Give each student one sheet of unlined paper and a supply of paper squares to use as markers.
2. Instruct the student to fold his paper in half four times to create his game card. (When opened, the paper's folds should create a grid of 16 spaces.)
3. Have the student randomly copy one category from the chart in each space on his paper, repeating a category if he desires.
4. Read the fact from the first card. Have each student determine the fact's category.
5. If the student has the matching category on his sheet, have him cover it with a marker. Announce the number on that fact card so students who covered that category can write the number on that marker.
6. Repeat Steps 4 and 5 until a student has four markers in a row horizontally, vertically, or diagonally.
7. Check the winner's matches for correctness by having him read aloud the numbers written on his four markers. If they correctly match the numbers on the facts you've read, declare him the winner. If not, continue play.

natural resources
population
economy
transportation
plants and animals
political divisions
manufacturing
communications
climate
culture
currency
government
education
religion
agriculture
history

Welcome To The Lake District

Dear Jacob,
Wow! Wish you were here to fish with me in Finland's Lake District. The hiking has been great, too!
The Lake District is in central Finland. It has thousands of lakes. Many boats travel on the lakes and rivers in the Lake District.
Jackson

Jacob Harvey
123 Curtis Drive
Anytown, U.S.A.
12345

Picturesque Postcards

Skill: Writing a description

Treat your students to this geography project worth writing home about! Give each student a 4" x 6" unlined index card, colored markers, and a 1" x 3/4" piece cut from a self-sticking nametag. Assign each student a landmark from a country currently being studied. Direct the student to draw a picture of the landmark on one side of his card and address the other side like a postcard, leaving space for a note. Next have him write the note, including a description of the landmark, its location, and its historic or geographic significance. Then, on the nametag piece, have the child design a postage stamp that's representative of that country and affix it to his postcard as a stamp. Pin these postcards on a bulletin board. With such picturesque postcards to admire, you might have to stop yourself from mailing them!

Unlikely Sports

Skill: Research skills, critical thinking

Bobsledding in Jamaica? Sounds nuts, but it's true. Share with students that despite an average temperature of 80°F, Jamaica sent a bobsled team to the Winter Games. Then divide students into groups. Have each group list the sports played in a country you're studying; then have it think about how that country's climate, topography, and culture might affect the playing of those sports. If the group thinks a sport is "unlikely" based upon one or more of the three factors, ask its members to determine what adaptations were made to make playing that sport possible. For example, even though the average temperature in Iceland is about 41°F, people there can swim year-round in heated indoor pools. Finally challenge each student to list three sports she would not expect to be played in that country and why. Provide time for students to share their lists.

Currency Conversion

Skill: Rounding decimals, multiplication

Shopping—a favorite pastime when visiting another country—can get tricky when a different currency is involved. For an exercise in converting the currency of the country you're studying, ask each student to bring in a weekly grocery-store circular. Then follow these steps:

1. Have each student draw a chart as shown below on a sheet of paper.
2. Tell students to pretend they each have $10 in U.S. currency. Have each student look in his circular and list the items he'd like to buy on the chart, making sure that they don't total more than $10. Next to each item, have him list its price and that price rounded to the nearest dollar.
3. Give each student a duplicated copy of the "Currency Trading" box from a copy of *The Wall Street Journal.* This section lists exchange rates and can be found by looking in the paper's index under "Foreign Exchange." (See the illustration at the right.)
4. Explain that the "Currency per U.S. $" column tells how much of the unit from a country is equal to one U.S. dollar. For example, according to the box it takes 5.4545 Finland markkaa to equal one U.S. dollar. Help students round 5.4545 markkaa to the nearest unit *(5 markkaa).* Point out that one U.S. dollar roughly equals 5 markkaa.
5. Write the following formula on the board: *price (rounded to nearest U.S. dollar) x currency per U.S. $ (rounded to nearest unit) = approximate price in foreign units.* With the class, use this formula to convert the rounded price of the first item to the unit of the country you're studying (for example, $2 x 5 markkaa = 10 markkaa). Repeat with other amounts.
6. Have each student convert the price of each item on his list and fill in the rest of his chart as shown.

If students need extra practice with multiplying decimals, don't ask them to round any of the numbers. Allow students to use calculators if desired.

FEBRUARY 22, 1999 EXCHANGE RATES

Country	U.S. $ equiv. Mon	U.S. $ equiv. Fri	Currency per U.S. $ Mon	Currency per U.S. $ Fri
Argentina (Peso)	1.0002	1.0002	.9998	.9998
Australia (Dollar)	.6083	.6243	1.6439	1.6018
Austria (Schilling)	.07925	.07959	12.618	12.565
Bahrain (Dinar)	2.6518	2.6518	.3771	.3771
Belgium (Franc)	.02702	.02714	37.015	36.840
Brazil (Real)	.8660	.8655	1.1548	1.1554
Britain (Pound)	1.6730	1.6720	.5977	.5981
Canada (Dollar)	.6794	.6798	1.4718	1.4710
Chile (Peso)	.002199	.002199	454.78	454.75
China (Renminbi)	.1208	.1208	8.2795	8.2796
Colombia (Peso)	.0007190	.0007190	1390.85	1390.85
Czech. Rep. (Koruna) Commercial rate	.03012	.02984	33.203	33.512
Denmark (Krone)	.1464	.1470	6.8313	6.8039
Ecuador (Sucre) Floating rate	.0001905	.0001905	5250.00	5250.00
Finland (Markkaa)	.1833	.1842	5.4545	5.4296

Item	Price in U.S. dollars	Price rounded to nearest U.S. dollar	Currency per U.S. $ rounded to nearest unit	Price in foreign units
crackers	$1.98	$2.00	5 markkaa	10 markkaa

Global Sharing With The Peace Corps

If you'd like your students to learn firsthand about another country and its culture, then the Peace Corps' World Wise Schools program is for you! This program—open to teachers of grades 3–12—matches your class with a Peace Corps Volunteer serving somewhere in the world. The letters and drawings your class sends to their Peace Corps friend can include tidbits about the class's activities as well as information about your city, state, and country. In turn, the volunteer's letters can provide your class with interesting and exciting facts about his or her corner of the world. Participating teachers also receive a resource packet that includes a videotape and study guide with teaching ideas about a country's geography and culture. If you are unable to commit to corresponding with a volunteer, you can still take advantage of the Peace Corps' global education resources. For more information, write: Peace Corps, World Wise Schools, 1111—20th Street NW, 2nd Floor, Washington, DC 20526. Phone: 1-800-424-8580. Web-site address: www.peacecorps.gov/ *(current as of 9-98).*

Barbara Spilman Lawson, Waynesboro, VA

Fact-Finding Sheets

Skill: Note-taking, writing paragraphs

Need a great aid to keep students from copying information when researching a country? Just give each student a copy of page 125. This sheet will guide each child's note-taking by helping him recognize the important facts to research. After the student fills in the sheet's boxes with notes, have him use those notes to write a paragraph for each box. With this handy guide, be prepared to see a marked difference in both note-taking *and* paragraph-writing skills!

Mary Ann Miller, Pleasant Grove Middle School, Texarkana, TX

Fact-Finding Sheet On _____

country

★ Location In World ★	★ Capital ★	★ Money ★
★ Type Of Government ★	★ Agriculture ★	★ Population And People ★
★ Head Of Government ★	★Most Important Industry★	★ Early History ★
★ Special Foods ★	★ Recreation ★	★ Education ★
★ Famous Citizen ★	★ Flag ★	★Official Language ★

- -

Note To The Teacher: Use with "Fact-Finding Sheets" on page 124.

All Set To Travel!

Finding out as much as you can about a place before you visit it can make the trip more pleasant and memorable. Complete the activities below to make sure your trip is nothing but fun!

PASSPORT

Destination:
_____ , _____
capital city   country

Departure:
_____ , _____
city   state/province

_____ , _____
month   date   year

Find out which unit of money is used in the country you'll visit.

_____

Hint: *Look for "Money" in the encyclopedia article about the country you're studying.*

Find the average temperature for the month you'll be traveling.

Hint: *Use an atlas.*

List the clothing you'll pack.

_____
_____
_____

Find out what time it is at your destination if your flight leaves at 1 P.M.

_____

Hint: *Use the world time zones chart in an encyclopedia.*

N
W   E
S

Locate the latitude and longitude of the capital city you'll visit.

_____   _____
latitude   longitude

Measure the distance from your home to your destination.

_____

Hint: *Use a piece of string and a globe. Then use the globe's key to change inches to miles.*

List three things a native from the country you're visiting could share with you about his or her country. Use the back if you need more space.

1. _____
2. _____
3. _____

Bonus Box: What souvenir could you bring back from your trip? On the back of this sheet, write a paragraph describing it and explaining why you bought it.

©The Education Center, Inc. • *THE MAILBOX® • Intermediate •* Feb/Mar 1999

Note To The Teacher: Provide an atlas, a globe, string, scissors, a ruler, and a set of encyclopedias for students' use.

This Must Be The Place!
Creative Map Activities That Really Hit The Spot

On the lookout for mapping activities that will keep intermediate kids tuned in? Just point your compass in the direction of the following fun-filled, hands-on learning ideas!

by Julia Alarie

Information, Please!
Skill: Reading a map

How much knowledge do your students already have about maps? Find out by presenting them with this challenge! Divide your class into groups of three or four students each, and have each group choose a recorder. Provide each group with a copy of the same map (political, physical, products/natural resources, or population density) of an area you're about to study. Also give each group a large sheet of paper. Instruct the students in each group to brainstorm everything they learn by studying the map. Have the recorder jot down each observation. After about ten minutes, compare all the information generated and check it for accuracy. Discuss how students discovered each fact. Proclaim the group with the most accurate information the "Official Class Cartographers"!

More Information, Please!
Skill: Comparing information on different kinds of maps

Extend the activity on the left below by giving each group a different kind of map of the same area. For example, provide one group with a population density map, another with a climate regions map, a third with a products or natural resources map, a fourth with a physical features map, and a fifth with a political map. Have the students in each group brainstorm all the information they can gather from studying their map. Check each group's observations for accuracy. Then compare the kinds of information acquired from the different maps. Lead the students to draw conclusions about the relationships among the facts gathered. For example: How does elevation affect population density? How is climate related to kinds of products? What natural features form boundaries? Now that's a booty of solid-gold learning!

Welcome To Rectanguland!
Skill: Using map symbols, following directions

Provide students with plenty of practice using map symbols and following directions with the reproducible on page 130. First go over the directions with students. Stress that they should complete steps 1 and 2 before beginning their maps. When all the maps are finished, compare and discuss the results; then have students color their finished products. Display the marvelous maps on a bulletin board titled "Rectanguland: You *Can* Get There From Here!" 127

Maps In The News
Skill: Current events, geography

What's often buried between the pages of today's news? Maps, mateys! Reserve a section of a wall or bulletin board on which to create a "Maps In The News" collage. Encourage students to be on the lookout for maps that accompany articles in newspapers and newsmagazines. Post the maps—along with their captions and the articles—as an ongoing reminder that maps are a big part of our everyday lives. In addition, post the following questions on the board to spark classroom discussions:

- What type of map is shown? (political, physical, population, products, etc.)
- What is the purpose of the map?
- On what continent does the news story take place? In what country? In which state?
- What type of story does the map accompany? (politics, culture, climate, disaster, etc.)
- List three facts you can learn from the map.

Can Someone Give Me Directions?
Skill: Cardinal directions

Using wall-mounted maps ("north is up, south is down") to teach cardinal directions is often confusing for students. To help them better understand the true cardinal directions, use colored masking tape or paint to make a compass rose right on your classroom floor. First get students' input to help you determine the actual directions; then make the compass rose accordingly. Since the compass is a permanent part of your classroom, refer to it whenever you're discussing directions.

CLEVELL HARRIS

Puzzled About Maps
Skill: Geography

Even intermediate kids think a good puzzle is worth its weight in gold! Turn any map—like those included in *National Geographic* magazine—into a floor map by gluing it onto a large piece of poster board. Use a different color of poster board for each map to make it easy to keep puzzles separate. After the map has dried, cut it into interesting shapes and store it in a labeled shoebox. Make map puzzles of any region you cover in social studies or of the settings of books the class is reading. Recruit parent volunteers to help you make these puzzles, which are perfect do-at-home projects!

Location, Location, Location!
Skill: Cardinal and intermediate directions

Give students practice in giving directions by playing Location. Choose a small but distinctive object in the classroom, such as a special eraser or figurine. Have your students close their eyes while one student places the object in a secret, but visible, location. Have students take turns asking directional questions to try to determine the object's location. For example:

- Is the object located in the northern part of the classroom?
- Is it southeast of the teacher's desk?
- Is the object located west of the aquarium?
- Is it near the northwestern corner of the classroom?

Let the first student to locate the object hide it for the next round.

Put Us On The Map!
Skill: Examining details on a map
Encourage students to dig into *every* detail of a regional map with this nifty investigation. Divide students into pairs and give each pair a copy of the reproducible on page 131. Also provide each pair with a map of the region you're planning to study. Go over the directions on the page with the class. Allow plenty of time for students to complete the activity; then have them share their findings with their classmates.

Pirate Ship!
Skill: Using coordinates and directions
All aboard for a kid-pleasin' game that is similar to Battleship®—but offers a few surprises for its sailors! Divide students into pairs. Provide each pair with four copies of page 132 and a die. (For durability, laminate one copy of the page for each player. Students can then use wipe-off markers.) Go over "To prepare to play" with students. Then discuss each step for playing the game. Be forewarned: the winner of Pirate Ship! may not feel like such a winner after all!

Pizza With A World View
Skill: Culminating activity
Celebrate the completion of your mapping unit by having students create delicious Hemisphere Pizzas. First choose a date; then check with your cafeteria manager to see if you can use the ovens that day. Next ask parent volunteers to donate ready-made pizza crusts, pizza sauce, cheese, olives, onions, peppers, pepperoni, and other pizza fixings—enough for four large pizzas.

On pizza-making day, divide your class into four groups. Assign a hemisphere (northern, southern, eastern, and western) to each group. Have students thoroughly wash their hands, and provide them with food-handlers' gloves. Then give each group a ready-made pizza crust, fixings, and a globe or map. Instruct each group to design a pizza that looks like its assigned hemisphere. While the pizzas are cooking, review the skills students learned during the unit. Then reward them with a *world*-class pizza party!

Welcome To Rectanguland!

Welcome to Rectanguland! It's a nice place to visit…if you can find it! And that's where your help is needed. Follow the directions below to make an accurate map of Rectanguland. Tourists all over the world are counting on you!

Compass Rose	**Key**				**Scale of Miles**
	forest	waterfall	capital	town	1 in. = 1 mi.
	desert	mining area	mountains	hills	
	river			lake	

Directions:

1. Look at each feature listed in the key. Draw and color a symbol for each feature in the box beside it.
2. Draw the compass rose. Include both cardinal and intermediate directions.
3. Now follow the steps below to make your map in the space above. Include each feature and its name.
   a. Rectanguland is a country shaped like a rectangle. (Surprised?) Its northern and southern borders are longer than its eastern and western borders.
   b. The Angular Mountains are located along the northern border.
   c. Winsome River flows down from the mountains in a southeasterly direction. Then it flows through Hiccup Hills.
   d. Winsome River forms Cascade Falls as it empties into Lake Linger. Lake Linger is near the eastern border.
   e. The capital city, Rightanglia, is located on the central western border of Rectanguland.
   f. The Great Piney Forest is also along the western border.
   g. The town of Needling is located at the northeast edge of the forest.
   h. Two miles south of Needling is its twin town of Noodling.
   i. In the south central area of the country is the DooWaka Desert.
   j. The mining center, with the town of Nugget at its center, is north of the desert.

Bonus Box: Find the area of Rectanguland. Round the length of each border to the nearest half-inch.

Names _____

Investigating a map

Put Us On The Map!

SCORE:

Directions for partners:

1. Each student writes his or her initials in the "letters" column, one letter per box.
2. With your partner, decide on a Bonus Category and write it at the top of the last column.
3. Explore your map together to find names of places that begin with the letters of your initials.
4. Score five points for each discovery! **Hint:** Words in columns 1, 2, and 4 should be proper names, like *Alabama (A)*, *Hudson Bay (H)*, and *New York City (N)*. Words in column 3 should be common nouns, like *mountain (M)*, *valley (V)*, *boundary (B)*, *state (S)*, etc.
5. Total up your score and write it on the map above.

letters (initials)	① political areas (countries, states)	② bodies of water (lakes, rivers)	③ landforms (mountain, valley, etc.)	④ cities and towns	⑤ Bonus Category
Player 1					
Player 2					

©The Education Center, Inc. • *THE MAILBOX®* • *Intermediate* • Dec/Jan 1998–99

Note To The Teacher: Use with "Put Us On The Map!" on page 129. Help students who may have difficulty selecting a Bonus Category by listing suggestions such as these on the board: Specific Mountain Ranges/Peaks, Airports, Counties, Historic Landmarks, National/State Parks, Colleges And Universities.

Pirate Ship!

To prepare to play:

1. Stand a book or two between you and your opponent so that you can't see each other's grids. Turn one copy of the grid over.
2. Name five prizes you would like to win. Your opponent writes each prize in a different oval on one of his or her grids. Your opponent then names five prizes he or she wants to win. Write each one in a different oval on one of your grids.
3. Next your opponent writes five dud prizes for you (rusty nails, rotten sneaker, etc.) in five different ovals on his grid. Write five dud prizes for your opponent on your grid.
4. Place your two grids beside each other. You will record your moves on the blank grid. You will record your opponent's moves on the prize grid.

The goal is to be the first player to find five prizes. To earn a prize, you must call out all the coordinate pairs that are enclosed by a prize oval. Remember: some prize ovals only have two coordinate pairs, while others have three.

To play:

1. Player 1 calls out a pair of coordinates, such as (D, 4). He marks the location with a small X on his blank grid.
2. Player 2 finds those coordinates and marks them with a small X on her prize grid. If the X falls inside one of the prize ovals, Player 2 says "hit." If the X doesn't fall inside a prize oval, Player 2 says "miss."
3. Player 1 then rolls the die. He may move one block at a time according to the roll of the die. For example, if a three is rolled Player 1 might say, "Move one block north from (D, 4), one block east, and another block east." Player 1 would now be at (F, 5). Player 2 marks the location of those coordinates on her prize grid with a small X and says "hit" or "miss". Player 1 also marks this coordinate pair on his blank grid.
4. Player 2 then takes a turn, calling out a pair of coordinates and then rolling the die.
5. When Player 1 takes his next turn, he can start with any pair of coordinates, not just his last pair.
6. When a player has earned a prize, the opponent says "Prize earned" but does not reveal the name of the prize.
7. Play continues until one player wins any five prizes. That's right—any five prizes!

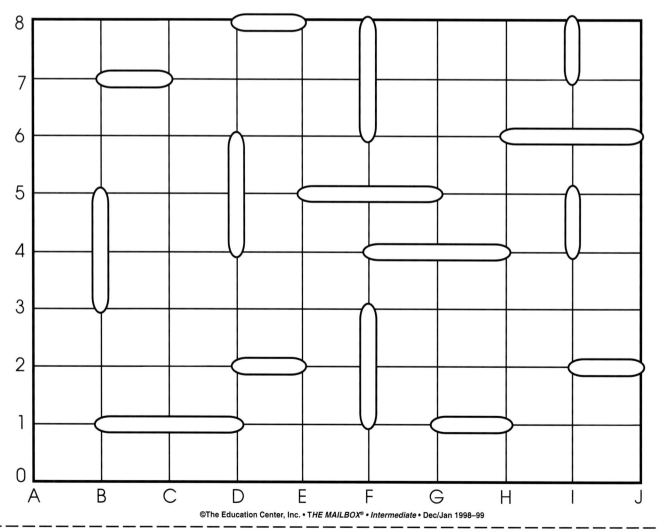

Note To The Teacher: Provide each pair of students with four copies of this page and a die. Use with "Pirate Ship!" on page 129.

STRIKING SOCIAL STUDIES GOLD!

Need a nifty idea to add some shine to your social studies lessons? Then dig right into this gold mine of skill-strengthening activities from our subscribers!

Philadelphia is both a city and a county.

Is that a fact or an opinion?

Philadelphia is the best city in Pennsylvania.

Is that a fact or an opinion?

Is That A Fact?
Skill: Research, recognizing facts and opinions

Use this fun activity to help students distinguish facts from opinions while studying any social studies topic. Pair students; then give each pair colored pencils or markers and two 8 1/2" x 11" sheets of white paper. Assign each pair a different topic from the unit being studied. Then direct the pair to research one fact on its topic and write a factual sentence about it at the top of one sheet of paper. Also have them draw a picture below this sentence to illustrate it and then write "Is that a fact or an opinion?" at the bottom of the sheet. Tell the pair to do the same with the second sheet of paper, but to write an opinion instead of a fact. When students are finished, collect the sheets, mix them up, and bind them into a class book with a title page. Share the book with the class, asking students to indicate whether each statement is a fact or an opinion, and why. It's a fact—this activity is a winner!

Lori Sammartino
Cranberry Township, PA

Picture-Perfect Postcards
Skill: Research, writing

Assess what students have learned about a state, region, province, or foreign country with these supersized postcards! Tell students that each of them has just won an all-expenses-paid vacation to a foreign country. Assign each student a place; then guide him through the steps below to complete the project. To vary the activity, have the student write a note that's persuasive instead of friendly.

Materials for each student:

encyclopedias or other reference materials	stapler
	glue
one 8 1/2" x 11" sheet of white paper	one 2" square of white paper
one 12" x 18" sheet of white construction paper	crayons, colored pencils, or markers
	pinking shears

Steps:

1. Research five to ten facts about your place, including information about its geography, history, climate, etc.
2. Use the facts to write an interesting note to someone you know.
3. Edit your note; then copy it onto an 8 1/2" x 11" sheet of white paper.
4. Staple the note onto the left half of the white construction paper.
5. Write the person's name and address on the right half of the postcard.
6. Use pinking shears to trim the edges of the paper square to resemble a stamp. On it, draw a picture—such as a flag, flower, plant, or animal—to represent your place. Also write the monetary unit of your place on the stamp.
7. Glue the stamp to the upper right corner of your postcard.
8. On the other side of the postcard, draw and color a scene that illustrates your place.

Sherry Ostroff, Burrowes Elementary, Lancaster, PA

Triarama Timeline
Skill: Sequencing historical events

Enhance the study of any historical period with this eye-catching, three-dimensional timeline! On the board, list the important events of the period you are studying. Assign each student a different event. Then give him scissors, glue, crayons or markers, construction-paper scraps, tape, and a copy of the triarama pattern on page 135. Have him complete the triarama as directed to illustrate his assigned event. Have him also write a paragraph about his event and tape it to his triarama as shown. Then have students pin the triaramas in the correct sequence on a bulletin board, along with a title and the date and name of each event. Be prepared—students will want to "tri" this activity again and again and again!

Kimberly Feldman—Gr. 6
Salt Brook Elementary
New Providence, NJ

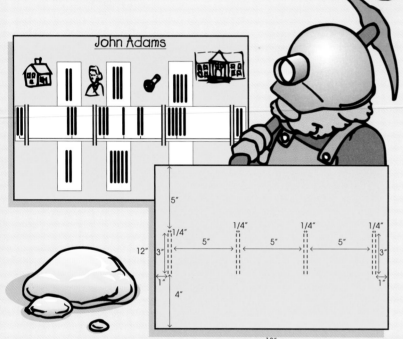

Mystery Regions
Skill: Reviewing U.S. regions

Review United States regions in style with this activity that results in some rather unique student newscasts! Divide students into groups, with one group per region. Have group members write clues about their region (without mentioning its name) to use in a news broadcast. Have one student in each group act as the anchorperson, another as a meteorologist reporting about the region's weather, and the others as reporters giving clues about the region. If desired, allow students to include clues in songs and commercials between segments of their newscast. Give students time to practice.

On the day of the broadcasts, list the regions on the board for each student to copy on his paper. As each group performs, have each member of the audience listen to the clues and identify the region being described by writing the name of the group's anchorperson next to that region on his paper. After all the presentations have been made, have each anchorperson reveal his group's region so students can check their papers.

Kathy Moses—Gr. 4, Pocono Elementary Center, Tannersville, PA

Time Weavers
Skill: Sequence, cause and effect

Have students understand how historic events could have shaped the lives of important people with this unique timeline activity. Assign each student a different important person from the time period or area you are studying. Have the student research significant dates in that individual's life and at least four major world events that could have impacted the person in some way. After the research has been done, review with students how a timeline is constructed. Then guide each student through the steps below to create his own time weaver. For a different type of timeline, see "Triarama Timeline" above.

Materials for each student:

one 3" x 18" strip of white paper (or adding-machine tape)   scissors
glue
one 12" x 18" sheet of construction paper   pen
crayons or markers
four 1" x 8" strips of white paper
ruler

Steps:

1. Measure and make cuts in the construction paper where shown by the dotted lines.
2. Beginning at one end, weave the 3" x 18" strip through the construction paper so that the 1/4-inch-wide cuts hold the strip in place.
3. Write the timeline for your person's life vertically on this strip as shown, beginning with his birth and ending with his death.
4. On the right end of each 1" x 8" strip, write a different world event and the year(s) it occurred.
5. Weave each strip under the timeline so that the writing is above the timeline and near a corresponding year in the individual's life. Glue the top and bottom of each strip to the construction paper to hold it in place.
6. Think of the effect that each world event had or could have had on your famous person. Write that effect on the bottom of each strip as shown.
7. Title your timeline and illustrate its important events with crayons or markers.

Terry Healy—Gifted K–6
Eugene Field Elementary, Manhattan, KS

Directions:

Pattern

Use with "Triarama Timeline" on page 134.

1. Cut out the square below.
2. Bring A/C to E by folding the square in half along the solid line to form a triangle. Fold it in half again along the dotted line to make a smaller triangle.
3. Unfold the square and cut along the dotted line.
4. Turn the square so that E is pointing straight up and the cut line is pointing downward. Use crayons or markers to draw the background for your scene on the large triangle above the solid line.
5. Bring C over to B and glue in place.
6. Glue A to D.
7. Use construction-paper scraps to make stand-up parts for your scene. Glue the parts to the triarama's base.

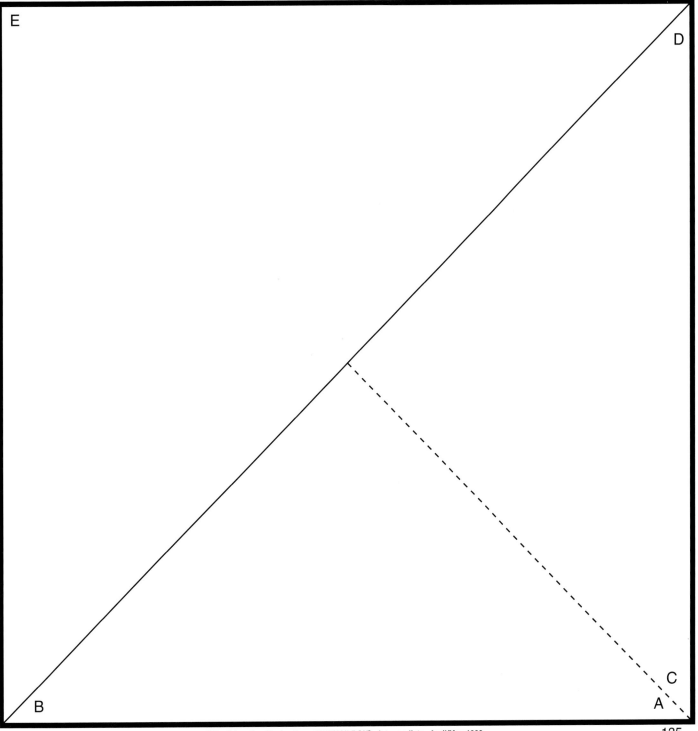

©The Education Center, Inc. • *THE MAILBOX®* • *Intermediate* • April/May 1999

135

ANCIENT CIVILIZATIONS OF LATIN AMERICA

EXPLORING THE MAYA, AZTEC, AND INCA EMPIRES

Marvel over the exceptional achievements of the Maya, Aztec, and Inca empires with the exciting activities, literature suggestions, and reproducibles that follow!

by Terry Healy, Manhattan, KS

Background Information: The Maya, Aztecs, and Incas developed some of the world's greatest civilizations. Artifacts reveal that their societies were far more advanced than other cultures at that time:

- The Maya, who lived in southern Mexico and Central America, were known for their advanced form of writing, place-value number system, and studies in astrology.
- The Aztecs set up their empire in central and southern Mexico. They were craftspeople who developed a calendar system and displayed exceptional engineering skills.
- The Incas, located in the Andes highlands of South America, excelled at architecture, built thousands of miles of roads and suspension bridges, and even terraced the land for their crops. They were also excellent potters, weavers, and metal workers.

When the Spanish arrived in the Americas, these empires began to fall. The Maya conquest began in 1500. The Aztecs fell in 1521 and the Incas in 1532.

THOSE INCREDIBLE INCAS!

Skill: Research skills

Imagine erecting structures of stone so finely cut that they needed no mortar to hold them together. Or making windows and doorways shaped like trapezoids, and amazing suspension and pontoon bridges—using only stone tools! Help students recognize the amazing achievements of the Incas with this research project. List the topics shown below on the chalkboard. Pair students; then assign each twosome a topic to research. After each pair has researched its topic, give the students the directions below along with scissors, pinking shears, a glue stick, a fine-tipped black marker, crayons, and two sheets of 9" x 12" construction paper (one pastel and one black). Display the resulting projects on a bulletin board titled "Those Incredible Incas!"

Steps:

1. Fold the colorful paper in half width-wise. Fold it in half again as shown.
2. Make diagonal cuts across two corners of the paper as shown.
3. Open the horizontal fold. Use pinking shears to trim the edges of the top half of the paper.
4. Open the paper. Fold back the two top halves to form flaps covering the bottom half of the paper.
5. Use the black marker to write "THEN" where shown. Above this label, illustrate the Incan accomplishment you researched. Then lift the flap and write a short summary of this feat on the paper below.
6. Label the right flap "NOW." Above the label, illustrate a modern version of the Incan accomplishment. Then lift the flap and summarize how the modern world accomplishes the same Incan feat today.
7. Glue the folded paper as shown on the black paper.

TOPICS:

Incan Agriculture And Irrigation

Math And Astronomy In The Incan World

Incan Bridge Building

Incan Road System

Incan Architecture

Incan Medicine

136

THAT'S THE WAY THE BALL BOUNCES
Skill: Writing step-by-step directions

If students want to know what a seriously competitive sport is *really* like, then tell them about the way the Maya and Aztecs played ball! Two teams of nobles in an I-shaped court would try to propel a solid rubber ball against a marker set in the center of each side of the court's walls or through vertical hoops. The players would hit the ball at high speeds from one side of the court to the other using only their hips, wrists, or elbows. Losers sometimes lost everything they had—even their lives!

For a creative-thinking challenge, have pairs of students invent a team game that's played with a small rubber ball and two hoops. Direct each pair to write a set of rules and step-by-step directions telling how to play its game. Then have the pair trade its rules and directions with another twosome. Ask each pair of students to read the directions carefully, make suggestions for revisions, and then return the directions to the authors. Collect the revised games to use during recess or at a special field day held at the end of your unit!

AZTEC ARTISANS
Skill: Following directions

If there's one thing that kept Aztec artisans busy, it was making decorative pieces of gold and silver! The Aztecs had no monetary system, so the highest classes wore these objects to symbolize their wealth. Turn students into skillful Aztec artisans by having them create golden ornaments of their own. Give each student a two-inch ball of air-drying clay, several layers of paper towels or newspapers, a dull pencil, a copy of the glyph patterns on page 142, gold or silver metallic acrylic craft paint, and a paintbrush. Direct the student to flatten and shape the clay into a 3/4-inch-thick circle on the paper. Have her use the dull pencil to make a glyph from the pattern page on the circle; then have her add a repeating design around the circle's edge. Allow the clay to dry overnight. The next day have the student paint one side of the circle, allow it to dry, and then paint the other side. Use these shiny projects to enhance an existing unit display or as a springboard for writing stories about a rich Aztec who lost a golden ornament like the ones created.

THE GIFT OF MUSIC
Skill: Comparing, contrasting, and writing myths

What would the world be like without the sound of music? It wouldn't have been as great for the Aztecs because music was very important to them. Read aloud the following picture books that tell how the Aztecs thought music came to the world: *Musicians Of The Sun* by Gerald McDermott (Simon & Schuster Books For Young Readers, 1997) and *How Music Came To The World,* retold by Hal Ober (Houghton Mifflin Company, 1994). After reading each myth, have students help you map it on the chalkboard. Next guide students to use the story maps to compare and contrast the two myths. Then list the shown topics on the board. Direct each student to write his own myth titled "How [topic] Came Into The World" to share with the class. If desired, have students compare and contrast myths written on the same topic. Or incorporate other Latin American tales into this activity using Lulu Delacre's *Golden Tales: Myths, Legends, And Folktales From Latin America* (Scholastic Press, 1996).

TOPICS:

Laughter	Clouds
Clocks	Rain
Calendars	Stars
Storms	Wheels
Games	
Fire	

STRINGING ALONG
Skill: Place value

Instead of stringing students along about how the Incas kept records, use this terrific hands-on project to make it perfectly clear! The Incas kept records with a device called a *quipu,* a long cord held horizontally from which hung a series of different-colored knotted strings. To demonstrate how the Incas could have represented 364 llamas on a quipu, draw on the chalkboard the illustration shown. Point out that the set of three dots represents 300, the six dots 60, and the four dots 4. *(Note: If the numeral had been 304, leaving a space for the tens would show that there were no tens.)* Next give each pair of students a 12-inch length of black yarn and one 18-inch length of yarn in each of the following colors: blue, red, yellow, green. Challenge the pair to create its own version of a quipu by following the steps below. To extend this activity, have each student use crayons or colored pencils to draw pictures of quipus representing numerals of higher place values (ten thousands, hundred thousands, etc.).

Steps:
1. Partner A holds the black yarn straight by holding one end in each hand.
2. Partner B ties the blue yarn near one end of the black yarn by folding the blue yarn in half, then folding its center loop over the black yarn. He then pulls the ends of the blue yarn through the loop, resulting in two lengths of blue yarn hanging from the black yarn (one for Partner A and the other for Partner B).
3. Partner B repeats Step 2 with the red, yellow, and green yarn.
4. Partners A and B take turns making knots in the colorful yarn using this code: blue = days until next birthday, red = score on last spelling test, yellow = pages in one of their textbooks, green = pages in current library book. For example, if there are 127 days until Partner A's birthday, he would make the following knots in his length of blue yarn: one knot (1 hundred, or 100) near the black yarn, two knots (2 tens, or 20) in the center, and seven knots (7 ones, or 7) near the bottom.

PICTURE THIS!
Skill: Critical thinking, art project

The Maya were the only ancient New World inhabitants to develop a true form of writing. They used picture symbols, or *hieroglyphs,* on pottery, walls, and ornaments, and in books called *codices*. The Aztecs also used hieroglyphs, but in a simpler style. Have students practice picture writing to help them recall interesting facts about the Maya and Aztecs. Give each student a sheet of light brown construction paper, colored markers, and a copy of page 142. Direct the student to choose glyphs from page 142—along with creating some of his own design—that help him tell something about Maya or Aztec life (see the suggestions below). Then have him draw his glyphs on one side of the brown paper and write the interpretation on the flip side. Next have him trade papers with a classmate, decipher his partner's glyphs, and flip the paper over to check. If desired, compile the papers into a class *codex* (book). Tape the papers together side to side and fold them accordion-style as shown. Add decorated front and back covers to complete the codex.

Codex Of Mayan And Aztec Life

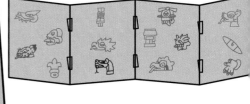

- Maya ceremonies, dances, and festivals were held in the centers of their cities.
- Only four Maya codices exist today. It is believed that hundreds more were destroyed by the Spanish.
- Priests and nobles were probably the only people who could read the Maya hieroglyphs.

- The Maya wore feather headdresses that made the wearers look like birds.
- Maya boys practiced battle skills.
- The Maya and Aztecs made dugout canoes by burning and digging out large trees.
- The Maya and Aztecs usually ate two meals per day.

Linking Literature With Latin America's Ancient Civilizations

Be sure to include the following outstanding children's books in your study of Latin America's ancient civilizations.

reviewed by Deborah Zink Roffino

Maya's Children: The Story Of La Llorona

written by Rudolfo Anaya
illustrated by Maria Baca
Hyperion Books For Children, 1997

Not far from the turquoise waters of a lake lying in the shadows of a Mexican volcano, you can hear the wailing sounds of La Llorona as she weeps for her children. In this retelling of an ancient Mexican myth—decorated with folk art in electric colors—Señor Tiempo (Father Time) plots to steal the children of Maya, beloved of the Sun God. When he succeeds, Maya spends eternity searching the lake, crying for her lost children. Don't skip the Author's Note, which offers interesting insight into this tale that is familiar throughout the Spanish-speaking Americas.

Quetzal: Sacred Bird Of The Cloud Forest

written by Dorothy Hinshaw Patent
illustrated by Neil Waldman
Morrow Junior Books, 1996

In the mountaintops above the mists of the cloud forest, the resplendent quetzal perches. His vivid green tail feathers trail as he takes flight and suddenly plunges back into the mists. Historians believe that this rare bird with its snakelike appearance gave birth to the Mesoamerican belief in the great god Quetzalcoatl, the feathered serpent. This detailed examination of the bird and the mythology surrounding it—generously illustrated with opalescent tones—explains how the Aztec civilization could have vanished due to the belief in this bird.

Beneath The Stone: A Mexican Zapotec Tale

written and photographed by Bernard Wolf
Orchard Books, 1994

This pictorial essay chronicles the lives of a modern Zapotec family living in the shadows of their ancestors in the Oaxaca Valley of Mexico. Work, school, family, feasts, and festivals are captured in expressive photographs and described in detail within the text. Rich with tradition, their village life reflects a blend of modern conveniences and ancient cultures.

The Lizard And The Sun

written by Alma Flor Ada
illustrated by Felipe Dávalos
Bantam Doubleday Dell
Publishing Group, Inc.; 1997

The lyrical text in this lovely book, written in English and Spanish, celebrates the sun, a focal point in the lives of indigenous people of Latin America. After the sun disappears for many days, the animals of the kingdom go in search of it. Eventually all give up except the tenacious emerald green lizard. Her persistence pays off and the life-giving light returns to the sky. The illustrations begin in the darkness, transform to brilliance, and offer scenes of the ancient pageantry of the Aztec world.

Order books on-line. www.themailbox.com

ANCIENT PYRAMID OF FACTS

If you were an ancient Inca, Mayan, or Aztec, you probably attended religious ceremonies that were held at a pyramid temple. Build your own pyramid to help you remember important facts about the Maya, Aztecs, and Incas!

Directions: Match each fact below with the culture it describes. Use encyclopedias to help you. Then write the fact on the corresponding pyramid wall. (Hint: Some facts will be written on more than one wall.) Next cut out the pattern. Fold it on the dotted lines and glue where directed to form a pyramid.

Worshipped gods and goddesses

Ate cornmeal pancakes

Empire centered in Andes highlands

Used llamas to carry their goods

Had no central form of government

Spoke a language called *Quechua*

Were conquered by the Spanish

Had their capital at the city of Tenochtitlán

Empire centered in Mexico

Empire centered in southern Mexico and Central America

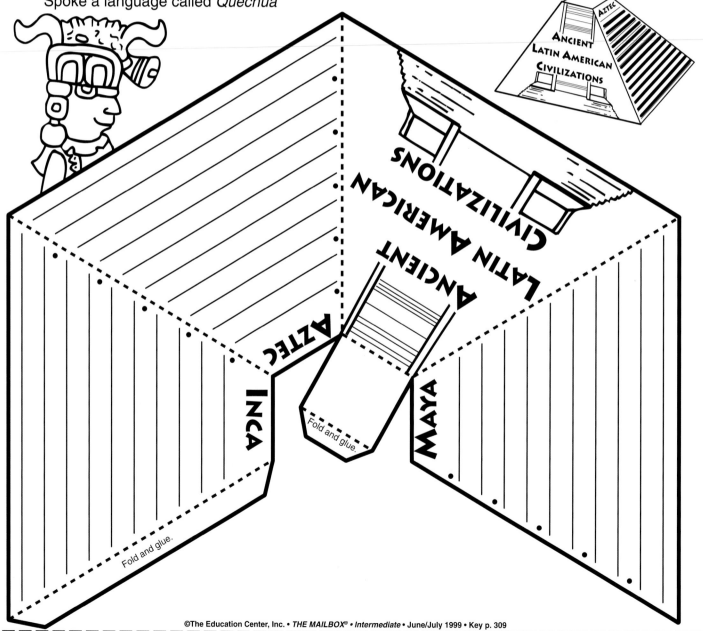

©The Education Center, Inc. • *THE MAILBOX*® • *Intermediate* • June/July 1999 • Key p. 309

140 **Note To The Teacher:** Provide students with scissors, glue, and encyclopedias to complete this activity.

GOIN' ON A DIG!

Much of what is known about the Maya, Aztecs, and Incas has been learned by studying artifacts from archaeological digs. Discover more about these ancient cultures and review parts of speech at the same time by taking part in a dig of your own!

Directions: Find 25 artifacts (**boldfaced** words) buried in the sentences below. List the words on the matching shapes. Here's a helpful hint: this dig consists of 8 nouns, 6 verbs, 5 adjectives, 3 adverbs, and 3 pronouns.

Nouns:

Verbs:

Adjectives:

Adverbs:

Pronouns:

1. Mayans thought that strapping babies to **boards** to make **their** heads longer made them more attractive.

2. The Maya **understood** the concept of zero long before it was understood in **Europe.**

3. To the Maya, Aztecs, and Incas, wearing bird feathers was a symbol of wealth—like having a **fancy** car or expensive clothes today.

4. The Maya, Aztecs, and Incas placed **masks** over their mummies to protect **them** in the afterlife.

5. The Incas believed that gold **was** the "sweat of the sun." They called silver the "tears of the moon."

6. Since the Incas had no form of **writing,** studying their pottery is a **valuable** way to learn about their culture.

7. Because they had no **animals** large enough to carry heavy loads, the Maya **carried** all their goods on their backs!

8. Aztec families **raised** turkeys for food, but **they** also ate small dogs!

9. To pay taxes, all **married** Inca farmers **dutifully** spent part of their time erecting buildings or constructing roads.

10. The Incas did not have the wheel. They **patiently** rolled **huge** building stones—some weighing many tons—on large log rollers for distances as long as 18 miles!

11. The Maya and Aztecs played a board game similar to **Parcheesi®.** They used beans for dice, stones for game pieces, and feathers and jewelry for prizes.

12. For protection, the Aztecs **built** their capital city, Tenochtitlán, in the center of a **lake.** They connected it to the mainland with removable-section bridges.

13. Each time a new baby was born, Inca families were given **more** land to farm.

14. Aztecs took steam baths in small buildings next to their homes. Each bathhouse was heated by a **fireplace.**

15. The poncho **is** a type of clothing from Inca culture that is **still** worn today.

Bonus Box: On the back of this page, list the kinds of items archaeologists find on digs.

Patterns

Use with "Aztec Artisans" on page 137 and "Picture This!" on page 138.

1. Crocodile
2. Wind
3. House
4. Lizard
5. Serpent
6. Death's-head
7. Deer
8. Rabbit
9. Water
10. Dog
11. Monkey
12. Grass
13. Reed
14. Ocelot
15. Eagle
16. Vulture
17. Motion
18. Flint knife
19. Rain
20. Flower

SCIENCE UNITS

WHO KIDNAPPED TED E. BEAR?

SOLVING A SCIENTIFIC MYSTERY USING CHROMATOGRAPHY

A young bear has been kidnapped, and students will need to observe and experiment in order to nab the nefarious kidnapper! Try this ready-to-use lesson plan about the science of chromatography to help students solve this puzzling case.

by Terry Healy

Materials:
4 coffee filters
3 black, water-based markers, each one manufactured by a different company
1 clear plastic cup of water for each group of four students
paper towels
scissors
rulers

STEP 1: TEACHER PREPARATION

1. Gather the materials on the list.
2. Label the markers "A," "B," and "C."
3. Use one of the markers (A, B, or C) to write the following ransom note on the first filter:

Dear Students,
 I have taken Ted E. Bear. If you are sly enough to discover who I am, you'll get your bear back.

 The Kidnapper

4. Label the three remaining filters "A," "B," and "C."
5. Use marker A to color a dot in each section of filter A, leaving about 1/2 inch between each dot and the edge of the filter. (See the illustration.)
6. Repeat Step 5 with markers B and C and the corresponding filters.
7. Duplicate one copy of page 145 for each group of four students.

STEP 2: DEFINING CHROMATOGRAPHY

Share the definition of *chromatography* from the reproducible on page 145 with students. Explain that chromatography will help them identify which marker matches the ransom note's ink.

STEP 3: SHARING THE SCENARIO

Read the following to your class: *A terrible thing has happened! Mr. Ted E. Bear has been kidnapped. The three suspects are Mr. Squirre Ell, Miss P. Q. Pine, and Master Kyle Otey. We've received a ransom note from the kidnapper.* (Read the ransom note to the class.) *By comparing the dyes used in each of the suspect's markers against the ink of the ransom note, we should be able to discover the kidnapper's identity.*

STEP 4: PERFORMING THE EXPERIMENT

Divide your class into groups of four. Direct each group to cut a 2" x 1" ink sample from filters A, B, and C, labeling each sample appropriately. Provide each group with a same-size sample cut from the ransom note and a small cup of water. Direct each group to carefully dip the lower edge of filter A's sample into the water for 10 seconds, making sure that the ink dot stays above the water level. Then have the group lay the sample in its correct place on page 145's chart to dry. Students should observe the water spreading through the sample. Have them repeat this process for each of the other samples.

STEP 5: DRAWING A CONCLUSION

Guide the groups in recording their observations on their reproducibles. Have the group members write down the colors seen on each filter sample. Then have them identify the kidnapper by comparing the ransom-note ink to each sample.

Dear Students,
I have taken Ted E. Bear. If you are sly enough to discover who I am, you'll get your bear back.

The Kidnapper

A

WHO KIDNAPPED TED E. BEAR?

Chromatography is the process that lets scientists separate a mixture into its different parts by their colors. The color record that results is called a *chromatogram.* This experiment will help you see what colors are mixed together to make each marker's ink.

Directions: Carefully dip just the lower edge of one sample into the water, **making sure that the ink dot stays above the water level.** Then lay the sample in its correct place on the chart to dry. Repeat this process for each of the other samples, including the ransom note.

Marker A	Marker B	Marker C	Ransom Note
Squirre Ell	P. Q. Pine	Kyle Otey	–?–

Conclusions: What colors were added together to make each ink mixture?

Marker A: _____

Marker B: _____

Marker C: _____

Which one best matches the ransom note: A, B, or C? _____

Who kidnapped Ted E. Bear? _____

Bonus Box: Pretend you are Ted E. Bear. On another sheet of paper, write a story describing how you were kidnapped and the feelings you experienced.

No Bones About It... Invertebrates Are Incredible!

Not having a backbone isn't as bad as it seems for some creatures. In fact, more than 95% of the world's animal population is spineless! Use the following hands-on activities and reproducibles to boost science-process skills and help students become "bone-fide" experts on invertebrates.

by Bonnie Pettifor

Invertebrates: 97, Vertebrates: 3

Begin this unit with a simple classification activity. Ask students to bring in safe items from home, such as plastic or stuffed toys, so that each team has at least 20 different objects. The next day divide the class into teams. Have each team study its items and then sort them into two groups by size, color, or any other categories. Explain to students that scientists have divided the animal kingdom into two main groups, one with backbones and the other without. The group with backbones, called *vertebrates,* makes up about 3% of all animals. The group without backbones, called *invertebrates,* makes up the other 97%. Since there is a great deal of difference between any two animals with backbones and any two without backbones, scientists have further divided both groups according to additional physical characteristics. Direct each team to subdivide one of its two groups into three subgroups and share its reasoning with the class. Use this activity again, with students bringing in different items, when studying a new group of living things.

Eight Fabulous Phyla

Introduce students to the animals that make up the eight largest phyla of invertebrates with this chart-making activity. Divide a large sheet of bulletin-board paper into eight columns, labeling it and listing examples as shown. Ask students to share what they know about each phylum. Add their comments to the chart. Next give each student a copy of the research activity on page 149 to complete as directed. As students learn more about invertebrates through their research, have them add information to (or delete information from) the class chart.

Sponges	Coelenterates	Flatworms	Roundworms	Segmented Worms	Mollusks
sheepswool sponge	jellyfish	planarian	vinegar eel	clamworm	clam
sulfur sponge	sea anemone	fluke	hookworm	earthworm	squid
Venus's-flower-basket sponge	coral	tapeworm	trichina worm	leech	octopus

146

It's Always Wise To Have Sharper Eyes

Keen eyes are all future "invertebrate-ologists" need for this simple exercise on observation! Pass around an interesting seashell and a hand lens, giving no directions other than telling students to look at it. Once each child has examined the shell, put it away. Then ask each student to list every detail he can recall about the shell. (If desired, have students also make detailed drawings.) As students share their recollections, point out that careful observation—combined with accurate note taking and drawing—is vitally important when doing scientific investigations. For another activity that sharpens observation and data-recording skills, see the reproducible "Candy-Worm Dissection" on page 150.

To adapt this activity to any science unit, follow the same procedure as above. Simply substitute the shell for an object related to the new unit. Don't worry if students get wise to this method—simply reduce the time allowed for looking at the object!

Spineless Math

Strengthen students' graphing skills with this hands-on encounter with backyard creepy crawlies. For each small group, fill a large Styrofoam® meat tray (donated by a local grocer) with the upper few inches of soil from under a rock, a log, or another object. Then guide the groups through these steps:

1. Spread out the soil on the tray.
2. Look for beetle larvae, earthworms, roundworms, slugs, pill bugs (also called roly-polies), centipedes, millipedes, ants, or other invertebrates in the soil.
3. Record the number of each invertebrate your group finds.
4. Make drawings of these invertebrates.
5. Record your group's observations about these invertebrates.
6. Use your group's data to create a bar graph of your findings.

Challenge all the groups to combine their data into a class graph. Post this graph above a terrarium set up by students for housing the invertebrates they found. Or return the animals to the area from which they were taken. For a great follow-up to this activity, see the reproducible on page 151 or "Bringing Up Baby" on this page.

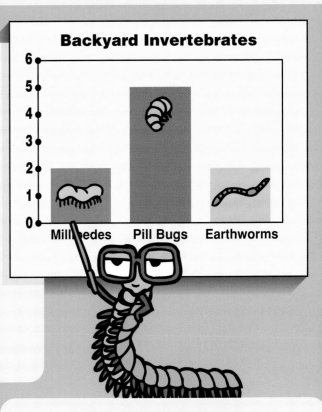

Backyard Invertebrates

	Echinoderms	Arthropods
	starfish	lobster
	sand dollar	insect
	sea urchin	spider

Bringing Up Baby

Interested in keeping an invertebrate as a pet in the classroom? Most invertebrates—such as land or water snails, earthworms, lady beetles, and mealworms—require very little attention once their natural environment has been duplicated. In return they supply lots of fascinating entertainment for students. *And* putting the care of these invertebrates in the hands of students helps teach responsibility. Specimens can be collected from nature, or live invertebrates can be ordered from a biological supply company (see the box below). And guess what? No 2:00 A.M. feedings to worry about!

For a catalog including invertebrates and other scientific supplies, contact:
Carolina Biological Supply Company
2700 York Road
Burlington, NC 27215
1-800-334-5551

BARRY
SLATE

Moovin' And Groovin'

How do some invertebrates move and eat? Find out with these three "inverte-GREAT" activities!

- **How A Sponge Eats:** Show students a natural sponge. Explain that this is really the sponge's skeleton that's been cleaned and dried. A live sponge has holes, or *pores,* through which water is squeezed to filter food. Let each student use a hand lens to examine the pores in a synthetic sponge. Then divide students into groups to complete the following experiment:

  Materials: 1 cup of water, 1 clear empty glass, 1 tablespoon of glitter, 1 large-holed synthetic sponge (large enough to cover the top of the glass), 1 plastic spoon, paper and pencil
  Steps:
  1. Use the spoon to stir the glitter (food) into the cup of water.
  2. Place the sponge over the empty glass.
  3. Predict what you think will happen to the food when it is poured on the sponge. Write your prediction.
  4. Slowly pour the food (glitter mixture) on the sponge.
  5. Carefully fold the ends of the sponge together; then squeeze the sponge so that the water from it goes into the empty glass.
  6. Record what happens to the food. *(The sponge filters the glitter from the water, trapping most of it in the sponge.)*

- **How A Squid Moves:** Explain that a squid travels by jet propulsion—taking water in and pushing it out—which moves it *backwards!* To demonstrate this unusual method of movement, squeeze the bulb end of a turkey baster. Put the tube end into a clear plastic tub of water. Release the bulb so that it fills with water. Tell students that this action mimics a squid taking in water under its mantle. Next squeeze the bulb, forcing the water out of the tube. Explain that this mimics the action of a squid as it pushes water out through a funnel under its head, making it move backwards.

- **Moving Into Research:** Follow up these two activities by assigning each student a different invertebrate to research (see the list on page 149). Have the student find out how his invertebrate eats, and also how it moves to catch prey and evade predators. Challenge him to share his findings in a presentation that includes a demonstration of how his animal moves.

Investigating Incredible Invertebrates!

Invertebrates are animals without backbones. Pretend that a group of aliens has come to investigate the different *phyla* (groups) of invertebrates found on Earth, and that *you* are on the committee to answer their questions!

To get ready to answer their questions, complete ___ activities by _____. Use the list of invertebrates below and your science text, library books, encyclopedias, or the Internet for help. Color one of the invertebrates on this sheet each time you complete an activity.

1. Choose one of these invertebrate phyla: Sponges, Coelenterates, Flatworms, Roundworms, Segmented Worms, Mollusks, Echinoderms, Arthropods. Write a paragraph describing the phylum's basic characteristics for the aliens. Include the names of several animals that belong to this group.
2. Make a model of any invertebrate to show the aliens. Be sure to label the invertebrate's parts.
3. Choose an invertebrate from the box below. Write a friendly letter from the invertebrate to the aliens. In the letter, have the invertebrate tell what it eats, how it gets its food, and where it lives.
4. Pretend a classmate is one of the aliens. Teach him the spelling and the definition of each of the eight largest phyla of invertebrates (Hint: they're listed in #1).
5. Make a detailed drawing of an invertebrate listed below in its environment as a souvenir for the aliens. Remember to label the invertebrate's parts.
6. Pretend you are an alien. Write an e-mail message to the chairman of the committee that is investigating invertebrates. In the e-mail, list five questions about invertebrates that you want answered during your stay on Earth.
7. Choose a partner. Work together to create a fun game that will teach the aliens ten interesting facts about one of the invertebrate groups listed in #1. Test your game with two other classmates.
8. Make a shape book about an invertebrate to give to an alien as a memento. Share the book with a younger student (before giving it to the alien, of course!).

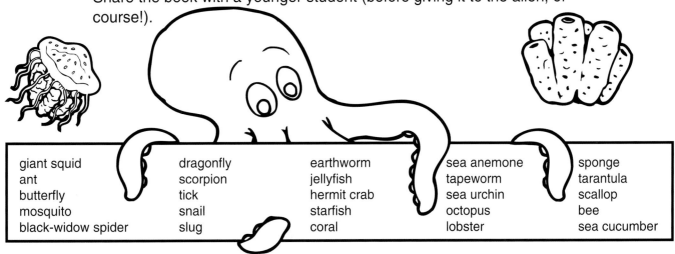

giant squid	dragonfly	earthworm	sea anemone	sponge
ant	scorpion	jellyfish	tapeworm	tarantula
butterfly	tick	hermit crab	sea urchin	scallop
mosquito	snail	starfish	octopus	bee
black-widow spider	slug	coral	lobster	sea cucumber

Note To The Teacher: Use with "Eight Fabulous Phyla" on page 146. Before duplicating, fill in the blanks with the number of activities to complete and the due date. Make one copy for each student. Use also with "Moving Into Research" on page 148.

Candy-Worm Dissection

How is a worm like a map? Believe it or not, they *are* alike! The 100–180 rings on an earthworm's body are like the lines on a map's grid. They help scientists locate the earthworm's organs. Scientists have learned this information through careful observation and a procedure called *dissection.* Dissection is the process of cutting into a dead animal to find out what its body is like inside. Follow the steps below to do a little dissecting of your own!

Materials: 1 Gummy Worm®, 1 plastic knife, 1 paper towel, 1 pencil

Steps:

1. Place the Gummy Worm® on the paper towel. Carefully count the number of rings on your worm. Record the number: _____.

2. Draw your candy worm in the space below. Show its exact number of rings.

3. Label the worm's rings in your drawing:
   Ring 3: Brain
   Rings 7–11: Five pairs of hearts
   Rings 17–18: Gizzard (stomach)
   (Note: Your candy worm won't have as many rings as real earthworms do! Add more rings to your drawing if you'd like.)

4. Carefully use the knife to cut the sections of the candy worm apart.

5. Look carefully at the outer surface of the candy worm. Also notice what the cut surface is like. Touch both surfaces. On the back of this sheet, describe the look and feel of these surfaces.

6. Use the information in Step 3 to label the drawing below with the names of the worm's organs.

7. Now eat your candy worm—it will taste much better than the real thing!

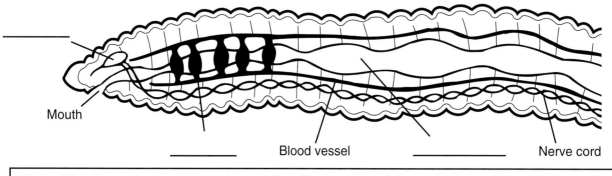

Mouth

_____ Blood vessel _____ Nerve cord

Bonus Box: Pretend you are an earthworm that's just been caught by a child. The child plans to use you as fishing bait! On another sheet of paper, write a story telling how you persuade the child to let you go.

©The Education Center, Inc. • *THE MAILBOX® • Intermediate •* Oct/Nov 1998 • Key p. 309

Home Sweet Invertebrate Home

Did you know that invertebrates prefer certain living conditions over others, just like people do? To learn more about the places that some invertebrates like to call home, follow the directions below with a partner.

Materials:
1 roly-poly bug (also known as a pill bug)
1 large, round white Styrofoam® plate
one 9" x 12" sheet of white construction paper
one 9" x 12" sheet of black construction paper
pencil
scissors
water
plastic wrap (enough to cover plate securely)
tape
1 toothpick

wet white circle

Steps:

1. Trace the plate on both the white paper and the black paper; then cut out the tracings.
2. Wet the white circle with water so that it has no dry spots; then press it to the bottom of the plate.
3. Fold the black circle in half; then tape this semi-circle to the plate at the edges as shown.
4. Put the roly-poly onto the uncovered part of the plate; then cover the plate completely with plastic wrap. If necessary, tape the plastic wrap to the plate's edges to prevent the roly-poly from escaping.
5. Use the toothpick to make several tiny airholes in the plastic wrap.
6. Put the plate in a place where it will be undisturbed for at least 30 minutes.
7. Decide which section—the light (uncovered) part or the dark (covered) part—you think the roly-poly will prefer. Record your prediction below.
8. After at least 30 minutes are up, uncover the plate and find the roly-poly. Was your prediction correct? Record your observations below.

My Prediction:
I think the roly-poly will like the _____ section.

My Observations:
I found the roly-poly in the _____ section. I think it chose this section because

_____

_____.

Bonus Box: Roly-polies prefer damp environments. Pretend you are a roly-poly. On the back of this sheet, write a conversation between you and a bee about why you prefer a damp home.

©The Education Center, Inc. • *THE MAILBOX® • Intermediate •* Oct/Nov 1998 • Key p. 309

Note To The Teacher: Use after "Spineless Math" on page 147. Roly-polies are found in damp places, such as under rocks and pieces of wood. Earthworms can also be used for this investigation. Duplicate one copy of this page for each pair of students. If desired, combine all the data and have students graph the results and draw conclusions.

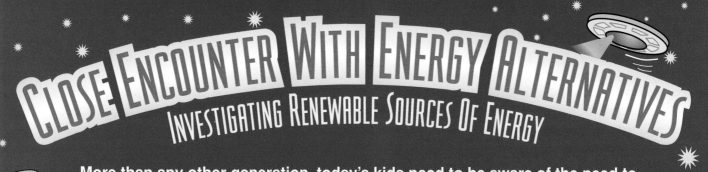

CLOSE ENCOUNTER WITH ENERGY ALTERNATIVES
INVESTIGATING RENEWABLE SOURCES OF ENERGY

More than any other generation, today's kids need to be aware of the need to become less dependent on nonrenewable sources of energy, such as oil and other fossil fuels. Give your students a close encounter with the world of renewable energy sources through the following out-of-this-world activities.

with ideas by Cynthia Wurmnest

SAVING SUNSHINE: SOLAR ENERGY

Searching for a renewable source of energy? Look up! Large amounts of energy from the sun hit our world every day. This energy can be used to produce electricity if properly collected, concentrated, and stored. Help students investigate the storage of solar energy with this activity that compares the heat-retaining ability of four substances. First divide the class into teams; then give each team a copy of page 155 and the following materials:

- 4 dark plastic trash bags
- 4 same-sized, clear plastic cups
- 4 different colored pencils
- equal amounts of dried pinto beans, shredded white paper, soil, and water
- watch or clock
- 4 twist-ties
- 4 thermometers*
- spoon

When all groups have completed the experiment as directed on page 155, meet together to discuss results and determine the most efficient heat-retaining material. (*If desired, perform the experiment as a class, holding each of four teams responsible for measuring the temperature of only one cup. Have teams share their data; then have each student complete his graph on page 155 and answer the questions.)

These Earth creatures are most friendly. See how they wave at us...

WORKING WITH THE WIND: WIND ENERGY

Throughout history, people have used wind energy to do many jobs, including produce electricity. To illustrate the wind's ability to generate an electrical current, obtain a galvanometer (check a local high school's science department) or a current detector (available at a hardware store for under $5.00). Position two large electric fans about six inches apart facing each other. Plug in one fan and turn it on HIGH. When the blades of the *unplugged* fan start to turn, touch the current detector to the metal ends of its plug. Surprise! The detector registers an electrical current.

Next display a picture of a windmill. Explain that windmills in history have provided power to pump water, grind grain, or generate electricity. Today's windmills, called *wind turbines,* are used to produce electricity. Ask, "What might be the advantages of wind energy?" *(It is free and produces little pollution; it doesn't have to be mined or pumped from the earth.)* Explain that wind speed must be greater than 7.5 miles per hour to produce electricity. Ask, "What might be wind energy's disadvantages?" *(Winds are too weak or infrequent in many places. Wind turbines are noisy and can be hazardous to birds. They can also interfere with TV and radio signals.)*

THAT'S HOT STUFF!: GEOTHERMAL ENERGY

Heat energy from deep inside the earth—such as that evidenced by geysers like Old Faithful—is called *geothermal energy.* Simulate the nature of a geothermal energy source with this simple demonstration. Position a table or desk at least five feet from where students are sitting. Turn a metal kitchen funnel upside down in a pan that has been filled halfway with water. Heat the pan on a hot plate or another safe heat source. As the water heats, it will come out of the top of the funnel. (Be sure to wear oven mitts and stand back from the table.) Turn off the hot plate; then explain to students that in many places around the world, hot water and steam like this come out from cracks in the earth's surface. Hot melted rocks underground heat the water to high temperatures and sometimes the water boils to produce steam. The steam can then be used directly or be harnessed to produce electricity. Ask students the following questions to further explore geothermal energy:

- How could geothermal energy be used to heat homes safely? *(Homes can be directly heated with the steam through radiators. Or the steam can be used to drive turbines in a power plant to make electricity.)*
- Why do you think this energy source is relatively inexpensive? *(The only cost to geothermal energy is the equipment to use it. The fuel is free.)*
- What might be drawbacks to geothermal energy? *(You have to be located near a geothermal source to take advantage of it. There aren't many geothermal sources near big cities where the need is greatest. Also, hot water and steam can't be transported over long distances without losing energy.)*

OOPS!
Heh, heh, heh,...

WORKIN' WATERWHEELS: WATER POWER

For centuries, people have used water to power machines. Today, water, or *hydroelectric,* power is used to generate electricity. Water power causes little pollution, plus the water used to generate electricity can meet other needs later. On the downside, few rivers have good locations for building power plants or dams. And locating power plants in wilderness areas can upset those environments forever.

Help students discover the power of water by having them construct and test their own simple waterwheels. Provide each pair of students with the half-page reproducible on page 156 and the materials listed on it. Help students follow the steps to make their own simple waterwheels. Then have them use their models to test three early types of waterwheels as described on page 156. At the end of the activity, discuss students' answers to the question at the bottom of the page. Point out that people improved on the primitive Greek mill waterwheel, resulting in the more powerful overshot waterwheel. Then have each student write in her science journal about a modern machine she would like to improve and the improvements she would make.

Yesterday And Today: Energy Conservation

That old horse-drawn carriage of 100 years ago didn't move as fast as our four-wheel-drive vehicles, but it also didn't cost much in terms of energy. For a fun exercise that gets your class thinking about the energy costs of progress, give each child a copy of the half-page reproducible on page 156. Have students or pairs of students complete the page. Then provide a sharing time to discuss their answers. As an extension, challenge student groups to design posters illustrating the contrasts between today's convenient, energy-guzzling machines and yesterday's inefficient, energy-saving devices.

On The Web

- *U.S. Department Of Energy's Energy Efficiency And Renewable Energy Network:* This helpful site contains background information for students, adventures with Energy Dog®, and more. Check it out at **www.eren.doe.gov/.**
- *Watt Watchers Of Texas:* This program makes elementary students aware of energy use and conservation both at home and at school. It also includes links to other sources of information on renewable energy. Find it at **www.wattwatchers.utep.edu.** *(Current as of 9-98)*

There's A Crisis In Techno Town!: Culminating Activity

Wrap up this unit with a fun simulation that provides an unforgettable review of renewable energy. Divide students into five groups. Choose one group to serve as the Town Council of Techno Town. Assign a renewable energy source to each of the other four groups: solar, geothermal, hydroelectric, and wind. Then read the following news release:

> Today Techno Town officials called a news conference to announce a series of public hearings on a recent energy crisis. Power outages have bothered this community recently, causing outraged citizens to lose the use of computers, home entertainment systems, and jet-train transportation into the town's busines district. Outages are blamed on the lack of fuel to run the Techno Town Power Plant, which generates all electricity for the community. Officials are expected to announce a competition among highly respected energy experts to choose a new alternative energy system for the town. Experts began arriving today. More details as they become available.

Announce that students will become the energy experts hired to propose a solution to Techno Town's problem. Each group must research its energy source, then prepare a presentation for the Town Council that includes an opening statement, a list of their system's advantages and disadvantages, a brief description of the equipment needed, and a closing statement.

On Presentation Day, give each student a copy of the note-taking form on page 157. Seat the Town Council together and instruct all students to take notes on each presentation. After the presentations, have the Town Council meet to discuss each energy source and make its decision. Require that the council write and issue a formal announcement giving reasons for its decision.

Saving Sunshine

WHEW!

Yikes! As the owners of Positively Plants Greenhouse, you and your team are spending a fortune heating the greenhouse on cold winter nights. It's time to save a little sunshine! One idea is to fill several big black barrels with something that will absorb solar heat during the day. Then you can use the heat to warm your greenhouse at night. But what substance will hold the most heat in the barrels?

To find out, perform the following experiment. (Your teacher will provide the materials.) After you complete Steps 1–8, answer the questions. Then enjoy your toasty warm greenhouse!

130°					
125°					
120°					
115°					
110°					
105°					
100°					
95°					
90°					
85°					
80°					

1   10   20   30

minutes after exposure

Color Code

☐ beans
☐ paper
☐ soil
☐ water

Steps:

1. Use the colored pencils to color in the Color Code boxes. Be sure to use a different color for each box.
2. Use the spoon to fill each cup with a different substance. Be sure the amounts are as equal as possible.
3. Put each cup into a separate trash bag; then use a twist-tie to close each bag around its cup.
4. Place the four cups in the sun for one hour.
5. After the hour is up, move the cups to the shade. Unwrap each cup from its bag.
6. Place a thermometer in each cup. Leave it there for one minute.
7. Check the temperature of each cup after one minute is up. Use the colored pencils and Color Code to plot the temperature on the graph.
8. Repeat Step 7 after 10 minutes, 20 minutes, and 30 minutes.

Questions: Write your answers on the back of this sheet.

a. Did all the substances absorb the same amount of solar energy? Explain your answer.
b. Which substance would be best to use to fill the barrels? Why?

Bonus Box: What might be a disadvantage to using solar energy? Write your answer on the back of this page.

©The Education Center, Inc. • THE MAILBOX® • Intermediate • Feb/Mar 1999 • Key p. 309

155

156

Yesterday And Today

A hundred years ago the old horse-drawn carriage didn't move as fast as today's four-wheel-drive vehicle. But it also didn't need gasoline to make it run. Nor did it hurt the environment the way today's vehicles do. Yes, that old horse-drawn carriage was slow, but it sure was an energy saver!

Can you match up an energy saver from yesterday with an energy user of today? Try to fill in each blank below. Complete blanks 10–12 with three pairs of your own. The first one is done for you.

ENERGY EFFICIENT

Yesterday	Today
1. horse-drawn carriages	1. cars and trucks
2.	2. electric stove
3. horse-drawn plow	3.
4.	4. vacuum cleaner
5. washtub	5.
6.	6. clothes dryer
7. candles	7.
8. mixing spoon	8.
9.	9. calculator
10.	10.
11.	11.
12.	12.

Bonus Box: On the back of this sheet, list ten electrical devices that you can't imagine living without. Then write a paragraph describing how you would cope without these devices if you had to do without electricity for one week.

©The Education Center, Inc. • *THE MAILBOX*® • *Intermediate* • Feb/Mar 1999 • Key p. 310

Note To The Teacher: Use with "Yesterday And Today: Energy Conservation" on page 154.

Which Waterwheel Works Wonderfully?

All through history, people have used waterwheels to help make power to run their machines. Investigate three early waterwheels with this wet and wild experiment!

Materials:
large, empty thread spool
4" x 6" index card
ruler
dishpan
scissors
masking tape
plastic drinking straw
squeeze bottle of water

Make your waterwheel:
a. Measure and draw four 1-inch squares on the index card. Cut out the squares.
b. Bend each square into an L-shape as shown above. Tape them to the spool to make your waterwheel's "fins."
c. Insert the straw into the spool's hole. Be sure the spool can spin loosely around the straw.

Test these types of waterwheels:
- *Greek mill:* Stand the waterwheel up in the dishpan as shown. Shoot a stream of water along the pan's bottom so that it touches the fins.
- *Undershot waterwheel:* Hold the straw horizontally over the pan. Shoot a stream of water under the wheel so that it touches the fins.
- *Overshot waterwheel:* Hold the straw as you did for the undershot waterwheel. Shoot a stream of water over the wheel so that it turns.

Which waterwheel would generate the most power?

Greek mill _____ undershot _____ overshot

©The Education Center, Inc. • *THE MAILBOX*® • *Intermediate* • Feb/Mar 1999 • Key p. 310

Note To The Teacher: Use with "Workin' Waterwheels: Water Power" on page 153.

There's A Crisis In Techno Town!

No power to run computers or video games! No electricity to keep refrigerators or air conditioners going! What is Techno Town to do now that it is running out of fuel to keep its power plant in business?

Fill in this chart with the main points that your group has found out about your assigned energy source. Then take notes during the other teams' presentations. Finally fill in the space at the bottom with your opinion about the best energy source for Techno Town. Be sure to give at least three reasons for your choice.

Renewable Energy Source	Advantages	Disadvantages
hydroelectric		
wind		
solar		
geothermal		

The best energy source for Techno Town is:

Note To The Teacher: Use with "There's A Crisis In Techno Town!: Culminating Activity" on page 154.

Looks Like Stormy Weather!

Hands-On Activities For Studying Storms

Your students may not be able to chase a tornado or fly an airplane inside a hurricane. But they can learn to track clues that will help them predict that a storm's on the way! Complement your studies of weather with the following creative activities, teacher demonstrations, and reproducibles on severe storms. *by Gail Peckumn, Jefferson, IA*

A Close-Up Look At How A Storm Develops

1 —Hot Air's On The Rise

How exactly does a hurricane develop? Three ingredients must be present.
- Warm water: During the summer and fall months, the sun continually warms tropical ocean waters.
- Moist air: Warm, moist air rises above the water and drifts up into the sky.
- Converging winds: Cooler air moves in to take the place of the rising warm air. As warm air continues to rise, the air pressure drops, making stronger winds.

Help students understand that warm air rises with the following demonstration:
1. Tape the bottom of one paper lunch bag to each end of a meterstick.
2. Balance the meterstick on your index finger. Hold it so that the opening of one bag is directly over a heat source (a lamp without its shade), but not touching it.
3. Ask students to observe what happens.

The air inside the bag will heat up, so the air expands and some of it escapes. This reduces the weight of the air inside the bag. The heavier, cooler air around the bag will exert a force on the lighter, warm air, causing the bag to rise. Remind students that they see warm, moist air rise when steam rises above boiling water. The same thing happens over warm ocean waters. The more heated water in the atmosphere, the more likely that a storm will occur.

2 —A Cold Front's Moving In

Cold air forces warm air upward, creating an area of low pressure. As warm, moist air rises, it can produce towering storm clouds. Show your students how this movement of cold air happens with the following demonstration. Remind students that since both air and water are considered fluids, water represents air in the demonstration.
1. Punch two holes in the bottom of a paper cup.
2. Secure the cup to the corner of a large, clear container (a plastic storage box or an empty aquarium) with duct tape. The bottom of the cup should be about two centimeters from the bottom of the container.
3. Fill another cup with ice-cold water and add a few drops of blue food coloring.
4. Fill the large container with hot water to about one centimeter from the top of the cup.
5. Quickly pour all of the cold, blue water into the cup. Have students view the bottom of the container to see what happens.
6. Have students touch the water in the paper cup that's inside the large container.

The cold, blue water will sink to the bottom of the container as it pushes up the hot water. The water in the cup will be warm because all of the cold water sank to the bottom of the container.

tape

cup with holes

plastic container

③ —Moisture's Building

Hot air can hold a lot of moisture. This moisture, in vapor form, rises in the atmosphere. Air temperatures become cooler with increased elevation, so all the moisture in the hot air starts to condense into clouds. The more moisture, the bigger the clouds. Demonstrate how hot air holds more moisture than cold air with the following activity:

1. Fill two glasses—one with hot water and the other with cold water and ice.
2. Let them sit for several minutes as students observe what happens.

Moisture will form on the outside of the cold water glass. Why? Because the cold water has cooled the air around the glass, and since cooler air cannot hold as much moisture as warmer air, the moisture in the air begins to condense into droplets on the glass.

Extend this demonstration by showing how clouds form.

1. Fill a small cake pan with ice.
2. Fill a large, widemouthed glass jar about 1/4 full of hot water.
3. Light a match and hold it down inside the jar for a few seconds; then drop it in. (This forms dust particles around which water vapor can condense.)
4. Place the pan of ice over the top of the jar.
5. Have students observe what happens.

Warm air will rise off the water in the jar, then cool and condense when it hits the pan of ice. The result will be the formation of a cloud near the top of the jar. Whenever there is a large amount of heated, moist air, it can cool and condense into huge cumulonimbus storm clouds, producing thunder, lightning, and rain.

> A tornado in Broken Bow, Oklahoma, carried a motel sign 30 miles and dropped it in Arkansas!

> In early times, people thought that lightning and thunder were signs of the gods' anger.

Pam Crane

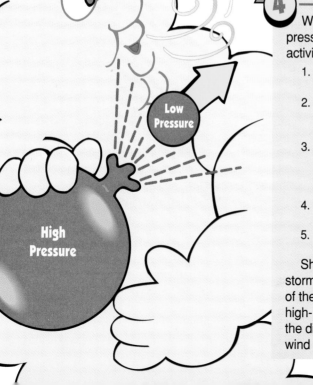

High Pressure

Low Pressure

④ —Pressure's Dropping

When stormy weather hits, high winds follow! Differences in air pressure cause winds. Demonstrate this concept with the following activity:

1. Blow a little bit of air into a balloon and hold the end so the air stays inside.
2. Ask your students where the air has greater pressure—inside or outside the balloon. *(inside)* Ask what will happen if you loosen your grip on the opening of the balloon. *(The air will come sputtering out.)*
3. Have a volunteer hold his hand in front of the balloon opening as you let the air out. Ask the class why the air left the balloon instead of staying inside it. *(Air moves from an area of high pressure to an area of low pressure.)*
4. Next fully inflate the balloon and hold its end. Ask students if the balloon has more air pressure inside than when you first blew it up. *(yes)*
5. Let out the air, as the same volunteer feels it escape. Ask the volunteer which time there was a stronger flow of air. *(the second time)*

Share with your students that this is what makes the wind in a storm blow—but on a much larger scale! Like the air that rushed out of the fully inflated balloon, surface air is always on the move between high- and low-pressure areas, trying to even them out. The bigger the difference in pressure between the two areas, the harder the wind will blow.

5—Lightning's Flashing

What exactly is lightning? Demonstrate for your students how lightning is formed on a smaller—and safer!—scale.

1. Blow up two large balloons and tie off the end of each one.
2. Tie a one-meter length of thread to each balloon.
3. Suspend the balloons from the top of a door frame so that they are about ten inches apart.
4. Label two sticky notes—one A and the other B—and attach a note to each balloon.
5. Have a student rub balloon A against her hair about a dozen times, then gently release the balloon.

The balloons will move toward each other and stay together. Why? Electrons are rubbed off the hair and collected on balloon A, giving it a negative electrical charge. Since like charges *repel* (push away) each other, the negative charges on balloon A repel the negatively charged electrons of balloon B. This causes the surface of balloon B to become more positively charged. Since the balloons now have opposite charges, they are attracted to each other.

Explain to your students that most scientists think this is what happens in a thundercloud. Light, rising water droplets and tiny pieces of ice collide with hail and other heavier, falling particles, creating electric charges. The heavier particles gain a negative charge; the lighter ones, a positive charge. The negatively charged particles fall to the bottom of the cloud and most of the positively charged particles rise to the top. Lightning occurs when these separated charges flow toward each other (or toward opposite charges on earth), creating an electric spark.

Hurricane comes from a Carib Indian word for "big wind."

When a snowstorm's winds reach 39 mph, it's called a *blizzard*.

Check out the following Web site (current as of October 1998) to learn more facts about lightning; plus read firsthand accounts from people who have actually been struck by lightning: **www.azstarnet.com/~anubis/zaphome.htm**

6—Thunder's Rumbling

Is that thunder rumbling in the distance? The bright light that we see in a flash of lightning is called a *return stroke.* Return strokes heat the air in their paths, causing it to expand very quickly. It then cools and contracts. This rapid expansion and contraction causes air molecules to move, which produces the sound waves that we hear as thunder. To help students "experience" thunder, provide each small group with a 1" x 8" plastic strip (cut from a transparency), a small lump of modeling clay, a large paper clip, a ruler, and a piece of wool (any item made of 100% wool). Then direct each group to follow these steps:

1. Use the clay to stand the paper clip upright.
2. Wrap the wool around the plastic strip.
3. Quickly pull the strip through the cloth at least three times.
4. Immediately hold the plastic near the top of the paper clip. What happens? Each group should hear a snapping sound. Why?

Electrons are rubbed off the wool and onto the plastic. The electrons cluster together until their energy is great enough to move them across the air between the plastic and the metal clip. The movement of the electrons through air produces sound waves, resulting in a snapping sound.

Other Stormy Weather Activities

The most dangerous place to be when a tornado hits is a mobile home.

How Do Meteorologists Know A Storm Is Coming?

With modern technology, meteorologists can now gather more information than ever before, using such weather instruments as *barometers, thermometers, anemometers, radar, weather balloons, computers,* and *satellites.* Help students better understand two of these methods with the following activities:

Infrared Radiation

1. Have students place sheets of different-colored paper in a sunny area outside. Place a thermometer in the middle of each sheet.
2. After 15 minutes, have students record the temperature reading for each color of paper.
3. Return to the classroom and discuss why the temperatures were different. *(Each color of paper absorbs and gives off different amounts of heat.)*

Explain to students that this is an example of infrared radiation. Just as some objects give off more heat than others, so do different areas of the earth and atmosphere. Weather satellites measure the heat given off by the earth and the atmosphere. These infrared images provide clues that help in weather and storm prediction.

Doppler Radar

1. Take your students outdoors.
2. Give one student a bell and direct him to go to a point about 50 yards away from the rest of the class.
3. Instruct that student to run toward the class while continuously ringing the bell, then continue running about 50 yards past you while still ringing the bell.
4. Ask your students what they noticed about the sound of the bell.

Students should notice that the sound began soft and low in pitch, but increased in loudness and became higher in pitch as the runner got closer to the class. Then it became softer and lower in pitch again as the runner ran past the class. Doppler radar works in the same way. It detects whether particles in the atmosphere are moving toward or away from a radar signal that has been sent out from an antenna on the ground. This radar is used to detect precipitation and wind circulation within clouds, so it's especially helpful in predicting tornado formation.

In 1900, the deadliest hurricane on record in the USA killed 6,000 people in Galveston, Texas.

Looking for great resources on storms? Check out:

- *Storms* by Seymour Simon (William Morrow And Company, Inc.; 1989)
- *Tornado* by Stephen Kramer (Carolrhoda Books, Inc.; 1992)
- *Lightning* by Seymour Simon (William Morrow And Company, Inc.; 1997)
- *Storms & Blizzards* by Mary Micallef (Natural Disaster series, Good Apple, 1985)
- *Hurricanes* by Dorothy M. Souza (Carolrhoda Books, Inc.; 1994)
- *The Magic School Bus Inside A Hurricane* by Joanna Cole (Scholastic Inc., 1996)

Link literature to your severe storms study with the exciting *Night Of The Twisters* novel unit on pages 194–199!

Now *That's* Incredible!

Did you know that in one day, a hurricane can release enough energy to power the United States for six months? Below are some more amazing facts about storms. Read each fact; then simplify the boldfaced math terms by

- adding, subtracting, multiplying, or dividing
- changing a word form to a numeral form
- reducing a fraction

Write your answers in the blanks. The first one has been done for you.

1. There are about **40,000 + 5,000** thunderstorms in the world each day. _45,000_

2. The temperature of the surface of the sun is about 10,800 degrees Fahrenheit. The air around a flash of lightning rises to about **5 x 10,800** degrees, or five times hotter than the sun! _____

3. Lightning strikes the earth about **ten million** times a day. _____

4. Lightning travels at a speed of up to **sixty thousand** miles per second. _____

5. Ocean temperatures have to reach **536 – 457** degrees for a hurricane to form. _____

6. In order to be classified as a hurricane, wind speeds have to be **37 x 2** miles per hour or more. _____

7. Winds in a tornado can reach up to **30 x 10** miles per hour. _____

8. Water droplets in clouds are so small that **100 x 100** could fit on the head of a pin. _____

9. One inch of rain is about the same as **90/18 to 144/12** inches of snow. _____

10. In 1967 Hurricane Beulah caused **7,100 – 6,959** tornadoes in Texas. _____

11. Since pilots started flying into typhoons and hurricanes in 1943, only **54/18** planes have been lost in these storms. _____

12. In 1969 Hurricane Camille dumped **243 ÷ 9** inches of rain in eight hours in parts of Virginia. _____

13. On March 18, 1925, tornadoes ripped through Missouri, Illinois, and Indiana, killing **394 + 295** people. _____

14. In 1989 destruction from Hurricane Hugo totaled about **seven billion** dollars. _____

15. In 1986 a storm of hailstones—each weighing over **two and two-tenths** pounds—killed **2 x 2 x 23** people in the country of Bangladesh. _____

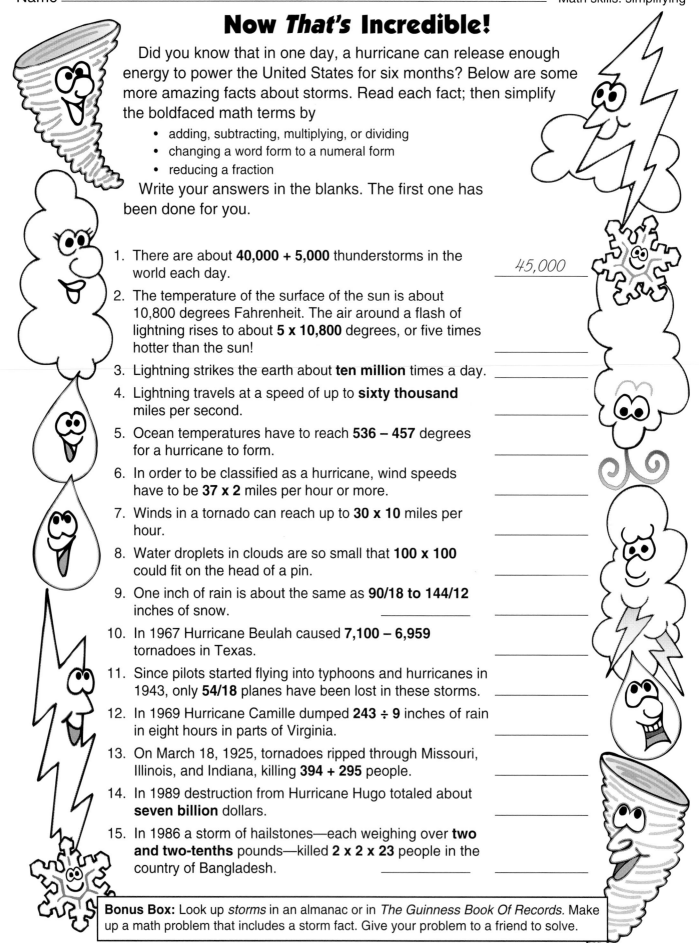

Bonus Box: Look up *storms* in an almanac or in *The Guinness Book Of Records*. Make up a math problem that includes a storm fact. Give your problem to a friend to solve.

©The Education Center, Inc. • THE MAILBOX® • Intermediate • April/May 1999 • Key p. 310

Stormy Effects

Storms are known for their terrible effects—on both people and property. See if you can complete the following cause-and-effect statements about storms. Read each cause; then choose a matching effect from the box and write it on the blank. Use encyclopedias, almanacs, your science textbook, and other resources to help you. The first one has been done for you.

Causes

1. Since the new hurricane was the fourth of the season, _____ *it was*
_____ *named David.*

2. The cloud was tall, dark, and anvil-shaped, _____

3. Because we had a blizzard warning, _____

4. Since the storm was called a *typhoon,* _____

5. Storm surges were predicted when the hurricane hit the coast, _____

6. Because thunderstorms pump lots of hot air from the earth's surface high into the air, _____

7. Since we have no basement, _____

8. Because Hugo was such a terrible hurricane, _____

9. Whenever I hear thunder, _____

10. We spotted a tornado while driving in a car, _____

11. Since the tornado was classified as an F-5, _____

12. There were 15 seconds between when I saw lightning and then heard thunder, _____

Effects

- we made sure we had blankets and food in the car before driving to town.
- they are called earth's "air-conditioning system."
- I know there has been lightning.
- so I knew the storm was three miles away.
- it was named *David.*
- so we evacuated the island.
- that name will never be used again.
- we knew houses and cars had been blown away.
- so we knew it was a cumulonimbus cloud.
- my family gathers in the bathroom in the center of our house during a tornado warning.
- so we stopped and took cover in a deep ditch.
- I knew that it wasn't located in the United States.

Bonus Box: When was the last time you were in a storm? On the back of this sheet, write three cause-and-effect statements about your experiences.

©The Education Center, Inc. • *THE MAILBOX®* • *Intermediate* • April/May 1999 • Key p. 310

163

IT'S A JUNGLE OUT THERE!
Studying Tropical Rain Forests

From the mossy floor to the lush canopy above, the rain forest is a remarkable environment that simply invites investigation. Lead your students on an exotic expedition through the rain forest with the following activities and reproducibles.

with ideas by Simone Lepine

*Look for helpful background information on rain forests in the yellow boxes.

Layer Upon Layer

The year-round growing season in the rain forest gives plants ample opportunity to grow...and grow…and grow! Four layers divide the rain forest into distinct areas:

- **Emergent Layer:** Towering over the rest of the canopy are the tallest of rain forest trees, a few reaching over 200 feet in height. Blown about by the wind, this layer is hotter and drier than the canopy beneath it.
- **Canopy:** Most animals of the rain forest live in this green and leafy layer, 80–150 feet above the ground. Large broad leaves catch and block both rain and sunlight.
- **Understory:** This layer extends about 40–50 feet from near the ground. It is made up of tall shrubs, mosses, algae, and fungi. Also found here are young trees whose growth has been stunted by the lack of sunlight.
- **Forest Floor:** In the dark, humid world of the forest floor live decomposers, such as termites and fungi, which quickly process the five tons of litter the other layers produce in a year. Animals such as jaguars, tapirs, and ocelots roam the floor hunting their prey.

The Invisible Tree

A tree that's 230 feet tall is hard to imagine—but not after doing this activity! Have each student cut a five-foot length of string. Then head outdoors or to the gym, taking along a tape measure and two orange cones or other markers. Once outside, follow these steps:

1. Have students lay their strings end-to-end in a line. Place a cone at both ends of the line. Ask, "How many feet of string do we have?" *(5 x the number of students)*
2. Tell students that a tree in the emergent layer can be as tall as 230 feet. Then ask, "How many more strings do we need to add to our line to equal 230 feet?" *(Forty-six five-foot lengths equal 230 feet.)* Have that number of students remove their strings from the line and lay them end-to-end behind one cone; then move the cone to the new endpoint.
3. After students have studied their invisible tree, explain that the canopy is about 150 feet above the ground. Challenge each child (except two helpers) to estimate where the canopy would fall on the tree and stand at that point beside the string. Have your helpers use a tape measure to discover the closest estimate.
4. Have students estimate where the understory (at 33 feet from the ground) would fall. Choose new helpers to measure and find the closest estimate.

As a fun extension, divide the class into pairs. Have each pair estimate the number of steps needed to walk the length of the tree; then have students test their guesses.

High-Rise Dioramas

Looking for a top-notch rain forest project? Look no further! Several weeks before the project, ask each student to bring in a shoebox and a paper-towel tube. Divide students into three large teams: Emergent Layer, Canopy, and Understory-Floor. Provide each team with reference books so students can research their assigned rain forest section. After the research is completed, regroup students into smaller teams of three, each with one person from each large group. Then have the teams follow the steps below:

Steps for the team:

1. Paint three paper-towel tubes brown to resemble a tree trunk. Let them dry.
2. Stack three shoeboxes atop each other. Decide as a group where to position the tree trunk (see the illustration). Then cut holes in the boxes and insert the tubes as shown. Use tape to secure the tubes to the boxes if necessary.
3. Give each group member the box for the layer he researched.

Steps for each team member:

4. Using art materials, create a scene in your box that includes at least four different animals and three plants that live in your rain forest layer.

When the three boxes are finished:

5. Stack the boxes in the correct order; then tape them together with masking or packing tape.
6. From green paper, cut out a treetop and other leaves to tape to the trunk and box as shown.

A Rain Forest Of Words

Do your students speak "rain forest-ese"? If not, help them learn with this vocabulary activity! Give each student a file folder and two to three copies of page 171. Post a list of rain forest words (see the sample list below). Then have the student complete each copy of page 171 as directed, storing the finished pages in her folder. When all copies have been completed, have the student cut out the pages along the bold lines and staple them inside her folder. Then let her decorate the front of the resulting book to complete her "pic-tionary" of rain forest words.

Possible words: bromeliad, buttress, camouflage, canopy, carnivore, cloud forest, consumer, crown, decomposer, deforestation, emergent tree, epiphyte, forager, fungi, herbivore, indigenous people, jungle, liana, niche, parasite, understory

Rain Forest Pocket Book

Fit a whole rain forest into a pocket? It's possible with this nifty research project! Duplicate page 168 on white construction paper for each student. Then guide the class through the following steps:
1. Fold the paper into three sections as shown so that the picture is on top.
2. Color the picture with crayons or colored pencils (no markers).
3. Cut the front page along the three dotted lines that divide the drawing; stop at the dots. Do **not** cut the back page.
4. Seal the bottom of each section with clear tape to make four small pockets. Then staple the left side of the book as shown.
5. Research the four layers of the rain forest. Write your notes on the inside pages of the book. As you come across other cool facts, write each one on a small piece of paper. Fold the paper and place it inside the appropriate pocket.

When the unit is completed, pair students; then have each child share her pocket book with her partner.

Animal Mystery Boxes

Turn report writing into a project that's more fun than a barrel of rain forest monkeys! Give each student a copy of page 170. Have him research a rain forest animal from the list on page 170 and complete the page. Then have him follow these steps to make an Animal Mystery Box about his critter.

Steps:

1. Cover an empty cereal box with white paper.
2. Cut one shape from construction paper. Label the cutout with "Rain Forest Mystery Animal" and your name. Then glue it to the front of your box.
3. Cut out additional shapes. Label each with a fact about your animal from page 170. Do not mention your animal's name in any fact.
4. Glue the cutouts onto all sides of your box. Add other decorations such as vines, leaves, etc.
5. Cut a 5" x 12" piece of white poster board. At the top, write "Pull up. Who am I?" as shown. At the bottom, write the name of your animal. In the middle, draw and color a picture of your animal.
6. Cut a five-inch slit in the top of the box. Insert the card so that only "Pull up" shows.

When all the boxes are done, have students place them on their desks. Tell students that they will be going on a jungle safari in the classroom; then invite students to wander around the room to examine the different boxes. Don't step on the anaconda!

Clevell Harris

Less Is...More!

So why all the fuss about protecting the rain forest anyway? Help answer that question with this eye-opening activity. Divide students into several groups. Give each group four rolls of pennies (one roll = 50 pennies). Direct each group to open two rolls and neatly lay the 100 pennies end-to-end on a flat surface. Explain that only about 6 percent of the earth's surface is covered by rain forests. Ask students how many of the lined-up pennies this figure represents *(six)*. Ask each group to move six pennies slightly away from the others in the line. Then ask how the rain forest area compares in size to the rest of the earth *(a very small area)*.

Next tell students that 50 percent of all species of animals and plants live in tropical rain forests. Instruct each group to open its two remaining penny rolls; then have the group's members stack 50 percent, or 50 pennies, atop the six pennies that represent the rain forest area. Have them stack the other 50 pennies atop the remaining 94 until they run out. Ask students, "How does the rain forest compare to the rest of the earth now?" Discuss why this ecological environment is so important. Follow up this discussion by having each student complete the reproducible on page 169.

For a great rain forest bulletin board, see page 29. And fill your classroom with a jungle of lush rain forest plants using the art activity on page 48!

WANTED: Rain Forest Botanist

Rain Forest Scientists

It's a bird! It's a plane! No, it's a botanist hanging from the rain forest canopy! Expose students to the types of scientists who study the rain forest—and sharpen their writing skills—with this activity. Divide the class into five groups: botanists, entomologists, ecologists, zoologists, anthropologists. Have each group research its scientist to find out what he/she studies and how to become an expert in that field. Then have the group write a classified ad, searching for a scientist in its field to work at a tropical rain forest lab. Direct each group to copy and illustrate its ad on a poster to display in the classroom. After groups have shared their posters, have each student choose one type of scientist and write a letter of application to the lab explaining why he would like to work there.

A Tropical Medicine Chest

The tropical rain forest is like a big medicine cabinet that we've just begun to clean out! About 25 percent of all medicines used today start from somewhere in the rain forest. That figure is amazing because man has studied only 2 percent of the 250,000 species of plants in these forests for this purpose. Some of the medicinal plants that have been discovered in the rain forest and the problems they help treat include the following:

- *Ouabain plant:* heart problems, rheumatoid arthritis
- *Indian yam:* rheumatoid arthritis, rheumatic fever
- *Chaulmoogra:* leprosy, skin infections
- *Calabar bean:* glaucoma, high blood pressure
- *Quinine (bark of red cinchona tree):* malaria
- *Curare:* multiple sclerosis (also used as a muscle relaxer during surgery)
- *Rosy periwinkle:* Hodgkin's disease, childhood leukemia
- *Moreton Bay chestnut:* HIV

A Pharmacy In The Forest

Help students understand the medical treasures hidden in the rain forest with this activity. Cut out 25 green paper leaves. Write "10,000" on each leaf; then give one to each of 25 students. Tell students that each leaf represents 10,000 different species of plants and that altogether the leaves represent the 250,000 plant species found in the rain forest.

Next display four empty pill bottles. Holding up one bottle, announce that about 25 percent, or one-fourth, of all medicines originate in the rain forest. Share the uses listed in the box above. Then explain that only about 2 percent of rain forest plants (about 5,000) have been studied. To represent this number, ask a student to tear her leaf in half and drop one piece into a pill container. Ask everyone to hold up their leaves to demonstrate how many species still hold potential for medical uses. Finally explain that 50,000 plant species in the rain forest become extinct each year. Ask how many leaves that number represents (five); then have five students throw their leaves in the trash. Discuss with students the implications rain forest destruction has for future medical research.

10,000
10,000
10,000
10,000
10,000
10,000

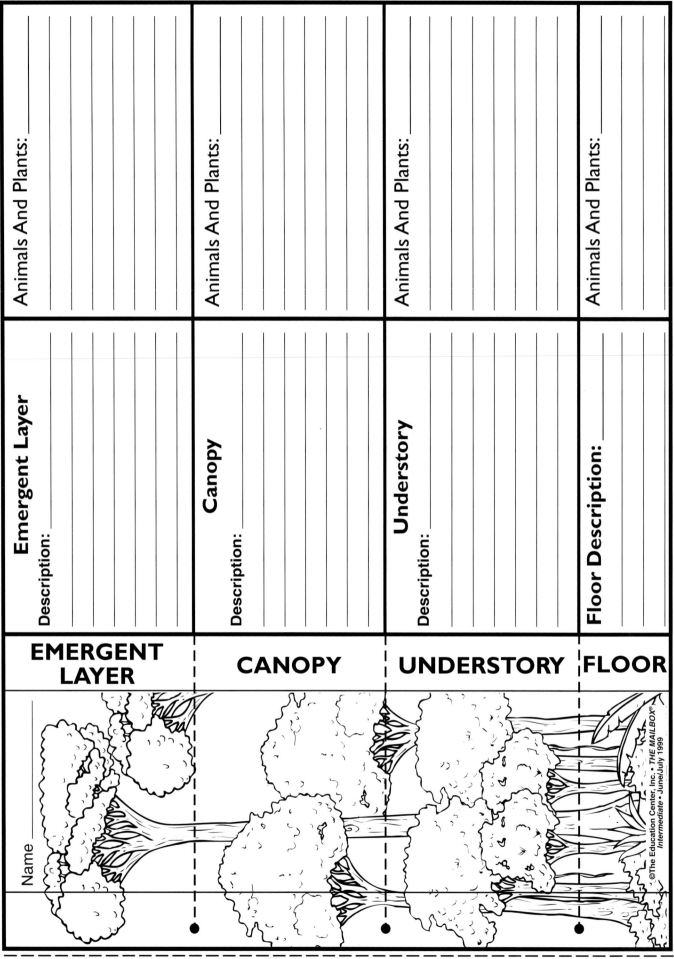

Animals And Plants: _____

Animals And Plants: _____

Animals And Plants: _____

Animals And Plants: _____

Emergent Layer
Description: _____

Canopy
Description: _____

Understory
Description: _____

Floor Description: _____

EMERGENT LAYER **CANOPY** **UNDERSTORY** **FLOOR**

Name _____

©The Education Center, Inc. • *THE MAILBOX*®
Intermediate • June/July 1999

Name _____

It's A Numerical Jungle Out There!

The rain forest isn't just filled with all types of plants and animals. It's also loaded with numbers, as you'll see from reading these math miniprojects. Choose _____ projects; then complete them by this date: _____.

A   Only 6% of the earth is covered by rain forests, yet more than 50% of the world's species of plants and animals live there! Use a metric ruler or meter stick to measure two lengths of string: one to represent 6% and one to represent 50%. *(Hint: Use a scale of 1% = 1 cm.)* Cut the two strings. Then tape the strings to the back of this paper. Next to your strings write a brief statement telling why this statistic is so amazing.

B   If you travel in Central and South America, you'll find 57% of the world's rain forests. About 25% are in Southeast Asia. The rest are in Africa. In the circle, draw a pie chart that illustrates these figures. Don't forget to label each piece of the pie.

C   What makes a tropical rain forest a tropical rain forest? First of all, there must be lots of, well, rain! Rain forests average 80 or more inches of rain a year. Another factor is temperature. The average yearly temperature in the tropical rain forest is about 80 degrees Fahrenheit. How do these figures compare with where you live? Use a local newspaper and other reference materials to help you fill in this chart.

	Tropical rain forest	**My area**
Yearly precipitation	80" and up	
Average temperature	80°F	
Humidity	80%	Today:

D   The rain forest is home to many species of plants and animals. For example, in just 2.5 acres of rain forest in the country of Peru, you could find nearly 300 species of trees! In that same amount of land in the state of Ohio, you would only find about 10 species. Use the key to fill in each box so that it shows the number of species of trees.

Peru   **Ohio**

KEY
▲ = 10 species

©The Education Center, Inc. • *THE MAILBOX®* • *Intermediate* • June/July 1999 • Key p. 310

Note To The Teacher: Use with "Less Is...More!" on page 166. Before duplicating, fill in the number of projects and due date. Provide students with the following materials: string, scissors, tape, metric rulers or meter sticks, and a local newspaper and other reference materials (such as an almanac or encyclopedia).

Critter Twitter

What's everyone twittering about? The mysterious
animals that live in the tropical rain forest, that's what!
Choose one animal from the box below. Then research
this critter and fill in the blanks.

1. Lives in a rain forest on this/these continent(s): _____

2. Invertebrate or vertebrate: _____

3. Level of the rain forest where animal lives *(check one):* ____forest floor ____understory

   ____canopy ____emergent layer

4. Size of animal when fully grown: _____

   _____

5. Eating habits: _____

   _____

   _____

6. Adaptations that help animal survive in the rain forest: _____

   _____

   _____

   _____

7. Description of animal's appearance: _____

   _____

   _____

   _____

8. Other interesting facts: _____

   _____

   _____

   _____

anaconda	cobra	kinkajou	sloth
anteater	flying lemur	macaw	spider monkey
armadillo	galago	marmoset	swallowbill butterfly
army ant	gibbon	ocelot	tapir
boa constrictor	harpy eagle	okapi	tarantula
bushmaster snake	howler monkey	paca	tarsier
chimpanzee	hummingbird	peccary	toucan
coati	jaguar	poison dart frog	tree frog

©The Education Center, Inc. • *THE MAILBOX® • Intermediate •* June/July 1999

170   **Note To The Teacher:** Use with "Animal Mystery Boxes" on page 166.

A Lush Lexicon

What's a *lexicon?* It's a dictionary—and now it's your turn to write your very own! Write each rain forest word on a leaf below. In the box next to the leaf, draw a picture to illustrate or represent the word. Then cut along the two dotted lines and fold back the flap. Write the definition of the word on the back of the flap.

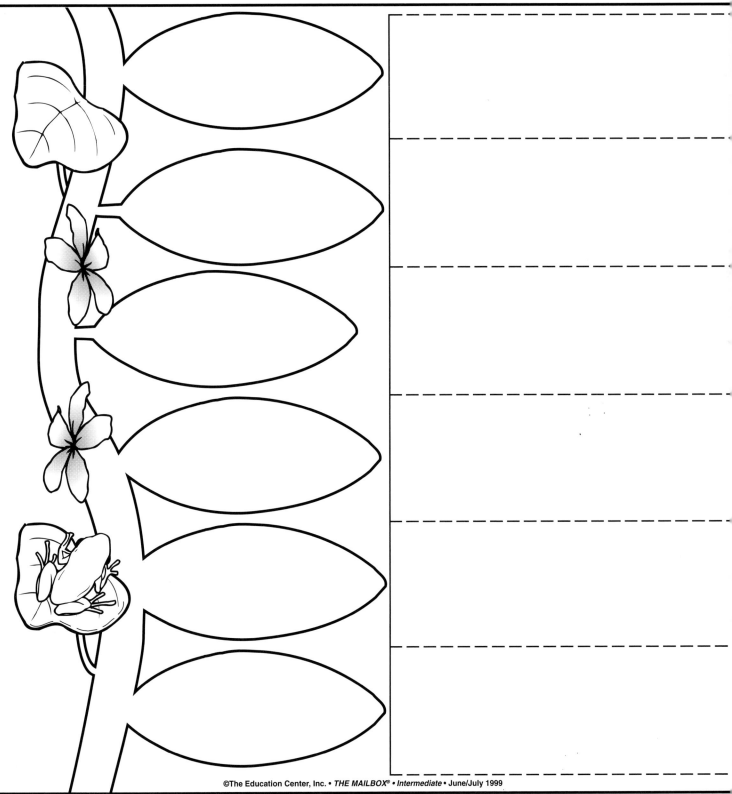

Somewhere Out There

Lost in space? Return to Earth by packing the following intergalactic activities into your next space unit!

by Hellen Harvey

Planet Poetry

Schedule a rendezvous between the nine planets and poetry with this fun writing activity! Divide students into nine groups, one for each planet. Have each group research to find five to ten facts about its planet. After the groups have gathered their facts, change orbits by forming five new groups: (1) Mercury and Venus, (2) Earth and Mars, (3) Jupiter and Saturn, (4) Uranus and Neptune, (5) Pluto. Direct each new group to write a *couplet*—two lines that rhyme—using a fact about the first planet for Line 1 and a fact about the other planet for Line 2. (Instruct the Pluto group to use two facts about Pluto for its couplet.) Encourage groups to write more than one couplet and choose the one they like best. When students have finished their couplets, compile the rhymes into a class poem as shown at the right.

Neighbors In Space

Mercury is the planet closest to the Sun;
Venus, called the morning star, is the brightest one.

Earth, our planet, is 4.5 billion years old;
Life probably never existed on Mars, we're told.

Jupiter is the biggest planet with the largest mass;
Saturn has an atmosphere that's mostly just one gas.

Uranus spins on its side as it orbits the Sun.
Named for the Roman god of the sea? Neptune's the one!

Pluto is the most distant planet of the nine,
To revolve around the Sun, it sure takes its time!

Is Anybody Out There?

Send students on a creative mission that just might convince aliens to pay our piece of real estate a visit! In the 1970s, unmanned space probes—the *Pioneer 10* and *11* and *Voyager 1* and *2*—attempted to communicate with other intelligent life-forms via engraved plaques and recorded messages. Have students design their own space probe plaques by following these steps:

1. Trace the bottom of an aluminum pie pan on white tracing paper. Cut out the resulting circle.
2. With a pencil, draw an object, a diagram, or a symbol that depicts the 90s in the circle. Include the object's name.
3. Tape the circle inside the bottom of the pie pan, drawing side down. Use a pushpin to punch holes through the paper and pan along the drawing's lines and the object's name.
4. Turn the pan over. Glue magazine pictures depicting life on Earth to the outside rim as shown.

Display the plaques on a bulletin board as a shining reminder of what's important to inhabitants of the third rock from the Sun!

Don't Mess With Gravity!

Astronauts must adapt to very different gravitational forces in space. Simulate this challenge by moving a chair to the front of the room. Place a glass of water on the floor next to the chair. Ask a student to lie across the chair with his stomach on the chair's seat and his head bent down toward the glass of water. Instruct the student to grasp the glass with his hands and take a drink. *(This will be difficult to do because gravity is pulling the water to Earth's center.)* Next place a straw in the glass and ask the student to drink the water using the straw. *(Earth's gravitational pull still makes this difficult to do, even though more force—the sucking action—is pulling the water toward the student's mouth.)* Follow up by having each student describe in his journal how difficult it must be for astronauts to perform ordinary tasks in space. Then challenge them to research the ways astronauts complete those tasks.

LITERATURE

☆ Now Playing: ☆

Blockbuster Book Projects Go To The Movies!

Find an intermediate kid and you're likely to find an avid moviegoer. So grab a bucket of popcorn, a soda, and the following book-report projects to turn your students' movie mania into an exciting reading adventure!

by Rusty Fischer

Casting Call

Make each student in your classroom a casting director with the following letter-writing activity. Tell each student that he has been hired to cast the lead actor in the movie production of the book he's just read. As the casting director, he needs to write a letter to persuade the male or female actor that he feels will best portray the main character to take the job. Direct each student to follow business-letter format and to include information about the main character, the setting of the story, and the basic plot. Encourage each student to also express to the actor why he or she is just perfect for the role. Have each student post his persuasive letter on a bulletin board with a magazine picture or original drawing of his star. (Now *there's* a way to get Brad Pitt into your classroom!)

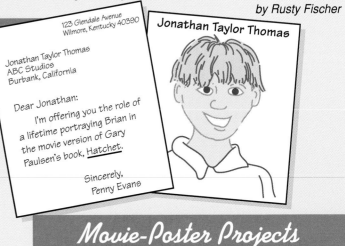

123 Glendale Avenue
Wilmore, Kentucky 40390

Jonathan Taylor Thomas
ABC Studios
Burbank, California

Dear Jonathan:
I'm offering you the role of a lifetime portraying Brian in the movie version of Gary Paulsen's book, Hatchet.

Sincerely,
Penny Evans

Jonathan Taylor Thomas

Movie-Poster Projects

Movie posters are just one way films are advertised to the public. Obtain a few appropriate movie posters from your local theater to display in the classroom. Then ask your students to describe what they see. Point out that a movie poster's job is to let the public know the title of the movie and the major actors in it, and to hint at the movie's plot to spark the moviegoers' curiosity. Distribute one sheet of white poster board and markers or crayons to each student. Instruct each student to create a movie poster for her novel, including the book's title and illustrations of its basic plot. Also direct the student to select one actor for each major character and illustrate them on the poster. Culminate the activity by having each student share her poster with the rest of the class while everyone munches on a moviegoer's meal of popcorn and soda. Have each student explain her illustration and why she feels the actors she selected are the best ones for the parts.

Soundtrack Selections

It's often the music that makes a movie so special. Play a recording of "The Circle Of Life" from the movie *The Lion King.* Have students explain why this song works so well as the movie's theme song. Then direct each student to think of a song that would work well as the theme song for his novel. Instruct the student to write the song's lyrics and explain in a brief paragraph how they fit the theme of the novel.

TUCK EVERLASTING

Is there really a fountain of youth?

Movie Scripts

A movie script gives the actors their lines, but it also gives them information on the setting and directions. Have each student select a scene in his novel in which the characters are engaged in dialogue, then write a script for this scene. Tell the student to begin the script with a basic description of the scene, the characters, and the setting. Then have him write the dialogue between at least two characters using the text in the novel as a guide. Tell the student to also include directions to the actors in parentheses informing them to express certain emotions or move in a specific direction. Extend the activity by having groups of students perform some of the student-written scripts. Quiet on the set!

Screamers!

A classroom full of screamers? You bet! A *screamer* is a tag line that moviemakers use to entice viewers to see a movie. Distribute several copies of your newspaper's movie section. Have students identify the screamer used to describe each movie. Then have students predict what each movie might be about. If a student has already seen a movie, have him tell whether the screamer was accurate or not and why. Next give each student a long strip of paper and markers or crayons. Direct him to write on the strip the title of a novel he's read and a one-line screamer that summarizes its plot. Have each student present his screamer to the class; then post the screamers on a bulletin board to entice students to read each book.

TUCK EVERLASTING
Fountain Of Youth Or Curse Of A Lifetime?

JUMANJI
Roll The Dice—I Dare You!

Critic's Corner

Turn your students into budding movie critics with the following activity. First have the class create a movie-rating scale such as the "thumbs-up/thumbs-down" system or the four-star rating scale. Then show your class the movie version of a novel or picture book you've recently read with the class (see the list below). Instruct students to watch the movie carefully to evaluate how well the producers stick to the book's original story line, the casting selections, and whether the movie is as good as the book. After viewing the movie, have each student use the class rating scale to critique it. Compile the results on the board for all to see; then have students explain why they gave the movie a positive or a negative review. As a follow-up, have each student write a paragraph telling why she thinks the novel she's read independently either has or has not been made into a movie.

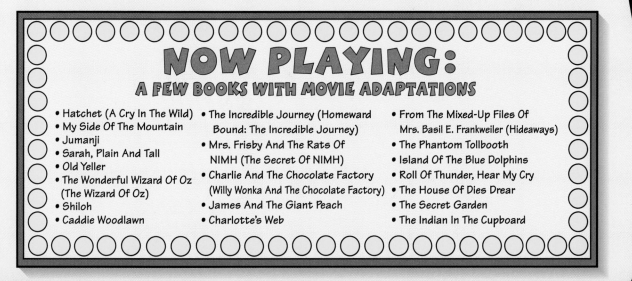

NOW PLAYING:
A FEW BOOKS WITH MOVIE ADAPTATIONS

- Hatchet (A Cry In The Wild)
- My Side Of The Mountain
- Jumanji
- Sarah, Plain And Tall
- Old Yeller
- The Wonderful Wizard Of Oz (The Wizard Of Oz)
- Shiloh
- Caddie Woodlawn

- The Incredible Journey (Homeward Bound: The Incredible Journey)
- Mrs. Frisby And The Rats Of NIMH (The Secret Of NIMH)
- Charlie And The Chocolate Factory (Willy Wonka And The Chocolate Factory)
- James And The Giant Peach
- Charlotte's Web

- From The Mixed-Up Files Of Mrs. Basil E. Frankweiler (Hideaways)
- The Phantom Tollbooth
- Island Of The Blue Dolphins
- Roll Of Thunder, Hear My Cry
- The House Of Dies Drear
- The Secret Garden
- The Indian In The Cupboard

There's A Boy In The Girls' Bathroom

An Award-Winning Novel By Louis Sachar

Bradley Chalkers believes in himself. He believes he's a monster. But then so does everyone else—except Carla, the new school counselor. With her help Bradley begins to see the good qualities that lie behind the monster mask he wears. Start your school year with Louis Sachar's humorous and insightful novel about self-esteem, honesty, facing fears, and trusting others.

ideas by Pat Twohey

Need Ideas For A Different Novel?
Many of the activities that follow can be adapted to use with other novels. Look for this symbol (✳) at the end of an activity, indicating that it can easily be adapted to use with other books.

Introducing The Book:
Terrific Titles Hunt

Introduce *There's A Boy In The Girls' Bathroom* and get your independent reading program off to a super start with this double-duty activity:

1. Point out to students that the title of Louis Sachar's novel makes you want to pick up the book and read it. Ask students to predict the book's plot based only on the title. List their predictions on chart paper.

2. Tell students they are going on a "Terrific Titles Hunt"; then head to the library. Have each student find and list five book titles that catch her eye.

3. Have each student make a bar graph listing her five titles; then have her poll classmates to find out which title they think is most appealing.

4. Have students share their completed graphs and discuss reasons for their favorite titles. Post the graphs in your reading center.

5. During the first month of school, have each student select one of the books listed on a graph and write a prediction about it based on its title. Then have her read the book and write a brief summary of it, comparing the actual events with her prediction.

6. After reading *There's A Boy In The Girls' Bathroom,* revisit students' earlier predictions. Discuss the effectiveness of Sachar's title. Encourage students to apply what they learned about book titles when titling their own stories this year.

Adapt this idea to use with any novel that has an unusual or a highly appealing title. ✳

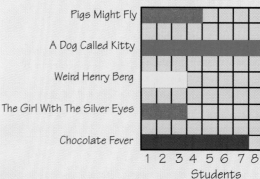

Throughout Reading

So What's The Problem?: Use the reproducible on page 180 to help students make predictions and analyze the conflicts in *There's A Boy In The Girls' Bathroom*. Share students' completed charts either at the end of the novel or periodically during reading. Use this reproducible with any novel your class is reading. ✳

Word For Word: Before reading, give each student a copy of the vocabulary reproducible on page 179. Have each student place a ✓ beside each activity(s) you want him to complete. Or use the words in spelling and vocabulary activities of your choice. To adapt this idea for another novel, list new vocabulary words by chapter; then add the directions and activities on page 179 to the list and duplicate a copy for each student. ✳

Writing Prompts: Use the following prompts to provide practice with writing skills as students read *There's A Boy In The Girls' Bathroom*:

Chapter 1: Sometimes I wish I were invisible…
Chapter 2: Here are my instructions for making and keeping a new friend…
Chapter 3: A special toy that comforts me when I'm sad…
Chapter 6: The worst day of my whole life…
Chapter 11: I agree with Bradley/Jeff about homework…
Chapter 15: Some of my best friends are imaginary…
Chapter 19: The time I told a really big lie…
Chapter 21: Some things I like about myself…
Chapter 26: Sometimes I get scared when…
Chapter 27: I'm afraid to try…
Chapter 29: I was so excited I couldn't sleep…
Chapter 33: Sometimes life is weird…
Chapter 38: Bradley's reaction to Carla's transfer was…
Chapter 44: The thing you have to remember about birthday parties is…
Chapter 46: I gave someone a gift from the heart…

After Chapter 2 Or 5:
Weaving A Good Friendship

Friendship, a recurring theme in this book, is the perfect topic for the start of a new school year. Introduce this theme early in reading by having each group make a chart as shown. Compile the groups' responses into a class chart. Then give each student six different-colored, 15-inch strands of yarn. Direct each student to knot her six strands together at one end, "weave" (pair and braid) the strands, and tie the unknotted ends together to make a friendship bracelet. After the weaving activity, have each student write a paragraph titled "How To Weave A Friendship" on a large index card. Post the cards and the class chart on a bulletin board. Adapt this idea to use with any novel that features the theme of friendship. ✳

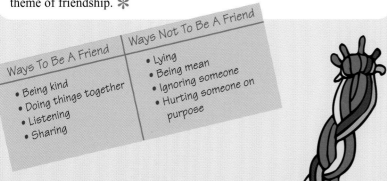

Ways To Be A Friend	Ways Not To Be A Friend
• Being kind • Doing things together • Listening • Sharing	• Lying • Being mean • Ignoring someone • Hurting someone on purpose

After Chapter 10: Map It Out

After Jeff gets lost in his new school and winds up in the girls' bathroom, Bradley decides he'd like to check out the forbidden place for himself! Reread chapter 6, which describes Jeff's embarrassing gaffe. Then reread chapter 10, in which it's clear that Jeff is still embarrassed. Ask students to share some of their most embarrassing moments and suggest ways to get over a major embarrassment. Then have each student draw a simple map of your school that would help a new classmate avoid the type of mistake Jeff made. Require each student to include a key on his map. Post the maps; then have the class choose one or more for your school's office staff to duplicate and distribute to new students.

After Chapter 21: Talking Musical Chairs

Carla wants to help Bradley believe in himself. Part of her plan has Bradley listing topics they can talk about. Use this event to build your students' self-esteem and help them get to know one another better:

1. Have each student list ten topics he would like to talk about with someone else.
2. Give each student a colored marker. Then have the class sit in two circles of chairs—with half of the students sitting in the inner circle facing the other half in the outer circle.
3. Have students sitting opposite each other swap lists. Direct the student in the inner circle (Student A) to choose a topic from the list of his partner (Student B) for the twosome to talk about for five minutes.
4. At the end of the discussion, have Student A draw a circle around the topic discussed on Student B's list.
5. Have Student B choose a topic from Student A's list to discuss. At the end of five minutes, have Student B circle the appropriate topic on Student A's list.
6. Ask each of the inner-circle students to move three chairs to the right. Have each outer-circle student move three chairs to the left. Then repeat steps 3–5. Remind students not to discuss a circled topic.
7. Continue until time runs out *or* each student has four circled topics on his list.

After Chapter 34: The *-LY* Connection

Along with humor and insight, there's even a little grammar in this terrific novel! Have each student take out his copy of page 179 (see the second activity in "Throughout Reading" on page 177). After reviewing the adjective/adverb connection, divide students into teams. Call out one of the 21 *-ly* adverbs on page 179; then challenge each team to write the adjective base word and a sentence using the adverb correctly. When time is up, have each group share its answers. Award one point for each correct base word and two points for each correct sentence. Continue until all 21 words have been called. Reward the highest-scoring team with a small treat or class privilege.

At The End Of The Book

Truth Busters: The characters in this book don't always tell the truth, which causes lots of problems for themselves and others. At the end of the novel, divide students into groups. Give each group a copy of the book; then ask group members to find examples of dishonesty in the text, listing the page number, the character who lied, and the lie for each example. After 20 minutes, have one group challenge another to find the lie on a specific page in the book. Give the challenged team two minutes to locate the lie and read it aloud. If it's successful award the team a point. If not have the challenging team read the lie before awarding it the point. Record the page number, lie, and speaker on the board. Continue until each group's list has been exhausted. Then discuss each lie. How did it affect the book's plot and characters? Finally have each student write about a time in his life when honesty truly was the best policy. Adapt this idea to use with any novel that features the theme of honesty. ✳

Page	Person Who Lied	Lie
4	Jeff	Said he'd never been to the White House, but he really had
7	Bradley	He said Mrs. Ebbel never gave him a note for his mother, but she did.

You "Gotta" Have Heart!: Help students analyze the book's characters and practice descriptive-writing skills with the reproducible on page 181. Or use the activities described in Parts 1 and 2 with any novel your class is reading. ✳

Name_____

There's A Boy In The Girls' Bathroom
Vocabulary

There's A New Word In The First Chapter
(And In A Few Other Chapters, Too!)

There's A Boy In The Girls' Bathroom is a great book—and one that's sure to pump up your vocabulary power! Use the words in the chart to complete the assigned activities.

Activities:

____ Choose 15 words from the list. Design a poster, a comic strip, or another project that will teach your class the meanings of the words.

____ After you read a chapter, write each of its new words below on an index card. On the back of the card, write the definition and a sentence using the word. As you read, use the flash cards to practice the words.

____ After you read chapter 1, color in the box beside each of its new words below. Use the new words to start an original story. After reading each chapter, color in the box beside every new word; then add on to the story, including the new words. After you finish the book, write an ending to your story.

____ Choose one column of words. Design a puzzle that will help someone learn the definitions of the words in that column. Make an answer key. Give your puzzle to a classmate to solve.

Chap.	Word	Chap.	Word	Chap.	Word
1	unfortunately	8	ferociously	24	stammered
1	bulging	9	hag	24	anticipation
1	unrecognizable	9	appreciate	24	flailed
1	distorted	9	poisonous	24	bellowed
2	suspiciously	10	blushing	26	desperate
2	counselor	10	automatically	26	exhaled
2	nervously	10	reflex	27	befuddled
3	hack	11	digest	27	genuine
3	ceramic	11	hesitated	28	inquisitively
3	scolded	11	manure	28	abruptly
3	barged	11	anguish	30	baffled
3	snickered	12	advice	31	mimicked
3	innocently	12	reluctantly	32	defiantly
3	glared	14	quickened	32	sincerely
3	flabbergasted	14	hysterically	32	dumbfounded
3	tolerate	15	massive	32	bewildered
3	asserted	15	romping	34	awkwardly
4	timidly	16	terrorizing	35	determination
4	drastic	16	cautiously	35	unreasonable
4	hopelessly	16	impolite	37	discipline
5	drizzling	18	intently	37	justified
5	overhang	19	shuddered	38	essence
5	modestly	19	quality	40	bizarre
6	clutched	21	restlessly	41	sternly
6	frantically	21	confidence	43	composed
7	grimaced	22	scoffed	46	replica

Note To The Teacher: Use with "Word For Word" on page 177. Provide each student with a copy of this page. Have students place a ✔ beside the activity(s) you want them to complete. Use also with "The -LY Connection" on page 178.

There's A Boy In The Girls' Bathroom
Reading comprehension, making predictions

Stories are often about problems and how the characters solve them. Understanding the problems that characters face and wondering how they solve them is part of the fun of reading. As you read the story, list each problem as you find it. Then predict how you think the problem will be solved. Later list how the problem was solved in the story. Staple notebook paper to this sheet when you run out of space.

So What's The Problem?

What is the problem?	How do you predict the problem will be solved?	How was the problem solved in the story?

So What's The Message? An author sends the reader a message when he or she writes a story. What message about life and living with others did the author send in this book? As you read, list your ideas in the box. Be ready to share and explain your ideas.

©The Education Center, Inc. • *THE MAILBOX® • Intermediate • Aug/Sept 1998*

Note To The Teacher: Use with "So What's The Problem?" on page 177. Provide each student with a folder in which to store his copy of this page as he reads. Discuss students' charts periodically as they read or at the end of the novel.

You "Gotta" Have Heart!

Part 1: The characters in *There's A Boy In The Girls' Bathroom* didn't always have a heart for one another. Think about the actions of each character below. Did the character treat others kindly? Write each character's name in the appropriate column. Beside the character's name, tell why you placed him/her in that column. Some characters may belong in both columns!

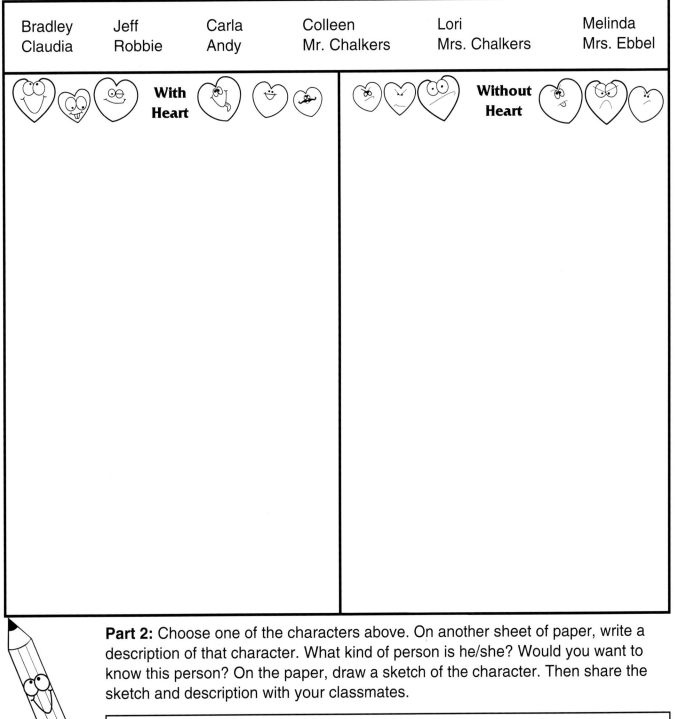

| Bradley | Jeff | Carla | Colleen | Lori | Melinda |
| Claudia | Robbie | Andy | Mr. Chalkers | Mrs. Chalkers | Mrs. Ebbel |

With Heart

Without Heart

Part 2: Choose one of the characters above. On another sheet of paper, write a description of that character. What kind of person is he/she? Would you want to know this person? On the paper, draw a sketch of the character. Then share the sketch and description with your classmates.

Bonus Box: Carla suggested that Bradley give Colleen a birthday gift from the heart. So he gave Colleen a replica of the human heart. Use an encyclopedia or other reference book to help you draw a diagram of the heart. Label the parts.

Knights Of The Kitchen Table

A Time Warp Trio Adventure by Jon Scieszka

Prepare your students to charge into adventure with the Time Warp Trio as they travel back in time to the Middle Ages in the hilarious *Knights Of The Kitchen Table.* Will Joe, Sam, and Fred survive their encounters with an evil knight, a smelly giant, and a fire-breathing dragon in order to save King Arthur and his court...and still make it back home? Don thy armor, mount thy horses, and ride at once into Camelot with the following creative activities and reproducibles.

by Lori Sammartino

Children's Books About The Middle Ages
Harold The Herald: A Book About Heraldry by Dana Fradon (Dutton Children's Books, 1990)
Eyewitness Books *Medieval Life* by Andrew Langley (Alfred A. Knopf, Inc.; 1996)
Eyewitness Books *Knight* by Christopher Gravett (Alfred A. Knopf, Inc.; 1993)
Knights In Shining Armor by Gail Gibbons (Little, Brown And Company; 1995)
Medieval Feast by Aliki (HarperCollins Children's Books, 1983)

After Chapter 2: Refresh students' descriptive-writing skills after reading chapter 2, which explains how the Time Warp Trio landed in the Middle Ages in the first place. Direct students to reread the description of Joe's special birthday gift. Point out the use of similes, descriptive adjectives, and details to paint a visual image of *The Book.* Then have each student write a descriptive paragraph about his idea of the perfect birthday gift. After students illustrate their paragraphs, assemble the finished pieces in a class booklet titled "The Perfect Gift." Allow students to take turns borrowing the booklet overnight to share with their families. Parents will love reading it—plus they may get some great gift ideas for their kids!

Before Reading: Set the stage for reading by transporting your students back in time more than 1,000 years to the Middle Ages—a time of castles and knights. Divide students into small groups and give each group a medieval book to read (see the suggestions above right). Assign each group a particular topic about the Middle Ages to concentrate on as they read, such as food, clothing, architecture, way of life, recreation, transportation, etc. After group members read a book, have them prepare a poster to share their findings.

Next ask students to think about how life was different in the Middle Ages compared to today. How would people of the present fit into the medieval culture? Or *could* they? What problems might they encounter trying to adjust their lifestyles? Record student responses on chart paper; then refer to the chart during the reading of the book. Do the book's characters have similar problems?

After Chapter 3: In chapter 3, the trio escapes the evil Black Knight by wearing him down. How else could they have solved this sticky problem? Teach children the basics of problem solving with this activity. First review the following problem-solving steps: (1) Identify the problem. (2) Identify the materials you have. (3) Brainstorm possible solutions and strategies. (4) Choose a strategy. (5) Use the strategy to solve the problem. Next have student groups brainstorm other solutions for how the trio could have escaped. Have groups share their solutions and discuss how the outcome might have been different if the trio had chosen a different strategy. Finally have students write different endings for chapter 3 based on their new courses of action. Repeat this activity after reading chapter 6 by having students suggest different ways the trio might have defeated Bleob the Giant.

After Chapter 4: In this chapter the boys introduce themselves to Sir Lancelot and his fellow knights as Sir Joe the Magnificent, Sir Fred the Awesome, and Sir Sam the Unusual. Challenge each of your students to make a medieval name for himself as well with the reproducible on page 185. Instruct students to follow the directions on the page, then cut out their completed shields. Display the shields on a bulletin board titled "The Medieval Me!"

After Chapter 5: In response to Merlin's challenge, Joe performs a card trick for King Arthur and his court. Have students reread the excerpt about Joe's trick. Then have each student use her expository writing skills to write directions for performing the trick. After students write their directions, divide them in pairs. Have each student practice the card trick, using only her partner's written directions; then select pairs to demonstrate the trick for the class. After each performance discuss areas that need revision. Let students revise their writing and then redo the trick. Everyone is sure to recognize the need for clarity in writing directions after this tricky exercise!

After Chapter 6: This chapter featuring Bleob the Giant presents a gigantic opportunity to practice important math skills!

- Bleob is said to tower at least 20 feet. Have students work in pairs to measure each other's height in feet and inches. Then mark off an area in your classroom that is 20 feet long. Have each student estimate how many of her own body it would take to equal Bleob's height.
- Have each student list several real things that measure about 20 feet.
- Have students measure and cut 20-foot strips of craft paper. Then have them work together in groups to draw Bleob, based on the book's description.
- Have students reread chapter 6 to solve this riddle: How many knights fell prey to Bleob? *(answer: 21 knights altogether)*
- Use the reproducible on page 186 to enhance students' real-life number-sense skills. The Bonus Box activity makes an excellent addition for students' math portfolios. At year's end have students rewrite their essays, adding new mathematical insights that they learned over the year.

Clevell Harris

After Chapter 7: Because of Sam's quick thinking, the three friends are saved from being crushed by the giant. Challenge students to demonstrate a little quick thinking on their own with a game called Don't Say Ummm. Cut small slips of paper and write a discussion topic (see the examples) on each. Put the slips in a paper bag. Call on one student at a time to pick a slip. Challenge her to speak on the topic for one minute nonstop, without saying "ummm," "er," or other similar hesitations. Is it hard to think fast on your feet? Ummm, you bet!

Why I deserve a raise in my allowance...
Why I do (or don't) believe in UFOs...
Why [sport] is the best sport to play...
Why [place] is the best place to vacation...
Why [title] is the best show on TV...
Why I'd like (or not like) to travel back in time...
Why I'd like (or not like) to ride on the space shuttle...
Why a/an [kind] is the best pet to have...
Why little brothers (or sisters) are such a pain...
Why I want to be a [job] when I grow up...
Why I should have a telephone (or other item) in my room...
Why I dislike [a kind of food]...
Why [problem] is the worst problem facing the Earth...
Why kids should never start smoking...
Why [problem] is the worst problem facing kids my age...

After Chapter 8: Missing cheeseburgers and TV, the trio begins to feel sad about being stuck in the Middle Ages. Have students think about items they would miss if they were time-warped to the Middle Ages. Instruct each student to list ten items along with his reason for choosing each one, then rank them in order of importance. Have students share their lists with the class. For a math extension, have students note common items in their lists, tally the number of students who mentioned each one, and then display their findings in graphs.

After Chapter 10: Having discovered the magical powers of *The Book,* the trio is now well aware of what a special birthday gift it is—and so are your students! Provide practice with the real-life skill of letter writing by having each student pretend to be Joe and write a thank-you letter to his uncle. Check for comprehension by having students mention in their letters their favorite parts of the adventure and other story details. To make this task even more authentic, encourage students to follow these steps to write their letters on scrolls like those used in the Middle Ages:

1. Crumple and then flatten out a 12" x 20" piece of a brown paper grocery bag.
2. Cut wavy edges around the bag to make it look old.
3. Write the final copy of your letter on the paper.
4. Roll up the completed letter and tie it with a piece of string or ribbon.

Dear Uncle Joe,
Thank you for the great gift you gave me for my birthday! The book is so cool. It sent Sam, Fred and me back to the Middle Ages where we had to outwit the Black Knight, an ugly giant, and a dragon! We also met Sir Lancelot, King Arthur, and Merlin. It was an adventure I will never forget. Thanks again for the wonderful book!
Sincerely,
Joe

At The End Of The Book: After completing *Knights Of The Kitchen Table,* have students think reflectively by completing the reproducible on page 187. Knowing what they know now, what items would have been helpful to have had with them if they had been trapped in the Middle Ages? Encourage each student to use his knowledge of the book to illustrate several items that he would have packed...if only he had known!

If your kids liked *Knights Of The Kitchen Table,* take heart! There are more great books in this series, taking the Time Warp Trio to the Old West, King Tut's tomb, and even a pirate ship!

The Medieval Me!

Back in the Middle Ages, each knight had his own special *coat of arms.* A coat of arms was a special design on a knight's shield. Knights learned to recognize each other's designs in battle so they wouldn't hurt a friend. Each coat of arms included special symbols. These symbols gave clues about the knight's personality, job, or special talents.

Now it's time for you to travel back in time to become a knight in the Middle Ages—kind of like Joe, Sam, and Fred! Of course, you'll need a coat of arms. First choose a new name for yourself. Write it on the coat of arms below. Then draw symbols on the coat of arms that tell something about your personality, interests, and special talents.

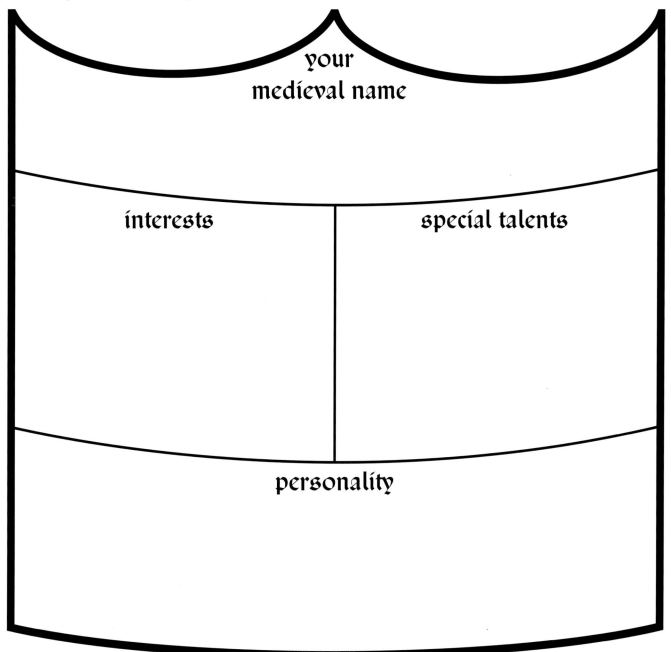

Bonus Box: What would it be like if you were a knight during the Middle Ages? On another sheet of paper, make two lists: "Things I Would Like About Being A Knight" and "Things I Would Not Like About Being A Knight."

The Knight Of Numbers

Can you become the "Knight of Numbers"? Search through chapter 6 of *Knights Of The Kitchen Table* to find examples of numbers and math words. List each phrase containing an example and its page number on the left banner. (You should find at least 15!) On the right banner, list examples of numbers you see in real life. Write the places where you see those numbers. An example has been done for you in each list.

Halt no longer, for the race is on to become the "Knight of Numbers"!

Numbers And Math Words In Chapter 6

page number	phrase
31	met <u>one</u> up close

Numbers In Real Life

place	example
telephone	0–9

Bonus Box: Use ideas from the banner on the right to help you write an essay. Tell how you use numbers every day of your life.

If Only I Had Known…

Pretend you're a member of the Time Warp Trio. You've just been given a chance to return to your medieval adventure—only this time, you get to pack a suitcase for the trip. Knowing how things turn out in the story, what would you pack in your suitcase so that you'd be better prepared this second time around?

On the suitcase, draw pictures of at least five items you would want to be sure to take with you. Then, on the back of this page, list your reasons for choosing each one. How would these items help you on your second adventure?

CAMELOT

Bonus Box: If you were allowed to return with one souvenir from your trip back in time with the Time Warp Trio, what would it be? On the back of this page, write a brief paragraph describing what you would choose and why.

Charlie And The
A Scrumdiddlyumptious Novel by Roald Dahl

Mix a kindhearted boy named Charlie Bucket, four other not-so-nice children, and the mysterious candymaker Willy Wonka, and what do you get? A chocolate-coated tale that's one of the most popular children's books around! Use the following activities to join Charlie and his companions as they tour the most amazing candy factory in the world.

by Simone Lepine—Gr. 5
Gillette Road Middle School
North Syracuse, NY

Introducing The Book

● *Charlie And The Chocolate Factory* contains a strong message about the virtues of kindness, generosity, and compassion—all demonstrated by Charlie Bucket. Likewise, it illustrates the downfall of those who are greedy, spoiled, rude, and foolish, like the four children who join Charlie on the tour. Before reading, discuss with students the meaning of *character trait*. Then divide a sheet of chart paper into two columns as shown. Have students brainstorm traits to list in each column. As students read, have them add to the chart any other traits demonstrated by the story's characters. Combine the chart with the following prompts for some scrumptious journal-writing sessions:

  • Choose two traits from the chart. In one paragraph tell how the traits are similar. In another paragraph tell how they are different.
  • Choose one trait. Tell about a time when you demonstrated that trait.
  • What three traits would you choose to have in a friend? Why?
  • Which trait did you demonstrate most yesterday? Explain.

Positive Traits	Negative Traits
sharing	greediness
honesty	lying
cheerful	grumpy
kind	hateful
responsible	spoiled

● To begin this math tie-in, send a note home to parents asking that each child bring his favorite candy bar to school on the day before you begin reading. (Offer the option of bringing a granola snack that contains only a small amount of chocolate; also purchase a few extra candy bars to have on hand.) On the special day, list the candy bars that have been brought, using tally marks to indicate repeats. Next divide the class into four groups. Have each group complete the following tasks; then save the candy bars to use in the following activity:

  • On a sheet of graph paper, create a bar graph or pictograph illustrating the candy bars that were brought to school.
  • Find the total number of calories in all of your group's candy bars. Then find the average number of calories per bar. Repeat for fat grams and sodium content.
  • Use a ruler to find the perimeter of each candy bar in your group.

● After the groups have completed the tasks above, instruct each student to carefully remove the outer wrapper of his candy bar. (Collect these to use with "After Chapter 1" on page 189.) Tell each student to break off only a 1" x 1" piece of his bar, eat it, rewrap the rest of the bar, and place it in his desk. Then read chapter 1, which tells how poor Charlie eats his candy bar to make it last a long time. After you finish the chapter, celebrate by letting students finish their candy bars.

Chocolate Factory

After Chapter 1: Help students learn the new words they'll encounter in this colorful story with a simple display. Enlarge one of the candy bars found on page 192; then duplicate multiple copies on construction paper. Divide the class into six groups and assign five of the book's chapters to each group. After the class has read a chapter, have the appropriate group list its new vocabulary words. Then have the group write each word and its definition on a candy-bar pattern and cut it out. Post the cutouts on a bulletin board labeled "Wonka's Wonderful Word Factory." Staple the candy-bar wrappers from the previous activity along the display's border. Continue adding words to the display as students read.

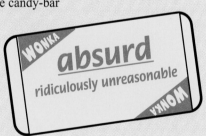

After Chapter 2: In chapter 2, Charlie's Grandpa Joe describes seven of Willy Wonka's fantastic chocolate inventions, but he doesn't mention any brand names for these products. As a class, brainstorm a list of actual product names. Discuss how these names often tell something about the product or grab a potential buyer's attention. Next divide students into groups. Challenge each group to create a brand name for each Wonka invention and write it on a separate index card. As students do this step, divide the chalkboard into seven sections—one for each invention. Have group 1 share its first brand name. Challenge the rest of the class to identify the product it names; then tape the index card in the appropriate column. Continue until all seven of group 1's cards are shared. Repeat with the other groups.

Color Crazy Caramels

Everlasting Always Tasty Great Gumballs

After Chapter 6: In this chapter, readers are introduced to the first two winners of the Golden Ticket contest. In a newscast introducing winner Veruca Salt, no mention is made that this little girl is spoiled rotten—though Grandpa Joe recognizes it immediately. Have students make inferences about what Veruca says or does that leads Grandpa Joe to that conclusion. Also have students draw conclusions about the other winner, Augustus Gloop. Then give each child a copy of page 193. Have students complete the chart as they read, drawing conclusions about the children's actions.

After Chapter 8: To help students empathize with Charlie's disappointment at not finding a Golden Ticket, conduct a mock class contest. To prepare, collect 100 index cards. Tell students that each of them will receive an index card. If the card has a sticker on it, its holder will receive a special prize. Place a card facedown on each child's desk with instructions not to turn it over. (Keep the undistributed cards for the following activity on page 190.) Tell students you have prepared 100 cards; then discuss the odds of winning *(1 out of 100, or a 1% chance)*. Ask students to describe their feelings as they wait to turn over their cards. List these responses on the board. Finally, have students turn over their cards and describe how they feel knowing that they didn't win. Write these responses on the board; then read chapter 9 together. At the end of the chapter, have students compare their "agony of defeat" feelings with Charlie's. Follow up this activity with the next idea at the top of page 190.

After Chapter 10: Before reading this chapter, place a sticker on each of the remaining cards from the previous activity on page 189. Tell students that they are going to finish the contest begun earlier because the winning card wasn't found. Discuss how their odds have improved since there are now fewer cards in the pile. Place one card facedown on each student's desk; then let students turn over their cards. Everyone's a winner! Give each student a chocolate chip or other small piece of chocolate; then have students describe how they felt when they flipped their cards over to discover they were winners. Write their responses on the board; then read chapter 11 and have students compare their "thrill of victory" feelings with Charlie's.

After Chapter 12: After Augustus, Violet, Mike, and Veruca find their tickets, their television interviews are described in great detail. But when Charlie wins, no interview is described in the book. Divide the class into pairs; then have each pair write a script of the unknown interview, including at least five questions and Charlie's responses. Before writing, you may wish to discuss Charlie's character traits as displayed so far and discuss how they might affect his responses. Have pairs read their scripts aloud, with one student acting as the television reporter and the other portraying Charlie.

After Chapter 16: In this chapter, readers are introduced to Willy Wonka's workers, the Oompa Loompas. After reading, write the following categories on the chalkboard: Country, Environment, Diet/Nutrition, Hobbies/Entertainment, Clothing, Current Status. As a class, fill in the basic facts about the Oompa Loompas for each category. Then divide students into groups. Challenge each group to write a short encyclopedia article about the Oompa Loompas. Before groups begin writing, you may wish to discuss how an encyclopedia article differs from the description given by Willy Wonka in the chapter. When students have completed their articles, provide time for sharing.

After Chapter 21: Imagine the implications if we could just chew gum for our meals! That's the almost-perfected invention shared in this chapter. Willy Wonka gives a great persuasive argument about the benefits of his chewing-gum meal. After reading the first five paragraphs of this chapter, have the class name all the positives of the chewing-gum meal—including their own ideas—as you list their responses on the board. Then give each student a piece of art paper. Challenge him to design an advertisement that will persuade people to try this state-of-the-art gum. When the posters are completed, display them in your school's cafeteria.

190

MEAL IN YOUR MOUTH CHEWING GUM

Meat! Potatoes! Dessert— All In One!

NO MORE DINNER DISHES TO WASH! TRY SOME TODAY!

After Chapter 27: Sharpen vocabulary and alliteration skills with an activity that's as easy as ABC! In this chapter, Willy Wonka describes his special Supervitamin Candy, which contains an array of vitamins—one for every letter of the alphabet! For fun, have each student list the alphabet down the left side of a piece of paper. Then have him complete the following sentence for each letter: "Vitamin __ makes you ____." When the lists are done, start with *A* and let each student read her sentence for it. Continue through the alphabet. You'll be sure to give the class a large dose of Vitamin G—guaranteed to make everyone giggle!

At The End Of The Book

● It's doubtful that anyone can read this book without daydreaming about candy! Put those daydreams to good use with this culminating project. Announce that Willy Wonka has hired each student as an inventor in his factory. Each student must create his next most amazing candy. First, have each student draw a design of his candy on paper; then have him use art materials to make a 3-D model. Also have the student write a description of his candy, including its name and ingredients. Provide several days for students to complete their projects. Then hold a Candy Convention during which each candymaker displays his model and description. After students have walked around and read about each other's inventions, wrap up this book in yummy fashion with the following candy-making activity!

HOMEWORK HELPER CANDY: One bite, and your brain goes into overdrive!

● Several days before the Candy Convention, brainstorm a list of candy ingredients that students could bring to school (as shown below). Have each student write a recipe for her own chocolate candy including items from the list. (Require that each recipe contain chocolate chips.) Ask parent volunteers to donate the ingredients and help with the activity. On the day of the convention, place the chocolate chips in slow cookers to melt. Set up a table at the front of the room that includes bowls of the other ingredients, plastic spoons, and small paper cups. Also cover student desks with aluminum foil topped by waxed paper, and give each child a tongue depressor. When the chocolate chips have melted, spoon some on top of each child's desk. The student comes to the front of the room to gather her recipe's ingredients. She mixes the items in her chocolate with the tongue depressor, forming the chocolate into a block. Then she wraps the block in the waxed paper and foil to cool. While the blocks are cooling, have each student name her candy and copy its recipe on paper. Duplicate the recipes later so students can compile their own candy cookbooks. When the candy has cooled, provide plastic knives so students can cut pieces to share with their classmates. *Maria Gonzalez—Gr. 4, Coral Reef Elementary, Miami, FL*

raisins
chopped peanuts
M&M's®
Cheerios®
peanut-butter morsels
minimarshmallows
caramels
Gummy Worm® candies
jelly beans

WONKA CANDY BARS

For more chocolaty fun, see the thematic activities on pages 228–229!

Name _____

A Chocolaty Review

Chapter(s): _____ **Pages:** _____

WONDERFUL WONKA WORDS

Look up these words in a dictionary. Write each word's definition on another sheet of paper. Then write a sentence using the word. Staple your paper to the back of this sheet.

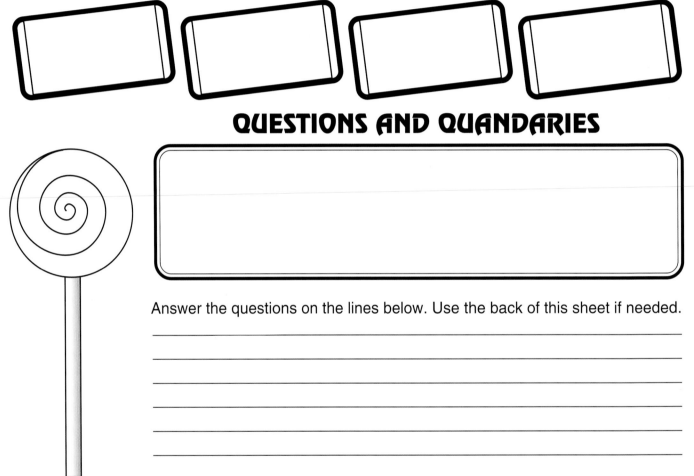

QUESTIONS AND QUANDARIES

Answer the questions on the lines below. Use the back of this sheet if needed.

_____
_____
_____
_____
_____
_____

Tasty Treat
Write your response to the Tasty Treat on the back of this sheet. If there is not room, write it on another piece of paper stapled to this sheet.

Note To The Teacher: Use this reproducible to review one or more chapters as students read the book. Make one copy. Write vocabulary words, comprehension questions, and a journal prompt or critical-thinking question (Tasty Treat) in the spaces provided; then make copies for your students. If desired, prepare these pages before students begin the book. On the first day of reading, give each student a folder containing his sheets for the entire novel.

Willy's Five Winners

In *Charlie And The Chocolate Factory*, five children find Golden Tickets in their candy bars. Five very different children, as you'll find out!
As you continue to read this book, fill out the chart below.

	Main Personality Traits	What happens to this character inside the factory?	How is this character different when he/she comes out of the factory?
 Charlie Bucket			
 Augustus Gloop			
 Veruca Salt			
 Violet Beauregarde			
 Mike Teavee			

Note To The Teacher: Use with "After Chapter 6" on page 189.

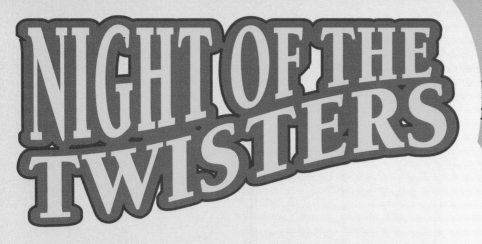

NIGHT OF THE TWISTERS

A Riveting Adventure By Ivy Ruckman

Imagine that in just a few moments everything you owned was destroyed. Such is the power of the tornadoes that star in the can't-put-it-down novel *Night Of The Twisters*. Use the following creative activities to join Dan Hatch and his buddies as they struggle to survive the harrowing night of the twisters.

with ideas by Terry Healy, Eugene Field Elementary, Manhattan, KS

Before You Read: Just Another Plain-Letter Day?
Skill: Graphing, completing a chart

As the book begins, Dan recalls that the day the tornadoes struck didn't appear to be a red-letter day. But later he would call it his "all-time worst black-letter day." Share with students that a *red-letter day* is a day of special significance and a *black-letter day* (as defined by Dan in the first chapter) is one that will "mess up your life." Next explain that the first six chapters of the book they'll be reading describe what happens to the characters between 5:00 and 9:00 PM on what appears to be just another ordinary, "plain-letter" day. Finally help students complete the following red-letter graphing activity:

Hour	Main activity	Category				
		Leisure	Study	Eating	Chores	Social
5:00–6:00 PM	Did homework; worked on science project	☐	☑	☐	☐	☐
6:00–7:00 PM	Ate dinner	☐	☐	☑	☐	☐
7:00–8:00 PM	Washed dishes and helped clean kitchen	☐	☐	☐	☑	☐
8:00–9:00 PM	Watched TV show; read library book	☑	☐	☐	☐	☐

Steps 1 & 2

Hour	Main activity	Category				
		Leisure	Study	Eating	Chores	Social
5:00–6:00 PM	Did homework; worked on science project	☐ 8	☑ 10	6	2	4
6:00–7:00 PM	Ate dinner	3	7	☑ 5	4	11
7:00–8:00 PM	Washed dishes and helped clean kitchen	7	12	1	☑ 8	2
8:00–9:00 PM	Watched TV show; read library book	☑ 15	6	1	2	6

Step 4

1. Display a transparency of the top half of page 197. Ask one student to describe his activities from the night before as you fill in the chart.
2. Have the class categorize each activity on the chart as you place a check mark in the small box in the appropriate column (see the illustration).
3. Give each student a copy of page 197. Instruct him to complete Part 1 for homework.
4. The next day call out the first category, "Leisure." Instruct each student who marked that category for his 5:00–6:00 PM activity to raise his hand. Count the total number of hands raised; then have each student record that number in the category's box as shown. Continue until all categories and time slots have been called.
5. Have each student choose one of the time slots (for example, 6:00–7:00 PM) and use the data in his chart to complete Part 2 of page 197.

After the class has read the first six chapters of the book, have each student complete a chart similar to the one on page 197 to describe Dan and Arthur's activities during the night of the twisters.

After "Six O'clock": Just Between Friends
Skill: Compare and contrast

In the first three chapters, the author paints a detailed picture of Dan and his best friend, Arthur. The two pals are very different, but their differences complement each other and strengthen their friendship. After reading these chapters, display the chart shown and divide students into pairs. Have each twosome copy and complete the chart; then bring the class back together to compare their charts. For homework, have each student complete another copy of the chart to compare and contrast himself with a good friend. Discuss the charts the following day. Ask volunteers to share why they think differences can actually help people get along.

	Dan	Arthur	Similarities	Differences
Physical traits				
Personality traits				
Favorite activities				
Family				

While You Read: Twister-Tale Journals
Skill: Writing, critical thinking

What's that blowin' in the wind? Lots of great writing ideas to fill the pages of your students' own twister-tale journals! Make a copy of the tornado pattern on page 198 for each child to use as a template. Have the student trace the template onto a sheet of tagboard and about ten sheets of notebook paper. Next have her cut out her tracings and staple the notebook-paper copies behind the tagboard cover. Finally have her decorate the cover with her name, the book's title, and other illustrations. While reading this novel, have students write about the following topics in their twister-tale journals:

- **After "As Told By Dan Hatch":** Dan wonders what it would be like if he were informed of a really bad day before it happened. Would this be a good thing or a bad thing? Give reasons for your answer.
- **After "Six O'clock":** How did the birth of Ryan affect Dan's life? What one event that has happened to you or your family has really affected your life? How?
- **After "Eight O'clock":** When signs that a bad storm is on its way start popping up, Dan gets a little worried. But Arthur doesn't seem bothered at all. If you had been at Dan's house that night, would you have reacted like Dan or like Arthur? Why?
- **After "Nine O'clock":** What fears did Dan and Arthur have immediately after the tornado hit? Would you have had the same fears? Why or why not?
- **After "The Next Hour Or So":** List what you think are the five most important needs of Dan, Ryan, and Arthur after the tornado strikes. Then number the items according to their importance (with "1" being the most important).
- **After "Eleven O'clock":** When a second tornado hits, Dan has to drive a police cruiser to headquarters. Would you describe Dan as a hero? Why or why not?
- **After "Early Morning":** When Dan finds his father, Mr. Hatch tells him that Mrs. Smiley had compared Dan, Arthur, and Stacey to sly foxes. To what animal would you compare yourself? Why?
- **After "As Remembered One Year Later":** Explain what you think Dan meant when he said this about Mrs. Smiley: "...her heart was too big to be housed in such an insignificant body."
- **At the end of the book:** What do you think is the most important lesson Dan learned from his ordeal? Why is this an important lesson?

Tie the reading of this adventure novel to a study of stormy weather with the "tornado-rific" unit on pages 158–163!

Milly's Twister-Tale Journal

Night Of The Twisters

After "Nine O'clock": Word Twister
Skill: Identifying descriptive language

Zero in on the imagery used in the fourth through sixth chapters with the following descriptive language idea that doubles as an art project. Provide each student with the materials listed; then direct him to follow the steps at the right. Hang the completed word twisters from your ceiling for a display that's sure to blow everyone over!

Materials for each student: a tagboard copy of the pattern on page 198; scissors; 5–6 cotton balls; a hole puncher; blue or black powdered tempera paint in an aluminum pan; glue; a length of string; black, blue, brown, and green colored pencils; paper and pencil

Bearing down on us
Roaring
Terror
Glass shattering
Blowing to pieces
Shrieking   Howling
Like a hundred freight trains
Ripped apart

Steps:
1. Scan chapters 4–6. On scrap paper, list any phrases that help you hear, see, and feel the approaching storm and the tornado.
2. Use the colored pencils to list the phrases on your tagboard twister. Add slanted lines around the words to resemble the turning of the tornado.
3. Pull apart the cotton balls. Dip the bottom edge of each stretched cotton ball into the tempera paint. Shake off the excess paint into the pan.
4. Glue the cotton balls to the top of the twister.
5. Punch a hole in the top of the twister. Tie the length of string through the hole.

After "Eleven O'clock": Steps To Safety
Skill: Reading comprehension, problem solving

After the tornado has passed, Dan, Arthur, and Ryan face many problems as they begin the daunting task of finding their families and surviving. Strengthen your students' comprehension skills as they review Dan's steps to safety with the following activity. Divide the class into four groups. Give each group two sheets of construction paper and a pair of scissors. Have the group trace one student's left shoe on a sheet of paper and cut out the tracing; then direct the group to follow the same steps to make a right shoe cutout.

Next have each group copy one of the following problems onto its left shoe cutout:

- Water is rising in the basement. The boys must get out but their way is blocked by debris.
- Ryan must be protected and cared for.
- Dan has to find his mom.
- Mrs. Smiley is trapped in her basement.

Direct each group to locate its problem in the seventh, eighth, or ninth chapter, and then write a summary of the solution on its right shoe cutout. After groups share their work, staple the footprint pairs on a bulletin board titled "Steps To Safety." Extend this activity by directing student groups to discuss the problems of finding food and fresh drinking water after a tornado. Have groups label additional foot cutouts with the problems and their solutions; then add these cutouts to the display.

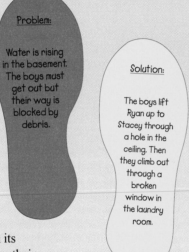

Problem:

Water is rising in the basement. The boys must get out but their way is blocked by debris.

Solution:

The boys lift Ryan up to Stacey through a hole in the ceiling. Then they climb out through a broken window in the laundry room.

After "Early Morning": The Twister Times
Skill: Writing a newspaper article

Author Ivy Ruckman begins this novel with a brief newspaper article describing the night of the twisters. Use this article as a springboard to publishing a student-written "Twister Times." First list the following questions on the board: Who? What? Where? When? Why? How? Explain to students that a news report must answer these questions quickly in the first part of the report. Reread the first page of *Night Of The Twisters* that includes the newspaper account; then have students identify the answers to the six questions on the board. Next brainstorm with the class a list of events in the book that would be good topics for newspaper reports. Some examples might include:

- Dan, Ryan, and Arthur's flight to the basement and their escape from it after the tornado
- The kids' rescue of Mrs. Smiley
- The trip in the police cruiser with Officer Kelly
- The Darlington family's experience during the tornado
- Aunt Goldie's mysterious rescue from the bowling alley

Assign a topic to each group or pair of students; then have each group write and illustrate a short article on its topic. Publish these articles in a class "Twister Times" newspaper. Provide copies for other classes as a way to encourage schoolmates to read this terrific twistin' tale.

At The End Of The Book: Hatch Family Album
Skill: Summarizing, predicting outcomes

Is a picture really worth a thousand words? It just might be with this great end-of-the-book activity! First divide the class into several groups. Give each group seven 4" x 6" blank index cards. Instruct the group to illustrate its cards as if they were photos of the following:

- The Hatch family before the tornadoes
- Dan and Arthur before the tornadoes
- The Hatch family three days after the tornado struck
- Life at Grandpa and Grandma Hatch's farm after the tornadoes
- The Hatch and Darlington families one year after the tornadoes
- The anniversary party held one year after the tornadoes
- Dan, Arthur, and Ryan three years after the tornadoes

Have each group staple together four sheets of black construction paper. Then have the group glue its "photos" and accompanying captions (written on white strips of paper) inside the resulting album, leaving the front of the first page blank to decorate as a cover. Display the finished photo albums in your school's media center to celebrate the conclusion to a "tornado-rific" tale!

Dan and Arthur enjoy their bikes just one day before the tornadoes hit.

Just Another "Plain-Letter Day"?

Part 1: In *Night Of The Twisters,* Dan thought that June 3 was going to be just another "plain-letter day." Boy, was he ever wrong!

What kind of day did you have yesterday? In the chart below, list the main activities you did between 5:00 and 9:00 PM. For each activity, put a check in the small box under the category that best describes it. You'll complete the rest of the chart and Part 2 in class with your teacher's help.

Hour	Main activity	Category				
		Leisure	Study	Eating	Chores	Social
5:00–6:00 PM						
6:00–7:00 PM						
7:00–8:00 PM						
8:00–9:00 PM						

Part 2: After you've completed the chart above, choose one time slot (for example, 5:00–6:00 PM). Create a bar graph below to show the number of classmates who participated in each category during that hour.

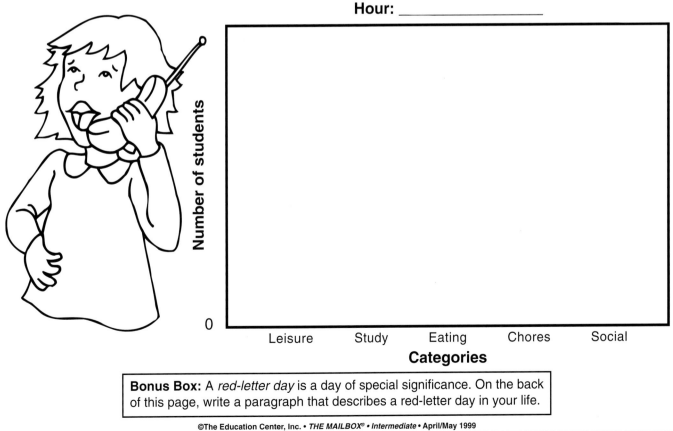

Hour: _____

Number of students

0

Leisure   Study   Eating   Chores   Social

Categories

Bonus Box: A *red-letter day* is a day of special significance. On the back of this page, write a paragraph that describes a red-letter day in your life.

Note To The Teacher: Use with "Before You Read: Just Another Plain-Letter Day?" on page 194. Provide students with rulers and crayons or colored markers.

Pattern

Use with the two activities on page 195.

Painting Without A Paintbrush

Part 1: In *Night Of The Twisters,* the author paints a picture of Dan's world during and after the tornado. But she doesn't use a paintbrush. Instead she uses words, especially a figure of speech called a *simile.* A simile compares two unlike things. It is introduced by the words *like* or *as,* as in "The tiger purred like a kitten." Finish each simile in the boxes below by filling in the blanks. In the last box, create your own simile picture to describe any topic you like.

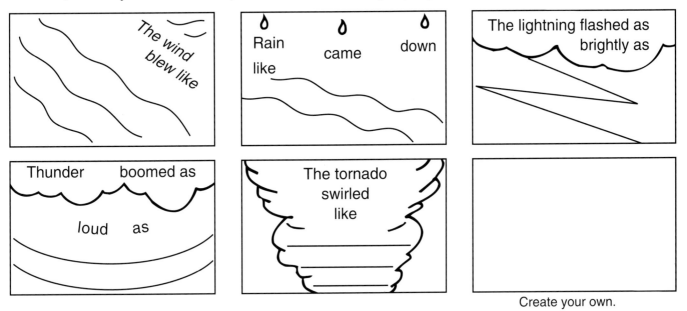

Create your own.

Part 2: The author paints pictures with another figure of speech called a *metaphor.* A metaphor compares two different things without using *like* or *as,* as in "That dog is a barking machine." Fill in the blanks below with words that could be used in metaphors about each object. The first one is done for you.

Bonus Box: Choose three of the words you listed in Part 2. On the back of this sheet, write a sentence using each word in a metaphor (for example: "The clouds were patches of cotton candy floating in the sky."). Remember: don't use *like* or *as* in your metaphors.

The Ballad Of Lucy Whipple

A Novel Of The California Gold Rush
by Newbery Award–Winner Karen Cushman

Triumph and tragedy are in store when California Morning Whipple—who changes her name to Lucy because she absolutely hates California—moves with her family to a rough-and-tumble mining settlement during the gold rush. Share this funny and poignant story of the women and children who were also players in this historic event; then complement its reading with the following creative activities and reproducibles.

by Michael D. Foster

While Reading: Dear Lucy...

Framing Lucy's refreshingly honest first-person narrative are her letters to Gram and Grampop, her grandparents back in Massachusetts. Lucy relates the daily events in her life, plus her thoughts, dreams, and reactions to them. As you read the book, let students practice their letter-writing skills and learn to think from a different perspective with this ongoing activity. After completing each chapter that includes a letter to Gram and Grampop, reread Lucy's letter and discuss it with your students: How did Lucy feel? What humor do they find in Lucy's letter? What sorrows? Next direct each student to write a reply to Lucy from either Gram's or Grampop's perspective. Have students write their letters in their reading journals so they can refer back to previous letters when writing new ones.

While Reading: The Rush Is On!

The setting of this book—the California gold rush of 1849—was a pivotal event in American history. Tie the reading of this novel to a study of this fascinating time period with the following ideas:

- Have students research the history of the gold rush by answering these questions: When and where was gold first discovered? How did people hear about the discovery? Where did the settlers come from? What were the effects of the gold rush on American society and politics? How did the gold rush affect California's population growth? What role did it play in California becoming a state? Provide each student with a sheet of yellow construction paper. Direct him to cut out a gold-nugget shape from the paper, then attach his research findings to the shape. Post the nuggets on a bulletin board titled "Gold Rush Riches."

- Have students research the two routes settlers used to reach California from the East: by boat down the East Coast and around South America, and by land across the continent. Then direct each student to pretend to be either the leader of a wagon train or the captain of a ship headed for California. Have the student create a travel poster that lists and illustrates the advantages of his method of reaching California—while also including the disadvantages of the alternate method. With their exposure to modern-day advertising, students should come up with some one-of-a-kind ad campaigns!

While Reading: A Gold Rush Dictionary

The Ballad Of Lucy Whipple includes many words and phrases that will probably be unfamiliar to students. As you share the story, have each child make a Gold Rush Dictionary of new words. Have the student list each word (see the list of sample words from the first three chapters below), a sentence that includes the word, a definition or synonym, and an illustration of the word. Since many of the words occur several times, students can refer to their dictionaries throughout the entire book.

Sample Words:

parlor
lean-to
saloon
lard
reticule
emigrant
steamer
boarding house
prospector
privy
trundle
chamberpot
general store
broadside
buckeyes

After Reading Chapters 1–5: Home Sweet Home?

Lucy's mother is determined that her family will be happy in their new home. But California Morning Whipple does *not* want to live in California! In fact, she hates it so much that she changes her name to Lucy and vows to find a way to return to her Massachusetts home.

To sharpen critical-thinking skills, have each child draw two compare and contrast T-charts on a large piece of white paper: one that compares California and Massachusetts from Lucy's point of view and one that compares the two areas from Mrs. Whipple's point of view. Have students refer to and list specific quotes from the book that support what they list in their charts. When the charts are finished, pair students; then have each twosome compare their charts.

Lucy's
Point Of View

California | Massachusetts

Mrs. Whipple's
Point Of View

California | Massachusetts

After Reading Chapters 6–8: Don't Jump!

Lucy has a vivid imagination, and it often causes her to jump to the wrong conclusions! Share with students how important it is to gather all the facts before drawing a conclusion. Then lead them in a discussion of the questions below. Remind students to support their answers with facts from the story.

- Does Mrs. Whipple read Lucy's letters to Gram and Grampop?
- What kind of student would Lucy be? Would she like school?
- What did Gram and Grampop write to Lucy about her plan to return to Massachusetts and live with them?
- Why does Lucy think Mr. Coogan is Rattlesnake Jake?
- Why does Lucy believe Mama has no plans to remarry?

After Reading Chapters 9–11: Lucy's Lending Library

Lucy begins lending her books to other people and has to make some rules for her "library"—some of which don't work! Have students work in groups to come up with at least five additional rules for Lucy's informal lending library. Direct each group to present its rules to the class and lead a discussion on the merit of each one. For example: Is the rule enforceable? Is it reasonable? Are there unexpected consequences that will prevent the rule from working as expected? After all groups have made their presentations, share with students the author's note at the back of the book, which includes information about the history of libraries in America and why they were so important to the settlers.

After Reading Chapters 12–15: Two Deaths, One Trial

Much happens in Lucky Diggins in these chapters, including two deaths and a trial. Use the following questions about these powerful events to start some lively class discussions. Or use them as writing prompts for students to respond to in their reading journals:

- How was honesty demonstrated in the mining camp regarding Lucy's books?
- Was Mrs. Flagg's trial fair? Was justice served? How was the law used to show mercy to Mrs. Flagg?
- Both Butte and Mr. Flagg died. Why was one viewed as a loss, while the other was viewed as a victory? Why did Butte's life seem to have more worth than Mr. Flagg's?
- Was Mrs. Whipple somehow to blame for Butte's death, since she brought her children to such a dangerous environment? Why or why not?

After Reading Chapters 16–17: The New Lucky Diggins

With the burning of Lucky Diggins, the residents of the mining community had to rebuild their town from scratch. Lead the class in a discussion of what buildings would be needed, besides the ones mentioned in the story. Then, in small groups, have students design the new town of Lucky Diggins on large sheets of art paper. Encourage students to use their imaginations as well as facts from the story to design their blueprints for the new community. Also have them keep in mind these factors as they design the new Lucky Diggins:

- the need for certain buildings (a store, for example)
- the resources that are available (materials had to be close at hand)
- potential for economic success (Will the business make enough money to survive in a mining town?)

For a long-term project, have students make scale models of the new Lucky Diggins based on their designs. Have students use assorted sizes of boxes, construction paper, and other art materials to complete their 3-D models.

After Reading Chapters 18–19: Three Options

All along, Lucy's goal has been to return to Gram and Grampop in Massachusetts and "civilization." Now she is presented with three choices: to go with her family to the Sandwich Islands, to return to Massachusetts, or to remain in Lucky Diggins. Review with students the concept of *pro and con* arguments—or how to look at an issue and decide what is good about it (pro) and what is bad (con). Then have each student make a pro and con chart for each of Lucy's three choices, describing the good as well as the bad points of each option. As a follow-up, ask students which choice they would have made—and why—if they were in Lucy's place.

Gold Rush Groups

Life in California was certainly different from life in Massachusetts! Lucy mentions and describes several things in her environment, from people and trees to animals and supplies. Classify each word below by writing it in the correct category. Some items will be written in more than one category.

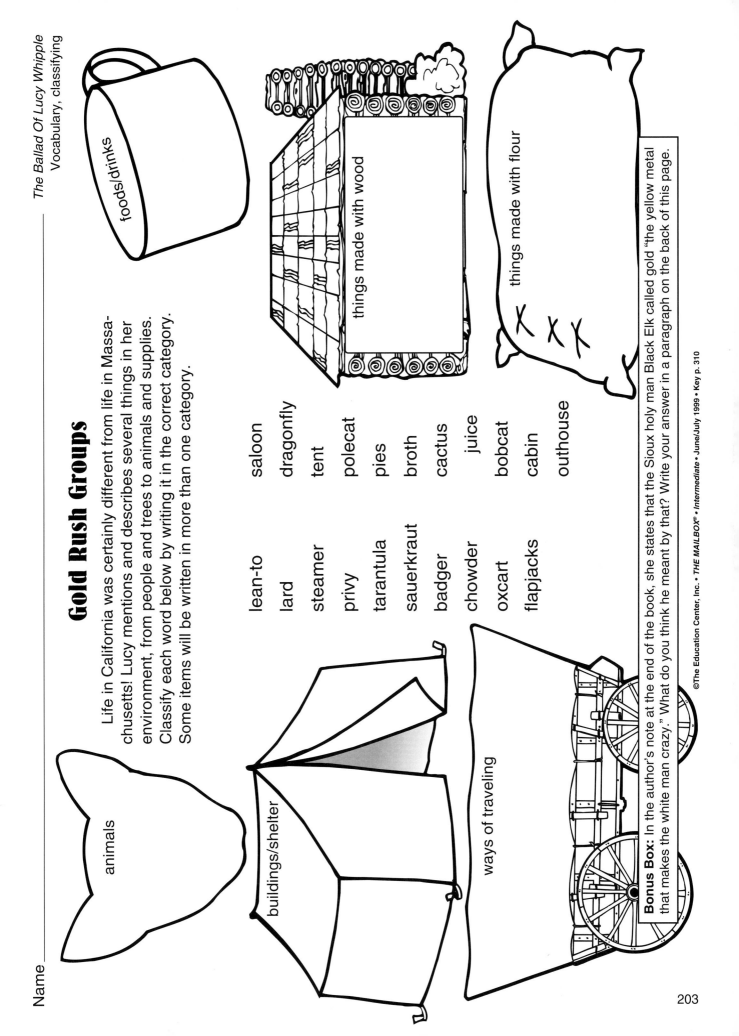

foods/drinks

things made with wood

things made with flour

animals

buildings/shelter

ways of traveling

lean-to   saloon
lard   dragonfly
steamer   tent
privy   polecat
tarantula   pies
sauerkraut   broth
badger   cactus
chowder   juice
oxcart   bobcat
flapjacks   cabin
                 outhouse

Bonus Box: In the author's note at the end of the book, she states that the Sioux holy man Black Elk called gold "the yellow metal that makes the white man crazy." What do you think he meant by that? Write your answer in a paragraph on the back of this page.

Welcome To Lucky Diggins' Trading Post!

Instead of paper money and coins, gold dust was used by the forty-niners to buy supplies in mining settlements. If gold is $36 per ounce, find out what the cost of each item below would be in dollars. Show your work in the blank space as shown. The first one is done for you.

Example: If the price of 1 dozen apples is 1/3 ounce of gold, then $36 ÷ 3 = $12.

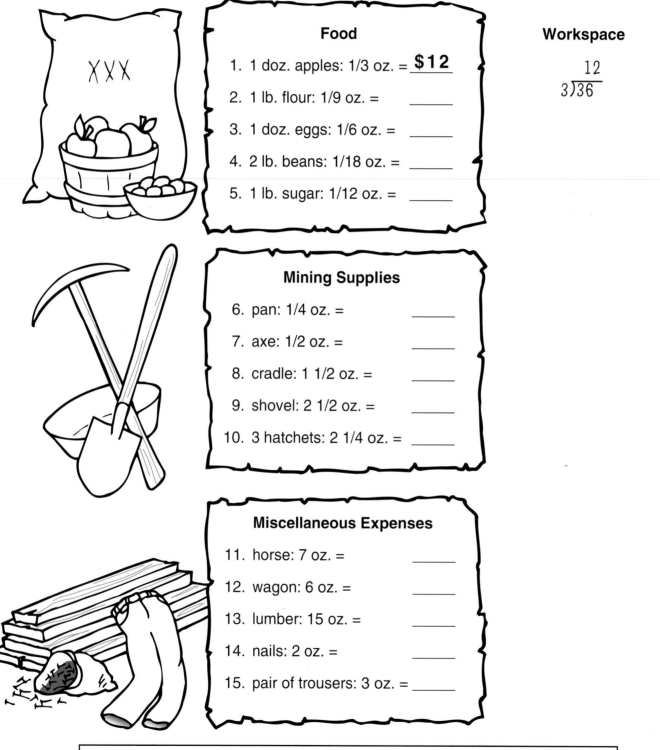

Food

1. 1 doz. apples: 1/3 oz. = **$12**

2. 1 lb. flour: 1/9 oz. = _____

3. 1 doz. eggs: 1/6 oz. = _____

4. 2 lb. beans: 1/18 oz. = _____

5. 1 lb. sugar: 1/12 oz. = _____

Workspace

$$\frac{12}{3\overline{)36}}$$

Mining Supplies

6. pan: 1/4 oz. = _____

7. axe: 1/2 oz. = _____

8. cradle: 1 1/2 oz. = _____

9. shovel: 2 1/2 oz. = _____

10. 3 hatchets: 2 1/4 oz. = _____

Miscellaneous Expenses

11. horse: 7 oz. = _____

12. wagon: 6 oz. = _____

13. lumber: 15 oz. = _____

14. nails: 2 oz. = _____

15. pair of trousers: 3 oz. = _____

Bonus Box: Suppose the price of gold doubled. How much would each food item then cost? Show your work and list your answers on the back of this page.

©The Education Center, Inc. • *THE MAILBOX® • Intermediate* • June/July 1999 • Key p. 311

Silver And Gold

Lucy found out that if she wanted something to happen, she had to *make* it happen. But sometimes things just happened on their own…or so she thought!

Read each pair of statements below. Decide which statement in each pair is a cause and which one is an effect. Remember:

- An *effect* is what happens as a result of a cause.
- A *cause* tells why the effect happened.

In each pair of statements, color the effect yellow—for gold. If the statement is the cause, color it gray—for silver. Happy mining!

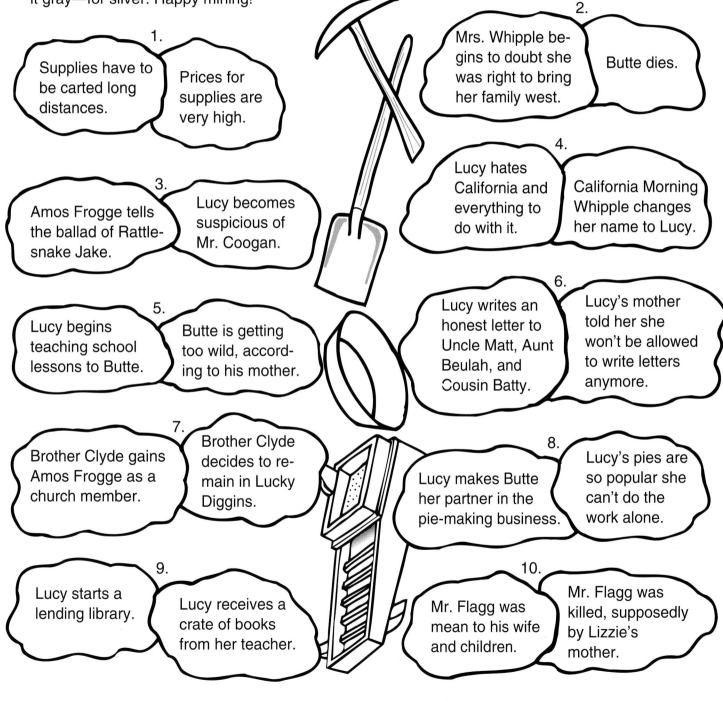

1. Supplies have to be carted long distances. / Prices for supplies are very high.

2. Mrs. Whipple begins to doubt she was right to bring her family west. / Butte dies.

3. Amos Frogge tells the ballad of Rattlesnake Jake. / Lucy becomes suspicious of Mr. Coogan.

4. Lucy hates California and everything to do with it. / California Morning Whipple changes her name to Lucy.

5. Lucy begins teaching school lessons to Butte. / Butte is getting too wild, according to his mother.

6. Lucy writes an honest letter to Uncle Matt, Aunt Beulah, and Cousin Batty. / Lucy's mother told her she won't be allowed to write letters anymore.

7. Brother Clyde gains Amos Frogge as a church member. / Brother Clyde decides to remain in Lucky Diggins.

8. Lucy makes Butte her partner in the pie-making business. / Lucy's pies are so popular she can't do the work alone.

9. Lucy starts a lending library. / Lucy receives a crate of books from her teacher.

10. Mr. Flagg was mean to his wife and children. / Mr. Flagg was killed, supposedly by Lizzie's mother.

Bonus Box: On the back of this sheet, list three effects of the gold rush on the area that would later become the state of California.

Stepping On The Cracks

An Award-Winning Novel by Mary Downing Hahn

It's 1944, and there's a lot going on for best friends Margaret and Elizabeth. Not only are both of their brothers fighting overseas in World War II, but the 11-year-old buddies are also engaged in a war of their own with archenemy Gordy Smith. Ironically it is because of Gordy that the girls learn more lessons about war and themselves than they ever thought possible. Use the following creative activities to enhance your reading of this award-winning historical-fiction novel.

by Carol Felts

Need Ideas For A Different Novel?
Look for this symbol (*) at the end of an activity, indicating that it can easily be adapted to use with other books.

Before Reading: World War II Lingo

Try this fun activity to introduce students to the World War II vocabulary that's peppered throughout this book:

1. Highlight each word listed on the top half of page 209 in your copy of the book.
2. Write each word on a sentence strip. Pin these strips on a bulletin board.
3. Write the definition of each word on a sentence strip; pin these strips on a wall or bulletin board opposite the word strips.
4. Introduce each word to the class; then have students try to select the correct definition. Emphasize that this will be just a guess since the students have yet to encounter the words in context in the book. After several students have guessed a definition, share the correct one. Continue for the remainder of the words.
5. As you read the novel aloud, stop at each highlighted word. Let the first student who can read aloud the correct definition from the wall move that sentence strip and pin it beside the matching word strip on the opposite wall. Have the remaining students copy the word and definition in their reading journals. Reward the first student with a small prize, such as a sticker or piece of sugar-free candy. *

panzer	a German tank used during World War II

After Chapter 4: Star Light, Star Bright

During the war, a family placed a blue star in its window to tell others that a loved one was fighting in the conflict. If the blue star was replaced by a gold one, neighbors knew that the loved one had died in the war effort.

Turn your classroom windows into a starry display with this critical-thinking activity. Duplicate the star pattern on page 209 onto tagboard to make several tracers. Have each student trace one star on blue paper and another on gold or yellow paper. Direct the student to write a question about the story on the blue star. Discuss the students' questions; then have each child cut out both of her stars and tape the blue one in a classroom window. Collect the gold stars to keep at your desk. When a student's question is answered as you read the book, have her write the answer on a gold star and tape it in the window beside her blue star. For a variation, have students make predictions about the book instead of writing questions. Use this idea with another book by using cutouts that represent an important element in the novel's plot. *

Why is Gordy such a bully?

Gordy is a bully because his father is so mean to him.

After Chapter 8: Touched By War

As students read this gripping novel, they'll soon see that the war affects almost everyone who lives in College Hill—which provides a perfect opportunity to discuss cause and effect. Begin by asking students how their lives would be affected if you decided to assign ten pages of homework every night (much like the girls' infamous sixth-grade teacher, Mrs. Wagner). Record their responses on the board. Explain that *because* of your homework assignment, the students would experience an *effect* on their lives. Ask if anyone in their families would be affected as well. Remind students that the war—even though it's happening a continent away—is taking a great toll on the people and the town of College Hill. Have students brainstorm some of the ways College Hill and its residents have been affected by the war; then have each student complete a copy of the cause-and-effect reproducible on the bottom half of page 210.

After Chapter 12:
Not As Simple As It Seems

Stepping On The Cracks is packed with interesting moral dilemmas—especially after the girls discover that the crazy man is actually Gordy's brother Stuart, who has deserted because he believes war is wrong. Examine the different points of view held by the book's characters with an activity that also sharpens important writing skills. Duplicate the top half of page 210 so that each student will have one activity when the page is cut apart on the dotted lines. Cut apart the activities; then place them in a container and have each student draw one out. After students have finished writing, group them according to their scenarios. Ask students to share their writings with their teammates; then have each group select the most persuasive and thorough piece to read aloud to the rest of the class. Adapt this idea to another novel by duplicating four dilemmas included in that book. ✳

After Chapter 16: Wish Upon A Star

After getting a glimpse into the Smiths' home and Stuart's hut, students will quickly see the difficulties faced by the book's characters. Help students understand the emotions of these characters with a star-studded display. Enlarge the star pattern on page 209 to full-page size. Duplicate a copy for each student. Have each child choose one character and write a paragraph describing what he or she might be wishing at this point in the story. After he has finished the paragraph, have the student glue his star on yellow or blue construction paper and cut it out, leaving a 1/2-inch border of construction paper. Post the stars on a bulletin board titled "Wish Upon A Star." Have students add small, gummed foil stars to the display for a shiny finishing touch. Use this activity with any novel that has characters who are facing tough decisions or dilemmas. ✳

If I were Margaret, I'd wish…

After Chapter 20: Hard On The Outside, Soft On The Inside

While reading chapters 17–20, prominently display a plastic egg in your classroom. Don't explain its presence except to tell students that it has something to do with the story. After students have read chapter 20, reread with them the section in which Margaret realizes "…I wasn't afraid of him [Gordy] anymore." Pick up the plastic egg; then ask each student to write a sentence or two describing how Gordy is like an egg. After students share their responses, explain that an egg has a hard protective shell (like Gordy's rough exterior, caused by his horrible home life). But the inside is soft and fragile—which is just how Margaret now sees Gordy.

Gordy On The Outside

Gordy On The Inside

Next divide the class into groups. Give each group an egg shape cut from white paper and one cut from yellow paper. Have a recorder for the group label the cutouts as shown. Direct each group to discuss how Gordy is like an egg, then list specific examples of Gordy's rough exterior on the white cutout. Direct the group to then list examples of Gordy's soft side on the yellow cutout. After about 20 minutes, have each group share its cutouts. Adapt this idea to use with any novel that has a character similar to Gordy (rough on the outside, soft on the inside). ✳

After Chapter 24: In Memory Of Jimmy

At the end of this chapter, Margaret and her family get the dreadful news that Jimmy has been killed in action. Although readers never meet Jimmy, they learn a lot about him from Margaret's recollections, as well as the letters and cartoons he sends home. Brainstorm with students some of Jimmy's characteristics (funny, sensitive, loving, artistic, etc.). Explain to students that a *eulogy* is a speech in praise of a person who has died. Tell students to imagine that College Hill is going to hold a special memorial service to honor those who lost their lives in the war, and Margaret has been chosen to eulogize her brother. Have each student or pair of students write a short eulogy from Margaret's point of view. Provide time for each student to read her eulogy aloud. If desired, play patriotic music softly in the background as students read their eulogies.

At The End Of The Book: Make Mine Murals!

Review the important events of this thought-provoking book with a fun art activity. With students brainstorm a list of important scenes from the book (or use the list below). Divide the class into groups of two to four students. Have each group choose a scene and draw a mural of it on a large piece of butcher paper. Encourage students to refer to the book for details about their scene. Also direct each group to describe its scene on an index card mounted somewhere on its mural. When the groups are finished, display the murals in order in your hallway. Adapt this culminating activity for any novel your class is reading. ✳

Possible Scenes:
- Chapter 4: Margaret and Elizabeth see Gordy and his friends near the hut for the first time.
- Chapter 7: Gordy and Elizabeth have a fight.
- Chapter 8: Elizabeth and Margaret get revenge on Gordy by trying to destroy the hut.
- Chapter 13: The girls go to Gordy's house for the first time and encounter the Smith family.
- Chapter 16: Elizabeth and Margaret play hooky from school to help care for Stuart in the hut.
- Chapter 17: In desperation, the girls take Barbara to the hut to help Stuart.
- Chapter 19: The girls and Gordy put Stuart on the bobsled to take him to the doctor.
- Chapter 22: Mrs. Baker confronts Mr. and Mrs. Smith at their house.
- Chapter 24: Margaret arrives home to discover her brother has been killed in action.
- Chapter 26: The girls witness the police arresting Mr. Smith.

Vocabulary List

Use with "World War II Lingo" on page 206. The number in parentheses indicates the page number on which the word can be found (taken from the paperback version of *Stepping On The Cracks* published by Avon Books, 1991).

★ **Hitler** *(2)*—Nazi ruler of Germany from 1933–1945
★ **Nazi** *(2)*—a supporter of Adolf Hitler and his beliefs
★ **knickers** *(6)*—loose-fitting short pants gathered at the knee
★ **drafted** *(14)*—enlisted in the army by the government rather than by choice
★ **bond** *(16)*—a certificate issued by the government that promises to pay its holder a certain amount on a certain date
★ **scrap** *(16)*—discarded metal collected during the war to be recycled
★ **foxhole** *(21)*—a pit dug to provide cover during battle
★ **tramp** *(22)*—a homeless person who travels on foot, and may beg for or steal food
★ **panzer** *(26)*—a German tank used during World War II
★ **pinup** *(27)*—a photo or poster of a pretty girl
★ **liberation** *(34)*—setting free
★ **oxfords** *(40)*—a type of laced shoe
★ **hobo** *(60)*—a homeless and usually poor person who wanders from place to place
★ **Victrola** *(64)*—a record player
★ **jitterbug** *(64)*—a type of dance popular in the 1940s
★ **deserter** *(70)*—one who leaves the military without permission
★ **furlough** *(98)*—a temporary time period during which a soldier has permission to leave the service
★ **conscientious objector** *(111)*—a person who refuses to serve in the military for moral or religious reasons
★ **Allies** *(127)*—50 nations, including the United States, China, the Soviet Union, and Great Britain; fought against Germany, Italy, and Japan
★ **ration** *(130)*—allow people to buy only a limited amount of food and other supplies
★ **AWOL** *(142)*—stands for "absent without leave"; absent from the military without permission
★ **Mussolini** *(152)*—Italy's leader during World War II
★ **Hirohito** *(152)*—Japan's leader during World War II

Pattern
Use with "Star Light, Star Bright" on page 206 and "Wish Upon A Star" on page 207.

Writing Scenarios

Use with "Not As Simple As It Seems" on page 207.

Pretend that you are Gordy. Your other brother, Don, has found out that you've been hiding Stuart. Write a letter to Don explaining why you decided to help your other brother hide out from the war.

Pretend that you are Stuart. To kill time while in the hut, you've been keeping a journal. Write a journal entry that tells about your feelings toward war.

Pretend that you are Margaret and you have just discovered Stuart in his hut. You really don't know if you should turn him in as a deserter or not. Write a letter to your brother Jimmy. Describe your problem and ask for his advice about what to do.

Pretend that you are Joe, Elizabeth's brother. You have just heard about Stuart being a deserter. Write a letter to Elizabeth explaining how you feel about war and Stuart's choice to desert.

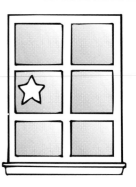

Name _____

Effects On Everyone

The people of College Hill are all affected by the war—even though it's taking place thousands of miles away! In the spaces below, write how each character is being affected by the war. Where the circles overlap, write one way that both characters are affected.

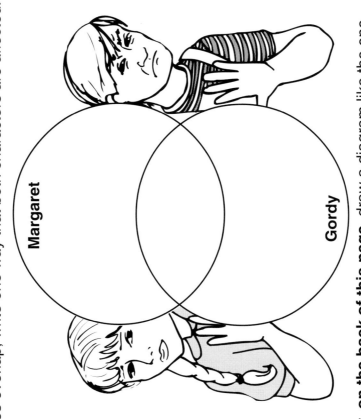

Margaret

Gordy

Now, on the back of this page, draw a diagram like the one above. Label one circle "Barbara" and the other "Stuart." Then fill in the diagram.

Bonus Box: Because there were shortages during the war, Margaret and Elizabeth had to give up certain things they loved. On the back of this page, list ten items you'd hate to have to give up.

Use with "Touched By War" on page 207.

210

OTHER CURRICULUM HELPERS

POINTERS

For Sharpening Study Skills

What's the best way to keep students on their toes with study skills? Point 'em in the right direction from the beginning and keep 'em on track throughout the year! Use the following great activities and reproducibles to sharpen your students' study skills at the start of the year or anytime.

ideas by Gail Peckumn and Cynthia Wurmnest

Stop, Look, Listen, And Learn
Skill: Active reading

Help students become active participants in the reading process. Point out that an active reader *stops* frequently and reflects on what he's reading, *looks* back over what he's read, and *listens* to his classmates' thoughts in order to *learn.* To practice this process, give each student pair a short, nonfiction article or book; then have students follow the steps below.

1. Look through the book's pages; then tell your partner what you already know about the book's topic and predict what kinds of information it contains.
2. Take turns reading aloud to each other for three minutes at a time, stopping at your teacher's signal. Restate to your partner one or more different facts from what was read.
3. Resume reading aloud in turn for five minutes, stopping at your teacher's signal. Ask your partner one or more questions about what was read. Repeat this step, this time reading for ten minutes.
4. Spend ten minutes drawing a quick sketch of something you learned while reading. Share your sketch with your partner.
5. Spend another five minutes summarizing for each other all that was read.

To help students remember what they read in their textbooks or other materials, use the reproducible on page 216.

The Gist Of It All
Skill: Listening, note taking, speaking

Put a twist on sharing "What I Did This Summer" stories by combining them with listening, speaking, and note-taking skills. Pair students; then have one child tell her partner about her summer while the other takes notes of the highlights. Next direct the storytellers to change partners and repeat the process, telling the same story. Then match the students who took notes on the same person and have them compare their notes about the classmate's summer story. After everyone has had a chance to do this activity, discuss with students how closely their notes compared. Conclude by having students use their notes to tell the class about one another's summers. Modify the activity to use anytime during the year by having students share weekend, holiday, or birthday stories.

This summer Darin went to a lake in Ohio.

They're All Ears!
Skill: Listening

Looking for formulas that produce a super-attentive class? Try the quick-and-easy listening activities below!

- Ask each student to read aloud a poem of his choice, deliberately omitting the title. Challenge the class to listen carefully, then try to guess the title.
- Give a student four or five oral directions in succession to remember and follow. For example, "Turn off the lights, write your name on the board, walk around Ben's desk three times, and then stand by the pencil sharpener." Vary the activity by allowing pairs of students to give directions to each other.
- Instruct each student to copy a short paragraph from any book, inserting an absurd detail somewhere in the paragraph. Next have her read her paragraph aloud to see if fellow classmates can identify the detail that doesn't belong.
- Select any picture; then give students detailed, oral directions for drawing it. For example, "Draw an island in the northeast corner of your paper, a small continent with a peninsula in the southeast corner,…" and so on. After giving all the directions, have students compare their pictures with the original and with those of their classmates.
- Modify the activity above by having each student draw a simple picture, such as one with geometric shapes. Then direct him to sit back-to-back with a partner and describe what he drew while his partner tries to reproduce it.
- Read sentences in which you insert one or more blanks to the class. For example, "The _____ bird swooped _____ and ate the _____." Have students repeat the sentence, supplying appropriate missing words.

A Thesaurus Is Not A Kind Of Dinosaur!
Skill: Using a thesaurus

This activity is sure to keep students' thesaurus skills from becoming extinct! Direct each student to list the names of five to ten close friends or family members. Next have him think of a complimentary predicate adjective to insert in a short sentence about each person, such as "Barb is <u>kind</u>" or "Tim is <u>smart</u>." After the student has completed the sentences, instruct him to find a synonym and an antonym in a thesaurus to replace each original adjective (for example, "Barb is <u>amiable</u>, not <u>malicious</u>"). Ask volunteers to share whether their original adjectives or the ones from the thesaurus best describe the persons on their lists.

Review Posters
Skill: Reviewing learned material

When it's time to study for a big test, use the team approach! A few days before the test, divide students into study groups. Then challenge each group to design a poster that illustrates the most important concepts and vocabulary in that chapter or unit. Provide time for groups to present their posters to the rest of the class; then display the posters so students can have a visual reminder of key concepts to study before the test—but don't forget to take them down on test day! *Julie O'Brien—Grs. 6–8, Princeton, IN*

213

Not Just ABCs
Skill: Alphabetizing, using a dictionary

Throwing in a few unexpected steps will spice up a review of alphabetizing skills! Review alphabetical order and its importance in finding entries in different resources, such as a dictionary, a thesaurus, an index, an encyclopedia, an atlas, a phone book, etc. Next have each student select a different letter of the alphabet and list 20 words from the dictionary that begin with that letter, making sure the words are *not* in alphabetical order. Pair students, instructing each child to alphabetize his partner's list. After his partner has checked his alphabetizing, direct each student to use the list to complete the following steps:

1. Write a definition for the 3rd, 11th, and 18th words.
2. Find the part of speech for the 5th, 9th, and 16th words.
3. Write a sentence for the 4th, 8th, and 13th words.

To extend this activity with encyclopedias and thesauruses, have students follow these steps:

For thesauruses:

1. Write a synonym for each of these words: numbers 3, 5, 8, and 15.
2. Write an antonym for each of these words: numbers 2, 7, 9, and 12.
3. Find the part of speech for each of these words: numbers 1, 6, 17, and 19.

For encyclopedias: (Have each student first list 20 topics that begin with his letter.)

1. Tell whether the 3rd, 11th, and 18th entries include a picture, map, or chart.
2. List the entry that comes before each of these entries: 2, 6, and 14.

Inspiring Inquiring
Skill: Choosing resources

This fun make-and-play game will help students decide which resources are the best ones to use.

1. Gather examples of the resources listed below; then write the list on the board. Review the list with students, pointing out that many of the resources are available through computer programs and the Internet.
2. Assign each student a different resource; then give him two small slips of paper. Have the student familiarize himself with the resource and then write two questions that could be answered using that resource. Collect students' papers and place them in a container.
3. Give each student a 5 x 5 grid as shown. Direct him to write "Free" in the middle square and the name of a different resource from the board in each remaining square.
4. Provide students with dried beans or small bits of paper to use as markers.
5. Draw a question and read it aloud. Direct students to cover a reference that could be used to answer that question. Explain that in some cases more than one resource can be used to find the answer, but that students should mark only one for each question. When a student fills a row or column, have him read his answers aloud. If his answers are reasonable, declare him the winner. Have students clear their boards to start a new round.

To give students more practice with choosing resources, see the reproducible on page 217.

dictionary	thesaurus
globe	travel brochure
almanac	index
copyright page	city map
calendar	newspaper
encyclopedia	bibliography
wall map	atlas
telephone book	product label
glossary	table of contents
TV schedule	flight schedule

		FREE		

A Web Is An Outline
Skill: Outlining from a web

Make outlining less intimidating for students by demonstrating how easy it is to turn a simple web into an outline. With input from students, use colored chalk on the board (or colored markers on a transparency) to web a chapter from a textbook the class is currently studying as follows:

1. Write the chapter's title as the center of the web. Circle it in red.
2. Write each topic within the chapter as a different branch off the title. Circle the topics in blue.
3. If there are subtopics for a topic, draw a different branch off the topic for each one. Circle the subtopics in green.

Next show students how to change the web into an outline:

1. Write what's circled in red as the title of the outline.
2. Write Roman numeral I, followed by one of the topics circled in blue.
3. Write a capital *A, B,* and *C* beneath Roman numeral I, each followed by one of the subtopics circled in green.
4. If necessary explain that further information about subtopics would be written in numerical order below the subtopics. Details beyond that would use lowercase letters.

Help students conclude that outlining, like webbing, is just another way of organizing thoughts and ideas. Then follow up by having each student make a web of his favorite team sport—including three subtopics—and then use it to write an outline.

"Betweensies"
Skill: Using guide words

Finding a word to sandwich between two other words will intrigue your game enthusiasts—and provide fun practice with guide words! Form two to four teams, numbering the players on each team. Position each team an equal distance from the board. Write two guide words from the list below on the board; then call out a number. Direct each team member with that number to run to the board and write a word that could come between those two guide words. Give two points to the first team to answer correctly, and one point to any other team answering correctly within 30 seconds. To continue play, write a new pair of guide words on the board and call out a different number.

cry–dog
parade–puddle
hen–hungry
lamp–lick
flour–gab
baby–beg

goat–hobby
second–swish
rash–riddle
shall–shut
tarnish–turtle
cat–clock

jam–jungle
walrus–wobble
donkey–dungeon
talent–teak
earn–empty
bend–bog

So if I can web, I can outline too!

State Government
I. Legislative Branch
  A. General Assembly
  B. How Laws Are Made
II. Executive Branch
  A. Governor
  B. Lieutenant Governor
  C. Secretary Of State
  D. Treasurer
  E. Auditor
  F. Attorney General
  G. Secretary Of Agriculture
III. Judicial Branch
  A. State Supreme Court
  B. District Courts
  C. Lower Courts
IV. Elections
  A. Public-Office Qualifications
  B. Voter Qualifications

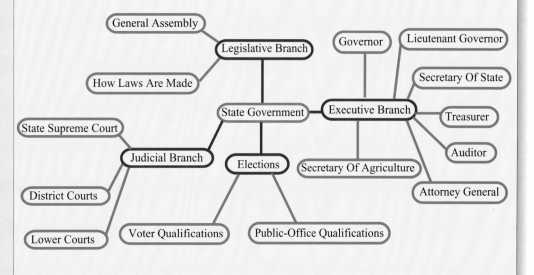

See page 218 for a sheet of helpful study-skill pointers that students can store right in their folders.

Note taking, summarizing

Chapter Chart

Study Point #1

Question/ Answer

Study Point #2

Summarize

This simple chart can help you remember what you read. As you read an assigned chapter, write a question for each page in the space below. Record the page number where the answer can be found. Then write the answer. When you've finished reading the entire assignment, write a few sentences telling what you learned in the Summary space. What an easy way to study!

Page Read	Question	Answer	Page Number Of Answer

Summary:

Bonus Box: Circle the new vocabulary words you used in completing the chart. Define these words on the back of this sheet.

©The Education Center, Inc. • THE MAILBOX® • Intermediate • Aug/Sept 1998

Note To The Teacher: Use with "Stop, Look, Listen, And Learn" on page 212. Give a copy of this chart to each student whenever he reads a chapter in his textbook. Have him keep his completed charts in a folder to use when studying for a unit test.

Research Roundup

Ol' Red needs help rounding up and branding his cattle. Use the resources listed on the sign below to answer each question. After you've written an answer and named the source that helped you, mark the cow below the question with a personal brand. Your job is done when all the cattle have been branded.

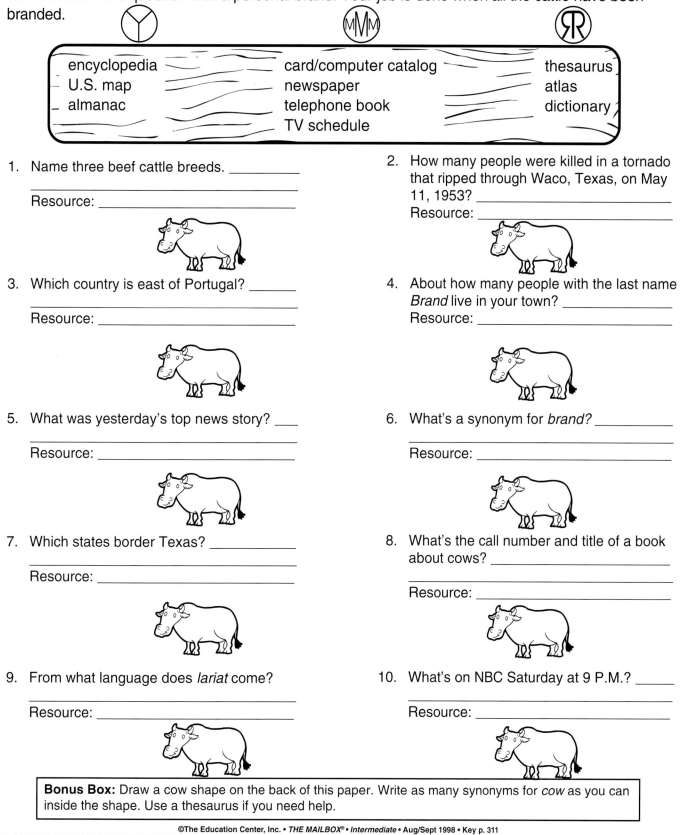

encyclopedia
U.S. map
almanac

card/computer catalog
newspaper
telephone book
TV schedule

thesaurus
atlas
dictionary

1. Name three beef cattle breeds. _____
   _____
   Resource: _____

2. How many people were killed in a tornado that ripped through Waco, Texas, on May 11, 1953? _____
   Resource: _____

3. Which country is east of Portugal? _____
   _____
   Resource: _____

4. About how many people with the last name *Brand* live in your town? _____
   Resource: _____

5. What was yesterday's top news story? ___
   _____
   Resource: _____

6. What's a synonym for *brand?* _____
   _____
   Resource: _____

7. Which states border Texas? _____
   _____
   Resource: _____

8. What's the call number and title of a book about cows? _____
   _____
   Resource: _____

9. From what language does *lariat* come?
   _____
   Resource: _____

10. What's on NBC Saturday at 9 P.M.? _____
    _____
    Resource: _____

Bonus Box: Draw a cow shape on the back of this paper. Write as many synonyms for *cow* as you can inside the shape. Use a thesaurus if you need help.

Pointers For...

Completing Assignments

- Know exactly what your assignment is and when it is due.
- Decide how much time you'll need to do the assignment.
- Plan a time to do the assignment.
- Choose a quiet place to work.
- Gather all the books, paper, pencils, markers, and folders you'll need to do the assignment.
- Read the directions for the assignment carefully.
- Decide how much of the assignment you'll finish before taking a break.
- Do the assignment neatly; then check it for mistakes.

Managing Your Time

- Make a daily to-do list. Number the tasks from most to least important. Cross out each task as you complete it.
- Use a weekly planner or a calendar to mark when different assignments are due. Plan your work and play time around these due dates.
- Work on your toughest assignments during the time of day when you work best.
- Make a hard assignment, such as a research project, easier by breaking it down into smaller parts. Decide how much of the assignment you'll need to finish by certain days in order to meet the due date.

Taking Notes

- Listen carefully.
- Write down only the important words and phrases.
- Use abbreviations and symbols whenever you can.
- Show the importance of your notes by numbering them from most important to least important.

Taking Tests

Essay Tests:
- Read the question twice to make sure you understand whether you are to *compare/contrast, define, describe, explain, list,* or *prove* your answer.
- Change the test question into the first sentence of your answer.
- Decide on the best order for the details of your answer.
- Write your answer as a paragraph. Reread your answer to make sure nothing was left out.

True/False Tests:
- Read the whole question before answering it.
- Look for words—such as *all, every, always,* and *never*—that often make a statement false.
- To mark an answer true, all parts of it must be true. If only part of a statement is true, mark it false.

Matching Tests:
- Read both lists before making any matches.
- Unless the directions say you can use an answer more than once, cross out each answer as you match it.

Multiple-Choice Tests:
- Read the directions to find out if you're to look for the *correct* answer or the *best* answer.
- Read *all* the answer choices before deciding on your answer.
- Look for tricky words such as *not, never, except,* and *unless* that can change a question's meaning.

Fill-In-The-Blank Tests:
- Count the number of blanks in each question to know how many words to write for an answer.
- Decide what word or number best answers that question and write it in the blank.

Note To The Teacher: Give a copy of this sheet to each student. Direct him to keep it in his folder or notebook to use as a reference.

Hot Off The Press!

Newspaper Activities Worth Crowing About!

Heard the scoop about the newspaper? It's just filled with a bundle of irresistible learning opportunities! Celebrate National Newspaper Week (the second week in October) with these newsworthy activities from our subscribers.

Headline News

Skill: Reading comprehension, main idea

Reading comprehension practice is as close as the daily headlines with this newsworthy idea! Cut one short article from the newspaper for each pair of students. Remove the headline from the article and number it. Mount the article onto a sheet of paper and number it to correspond with its headline. Have each student pair read its article to determine the main idea. Then have the twosome write an appropriate headline at the top of the page. Finally let the pair compare its headline to the one written by the actual journalist. *Terry Healy—Gifted K–6, Eugene Field Elementary, Manhattan, KS*

Everybody's Got One!

Skill: Point of view

Understanding different points of view can be confusing for students. Make it easy with the following newspaper activity. Collect copies of several different newspapers that are featuring the same lead story. Photocopy the stories. Have students read the stories, then brainstorm a list of the facts that are the same in all versions. Make a separate list of details, quotes, comments, or opinions that are included in some, but not all, of the reports. After discussing the differences in the stories, have students decide which version presents the most accurate picture of the actual event. *Julia Alarie—Gr. 6, Essex Middle School, Essex, VT*

Number Trivia

Skill: Reading for details

There's nothing trivial about this clever newspaper activity! Divide the class into small groups. Give each group a section of a newspaper and a supply of index cards. Direct the group to scan its section and write a list of "How many?" questions that can be answered from information in an article or ad (for example, "How many Supreme Court justices are there?" or "How many miles long is the Mississippi River?"). Direct the group to write each question on the front of an index card and its answer on the back. After discussing the correct answers, place the cards at a center for individual play. Or keep them at your desk to use as a nifty free-time filler. *Denise Amos—Gr. 4, Crestwood Elementary, Crestwood, KY*

Comical Conclusions

Skill: Drawing conclusions

Turn to the funny pages to teach students how to literally draw conclusions! Cut several comic strips from the newspaper. Snip the final frame from each strip. Next glue each comic strip (minus the last frame) to a sheet of construction paper. Place the sheets in a writing center. Direct each student who visits the center to select one sheet and draw her conclusion about the missing frame's events on a piece of paper. Students will love exercising their funny bones as they become conclusive comic strip writers! *Terry Healy—Gifted K–6*

How Does The Paper Measure Up?
Skill: Measurement

Enhance students' understanding of measurement with this easy-to-do activity. Divide a large piece of bulletin-board paper into these four types of measurement: length, weight, area, and volume. Provide each group of four students with a newspaper. Direct the group to look through its paper and find four examples of each type of measurement. Have the group cut out the pictures or text that include the measurement examples and glue them onto the chart in the appropriate sections. *Denise Amos—Gr. 4, Crestwood Elementary, Crestwood, KY*

Length	Weight	Area	Volume

Storage Solution

Storing newspapers is a snap with this tip! Since most activities work best with specific types of articles (such as the sports section, comics, etc.), simply group papers by section instead of edition when storing them! *Denise Amos—Gr. 4*

On The Cutting Edge
Skill: Science

Trying to stay current with science's latest discoveries and technology? Keep yourself and your students on the cutting edge with this idea. Provide each group of students with a newspaper. Have the group clip articles about the most recent scientific developments and place them in a notebook in your science center. Discuss with students how each development might affect daily living. Continue to add articles to the notebook throughout the year. When science fair time rolls around, allow students to use the articles as starting places for project ideas. *Terry Healy—Gifted K–6, Eugene Field Elementary, Manhattan, KS*

Movie Madness
Skill: Elapsed time

Create a little movie madness with the following activity on elapsed time! Provide each student with a movie section of the newspaper. Explain that the student will be allowed to spend from noon until midnight at the movies. Have her use the movie section to create a master schedule of the films she will view, making sure that no times overlap. Have each student share her movie itinerary; then display each one on a bulletin board titled "Time For Movie Madness!" *Phyllis Ellett—Grs. 3–4, Earl Hanson Elementary, Rock Island, IL*

Animals In The News
Skill: Animal classification

Use the newspaper as a handy resource during your animal classification study. Have each student divide a notebook into the five classes of vertebrates; then challenge him to use the newspaper to collect news articles, classified ads, and photographs of animals for each vertebrate group. Besides newspaper pieces, have the student also include a scientific description of each animal group represented in his notebook. As an extension, have the student expand his notebook to include invertebrates. *Phyllis Ellett—Grs. 3–4*

Wanted: Unclassified Details
Skill: Critical thinking, narrative writing

Develop critical-thinking skills with this writing activity using classified ads. Cut out one interesting classified ad for each student. Tape each ad to an index card. Have the student read his ad and think about the events that might have led up to the placement of the ad in the newspaper. As an example, read the classified ad shown below to the class. Then ask questions, such as "Who do you think bought the present?" or "Why was the present being given?" Direct each student to create characters and a plot that explain why the ad was placed. Here's one time when the best place to begin a story is at the end!

Julia Alarie—Gr. 6, Essex Middle School, Essex, VT

Lost Present San Francisco sweatshirt inside, wrapped with yellow cow paper and red bow. Last seen on upper Main Street. Call 363-9876.

Newspaper Poetry
Skill: Writing poetry

Roll the poetry press with this creative-writing activity! Cut out a variety of headlines, sayings, and words from the newspaper. Equally divide the cutouts into plastic zippered bags. Provide each group of two to four students with one bag of clippings, a sheet of poster board, glue, and colorful markers. Instruct each group to create a poem using only the words from its bag. Then have the group glue the poem onto the poster board, and add a title and illustrations. Laminate each group's poem and display it in the classroom or hallway for others to read. *Killeen Jensen—Gr. 6, Tallulah Falls School, Tallulah Falls, GA*

HELP WANTED

In need of a large, black bird who prefers living in open areas, on farmland, at the edges of woodland, and in parks. Clever, alert bird who speaks in 23 crow calls. Diet varies from corn and wheat to insects, small birds, and rodents.

Giggle Over Grammar
Skill: Parts of speech

Students are sure to get a giggle out of grammar with the following activity! Give each child one comic page from the newspaper. Have her choose three comic strips, cut them out, and mount them onto a large sheet of construction paper. On a separate sheet of paper, have her create a chart that lists all the nouns, verbs, adjectives, and adverbs found in the three comic strips. What a fun way to practice the parts of speech! *Michelle Discenza—Gr. 5, Morrisville Year-Round Elementary, Morrisville, NC*

There Can Never Be Another You!
Skill: Descriptive writing, characterization

Here's a fun and easy way to encourage your students to write precise characterizations. Begin by telling students that they have all been selected to spend a year on a space station. Now you and their families need temporary replacements for them at school and at home. Read some sample "Help Wanted" ads from the newspaper. Tell each student to think about the kind of person he is at home and at school. Then have him write an ad describing the characteristics of the person who could take his place for a year. Post the ads on a bulletin board titled "There Can Never Be Another You!"*Julia Alarie—Gr. 6*

FACTS

F	A	C	T	S
		FREE SPACE		

CARD NUMBER _____ NEWSPAPER PAGE _____

QUESTION:

ANSWER:

Create A Business Ad

Skill: Propaganda techniques

From antiques to auto parts, the newspaper advertises just about anything! Gather a variety of advertisements from several newspapers. Divide the class into groups of three to four students. Provide each group with several ads to study. Challenge students to gather information about each ad based on the following questions:

- What is the ad trying to sell?
- What incentive or advantage does the ad offer to the buyer if he buys from this particular business?
- What is visually appealing about the ad?
- After reading the ad, what piece of information stays in your mind?
- In what ways does the ad tempt the buyer?

Bring together the findings of each group by making a chart with students that lists the most effective qualities used in the ads. For example, maybe an eye-catching border caught the reader's attention or alliteration caused a key phrase to stand out in the reader's mind.

Next have each group choose a product that it would like to market. Direct the group to design a newspaper ad for the product using the criteria above discussed by the class. Conclude the activity by having the class vote on the most appealing advertisement. *Debbie Erickson, Waterloo Elementary, Waterloo, WI*

Newspaper FACTS Bingo

Skill: Reading, listening

Help students improve their reading and listening skills with a kid-pleasin' game of Newspaper FACTS Bingo:

1. Give each student one blank bingo card and two question cards as shown, plus two pages of a newspaper. (Give the same two pages to each student.) Also provide a handful of markers, such as dried beans or popcorn kernels.
2. Have each child write a question, an answer, and the page number for each newspaper page on one of her question cards.
3. Collect all question cards and number them.
4. Have each student program her bingo card by writing random numerals in each space (from 1 to the highest numbered question card).
5. Select a card. Read its question, the card number, and the page where the answer can be found.
6. Allow 30 seconds for each student to skim her newspaper page for the answer. Direct her to record the card number and answer on a blank sheet of paper. If the card number is on her bingo card, have her cover that space.
7. Continue until a player covers five spaces in a row and shouts, "Facts!" If the player correctly answered each of the questions in her covered row, declare her a winner and resume the game. *Thomas W. Davis—Gr. 6, Pioneer Park Elementary, Lawton, OK*

The triangle pattern:

Who? _____

What? (2 words) _____

When? (3 words) _____

Where? (4 words) _____

Why? (5 words) _____

Mother Goose In The News

Skill: Writing a newspaper story

Extra, extra! Read all about the escapades of nursery rhyme characters with this activity on writing a newspaper story. Post several nursery rhymes on a bulletin board titled "Mother Goose News." Direct each student to select one of the rhymes; then have him write a news story including information on the who, what, where, when, and why of the rhyme's event. Encourage the student to add a catchy headline to his news story. Post each finished article next to its matching nursery rhyme on the bulletin board. *Terry Healy—Gifted K–6, Eugene Field Elementary, Manhattan, KS*

SPIDER SCARES LITTLE MISS MUFFET!

"Tri" A New Angle

Skill: Summarizing a news story

Challenge students to try a new angle on summarizing with the following idea! Instruct each student to choose one current-events article from the newspaper. After reading the article, direct the student to summarize his story on a copy of the triangle pattern shown. Have students cut out their triangles and glue them to slightly larger construction-paper cutouts. Display the triangle summaries on a bulletin board titled "Give Summarizing A 'Tri'!" *Leigh Taylor Bowman, David Youree Elementary, Smyrna, TN*

NEWSPAPERS?
WHY
READ
SPORTS
HUMOR
SERVICES

The News Near And Far

Skill: Types of newspaper stories

Increase your students' knowledge of the types of newspaper stories with this poster-perfect activity! Begin by sharing with students samples of *local, state, national,* and *international* news articles. Next give each cooperative group a newspaper, making sure each group's paper is for a different day of the week. Have the group peruse its paper and find at least one example for each of the four categories. Then direct the group to glue its articles onto a piece of poster board and label each with its category. Conclude the activity by having each group present its poster to the class. *Elizabeth Day—Gr. 5, James Tansey Elementary, Fall River, MA*

Why Read Newspapers?

Skill: Uses of the newspaper

Introduce students to the many uses of the newspaper with the following bulletin board. Display the title "Why Read Newspapers?" in a crossword format as shown. Trace and cut out letters from an old newspaper to spell words relating to the newspaper—such as *humor, entertainment, sports, news,* and *services.* Add these words to the board. Use the display to springboard a discussion about the many uses of the newspaper. After the discussion, have student groups cut out examples that represent each newspaper use on the display. *Pat Landreth—Gr. 5, Pershing Elementary, Fort Leonard Wood, MO*

Something To Crow About!

The newspaper has all sorts of interesting articles worth crowing about! Stick your nose in a newspaper and choose one article. Read the article carefully. Then answer the questions below.

Title Of Newspaper: _____

Day: _____   Date: _____

Who: Who is this article about? What specific names are mentioned in the article? _____
_____
_____

What: What is this article about? *(Give a brief summary of the article.)* _____
_____
_____
_____

What's the big deal? *(Why is this important to my class, my state, my country, or the world?)* _____
_____
_____
_____

What did you already know about this situation before reading the article? _____
_____
_____

What do you think will happen next? *(in one week, one month, one year)* _____
_____
_____

When: When did the event(s) in this article occur? _____
_____
_____

Where: Where did the event(s) in this article occur? _____
_____
_____

Why: Why do you think this happened? _____
_____
_____

Note To The Teacher: Provide each student with a recent newspaper and one copy of this page. After he completes the activity, have each
student cut out his article and attach it to the back of this page. You may wish to have students complete this activity over several days.

FLYING THE COLORS!

Flags—who doesn't love watching these bold, colorful, and majestic banners unfurling in the breeze? Use the eye-catching allure of flags and the following high-flyin' activities to boost skills in reading, writing, research, and more!

by Wanda Humphries, Blanchard, OK

HONORING OUR FLAG
SKILL: RESEARCHING THE U.S. FLAG

What are the proper ways to honor our national flag? Let students find out for themselves with this class research project. Share with students what the colors, stars, and stripes in our flag represent *(red— hardiness and courage; white—purity and innocence; blue—vigilance, perseverance, and justice; stars—the 50 states; stripes—the 13 original colonies)*. Then divide students into groups of two or three. Have each group use encyclopedias and other reference materials to research a different topic from the list below. To present their findings, have each group write and illustrate a short report to share with the class. After the groups make their presentations, follow up by having each student complete the reproducible project on page 227 to become even more of an expert on flags!

- the appropriate times (days of the week, time of day, weather conditions) to fly the U.S. flag
- holidays during which it is appropriate to fly the flag
- the appropriate places and method for flying the flag outdoors
- the appropriate places and method for hanging the flag indoors
- the proper way to raise and lower the flag
- the meanings of these phrases: *breaking the flag, striking the flag, dipping the flag, flying upside down, flying at half-mast*
- the proper way to carry the flag
- the proper way to salute the flag
- prohibited and permitted uses of the flag
- the proper way to care for the flag

SPELLING WITH FLAGS
SKILL: SPELLING PRACTICE

Let students' fascination with flags spill over into spelling with this fun activity! Refer to an encyclopedia to make a poster of the international alphabet flags. Display the poster in your classroom. Explain to students that these flags stand for letters of the alphabet and are used to send messages from one ship to another at sea. Allow students to practice their spelling words by drawing the flags that spell their words with colored pencils or crayons. Vary this activity by having each child write five or more of her spelling words on paper using the international alphabet. Then have students swap papers and decode their classmates' words.

FLAG DRAWING TO THE LETTER
SKILL: WRITING ACCURATE DIRECTIONS

Help students see the importance of giving accurate directions with this writing activity. Give each student a ruler, crayons or markers, and a 9" x 12" sheet of white construction paper. Have him use the materials to design a flag of his choice. After he completes his flag, ask him to write a paragraph telling how to draw it, including measurements of the flag's dimensions and placement of any symbols. After students have finished writing, collect their paragraphs and give them to another teacher in your grade level. Ask this teacher to have her students follow these written directions to draw the flags; then have her return the directions and resulting drawings to you. When the papers are returned, distribute them to your students. Ask each child to compare the second flag drawing to his original. Students will quickly see the importance of writing clear and specific directions.

225

FLAGGING DOWN THE NEWS
SKILL: READING AND SUMMARIZING CURRENT EVENTS

Use stickers of flags from different states and countries to get students stuck on reading daily newspapers! Divide students into groups of five. Give each group a variety of stickers and 15–20 sheets of newsprint stapled together to make a scrapbook. Ask each group to title its book "Flagging Down The News" and use several stickers to decorate the cover. Have the group also place a single flag sticker at the top center of each right-hand page. Direct each student to be on the lookout for newspaper articles from the states and countries of the flags in his group's book. When a student finds an article, have him bring it in, glue it in his group's scrapbook on the correct page, and summarize it on the facing page. If desired, have groups keep track of the places they're reading about by labeling or coloring them in on a class map. After two weeks, give a small treat to the group that reads and summarizes articles from the largest number of places. *(Note: If you can't find flag stickers, check in an encyclopedia for illustrations of world flags.)*

Barry
Slate

FLAG MOBILES
SKILL: RESEARCHING OTHER COUNTRIES

Expand your flag unit to include other countries and get a brigade of flag mobiles to brighten your classroom! Pair students; then assign each pair a different country. Have each pair:
- staple two 9" x 12" sheets of white construction paper together and illustrate both sides with a model of its country's flag
- research its country and write several fascinating facts on small paper squares that match the country's flag colors
- attach the facts to the bottom of the flag with yarn and transparent tape
- present the mobile and information to the class

After students present their mobiles, hang the projects from your classroom ceiling. To vary this activity, have students research flags related to historical events, such as the Spanish flag carried by Columbus or the flag that flew over the Alamo. On the squares that dangle from the mobiles, have students write information about the event or about the person most associated with it.

226

CREATING A CLASS FLAG
SKILL: DETERMINING ATTRIBUTES

Challenge students to become designers of flags with a whole lot of class! Explain that a flag's colors and symbols have special meanings; then list this information on the board as shown. Next help students think of terms such as *hardworking* and *helpful* that describe the class's attributes. Also discuss colors and symbols that might represent those characteristics. Then divide the class into groups of four. Give each group a 12" x 18" sheet of white construction paper, crayons, scissors, glue, and assorted colors of paper scraps. Direct each group to use its materials and the list of attributes on the board to design a flag with colors and symbols that represent the class. When everyone is finished, have each group present its flag to the class and give their reasons for using particular colors and symbols. Then "fly" a different flag in your room each week until all the flags have been properly displayed.

Color/symbol	What it stands for
red	courage
white	purity
blue	loyalty
green	growth
rising sun	hope for the future
coat of arms	the historical past

A Handbook On Flags

Complete the steps in Parts A and B below to create your very own handbook on flags.

Materials:

encyclopedias or other reference books
16 sheets of 8 1/2" x 11" white paper
crayons, markers, or colored pencils
ruler

pencil
scissors
hole puncher
yarn

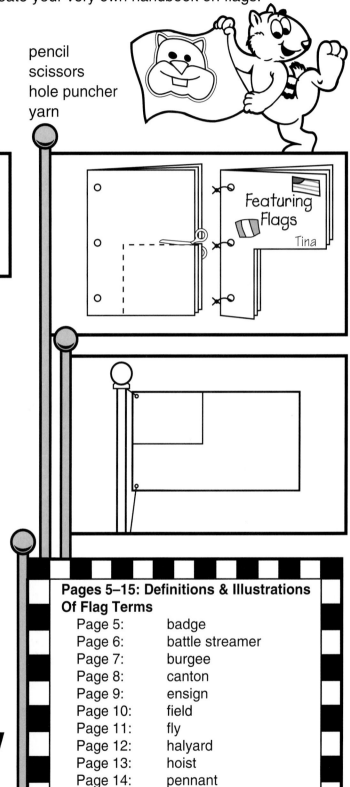

Part A: Making And Assembling The Pages
1. Cut and hole-punch each page as shown.
2. Tie the pages together with yarn.
3. Write your name and a title on the book's cover (top sheet). Decorate the cover.
4. Number the remaining pages 1–15.

Part B: Completing The Pages
Page 1: Diagram Of A Flag
Draw a simple flag (see the illustration), then label it with the following parts:
   a. staff
   b. staff ornament
   c. hoist
   d. halyard
   e. canton
   f. field
   g. fly
   h. fly end

Pages 2–4: Kinds Of Flags
   Page 2: example of a national flag
   Page 3: example of a U.S. state flag
   Page 4: example of a signal flag

Bonus Box: Add additional pages to your handbook for these terms: *fimbriation, guidon, standard,* and *vexillology.*

Pages 5–15: Definitions & Illustrations Of Flag Terms
   Page 5:   badge
   Page 6:   battle streamer
   Page 7:   burgee
   Page 8:   canton
   Page 9:   ensign
   Page 10:   field
   Page 11:   fly
   Page 12:   halyard
   Page 13:   hoist
   Page 14:   pennant
   Page 15:   staff

©The Education Center, Inc. • THE MAILBOX® • Intermediate • April/May 1999 • Key p. 311

Note To The Teacher: Use with "Honoring Our Flag" on page 225. Provide students with encyclopedias or other reference books to complete this project. If desired, adapt this activity by assigning only the parts you wish students to complete and adjusting the number of sheets of paper in the materials list.

CHOCOLATE
—HOW SWEET IT IS!

Take America's favorite flavor and mix it with the following thematic activities, and what do you get? A scrumptiously sweet array of thematic activities on America's favorite sweet treat: chocolate!
ideas by Julia Alarie

Descriptive Drops
Skill: Adjectives, creative writing

This bulletin-board idea is bound to make mouths water in no time! Cover a bulletin board with brown craft paper. For each student, cut out a large, chocolate-drop shape (like a Hershey's® Kisses® candy) from aluminum foil. Mount each cutout on the board titled "How Sweet It Is!" Then give each student a 2" x 11" strip of white paper. Instruct the student to write an adjective or a phrase that describes chocolate on the left end of her strip and her name on the right end. Have each student read her strip to the class, then attach it to her chocolate-drop cutout. For a chocolatey-sweet writing activity, challenge students to use these words and phrases with the following prompts:

- It was a day like any other. That is, until I picked up my pencil and it turned to chocolate! I…
- When my mom said we were having chocolate for dinner, I…
- What's that noise? It sounds like it's coming from my bag of M&M's®!
- It was the strangest candy-bar wrapper I'd ever seen. It…

The Story Of My Life
Skill: Research skills, narrative writing

Blend fact with fantasy in this activity that sharpens writing and research skills. Gather research materials about chocolate. Provide time for students to research and gather information. After research has been completed, explain to students the literary technique of personification: attributing the personalities and actions of humans to things that are not human. Instruct each student to use personification and the data he's collected to write an autobiography of a cocoa bean. Encourage the student to write the autobiography as an interesting life story that might be published in a magazine or presented as a picture book for younger children. Bind the completed stories in a class book titled "The Story Of My Life As Told By A Famous Flavor."

Chocolate Ads
Skill: Propaganda techniques

Help students understand the media's power in advertising a product like chocolate with this thought-provoking idea. About a week before this activity, tell students to be on the lookout for newspaper and magazine advertisements for chocolate. Have students bring in the ads on the day of the activity. Discuss the following four different types of advertisements:

- **Testimonial**—an important or famous person endorses the product
- **Bandwagon**—the buyer is urged to join the winning team; don't be left out
- **Vanity/Transfer**—using the product will make you popular, beautiful, cool, etc.
- **Scientific**—scientific research is used to endorse the product

Write the four categories on the board. Then have each student share one of his ads and tape it under the appropriate category on the board. After each student has shared an ad, discuss the effectiveness of the ads. Finally divide students into pairs. Have each pair create a magazine or television ad—using one of the four types of advertising discussed earlier—for the newest perfection in chocolate confection: Ultimate Bars. Schedule a time for each pair to present its ad. Challenge the class to determine which advertising technique each pair used.

"Chocola-Talk"
Skill: Prefixes and suffixes

You've heard of languages such as French, German, and Spanish—but how about "Chocola-talk"? Introduce students to this new language with an activity that reviews suffixes and prefixes. List several common suffixes and prefixes on the board, such as -ful, -less, -able, -ology, -ist, ex-, re-, semi-, and pre-; then review their meanings. Next assign one of the "Chocola-talk" words below to each student. Instruct the student to write his assigned word in large letters at the top of a sheet of drawing paper. Then have him use the prefix and/or suffix in his assigned word to create a definition for the word. Have him write the word's definition, its pronunciation, and its part of speech underneath the word. Next instruct him to illustrate the word and write a sentence using it. Compile students' pages into a
" 'Chocola-Talk' Picture Dictionary." Encourage students to use the "Chocola-talk" words to sweeten their writings during your chocolate study.

"Chocola-Talk" Word Bank

prechocolate	chocolater
chocolating	chocolatest
underchocolated	chocolatology
postchocolate	chocolateness
antichocolate	extrachocolated
superchocolate	interchocolate
semichocolate	minichocolate
unchocolate	outchocolated
nonchocolate	thermochocolagraph
exchocolate	chocolatization
dechocolated	polychocolated
overchocolated	rechocolate
prochocolate	chocolatehood

This Takes The Cake!
Culminating Activity

As a culminating activity to your chocolate unit, throw a cake-decorating contest! Recruit parent volunteers to help gather and prepare the following supplies for each group of students:
- 1 unfrosted chocolate cake (an 8-inch-diameter round layer)
- 1 can of chocolate frosting
- 1 tube of colored cake-decorating icing and a decorating tip for the tube
- sprinkles and other decorating supplies
- paper plates (one for the cake and one for each student)
- plastic knives and forks
- napkins

Divide students into groups of three or four. Allow a set amount of time for decorating; then let the fun begin! Recruit a panel of judges made up of parents and school staff to distribute awards for The Most Beautiful Cake, The Most Unusual Cake, The Funniest Cake, The Cake With The Best Message, and other unique categories. Take a photograph of each group's creation; then conclude the activity by having students sample their hard work!

Once Upon A Chocolate Time...
Skill: Creative writing

Encourage students' creativity by challenging them to rewrite favorite fairy tales, adding a chocolate touch. Brainstorm a list of common fairy tales with your class. Then divide students into pairs. Instruct each pair to select one fairy tale to rewrite, incorporating chocolate into the story. To help get pairs thinking in the right direction, suggest a few titles, such as Jack And The Cocoa Bean Stalk, King Midas And The Chocolate Touch, and The Elves And The Chocolate Maker. Also suggest that students make subtle changes in story lines instead of rewriting entire tales. For example, the king in Rumpelstiltskin could order his new bride to spin straw into chocolate instead of gold. Schedule a time to have each pair read its revised tale to the rest of the class. As a treat serve assorted chocolate snacks after the readings.

Chocolatology
(chä - k(ə) - lət - ä - lə - jē) n.
The scientific study of chocolate.

A major breakthrough in chocolatology occurred when Dr. Chip accidentally dropped a chocolate bar into a jar of peanut butter.

Be sure to check out the Charlie And The Chocolate Factory book unit on pages 188–193!

REMEMBER THIS!

Memory Tricks That Help Students Remember Important Facts

Remember the silly sentence that helped you learn that Jupiter is closer to the Sun than Saturn? Or the acronym that reminded you of the names of the Great Lakes? Share the following memory tricks from our contributors with your sometimes-forgetful students. They'll never forget the tricks—or *you* for making the learning so much fun!

LANGUAGE ARTS

Remember: P before Q!

- **Rx For Punctuating Dialogue:** When writing dialogue, it's tough for students to remember that punctuation marks that end or interrupt a quotation—such as commas, question marks, and exclamation marks—should go inside the second set of quotation marks (for example: *Mary stated, "An elephant never forgets!"*). Just tell students to remember that since the letter *P* comes before *Q*, the punctuation mark comes before the quotation mark. That should do the trick!

Kim Renfro—Gr. 5, Reisterstown Elementary
Reisterstown, MD

- **Endangered Vowels:** Want students to know exactly what to do when adding a suffix to a word ending in silent *e?* Tell them that the five vowels have now been added to the endangered species list and, therefore, should be conserved and not wasted! Convince students that when they add a suffix beginning with a vowel to a word ending in silent *e,* they should "save," or conserve, the *e* by dropping it to avoid having two vowels (an *e* and an *a*) together. For example, to add *-able* to *love,* drop the *e* in *love* (conserving it) to make *lovable.* Then explain that they can keep the silent *e* in a word when the suffix doesn't begin with a vowel. For example, to add *-ment* to *retire,* keep the *e* to make *retirement.*

Aileen Flaherty—Gr. 5, Woodburn Elementary
Falls Church, VA

MISCELLANEOUS

- **Knuckle Months:** This trick will have students knuckling down to remember the number of days in each month! Have each student hold her hands out in front of her palms down, making two fists as you sketch the illustration shown on the board. Ask students to count the eight knuckles and note the spaces as you label them left to right to represent the months as shown. Explain that the months represented by knuckles have 31 days. Ask students to note the label of the first space on the left hand (February); then tell them to remember that it has the fewest days of any month (28, or 29 in a leap year). Continue by pointing out to students that the next four spaces represent months that have 30 days.

J F M A M J J A S O N D

Susan Phillips, Harwood, ND

- **Silent As A Mouse:** Need students to work quietly for a while? Purchase a stuffed mouse and introduce him to your class as SAAM (Silent As A Mouse). Whenever you want to signal this message to students, just place SAAM on the chalkboard tray or clip him to a wire hung in front of the classroom.

MJ Goewey, River Road Elementary, Eugene, OR

Shhh...

Huron

Ontario

Michigan

Erie

Superior

- **Great Lakes Acronym:** Use a simple word—*homes*—to help students remember the names of the five Great Lakes: *H*—Huron, *O*—Ontario, *M*—Michigan, *E*—Erie, *S*—Superior. Just suggesting the phrase "home sweet home" will bring the names of these lakes instantly to students' minds!

Luree DuChene—Gr. 4
Bates School
Woodhaven, MI

- **Meeting Mimal:** Help students recall five key Midwest states by introducing them to a character named Mimal. On a U.S. map, outline the five states shown. Point out that Minnesota is Mimal's hat, Iowa forms his face, Missouri is his belly, Arkansas forms his legs, and Louisiana contains his boots. Have each student make his own picture of Mimal by outlining these states on a copy of a U.S. map. Follow up by having students write creative stories about Mimal's adventures in the Midwest.

Therese Durhman—Gr. 5, Mountain View Elementary
Hickory, NC

SCIENCE

- **Simplifying Simple Machines:** The first letters of the words in this silly sentence make learning the names of simple machines a piece of cake! Write "I like playing soccer with Will" on the board. (If desired, personalize the sentence by substituting the name of a current student whose name starts with *w* for *Will*.) Underline the letters as shown; then list each letter and the simple machine it represents below the sentence. It's so simple!

Tamara King—Gr. 5
Appleton Village School
Appleton, ME

Inclined plane

Lever

Pulley

Screw

Wedge

Wheel and axle

- **Planet Placement:** Use this silly sentence to help your students remember the correct order of the planets from the sun: "My very exciting mother just sat under Nancy's poster." All students have to do is match the first letter in each word with the name of a planet!

Melissa Kienzl—Gr. 4, Pleasant Valley Elementary
Kunkletown, PA

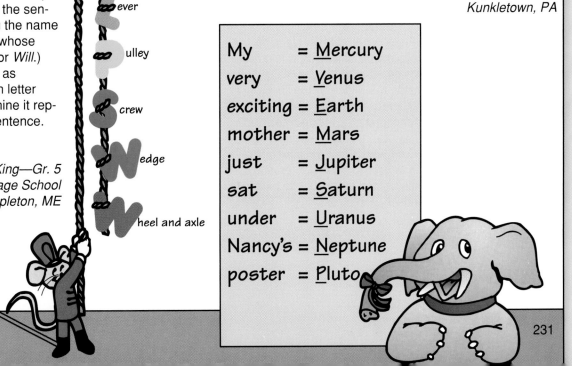

My	= Mercury
very	= Venus
exciting	= Earth
mother	= Mars
just	= Jupiter
sat	= Saturn
under	= Uranus
Nancy's	= Neptune
poster	= Pluto

$9 \times 8 = 72$

- **Finger Calculators:** Have students let their fingers do the calculating to master multiplying by nine! To demonstrate how to multiply 9 x 8 using your fingers, hold both hands up and bend down the eight finger (the middle finger of your right hand). Explain that this bent finger represents the multiplier *8*. Wiggle each finger in turn as you count left to right from 1 to 7 to reach the bent finger. Explain that these seven fingers represent seven tens, or 70. Then count the two fingers to the right of the bent finger, explaining that these fingers represent two ones. So the product of nine times eight is 72. It won't take students long to get the hang of this trick!

Tammie Boone—Grs. 5–6, Sheldon Middle School, Sheldon, IA

I'm MADD about this memory trick!

$$\begin{array}{r} \overset{2}{2}6 \\ \times 4 \\ \hline 4 \end{array}$$

- **MADD About You!:** A teaching gimmick disguised as a simple warning can help students remember to multiply before adding in a regrouped number. Tell students when you say, "Don't make me MADD!" that you're not upset—you're just prompting them to <u>multiply</u> first, then <u>add</u>. For example, in the problem shown, students should multiply 2 times 4 before adding in the 2 that was carried. As a visual reminder, post MADD's meaning: <u>M</u>ultiply first, then <u>ADD</u>!

*Debra Dellinger, Deyton Primary School
Spruce Pine, NC*

$$\frac{7}{4}$$

$$\begin{array}{r} 1 \text{ r } 3 \\ 4\overline{)\,7} \\ -4 \\ \hline 3 \end{array} = 1\frac{3}{4}$$

- **Tumbling Fractions:** If students are struggling with changing improper fractions to mixed numbers, this silly story can set them straight! Write an improper fraction such as 7/4 on the board. Then tell students this tale as you point to the numerals and demonstrate the steps: *The denominator 4 is a little guy who has a much larger guy—the numerator 7—standing on his shoulders. Since this little guy can't hold up a big fellow like the numerator, the 7 falls off the little guy's shoulders and into the division house. The little guy teases him by saying, "Nanny, nanny, pooh, pooh! I'm going to divide you!" Then the little guy divides himself into the numerator to make a mixed number!* Silly as it sounds, it works!

*Kim Renfro—Gr. 5
Reisterstown Elementary
Reisterstown, MD*

- **Why Did Dad Make Nachos?:** This probing question can help students remember the steps for finding fractional parts of whole numbers. To explain what the first letter of each word in *<u>W</u>hy <u>d</u>id <u>D</u>ad <u>m</u>ake <u>n</u>achos?* stands for, demonstrate how to find 2/3 of 21 as shown. Not only does this trick work, but it also encourages students to create their own sentences to fit other functions!

*Anne D. Petersen—Gr. 6, Blue Ridge Elementary
Harpers Ferry, WV*

$$\frac{2}{3} \text{ of } 21$$

$$21 \div 3 = 7$$

(<u>w</u>hole number 21 <u>d</u>ivided by the <u>d</u>enominator 3 equals 7)

$$7 \times 2 = 14$$

(7 <u>m</u>ultiplied by the <u>n</u>umerator 2 equals 14)

- **Moving Decimals:** Are your students stumped by which direction to move the decimal when multiplying or dividing decimals by multiples of ten? This simple explanation will make it crystal clear! Help students generalize that since the letter *d* is at the left end of the alphabet, they should move the decimal point to the *left* when dividing. Likewise, since the letter *m* is closer to the right end of the alphabet, they should move the decimal point to the *right* when multiplying. You'll be amazed at how easily students grasp this confusing concept!

Rhonda H. Hattaway—Gr. 5
Red Level School, Red Level, AL

Kiss Henry Dirk's mother during cow milking.

- **Ordering Metric Units:** If your students wrestle with ordering metric units correctly by size, then this hilarious sentence will end their conflict! Write this sentence on the board: *Kiss Henry Dirk's mother during cow milking.* Underneath the sentence, record which metric unit the first letter of each word represents as shown. Then display the sentence in a prominent place until students no longer need it as a reminder.

Tammie Boone—Grs. 5–6, Sheldon Middle School, Sheldon, IA

Slow down!
(To change from <u>s</u>maller to <u>l</u>arger units, <u>d</u>ivide.)

Lost some money?
(To change from <u>l</u>arger to <u>s</u>maller units, <u>m</u>ultiply.)

- **Making Metric Conversions:** If converting one metric unit to another is tripping up your students, then use a few simple words to come to their aid! Tell students to remember the sentence *Slow down!* so they'll remember this tip: when changing from <u>s</u>maller to <u>l</u>arger units, <u>d</u>ivide. Then have them remember the question *Lost some money?* to help them remember that when changing from <u>l</u>arger to <u>s</u>maller units, they should <u>m</u>ultiply. When learning is made this simple, converting units is a snap!

Lisa Carlson—Gr. 4, Bear Path School, Hamden, CT

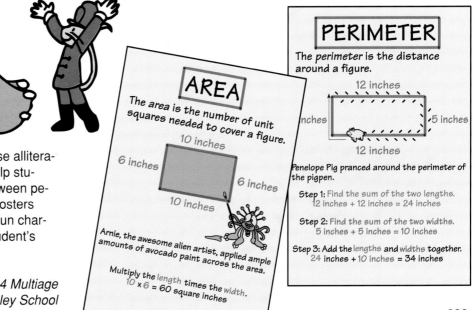

AREA

The area is the number of unit squares needed to cover a figure.

10 inches
6 inches
6 inches
10 inches

Arnie, the awesome alien artist, applied ample amounts of avocado paint across the area.

Multiply the *length* times the *width*.
10 x 6 = 60 square inches

PERIMETER

The *perimeter* is the distance around a figure.

12 inches
inches
5 inches
12 inches

Penelope Pig pranced around the perimeter of the pigpen.

Step 1: Find the sum of the two lengths.
12 inches + 12 inches = 24 inches

Step 2: Find the sum of the two widths.
5 inches + 5 inches = 10 inches

Step 3: Add the lengths and widths together.
24 inches + 10 inches = 34 inches

- **Picturing Perimeter And Area:** Use alliteration and eye-catching posters to help students remember the difference between perimeter and area. Display the two posters shown. One quick glance at these fun characters will be all it takes to jog a student's memory about perimeter and area!

Kerry and Linda Scaletta—Grs. 3–4 Multiage
Frank C. Whiteley School
Hoffman Estates, IL

FILL 'ER UP!

Our Subscribers' Favorite Five-Minute Fillers

$8 + 1 - 7 \times 3 + 4 - 6 = ?$

4!

Strings Of Math Facts

Skill: Mental math

Got a little time to spare before the next lesson? Fill it with some quick mental-math practice! Call out a multistep problem with an answer of 10 or less; then have students show the answer with their fingers. Begin with simple problems, such as $5 + 3 - 2$. Then gradually advance to a more difficult problem, like $4 + 2 - 3 \times 1 + 5 + 2 - 4$. Scan the classroom to identify students who are having trouble solving the problem. If several students are having difficulty, quickly throw out a problem, such as 6×0, to get everyone back on track.

Susan Conway—Gr. 4, Holliston Middle School, Holliston, MA

I'll Give The Answer...You Give The Question!

Skill: Reviewing concepts

For a filler that takes its cue from a popular television game show, give students an answer and have them come up with logical questions to match it! For example, provide an answer related to social studies, such as "George Washington." Students could respond by asking, "Who was the first president of the United States?" or "Who commanded the Continental Army during the Revolutionary War?" Accept any question that fills the bill. You'll have given students a quick review *and* assessed them at the same time!

Lori Brandman—Gr. 5, Shallowford Falls Elementary
Alpharetta, GA

Kids And Questions

Skill: Critical thinking

Fill spare minutes with the help of The Kids' Book Of Questions by Gregory Stock, Ph.D. (Workman Publishing Co., Inc.; 1988). Choose from more than 250 questions about topics such as bravery, why parents act the ways they do, and what gets on students' nerves. Be prepared for a lively discussion every time you crack open this handy resource!

Patricia Altmann, Carmel, NY

scratch scratch

What is the hardest thing about growing up?

License-Plate Patter

Skills: Critical thinking, decoding

It's Where YOU Live!

DSINER

YOUR STATE

Encourage students to don their thinking caps with this brain-teasing time filler! Copy a message from a vanity license plate onto a pattern of your state's plate (see the illustration). Post this plate in a visible spot in the classroom. Challenge students to decipher its message and tell why they think the driver of the vehicle wanted that particular word or phrase on his license plate. Honk if you love this fun filler!

Judy Lamac—Grs. 3–4, Pleasant Hill School, Palatine, IL

Touch Three

Skill: Listening

Spend extra minutes between subjects strengthening students' listening skills. Name or describe three items in your classroom. (For example, say, "I see an object that is yellow and round, an object that is square, and an object that is rectangular and tan.") Select a child to stand up and touch the objects you named. If the student touches all three objects, allow her to describe three different objects for a classmate to touch. If the student does not touch all three objects, have her choose someone to take her place. To make this game more challenging, require that the student touch the objects in the correct sequence!

Stacy L. Fritz—Grs. 2–6, Lehigh Carbon Community College, Kutztown, PA

elephant
trip
pretty
yellow

String Of Words

Skill: Building vocabulary

Spend a spot of free time with a quick round of this vocabulary-stretching game! Write a vocabulary word from a current unit on the chalkboard. Direct each student to write a word on his paper that starts with the last letter of the word on the board. For example, if you wrote envelope, the student could write elephant. Have students add to their lists, starting each word with the last letter of the preceding word. Declare the student with the longest list the winner. As an extra challenge, require that the words students write have four or more letters or that they be related to a particular unit of study.

Patricia Altmann, Carmel, NY

Continental Lineup

Skill: Reviewing geographical features

Fill the minutes before lining up your class with a quick geographical review. Divide students into six teams; then assign each team a different continent (excluding Antarctica). Have each group member name a different country, city, or geographic feature found in his assigned continent. Award a point for each correct answer. Then line the groups up in the order of their point totals!

Terry Healy—Gifted K–6, Eugene Field Elementary, Manhattan, KS

a s t n r d

sat
tan
rat
ran
strand

Jumbled Letters

Skill: Building vocabulary

The only materials you'll need for this fast-paced filler are vowels and consonants! Divide your class into groups of three to four students. Have one group select one vowel and five consonants for all groups to use. Direct each group to build as many words from those six letters as possible (with or without repeating letters) before time is up. Have a dictionary handy to check any questionable words. Declare the team that builds the most words the winner. To vary this activity, allow teams to earn bonus points for every word they use correctly in a sentence.

Rosemary Linden—Gr. 4, Royal Valley Elementary, Hoyt, KS

Odd One Out

Skill: Critical thinking, reviewing subject matter

What can you do with an extra minute or two? Give students one dose of thinking skills and one of review! Prepare a list of three- or four-word sets of related terms from a current unit of study. To each set, add an unrelated word (see the examples). Then divide your students into two teams. Read aloud one set of words. Award one point to the first team to both identify the unrelated word and tell why it does not belong. Play as long as time permits or until all the word sets have been used.

Terry Healy—Gifted K–6
Eugene Field Elementary
Manhattan, KS

noun, verb, adjective, abbreviation

reaper, thresher, plow, trolley car

Jamestown, Plymouth, Los Angeles, St. Augustine

Harriet Tubman, Frederick Douglass, Jefferson Davis, William Lloyd Garrison

executive, politician, judicial, legislative

Brain Games

Skill: Reviewing subject matter

Enlist the help of your students' parents to provide plenty of learning for every extra minute. Early in the year, ask parents to donate commercial trivia games that include question cards appropriate for intermediate students, such as Brain Quest®. (Also look for games at yard sales and discount stores.) When you have a break in the class routine, pull out a few question cards and challenge students to come up with the answers. Award one point for each correct answer and three points for each correctly answered question that relates to a topic the class has recently studied.

Mary T. Spina—Gr. 4
Bee Meadow School
Whippany, NJ

Who was the sixteenth president?

Book Talks

Skill: Reading motivation

Got some time to spare before the next lesson? How about advertising a great book! Pull a novel you think students shouldn't miss from your classroom library and present a brief book talk about it. Then read aloud a short portion of the book that is sure to grab students' interest. Your efforts will be well worth it when you discover a child taking the bait and digging deep into the book's covers!

Patricia Altmann
Carmel, NY

The Hot Seat

Skill: Oral communication

Cat got your tongue? Not with this fun filler! Give each student a slip of paper to label with a topic she thinks would be fun or interesting to talk about. Collect the slips in an empty coffee can labeled "Hot-Seat Topics." Also place an empty chair labeled "Hot Seat" at the front of the room and another labeled "Thinking Chair" in the back. When you have a few spare minutes, ask a volunteer to pull a slip from the can; then direct her to sit in the Thinking Chair to ponder what she'd like to say about the slip's topic. After two minutes, have the student move to the Hot Seat. Then have another classmate pull a slip, move to the Thinking Chair, and plan his talk while the Hot-Seat child speaks for two minutes on her topic. At the end of the first speaker's turn, have the Thinking-Chair child move to the Hot Seat and start talking. You can bet everyone will be talking about this terrific time filler!

the school dress code

pollution

pets

little sisters

the Green Bay Packers

Pat Twohey–Gr. 4, Old County School, Smithfield, RI

Magnetic-Letter Spelling
Skill: Spelling

Here's a time filler that's sure to attract a strong interest in spelling! Affix two sets of magnetic letters to your chalkboard, arranging one set on each half of the board. Divide your students into two teams; then have one player from each team come to the board. Call out a spelling word and direct these two players to arrange the magnetic letters to spell the word. If the word requires duplicates of any vowel or consonant, direct the players to write in those letters with chalk as needed. The first player to spell the word correctly earns one point for his team. Play as long as time allows or until every student has had a turn. Declare the team with the most points the winner.

Patricia Altmann
Carmel, NY

Daily Chuckle
Skill: Interpretive reading, vocabulary

Use a little lighthearted humor to sharpen reading and vocabulary skills with this easy-to-do idea. Save favorite comic strips and cartoons you've read in a special file. Or invite your students to bring in their favorite strips. Each morning post a different strip; then challenge students to be ready to explain the comic's joke to the rest of the class. Point out that a student may need to head to the nearest dictionary if the strip contains a new vocabulary word. During the day, choose a child to read and interpret the strip for the class. Not only does this activity improve interpretive reading and vocabulary skills, but it also provides a great opportunity to share a giggle or two with your students.

Judy Lamac—Grs. 3–4
Pleasant Hill School
Palatine, IL

What If...?
Skill: Predicting outcomes

For a time filler that's anything *but* run-of-the-mill, have students ponder "What if…" questions. In advance, make a list of questions that inspire students to imagine what the world might have been like if specific historic events had turned out differently. For example, what if Columbus had sailed east instead of west? Or if Benjamin Franklin hadn't flown his kite and discovered electricity? Write each question on a different index card. Whenever there's extra time between subjects, pull out a card to read aloud. Have each student respond to the question by writing a three- to four-sentence answer on his paper. Collect students' completed papers; then read aloud the responses. What if...students ask to do this activity again and again?

Terry Healy—Gifted K–6
Eugene Field Elementary
Manhattan, KS

What if Columbus had sailed east instead of west?

Whaddaya Think?

Skill: Critical thinking, constructing a bar graph

Use this double-duty time filler to hone critical-thinking skills and provide practice with bar graphs! First develop a list of yes/no questions from a current unit the class is studying or from a favorite novel. For example: Was Columbus a hero (or a villain)? Are all squares rectangles? Should Matt have gone with Attean and his tribe when winter came? Next write one question from your list and its responses on the board as shown. Give each student a sticky note on which to explain his answer. Randomly select several students to share their answers and the reasons for their responses. Then have each student in turn come to the board and place his sticky note in the appropriate row. The result will be an instant graph of students' opinions. If time permits, ask another question and build a second graph.

Terry Healy—Gifted K–6
Eugene Field Elementary
Manhattan, KS

What's The Password?

Skill: Building vocabulary

The next time you've got some extra time between subjects, play a quick game of "Password"! Divide students into two teams. Have one player from each team come to the board and sit with his back to it. Write a word, such as *flag,* on the board. Have one member from Team A give his teammate a one-word clue (for example, *stripes*) to help his teammate identify the word. Do not allow hand gestures or sounds to be used in clue giving. If the player correctly identifies the word, award one point to Team A; then write a new word on the board and give Team B a turn. If the player can't correctly identify the word, have a member of Team B give a second clue (for example, *stars*). Continue until the word on the board is guessed. Use this game to review general or seasonal vocabulary words, or to review new words in social studies or science.

Susan Conway—Gr. 4
Holliston Middle School
Holliston, MA

Sweet Dismissals

Skill: Reviewing the day's activities

Sending students home at the end of the day will have its sweet reward with this activity! While packing up, have students share facts or information they learned during the day with the class. To sharpen listening skills, require that each student who participates must not repeat a fact already given by a classmate. Reward each child who shares a fact with a piece of sugarless candy. Not only will your students satisfy their sweet tooths, but you'll sneak in a quick review and some great practice with listening skills!

Lori Brandman—Gr. 5
Shallowford Falls Elementary, Alpharetta, GA

GAME PLANS

GAME PLANS

Coordinate Grid Tic-Tac-Toe

Reinforce the basics of coordinate graphing with this fun variation of tic-tac-toe. On the chalkboard or overhead projector, draw a 7 x 7 grid as shown. Place a dot at one of the graph's intersections to indicate the origin (x, y = 0, 0). Then divide your class into two teams. Have the teams take turns giving you a coordinate pair. Mark an X for Team 1 and an O for Team 2 at the intersection indicated by the coordinate pair given by the group. When a team gets four marks in a row vertically, horizontally, or diagonally, circle that row and award the team a point. Continue marking Xs and Os on the grid and awarding points until it is no longer possible for a group to get four in a row. Tic-tac-toe was never more "math-tastic"!

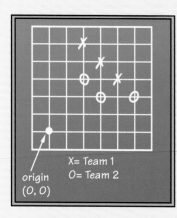

X = Team 1
O = Team 2

origin (0, 0)

Game Variations:
- Don't explain to students how to find a coordinate pair location on the grid. Instead, have them figure out how to indicate the coordinates by studying where each mark falls on the grid.
- Have the grid blocks represent increments of two, five, or ten rather than one.
- Move the origin up and to the right to incorporate an area of negative integers.
- Laminate sheets of grid paper; then place dry-erase markers and the grids at a learning center so students can play in their free time.

Beth Gress—Gr. 6, Mt. Gilead, OH

Zowie!

Reviewing parts of speech has never been easier than with this fast-paced game! Direct each student to fold a lined sheet of paper into four vertical columns; then have him label the columns with the words *Adjective, Noun, Verb,* and *Adverb* as shown. Call out a letter of the alphabet. Have each student write one adjective, one noun, one verb, and one adverb that begin with that letter in the columns. The first student to fill in the line for that letter jumps up and calls, "Zowie!" Write the student's words on the board to check for accuracy. Then let that student call out a letter for the next round. After students have played several rounds, collect the papers and check to see who may need extra help. Zowie! What positively perfect parts-of-speech practice!

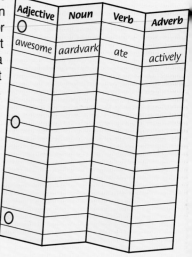

Adjective	Noun	Verb	Adverb
O			
awesome	aardvark	ate	actively
O			
O			

Pat Twohey—Gr. 4
Old County Road School
Smithfield, RI

Dingbat

Use this nifty adaptation of Old Maid to help your students review the states and their capitals. Label index cards with the states and capitals (one capital or state per card). Label one card with the word *Dingbat* to use as the "Old Maid." Make several of these card sets. Divide your class into groups of three to six players. Give each group a set of cards. Select one child in each group to deal the cards in her deck to her group members. Before play begins, have each student discard from her hand any correct matches of a state and its capital. Have the player to the left of the dealer begin play by selecting a card from another player, continuing to discard any matches she may have. Continue play in this fashion. The first student with no cards and all of her matches correct wins the game. Provide a key so students can check their matches. If you make additional sets of Dingbat cards, this game can be just the "ding" for reviewing lots of other skills!

Killeen Jensen—Gr. 6
Tallulah Falls School
Tallulah Falls, GA

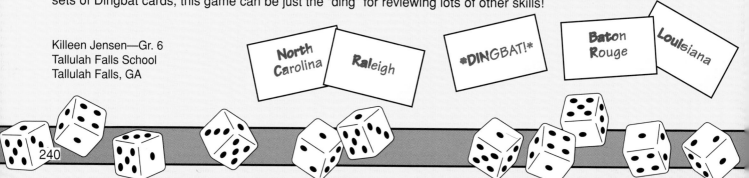

North Carolina | Raleigh | *DINGBAT!* | Baton Rouge | Louisiana

Sentence Relay

This whole-class game will make practicing punctuation and capitalization "ree-lay" fun! Write sentences from a current class novel or the newspaper on index cards (one sentence per card), omitting all punctuation and capitalization. Divide your class into two teams. Have each team form a relay line at the chalkboard. On your signal have the first student in each line choose a card and write its sentence on the board, inserting the correct punctuation and capitalization. When he's finished, have the student go to the back of his team's line; then have the next teammate in his line choose a card. Allow a player to make corrections to his team's sentences, if needed, during his turn. Continue play until all players have had a turn. Give teams one point for each correct sentence. Declare the team with the most points the winner.

Christine Juozitis—Gr. 4
Thomas Jefferson School
Binghamton, NY

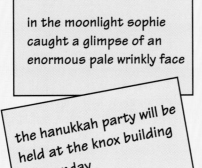

in the moonlight sophie caught a glimpse of an enormous pale wrinkly face

the hanukkah party will be held at the knox building on monday

Reviewing In The Round

What do you get when you combine a circle of students, a gift-wrapped package, and music? A unique way to review any subject! To prepare for this game, write review questions on slips of paper. Place a class supply of homework passes inside a box; then wrap this box with layers of gift wrap (one layer for each question). As you wrap, tape a review question outside each layer of gift wrap.

To play, seat students in a circle. Start the music and have students pass the gift clockwise around the circle. When the music stops, ask the student holding the gift to read aloud the question taped to the outside. If he answers the question correctly, allow him to unwrap that layer of gift wrap. Also tell him to hang on to his question slip. If he answers incorrectly, have him pass the gift to the player on his left. After the question has been answered correctly, restart the music and continue play. Let the student who correctly answers the last question open the box and hand out homework passes to classmates holding question slips. What a fun way to wrap up a review game!

Miriam Krauss—Gr. 5, Bais Yaakov Of Brooklyn, Brooklyn, NY

Strategic Spin-Off

Need a fun game for a rainy day? Pair students; then give each pair a laminated hundreds chart, a paper clip, red and blue paper squares, and a cut-out circle divided into 12 sections as shown. Have each player choose one color of paper squares to use as markers. Then share the following directions with your students:

Steps:
1. In turn, make a spinner with the paper clip and a pencil (see the illustration).
2. Spin twice and combine the digits you spin to make a numeral. For example, spinning the digits 3 and 2 could result in 32 or 23; spinning 0 and 7 could make 07 or 70.
3. Cover that numeral's square on the hundreds chart with one of your markers. To cover 100, you must spin "Lose a turn" twice in one turn.
4. If the only numerals you can create are already covered, your turn is over.
5. Continue playing until one player covers four numerals in a row in any direction or until time is up. If time is called before a player gets four numerals in a row, the player with the most covered squares is the winner.

Sandra Hillstrom—Gr. 5, Lincoln School, Spring Valley, IL

1	2	3	4	5	6	7	8	9	10
11	12	13	14	15	16	17	18	19	20
21	22	23	24	25	26	27	28	29	30
31	32	33	34	35	36	37	38	39	40
41	42	43	44	45	46	47	48	49	50
51	52	53	54	55	56	57	58	59	60
61	62	63	64	65	66	67			
71	72	73	74	75	76				
81	82	83	84	85	86				
91	92	93	94	95	96				

GAME PLANS

The Directions Game

Use this fun whole-class game to reinforce cardinal and intermediate directions! Send one student just outside your classroom door. Select another child to identify an object inside the room. When the first student returns, begin calling on his classmates one at a time to lead him to the object using cardinal or intermediate directions. For example, one student might say, "Go north five steps." Another child may offer, "Walk eight steps southeast." When the student finds the chosen item, let him choose the next player to leave the room.

Sherri Kaiser—Gr. 4
Walnut Grove Elementary
Suwanee, GA

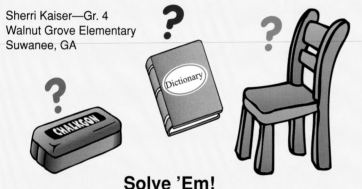

Solve 'Em!

Energize your next math review with this spin-off of the popular classroom game Seven Up. Have each student write his name and a math problem on one side of an index card; then have him write its solution on the back. Next choose ten students to be "up." Have these students stand in front of the class while the others put their heads down on their desks. Direct each up student to lay his index card on the desktop of a classmate whose head is down. When each up student has given his card away, call, "Solve 'em!" A student with a card on his desk solves that card's problem on scrap paper and turns the card over to check his answer. If correct, he changes places with the student who wrote the problem. If incorrect, he remains in his seat. Before advancing to round 2, solve each problem together on the board. Also allow each up student to write another problem on a second card.

Marsha Schmus—Gr. 4, Chambersburg, PA

Spelling Battleship

Make spelling memorable with a game that spells *F-U-N!* To prepare, write each child's name on a slip of paper and place it in a container. Make a master of the gameboard shown below; then make several copies. Also draw a large copy of the gameboard on chart paper and post it on the chalkboard.

On game day, prepare one copy of the gameboard by writing each of the week's spelling words in a square. Also have students draw their own grids on their papers using the chart as a guide. Then follow these steps to play:

1. Pull a name from the container and let that student guess a coordinate pair, such as "G, 6." If it's a *miss* (a square without a spelling word in it), say, "Miss." Have each student x out that space on his grid while you do the same on your master copy.
2. If it's a *hit* (a square with a spelling word in it), say, "Hit." Then call out the word and have each student write it on his grid in the box that was called. Have the student who made the hit spell the word aloud. If he spells it correctly, that ship is sunk, and each student circles it on his grid. If the word is misspelled, another student calls that coordinate and tries to spell the word.
3. The game ends when all the words have been spelled correctly, or sunk. When the class sinks all of your ships, award one point, with ten points earning the class ten extra minutes of recess!

Game Variation: Instead of spelling words, write the names of states in the grids. Have students name a state's capital to sink it.

Matt Schoenfelder—Gr. 5, Schaeffer Elementary, Lancaster, PA

	1	2	3	4	5	6
A				treaty		tremble
B		tardy				
C			treachery			trapeze
D					talent	
E		treatment				
F				token		
G	tousled					tour

Spelling Battleship

Lifesavers...
Management Tips
For Teachers

LIFESAVERS...
management tips for teachers

First-Day Folders

Need an effective system for organizing the mountain of papers that are sent home the first day of school? Purchase one pocket folder for each child and write his name on the front. Place papers that don't need to be returned in the left-hand pocket. Place papers that need to be filled out and returned in the right-hand pocket. (Make a few extra folders for new students who arrive later in the school year.) Have students return the folders the next day with the completed paperwork inside. Simply pull and sort the forms from each returned folder. Then use the emptied folders as portfolios, for storing computer lab work, or as homework folders.

Nancy Curl—Gr. 6, Olson Middle School, Tabernacle, NJ

Easy Anecdotal Records

Keep track of student behavior with this simple idea. List each student's name down the left-hand side of a lined sheet of paper; then draw a dateline at the top of the page. Duplicate a supply of this sheet. At the beginning of each day, date a clean sheet and place it on a clipboard. Throughout the day, make notations on positive and negative behaviors you observe for each child. At the end of the day, place the completed sheet in a three-ring binder. You'll be surprised at how this easy idea will help you focus on each child, as well as how informative the charts are at parent-conference time.

Diane Moser—Gr. 5
Sangre Ridge Elementary, Stillwater, OK

Quick Plans

Want to make writing lesson plans practically painless? I purchase a three-ring binder, a supply of photo-album filler pages (each of which holds six 3" x 5" photographs), and six different-colored packs of 3" x 5" index cards. Next I assign each subject area a different color. On the front of each card, I write a lesson's objective and assignment. On the back, I list the materials and directions. Then I slide the six cards into the slots of one album page. If I get behind in a lesson, I just pull out that card and move it to another day's page. No more erasing, whiting-out, or crossing out big blocks in my plan book. At the end of the month, I pull out the cards and store them in a file box for next year.

Kim Brown—Gr. 4
Bixby, OK

Red Light/Green Light

How do you quickly remind students when and when not to talk in class? Simply use the red light/green light system! Have students brainstorm a list of times when it's okay to talk softly in class. List these times on a large green poster-board circle. Then brainstorm a list of times when it's not okay to talk in class. List these times on a large red poster-board circle. Glue the circles together back-to-back; then display the stoplight in the room. Throughout the day flip to the appropriate color as a reminder.

Rosemary Linden—Gr. 4
Royal Valley Elementary
Hoyt, KS

Whose Job Is It Anyway?

Assigning classroom jobs has never been easier than with this handy helpers display. Tack one large calendar for each classroom job on a bulletin board. Post the name of a different job above each calendar. Beneath each calendar staple a brief description of the job. Assign students to class jobs by writing a name (or names, depending on the job) in each school-day box on each calendar. That should stop all cries of "Whose job is it anyway?"

Andrea McMahan
Munford Middle School
Munford, TN

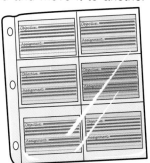

LIFESAVERS...
management tips for teachers

Chart And Poster Notebook

Organize your charts and posters in a snap! Begin by sorting charts and posters by subject. Take a picture of each; then mount the photos in a notebook, divided and labeled by subject. Store the charts and posters in a large flat box, one for each subject area. When it's time to teach a new lesson, you'll have a quick reference of the materials you have on hand.

Sherri Roberts—Gr. 4, Roosevelt Traditional School
Hutchinson, KS

Pick A Partner, Any Partner

Looking for a new way to pair partners for class activities? Simply take a photo of each student; then cut out each child's body and mount it on a 2" x 4" strip of paper. Laminate the paper strips. When you need to pair students, hold the photo strips facedown in your hand like a deck of cards and allow each student to draw a strip. What a picture-perfect way to place students into pairs!

Christine King—Gr. 5
The Grammar School
Wilbraham, MA

Stop Signs

Encourage students to put a stop to inappropriate behavior with the following idea. Cut several small stop sign shapes from red poster board. Label the signs with white chalk or crayon before laminating them. If a student misbehaves during a lesson, place a stop sign on her desk. When the behavior stops, remove the sign. If the sign is still on the desk at recess time, the student loses part or all of her recess. The stop sign serves as a silent warning without any interruption in a lesson.

Brenda Fendley—Gr. 4, Blossom Elementary, Blossom, TX

Class Captain

Finding yourself frustrated by the everyday tasks that nibble away at precious planning time? Place a laminated checklist of daily jobs—such as taking attendance, erasing the board, and passing out school notices—in a binder. Each morning choose a student to be the day's class captain. Instruct the class captain to use a wipe-off marker to check off each job as he completes it throughout the day. The next morning wipe the checklist clean and choose another child to be the day's class captain. Now that's a time-saver worth saluting!

Paige Baker—Gr. 4, Barrington Elementary, Austin, TX

Is It Done Yet?

Project-based instruction is becoming more and more popular in the classroom. Help your students evaluate their projects before turning them in with this idea. When a project is first assigned, give students the requirements and criteria that will be used to grade it. Then share the following acronym to help students know when their projects are "done": **D**etails, **O**riginality, **N**eatness, **E**diting. Provide each student with a copy of the checklist on page 251. Discuss each term so that the student knows exactly what is expected of him. Before turning in his final project, have the child complete the checklist and attach it to his project. With this easy-to-use form, students will gain important insight about the qualities of a good finished project.

Meg Turner
Durham, NC

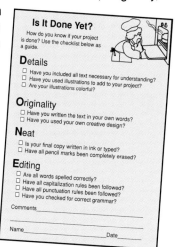

Is It Done Yet?
How do you know if your project is done? Use the checklist below as a guide.

Details
☐ Have you included all text necessary for understanding?
☐ Have you used illustrations to add to your project?
☐ Are your illustrations colorful?

Originality
☐ Have you written the text in your own words?
☐ Have you used your own creative design?

Neat
☐ Is your final copy written in ink or typed?
☐ Have all pencil marks been completely erased?

Editing
☐ Are all words spelled correctly?
☐ Have all capitalization rules been followed?
☐ Have all punctuation rules been followed?
☐ Have you checked for correct grammar?

Comments_____

Name_____Date_____

LIFESAVERS...
management tips for teachers

Pick A Partner

Forming cooperative groups is a cinch with this simple idea. All you need is a set of index cards.

- For pairs, program pairs of cards with synonyms, antonyms, homophones, states and capitals, or number-sentence parts (such as "5 x 6 =" and "30").
- For groups, program sets of index cards (four cards for forming groups of four, five for groups of five, etc.) with such items as geometric shapes, foods in the food groups from the Food Guide Pyramid, and colors.

Laminate the cards and store each set in a labeled Ziploc® bag. To change groups or partners, place a set of cards in a container and shake it well. Then have each child draw a card and find its mate(s). If you have an odd number of students, add a "Free Choice" card to each batch, which allows its holder to work with the pair or group of his choice.

Carol Unanski—Gr. 4, Indian Hill Elementary, Holmdel, NJ

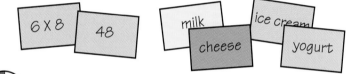

Address Labels

Keep levels of communication high and writer's cramp low by using mail-order address labels. Order labels that are printed with the phrases you write most often on students' papers. Each time you stick a label on a paper, check the phrase that's appropriate as shown. Or order labels with just two lines, each a different phrase; then cut each label in half to get two different stickers. What a simple and inexpensive way to communicate with students and parents!

Natalie S. Leatherman—Gr. 5, Pioneer Park Elementary
Lawton, OK

> ✓ Parent Signature Needed
> Messy: Resubmit
> Late Work Not Accepted
> Add More Details

> You are improving!
>
> Keep working hard!

Missing-Assignments Notebook

Tracking missed assignments is hassle-free with this management technique. Write "Missing Assignments" on the cover of a spiral notebook. In alphabetical order, write the name of a different student at the top of each notebook page. Keep the notebook at your desk. Whenever a student fails to turn in an assignment, list it on his page. When the assignment is turned in, cross it out.

Doreen Placko—Gr. 5, St. Patrick School, Wadsworth, IL

Lightweight Journals

Use this handy idea to make journals that are easy to cart home for grading:

1. Purchase five cardboard magazine boxes. Label them A–E.
2. Purchase a class supply of two-pocket folders in five different colors. Put one of each color of folder in each box. Label the folders in each box with its letter as shown. (If you have more than 25 students, increase the number of boxes or add another color of folder.)
3. Label each folder with a student's name.
4. In each folder place a month's list of journal prompts and a supply of writing paper.

During journal writing each day, have each student get his folder, write, and replace the folder in its box when he finishes. When it's time to take a look at students' journals, you carry home featherlight folders instead of heavy notebooks!

Terry Castoria
Frank Defino Central
  School
Marlboro, NJ

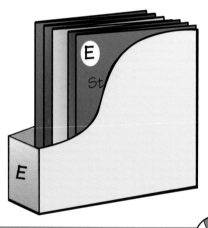

Student ID Cards

Keep track of your students in a snap with this teacher-tested idea. Obtain a photo of each student; then glue the photo to an index card labeled with the student's name and your name. When a student leaves the room for any reason, have him place his identification card on a bulletin board labeled with different destinations (office, restroom, speech class, etc.) to indicate where he is going. When on a field trip, pin the student's card to his clothing or hand it to a chaperone so she can quickly identify the students for whom she's responsible.

Jaudon Marlette—Gr. 4, Arbor Ridge Elementary, Orlando, FL

Ty Jones
Miss Johnson's
Room

Turn to page 250 for a terrific form to help with planning your units!

LIFESAVERS...
management tips for teachers

May I Borrow A Pencil?

If you're a bit tired of hearing "May I borrow a pencil?", here's an idea that will stop "lead lifters" in their tracks! Divide your class into teams; then select one person in each group to be the Supplies Steward. Put several pencils into a separate container for each team. (Try using empty coffee or frosting cans, baby-wipes boxes, or large butter tubs.) Have each team decorate its container; then hold a contest to choose the winning design. Reward the winning team with a supply of seasonal pencils with which to stock its container. Hold each Supplies Steward accountable for his team's pencil supply. Rotate stewards weekly, and watch your students get the point about being responsible!

Pat Twohey—Gr. 4, Old County Road School, Smithfield, RI

Count Their Corrections

Help your students learn from their mistakes with this grade-A tip! Begin by asking each student to find and circle her errors on a recently graded math test. Have the student explain her mistakes in writing; then have her detail the correct process or missed fact and redo the problem correctly. Grade and score the test again and average the two scores together for the final grade. Now you'll see a score that represents *true* learning!

Jane Mills—Gr. 5
Norman Rockwell School
Redmond, WA

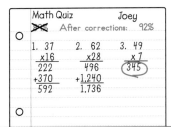

Too Many Interruptions?

Do you encourage your students to go to each other with questions before coming to you? Then it's likely that sometimes your helping students are interrupted so frequently that they struggle to get their own work done. To curb this problem, duplicate the patterns on page 252 on bright yellow paper (one copy for every three students). Have each student cut out a smiley pattern and "Shhh!" pattern and glue them back-to-back onto a tongue depressor as shown. Attach a piece of magnetic tape to each side of the depressor so it will stick to the side of a student's desk. If a student is open to questions, he displays the smiling face. But if he doesn't want to be distracted from his work, he displays the "Shhh!" face to gently signal classmates not to interrupt him for a while. Try using one of these management tools yourself the next time you need a little quiet time too!

Barbara Wilkes Delnero—Gr. 4
Tuckerton Elementary
Tuckerton, NJ

Check This Out!

Solve the mystery of managing your classroom library with this easy-to-use system. On each of several library-card pockets, write a range of alphabet letters, such as *A–F*. Attach the pockets to the side of your filing cabinet or desk with magnetic tape. When a student wants to check out a book from your library, have him write his name and the book's title on an index card, then place the card in the pocket that includes the letter of his last name. The result is a classroom card catalog that's no mystery to manage!

Jill Lynn Perry—Gr. 5
Mason Corinth Elementary
Williamstown, KY

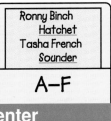

Assignment Center

Add function to your classroom walls with this timely tip. Decorate a large bulletin board to look like a calendar. Also make a seasonal header for each month. At the beginning of a new month, mount the appropriate header above the calendar. Then, before dismissal each afternoon, write that day's date and activities on an index card using different-colored pens: activities in black ink, notes in green, and assignments in red. Staple this card in the corresponding space on your calendar. Beside the display, place an assignment box containing folders labeled by subject. Fill the folders with corrected papers that were handed out while a student was away or work that an absent child needs to complete. After an absence, a student simply checks the assignment center and box to make up the work he missed.

Tamara Benning
Albany, OR

247

LIFESAVERS...
management tips for teachers

Five In From The End

Eliminate the problem of running out of classroom forms and worksheets with this easy idea. Laminate one copy of each reproducible you use for games, reading, group work, etc.; then place it in the proper file folder five in from the end. When a student goes to get a reproducible from a folder and sees that the next one is the laminated sheet, instruct him to place it on your desk. Not only will the laminated sheet signal you to run off more copies, but there will also still be some reproducibles left in the folder for other students to grab that day.

Barbara Wilkes Delnero—Gr. 4
Tuckerton Elementary, Tuckerton, NJ

Simple Sticker Storage

Solve the sticky problem of sticker storage with this organizational tip! Take advantage of your summer months to transform a greeting card organizer into a handy tool for sorting and storing stickers. Use each month's individual pocket to store stickers for that month or season. Relabel the summer months' pockets for specific themes or curriculum areas, such as "Oceans" or "Math." Place grading or reward stickers in any unlabeled pockets. By getting organized over the summer, your stickers will be ready to use throughout the coming school year.

Patricia A. Faria—Gr. 6
St. Angela School
Mattapan, MA

Pencil Jars

Make sure you're including everyone in class discussions with an idea that makes a point about participating. Write each student's name on a seasonal pencil at the beginning of the month; then place all of the pencils in a jar. When you need a response to a question, pull a pencil out of the jar and read aloud the name written on it. After that student responds, put her pencil in a second, empty jar so you won't call on her again. The next day simply switch jars and repeat the process. At the end of the month, give each student her pencil so she'll really get the point about how important class participation can be!

Missy Jones
Farmington, KY

248

Stamp Contest

Use reward stamps to reinforce positive behavior with this first-class activity! Divide an 8 1/2" x 11" sheet of paper into two-inch squares. Label each square with your name and a cute slogan, such as "Success Stamp." Duplicate a class supply of these squares on colored paper and cut them apart. Give a stamp to a student each time you see him use positive behavior in your classroom. Then, each Friday, hold a contest during which students are free to place as many stamps as they wish inside a special container. Remind them that entering is risky, however, since all stamps which have been entered are destroyed after each contest. Choose two stamps from the container and award inexpensive/cost-free prizes, such as books, free homework passes, and snacks to the lucky winners. Then post the winners' names on a bulletin board titled "First-Class Students!"

Helene Singer—Gr. 4
Holbrook Road School
Centereach, NY

Monthly Book Tip

Never miss out on another great monthly idea again with this simple tip! Duplicate the table of contents from each of your monthly idea books; then attach it to the plan book page for a week or more before the new month begins. The copy will remind you to pull your book to find ideas for the upcoming month. You'll have plenty of time to copy worksheets, gather supplies, and make new bulletin boards. Plus, by the end of the month, you'll have a ready-made monthly unit for next year!

Sharon Abell—Gr. 6
Winston-Salem, NC

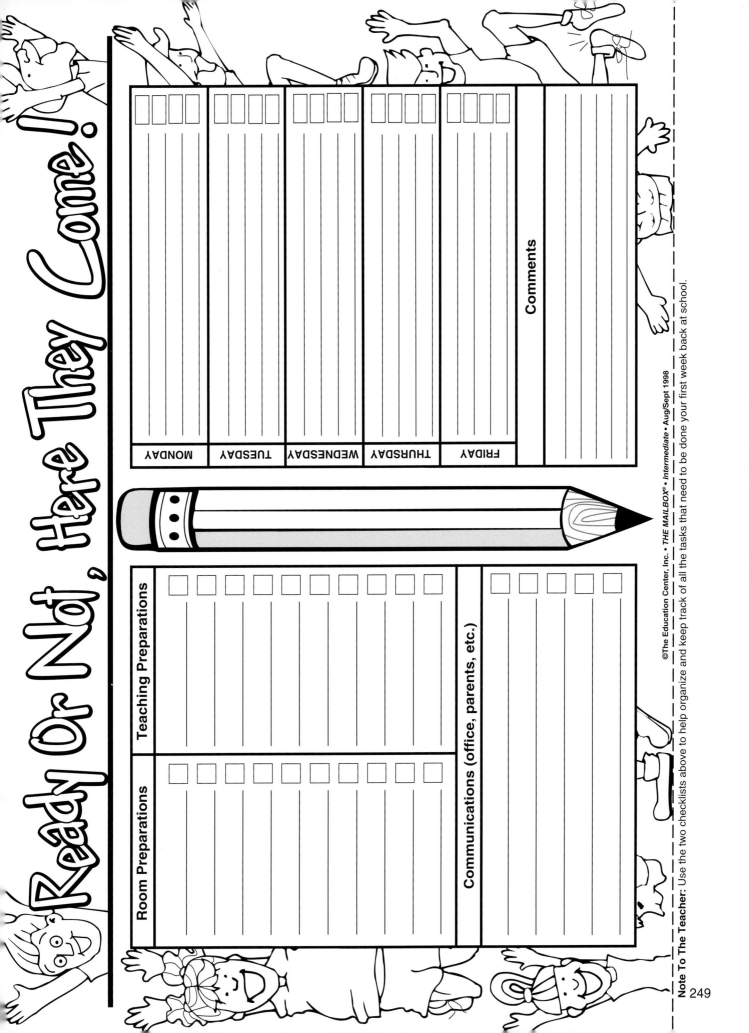

Ready Or Not, Here They Come!

Room Preparations
☐ ☐ ☐ ☐ ☐ ☐ ☐ ☐ ☐ ☐

Teaching Preparations
☐ ☐ ☐ ☐ ☐ ☐ ☐ ☐ ☐ ☐

Communications (office, parents, etc.)
☐ ☐ ☐ ☐ ☐ ☐

MONDAY	TUESDAY	WEDNESDAY	THURSDAY	FRIDAY	Comments
☐☐☐☐	☐☐☐☐	☐☐☐☐	☐☐☐☐	☐☐☐☐	

Note To The Teacher: Use the two checklists above to help organize and keep track of all the tasks that need to be done your first week back at school.

Unit-Planning Web

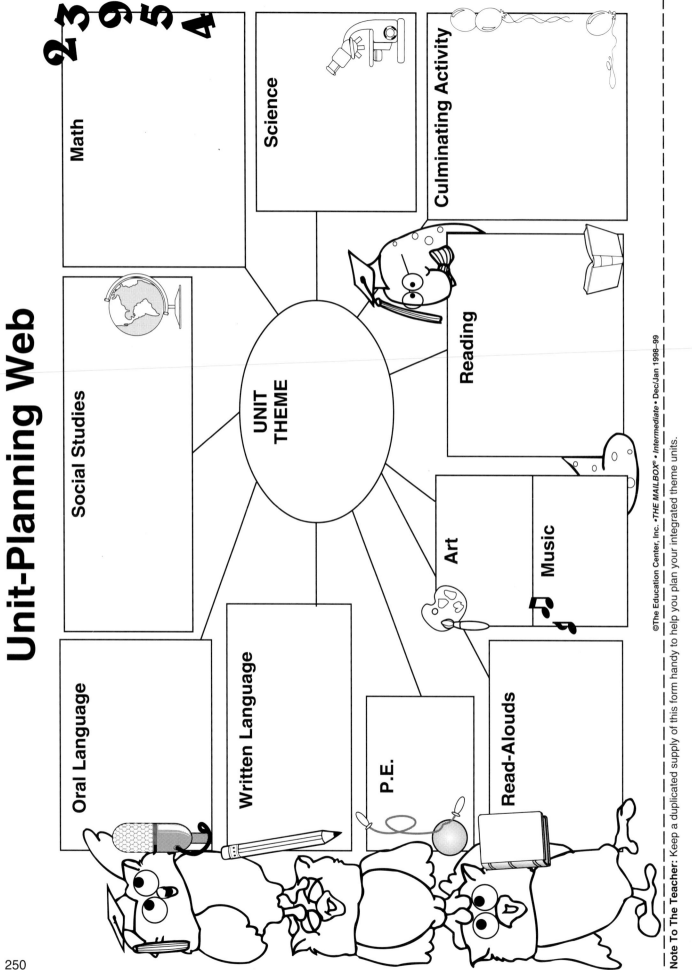

Math

2 3 6 5 4

Science

Culminating Activity

Social Studies

UNIT THEME

Reading

Oral Language

Written Language

P.E.

Art

Music

Read-Alouds

©The Education Center, Inc. • *THE MAILBOX® • Intermediate* • Dec/Jan 1998–99

Note To The Teacher: Keep a duplicated supply of this form handy to help you plan your integrated theme units.

Is It Done Yet?

How do you know if your project is done? Use the checklist below as a guide.

Details

- [ ] Have you included all text necessary for understanding?
- [ ] Have you used illustrations to add to your project?
- [ ] Are your illustrations colorful?

Originality

- [ ] Have you written the text in your own words?
- [ ] Have you used your own creative design?

Neatness

- [ ] Is your final copy written in ink or typed?
- [ ] Have all pencil marks been completely erased?

Editing

- [ ] Are all words spelled correctly?
- [ ] Have all capitalization rules been followed?
- [ ] Have all punctuation rules been followed?
- [ ] Have you checked for correct grammar?

Comments _____

Name _____ Date _____

©The Education Center, Inc. • THE MAILBOX® • Intermediate • Oct/Nov 1998

Is It Done Yet?

How do you know if your project is done? Use the checklist below as a guide.

Details

- [ ] Have you included all text necessary for understanding?
- [ ] Have you used illustrations to add to your project?
- [ ] Are your illustrations colorful?

Originality

- [ ] Have you written the text in your own words?
- [ ] Have you used your own creative design?

Neatness

- [ ] Is your final copy written in ink or typed?
- [ ] Have all pencil marks been completely erased?

Editing

- [ ] Are all words spelled correctly?
- [ ] Have all capitalization rules been followed?
- [ ] Have all punctuation rules been followed?
- [ ] Have you checked for correct grammar?

Comments _____

Name _____ Date _____

©The Education Center, Inc. • THE MAILBOX® • Intermediate • Oct/Nov 1998

Note To The Teacher: Use with "Is It Done Yet?" on page 245. Duplicate one half-page checklist for each student.

Write On!

Ideas And Tips For Teaching Students To Write

See My Van Go!

Turn the beloved American minivan into a truly artistic writing experience! Locate and display a picture of artist Vincent van Gogh. Explain to your class that a long-lost cousin of Vincent's has just opened an auto-styling shop named Van Go! Vincent's cousin believes the sides of a van are the perfect canvas for creating a masterpiece. Distribute a copy of the van pattern on page 259 to each child (enlarge the pattern if desired). Instruct each student to use her imagination to decorate her van with crayons or markers. After the artwork is complete, direct the student to write the story of her van. Where has it traveled? Who have been its most interesting owners? What adventures has it had? Place the completed stories and motorized masterpieces on a bulletin board titled "See My Van Go!"

Terry Healy—Gifted K–6, Eugene Field Elementary, Manhattan, KS

I love my Kermie
And have my own show.
Moi is so beautiful.
You should know!
Who am I?

Paper-Bag Busts

Motivating even your most reluctant writers is in the bag with this creative-writing activity! Instruct each student to research a famous person or character. Then have him construct a bust of that person using a small paper lunch bag and various art materials. After completing his bag bust, have each student write a poem, paragraph, or rhyming riddle about his character's identity. Finally allow each student to share his bag and writing with the class.

Donna Brasher—Gr. 4
Cherokee Elementary
Guntersville, AL

Rough Drafts On Yellow

Eliminate confusion between works in progress and final copies with the following idea. At the beginning of the school year, ask each student to contribute a yellow legal pad to the classroom. Have students use the yellow paper for writing rough drafts and editing. The extra length of these pads provides more space for making changes. After all editing and revisions are complete, have students write their final copies on white composition paper.

Nancy Curl—Gr. 6
Olson Middle School
Tabernacle NJ

Monthly Management

Looking for an easy way to manage your writing program? Tired of endless student drafts and revisions with no perfected final product? Then try this management strategy! Begin by choosing eight writing themes, one for each month of the school year. Next choose two skills and one part of speech to emphasize throughout each monthly theme. Create a chart as shown and provide each student with a copy. Direct each student to take her monthly writing piece through all stages of the writing process. At the end of the year, each child will have at least eight written masterpieces in her portfolio!

Ben Fromuth—Gr. 4, Penrose Elementary, Colorado Springs, CO

	September	October	November
Monthly Theme	Letters	Autobiographies	Interviewing
Skill 1	parts of a letter	sequencing	questioning
Skill 2	paragraphs	expressing thoughts, feelings	researching
Part Of Speech	nouns	verbs	adjectives
Perfected Product	letter	autobiography	family history album

Write On!

run
big
fun
bad
nice
said
look
happy

Ideas And Tips For Teaching Students To Write

R.I.P. Thesaurus

Watch students' vocabularies grow by having them create "spooktacular" personal thesauruses! Provide each student with a folder. At the beginning of each week, brainstorm with your class one common, overused word that needs to be "put to rest" (see the list shown at the left). Distribute one copy of page 260 to each student. Have the student write the overused word at the top of the page. Next have him use a thesaurus to find and list synonyms to use in place of the word. Then have the student complete the bottom of the page as directed. Before filing the page in his thesaurus folder, have him cut up the vertical alphabet row to the letter that the word begins with as shown. Then have him place the page in his thesaurus folder alphabetically. After a word is "put to rest," encourage students not to use it in their writings.

Maria Gonzalez—Gr. 4, Coral Reef Elementary, Miami, FL

The Writing Rack

Need an easy and fun way to get your students organized for writing? Purchase a folding, wooden laundry rack and attach to it a colorful sign labeled "Our Writing Rack." Collect a class supply of clothespins; then write a student's name on each one. As each student completes a rough draft of a writing project, have her clip her paper to the rack. Explain to your class that good writers let their ideas and writing "dry" overnight. The next day have each student unclip her paper and create a final draft. The Writing Rack not only keeps everyone from losing her rough draft, but also is a handy tool for checking student progress at a glance.

Betsy Rumberger—Gr. 4
Harrisburg Academy
Wormleysburg, PA

Fairy-Tale Envelope Books

Bring a new twist to familiar fairy tales with this letter-perfect book-writing activity. Create a book for each student by cutting the flap from each of five letter-sized envelopes. Punch two holes as shown in each envelope; then bind the five e n - velopes together with yarn or ribbon, and give the booklet to a student. Next read a fairy tale aloud to your students. Instruct each child to write four letters, each from one character to another addressing certain issues in the story (for example, a letter from Cinderella to her stepmother telling about her wedding to the prince). Have each student fold his letters and put one in each envelope, leaving the first envelope empty to decorate as a cover. As a finishing touch, have him draw "photos" on blank index cards to include with his letters. What a happy ending to a great project!

Heidi Graves and Darby Herlong—Grs. 4 & 5
Wateree Elementary
Lugoff, SC

Our Writing Rack

Letters From Cindy

by Nicole

Write On!

Ideas And Tips For Teaching Students To Write

It's Not Just Blue!

It's Not Just Blue!
teal
sky
periwinkle
midnight
navy
turquoise
aquamarine

It's Not Just Big!
gigantic
enormous
huge
colossal
magnificent

Improve the vocabularies of your creative writers with this easy-to-do activity. Begin by labeling a piece of chart paper "It's Not Just Blue!" Discuss with students the color blue and its many shades and intensities. Brainstorm other names for *blue,* such as *teal, sky, periwinkle,* or *turquoise.* Write these words on the chart; then have students write sentences that include them. Help students realize that their writing becomes more descriptive when more detailed words are used. Create charts for other overused words, such as *nice, pretty, big, fast,* etc. Post these charts around the room as quick references for students while they write.

Sandra Preston—Gr. 5, Albany Magnet School of Humanities, Albany, NY

Autobiographical Newspaper

Extra! Extra! Link autobiography and newspaper writing with this kid-pleasin' activity. Begin by explaining to the class that each student will write his own autobiographical newspaper, filled with articles that tell information about himself. Then list the following titles on the chalkboard:

- The Cry Heard Around The World—The Day I Was Born
- Favorite Things To Do
- Friends, Relatives, And Neighbors
- Favorite Foods
- Early Years

- Places To Go
- Favorite Pets
- Favorite TV Shows And Movies
- Feeling Good About Myself
- In The News

- Cars Of The Time
- Mom And Dad Are Special
- Reading Time
- When I Grow Up
- My Room

Have each child choose a specified number of titles from the chalkboard and write articles for them. Then have him type his articles on the computer, using clip art to illustrate his paper. Once these newspapers are hot off the press, provide time for students to swap copies so they can read each other's "rags"!

Betty Bowlin, Henry Elementary, Ballwin, MO

Elaborating With Pizza

Teach the technique of elaboration by turning to something students love: pizza! Use this tasty treat as a concrete way to show students how adding detail creates layers of meaning that make their writing clear, precise, and interesting. Post a copy of the chart shown. Then provide each student with the ingredients listed in the recipe below, along with a paper plate, a plastic spoon, and a few paper towels for cleanup. As students assemble their pizzas, go over the chart to show how each pizza-making step illustrates the degree of elaboration used in writing. Conclude by baking the pizzas in one or more toaster ovens; then let students dig into their tasty teaching tools!

Joy Fullen—Gr. 4
Acton Elementary
Dallas, TX

Directions	Degree Of Elaboration	Explanation
Put muffin on plate.	Bare writing	No extension or elaboration.
Spread pizza sauce on muffin.	Extended	Minimally elaborated. A specific piece of pertinent information is linked to an idea.
Sprinkle cheese on top of sauce.	Somewhat elaborated	Other specific pieces of pertinent information are linked to an extension.
Arrange pepperoni slices on top of cheese.	Moderately elaborated	Idea is explained in greater detail.
Add olives, green peppers, and any other toppings. Bake at 350°F until cheese is bubbly.	Fully developed	A variety of elaboration techniques are used to make the meaning clear.

Elaboration Pizzas

Ingredients for each student:
1/2 English muffin
1–2 T. pizza sauce
pepperoni slices
grated mozzarella cheese
other toppings: olives, green-pepper slices, sliced mushrooms, chopped onions, etc.

Write On!

Ideas And Tips For Teaching Students To Write

The Haunted House

The house was old and run-down. Its windows were broken and...

Picture This!

Link descriptive writing, imagery, and literature with this simple activity. Have each student write a paragraph describing the setting of the novel he's currently reading. Next have him exchange paragraphs with a partner. Have each student draw the setting described in his partner's paragraph. If a student hasn't written in detail, his partner will have a hard time picturing the setting. Students will easily see the importance of using detailed descriptions in their writings. Display each student's paragraph with his partner's interpretation on a bulletin board titled "Picture This!"

Julie Gartner—Gr. 6, Virginia Lake School, Palatine, IL

When I was young in Manhattan, my father became a police officer. He took me to where he worked...

—Yashira

When I Was Young In...

Integrate autobiographical literature into your writing curriculum with this idea. Read Cynthia Rylant's picture book *When I Was Young In The Mountains* aloud to your students. Emphasize the repetition of the words "When I was young in the mountains…" and discuss how it provides a pleasing rhythm to the listener. Write the sentence starter "When I was young in _____" on the board. Have each student copy it at the top of a piece of notebook paper. Then have him write the name of his hometown in the blank and add several sentences describing a specific sight, sound, aroma, or memory that he can recall from growing up. Give the student a sheet of unlined paper and have him illustrate his memory. Bind the students' recollections and illustrations to make a memorable class book!

Millie Ryan—Gr. 5, P. S. 195, Rosedale, NY

My Tall Tale
by Lisa

We're "Lion"!

Encourage your students' love for exaggeration with an activity that mixes writing with art. Follow the steps below.

Materials for each student: one white paper plate, one sheet of notebook paper, scissors, glue, black and orange markers or crayons, two medium-sized wiggle eyes, orange yarn

Steps:

1. After a discussion on the importance of telling the truth, read a tall tale, such as *Pecos Bill* or *Paul Bunyan,* to your class. Emphasize the use of hyperbole, or exaggeration.
2. Pass out the paper plates and scissors. Have each student cut a piece of notebook paper to fit the concave side of her plate.
3. Have each student write a rough draft of a brief, original tall tale.
4. After the student has proofread and made any necessary corrections, have her copy her final draft onto the circular sheet of paper and then glue it to the concave side of her plate.
5. On the other side of the plate, have the student draw the nose and mouth of a lion and then color the plate orange.
6. Have the student glue on the eyes and the pieces of yarn for the mane. Hang this "lion" story on a clothesline or from your ceiling for everyone to enjoy.

Darby Herlong—Gr. 5, Wateree Elementary, Lugoff, SC

Write On!

Ideas And Tips For Teaching Students To Write

Letter-Box Story

Box up some fun with this unique creative-writing idea! Have each student bring in a shoebox or cereal box. Assign each child one letter of the alphabet, repeating some if necessary. For homework, have each student find five objects starting with her letter to put in her box and bring back to school. The next day, have her write a short story or poem incorporating as many words beginning with her letter as she can, including the five objects from home. As a final step, have each student decorate her box and share its story with her classmates. Display the finished letter boxes and stories at a center or in your school's media center.

Ingrid Wolf—Gr. 4
Catholic Central School
Appleton, WI

Beanie Babies™ Bags

Your students will be "bagging" for homework with this fun journal-writing activity! Collect several Beanie Babies™, plus a spiral-bound notebook and inexpensive canvas bag for each stuffed animal. Use a marker to write your name on each toy's tag and on the cover of its notebook; then use fabric paint to write the Beanie Baby's name on the outside of the bag. Also decorate the notebook cover with stickers that match the stuffed animal's theme. (Make these bags during the summer months, and you'll be ready to use them in August.) On Friday send home each bag with a different student. Instruct each child to write about what she did with the toy over the weekend, encouraging her to create fun and imaginative stories of their time together. Rotate the bags so that everyone gets the chance to have a Beanie Baby adventure!

Meshell Kibelkis
Kolmar School
Midlothian, IL

Goofy Gazette

Stop the presses with this bulletin board that becomes a creative-writing activity! Begin by covering your bulletin board with newspaper pages; then divide it into thirds with a marker and label the three sections "News," "Sports," and "Entertainment." Briefly discuss these sections of your local newspaper with students. Next cut slips of paper large enough for at least two sentences and label each with one of the headings. Give one slip to each student; then direct her to write a fun or an inventive headline on the back of the strip as shown. When each student is finished, collect her slip, fold it, and give it to a different classmate. After brainstorming, have the classmate write a brief, funny article to go with his new headline. Collect the stories and headlines; then staple them to your bulletin board under the appropriate headings. Not only will you have a great-looking display, but your class will have just written their own "goofy gazette"!

Rusty Fischer
Tropical Elementary
Merritt Island, FL

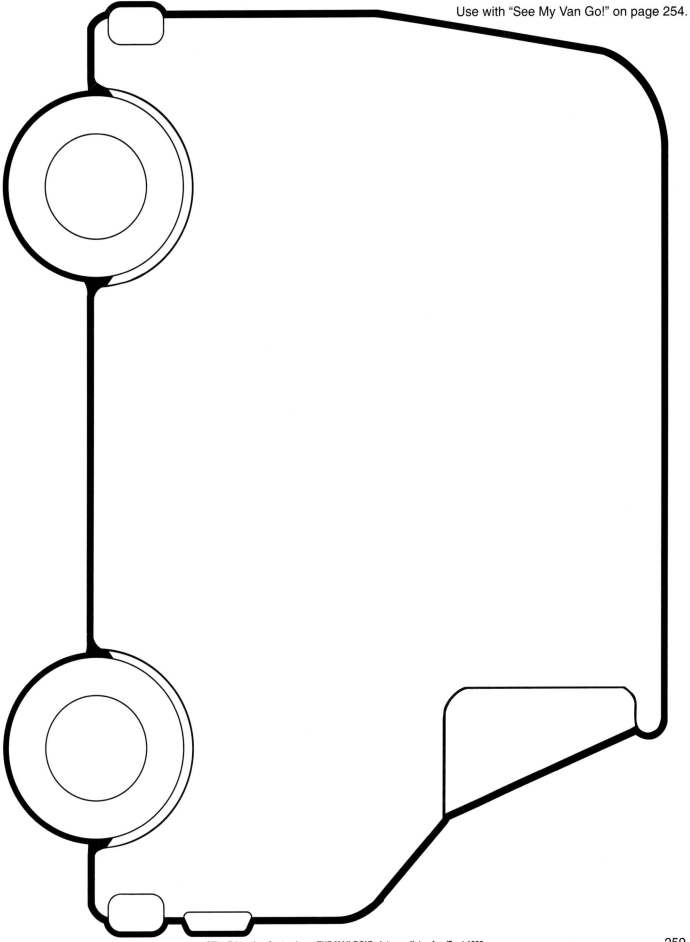

R.I.P.

_____
(overused word)

Survived by:
(synonyms)

_____   _____
_____   _____
_____   _____
_____   _____
_____   _____
_____   _____
_____   _____

Directions: Choose three of the synonyms listed above. Write a sentence using each one correctly.

1. _____
   _____

2. _____
   _____

3. _____
   _____

A
B
C
D
E
F
G
H
I
J
K
L
M
N
O
P
Q
R
S
T
U
V
W
X
Y
Z

Seasonal Ideas & Reproducibles

Seasonal Sampler

Seasonal And Holiday Activities For The Classroom

Get ready for August's back-to-school fever and some of September's special days with this irresistible collection of seasonal ideas and reproducibles.

Back To School

Toilet-Paper Tattle

This getting-to-know-you activity is a real attention grabber! Distribute one roll of toilet paper to every group of four to six students. Without any explanation, direct each student to take as many sheets as he thinks he needs and then pass the roll to the next child in his group. Have each student count his sheets and write that number of little-known facts about himself—such as having seen the *Star Wars* video 56 times—on loose-leaf paper. Have students share their completed lists. Then follow up with questions such as "What new things did you learn about your classmates?", "Would you like to do any of the things you heard about?", and "What funny (happy, surprising, sad, etc.) things did you learn?" With this fun-filled activity, your students will be rolling in information about one another! *Lisa Waller Rogers, Austin, TX*

Stand Up And Be Recognized!

Spark new friendships and build camaraderie with this easy getting-to-know-you activity. Have each student complete the reproducible on the top half of page 264; then have him cut out the clues, fold them in half, and place them in a container provided by you. Each day during the first week of school, gather students in a large circle on the floor and read aloud 10–20 clues one at a time. After you read each clue, direct its writer to stand. As clues are read, your students will quickly identify classmates with whom they share something in common. What an uncommonly great icebreaker! *Joy A. Kalfas, Palatine, IL*

Guessing-Game Bulletin Board

Arm yourself with a camera to produce a winning bulletin board that helps students get to know their classmates. Take a snapshot of each child during the first week of school; then have him copy and complete the information that's shown below on an index card. Mount each photo and its card on a bulletin board titled "Who Am I?" Next staple a paper flap over each snapshot to conceal it. No student will be able to resist reading the clues, taking a guess, and lifting the flap to see if his guess is right! *Lisa Waller Rogers*

Who Am I?

Who Am I?

My first and last names have a total of _____ letters.

I've attended this school for _____ years. (Write the number as a math sentence.)

My favorite TV show is _____.

My favorite food is _____.

My favorite day of the week is _____.

My favorite fast-food restaurant is _____.

My favorite commercial is _____.

My first name comes ___ alphabetically on the class roll.

A-Hunting We Will Go!

Foster an environment in which feelings of familiarity and acceptance can grow with this back-to-school scavenger hunt. Give each student a copy of the bottom half of page 264 to complete as directed. Afterward bring the class together to analyze the results, asking questions such as:

- Which categories were the easiest to match?
- Did you find a match for every category? If you didn't, is that important? Why?
- What things did you have in common with your classmates?
- Which findings surprised you?

You can bet that everyone will know his classmates better after this extraordinary excursion! *Daniel Kriesberg—Gr. 4, Locust Valley Intermediate School, Locust Valley, NY*

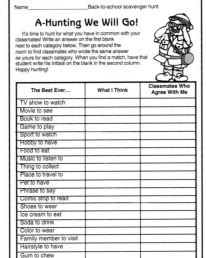

Name_____Back-to-school scavenger hunt

A-Hunting We Will Go!

It's time to hunt for what you have in common with your classmates! Write an answer on the first blank next to each category below. Then go around the room to find classmates who wrote the same answer as yours for each category. When you find a match, have that student write his initials on the blank in the second column. Happy hunting!

The Best Ever...	What I Think	Classmates Who Agree With Me
TV show to watch		
Movie to see		
Book to read		
Game to play		
Sport to watch		
Hobby to have		
Food to eat		
Music to listen to		
Thing to collect		
Place to travel to		
Pet to have		
Phrase to say		
Comic strip to read		
Shoes to wear		
Ice cream to eat		
Soda to drink		
Color to wear		
Family member to visit		
Hairstyle to have		
Gum to chew		

"You-Nique" Deskplates

Use personalized license plates as the springboard for creating unique back-to-school deskplates. Discuss vanity license plates with students, asking them to share examples of ones they've seen. Point out that these plates use numbers and letters to form special messages about a car owner's personality, hobbies, and abilities. Next give each student a small, cleaned Styrofoam® meat tray. Have the student pencil a message of eight or fewer letters/numbers on the tray that communicates a personal interest or ability. Direct the student to decorate his design with permanent markers license-plate style. Affix the completed desk-plates to the front of students' desks to identify their assigned seats and help students learn more about their classmates.

Germaine Johnson #34 SOCKRKID Glendale Mustangs

Signing Of The U.S. Constitution

Calling All Reporters!

Call students' attention to an important date in history—the signing of the United States Constitution on September 17, 1787—with a creative newspaper-reporting activity. First read aloud *Shh! We're Writing The Constitution* by Jean Fritz (The Putnam Publishing Group, 1987). Then have each student pretend to be an on-the-spot reporter covering the signing of this important document. Challenge each child to write a newspaper headline and an eyewitness account telling about the events he observed on September 17, 1787. Mount students' articles around a copy of the U.S. Constitution (obtained at your local public library) on a bulletin board titled "Hot Off The Patriotic Press!"

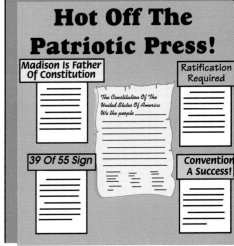

Hot Off The Patriotic Press!

Madison Is Father Of Constitution

Ratification Required

The Constitution Of The United States Of America We the people

39 Of 55 Sign

Convention A Success!

Labor Day

Career Shopping

Mark the celebration of Labor Day with a writing activity that causes students to think of future careers. Share that this holiday—celebrated the first Monday in September—honors all workers and was first observed in New York City with a parade on September 5, 1882. Have the class brainstorm a list of careers as you write it on the board. Next direct each student to choose three careers at which she thinks she could be successful. Have her explain in a paragraph why she feels she could succeed at these jobs and include personal attributes to support her reasons. Allow each student to share her writings with the class the next day. Encourage students to make or bring props—such as special clothing or tools used in their chosen professions—to share during the presentations.

Architect Interior Designer Textile Designer

A-Hunting We Will Go!

It's time to hunt for what you have in common with your classmates! Write an answer on the first blank next to each category below. Then go around the room to find classmates who wrote the same answer as yours for each category. When you find a match, have that student write his initials on the blank in the second column. Happy hunting!

The Best Ever...	What I Think	Classmates Who Agree With Me
TV show to watch		
Movie to see		
Book to read		
Game to play		
Sport to watch		
Hobby to have		
Food to eat		
Music to listen to		
Thing to collect		
Place to travel to		
Pet to have		
Phrase to say		
Comic strip to read		
Shoes to wear		
Ice cream to eat		
Soda to drink		
Color to wear		
Family member to visit		
Hairstyle to have		
Gum to chew		

©The Education Center, Inc. • THE MAILBOX® • Intermediate • Aug/Sept 1998

☆ ☆ Introducing Me! ☆ ☆

Clue others in on what makes you tick by completing the sentences below. Next cut the clues apart on the dotted lines. Fold the clues in half and place them in the container provided by your teacher. Then get ready for a fun getting-to-know-you activity for the whole class!

1. What I look forward to most about the first day of school is _____ .

2. I can't _____ , but I'm really good at _____ .

3. All it takes to make me happy is _____ .

4. The way I spend free time is _____ .

5. If I were planning my favorite meal, it would include _____ .

6. If I were giving an Emmy for the best TV show, I'd award it to _____ .

7. My most prized possession is _____ .

8. If I could be like another person, I'd choose _____ .

9. If I could own only one book, I'd want it to be _____ .

10. To cheer myself up, I _____ .

©The Education Center, Inc. • THE MAILBOX® • Intermediate • Aug/Sept 1998

Note To The Teacher: Use "Introducing Me!" with "Stand Up And Be Recognized!" on page 262. Provide students with scissors. Use "A-Hunting We Will Go!" with the activity on page 263.

Miss Pickwell's Puzzlers

Priscilla Pickwell takes great pride in creating puzzles to perplex students during the first days of school. See if you can solve the puzzles she's giving this year's class!

Puzzle #1

Solving this puzzle will let you in on a little secret! Start reading from one of the letters in the top row. Move to the right, left, up, or down to discover this secret. Hint: You can't move diagonally!

I	N	B	K	S
N	G	O	O	A
R	T	S	E	R
A	O	Y	T	H
E	L	E	K	E

The secret:

_____
_____
_____
_____
_____

Puzzle #2

Some schoolchildren visited the chimpanzee section at the city zoo. They gave the zookeeper this challenge: Name ten three-letter words that are chimpanzee body parts. The keeper had no problem coming up with ten words. Can you?

____ ____ ____ ____ ____

____ ____ ____ ____ ____

Puzzle #3

Use the grid on the right to rearrange the numbers in the other grid so that the same number does not appear twice in any row, column, or diagonal. If the numbers are arranged correctly, each row and column totals 100. Good luck!

0	10	30	0	40
20	20	40	20	10
40	10	30	40	0
30	0	10	30	10
40	20	0	30	20

Puzzle #4

Hidden in this puzzle is a word that completes Miss Pickwell's advice about homework. Compare each pair of numbers. Then circle the number that is greater. Write the letter above the circled number in its corresponding blank below to read the message.

	T		B
①	1,610	or	1,601

	W		A
②	27,770	or	27,707

	D		I
③	4,500	or	4,550

	J		O
④	36,005	or	36,050

	H		J
⑤	580,070	or	508,070

	T		H
⑥	882,222	or	822,882

	U		E
⑦	55,489	or	54,895

DON'T
LEAVE
HOME

___ ___ ___ ___ ___ ___ ___
2   3   6   5   4   7   1

IT!

Seasonal
Holiday And Seasonal Activities

Fill the exciting days of October and November with
this creative collection of fall ideas and reproducibles!

Halloween

Haunted House Book Reports

Shrieks and groans may not come from these houses, but great book reviews surely will! Ask a local pizzeria to donate a class supply of pizza boxes. Have each student read a mystery; then have her attach a written book report to the interior of a box she has decorated like a house to re-create the book's setting. Suggest that each student use a variety of art materials—from cotton to plastic spiders to twigs—to decorate her house in a hauntingly "ghost-tacular" way! (For another great box project, see "Cereal-Box Diorama" on page 40.) *Lucy Cruz—Gr. 6, Berkeley School, Bloomfield, NJ*

The House Of Dies Drear

"Spook-tacular" Banners

Decorate for Halloween with student-made banners that are frighteningly simple to make!

Materials for each banner:
9" x 12" piece of black felt
scraps of orange and white felt
scissors
fabric glue
6 small black beads
cardboard tube from a dry cleaner hanger, cut to a 12" length
4 small black buttons
28" length of orange yarn

Steps:
1. Cut out letters that spell "BOO" from orange felt. Glue the letters down the center of the black felt.
2. Glue two buttons to the *B* as shown. Glue one button in the center of each *O*.
3. Cut three objects (ghosts, spiders, jack-o'-lanterns, leaves, cats, etc.) from white felt. Glue two small beads on each object to represent eyes.
4. Glue the white felt cutouts on the banner. Let the glue dry.
5. Fold the top edge of the banner over the cardboard tube. Glue the edge to the back of the banner.
6. Make the hanger by tying each end of the yarn to the ends of the cardboard tube.

Colleen Dabney—Grs. 6–7, Williamsburg Christian Academy, Williamsburg, VA

Coat-Hanger Characters And Conversations

Welcome Halloween with a host of characters that can be as mild mannered or scary as you wish! To make one character, cut a leg from an old pair of panty hose (brown for a scarecrow, white for a ghost, black for a cat). Bend a wire coat hanger in a desired shape; then insert the hanger into the toe of the hose. Tie the cut end of the hose into a knot below the hanger's hook. Glue face and hat cutouts to the project and allow to dry. Hang the completed characters in the classroom. As a writing and grammar extension, pair students and have them write a conversation between their two characters.

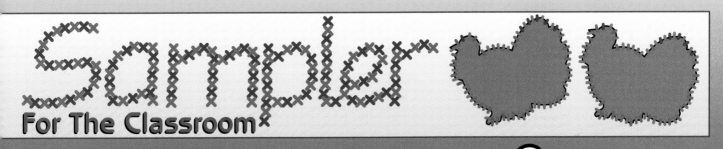

Sampler
For The Classroom

Nutrition In A Sandwich

Tease students' taste buds *and* review the Food Guide Pyramid with this creative activity. Share with students that November 3—Sandwich Day—is set aside to honor John Montague, Fourth Earl of Sandwich, the inventor of the sandwich. Invite students to tell about the best or worst sandwiches they have ever eaten. Then challenge each child to illustrate and list the ingredients of a tasty sandwich he would like to be served in your school's cafeteria. Require each student to include an item from each section of the Food Guide Pyramid in his sandwich. If desired, have students vote for the sandwich they think would win Earl Montague's "Medal Of Nutritional Merit." (For another terrific Sandwich Day activity, see "Sandwich Day Smorgasbord" on page 295.)

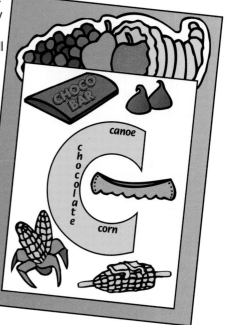

National Children's Book Week

An Overall Good Book

Promote the "Books Go Everywhere!" theme of National Children's Book Week (November 16–22) with this nifty idea. Brainstorm with students all the places that books can

go, such as to a park, on an airplane—even in a pocket! Then give each student a 1 1/2" x 7" piece of white poster board. Have him decorate the paper as a bookmark that highly recommends a book he's read. Meanwhile pin a pair of toddler-size overalls to a bulletin board titled "Overall Good Books!" Place the completed bookmarks in the overall's pockets. Suggest that each student take a bookmark to mark his place in the next overall good book he reads.
Susan Keller—Gr. 5 Reading/Language Arts, Plumb Elementary, Largo, FL

Thanksgiving

Native American ABCs Of Thanksgiving

Honor our nation's Native Americans for their contributions to our culture with this collaborative class project. Together make a list of items given to us by Native Americans. List each item by its letter of the alphabet (for example, *C—canoe, chocolate, corn*). Next have students make or bring in magazine pictures or package labels of the items listed. Direct students to cut out and glue a different letter of the alphabet to sheets of construction paper, labeling each letter with the words listed for it. Then have students glue their collection of pictures on the corresponding sheets (see the example). Display the sheets in alphabetical order on a wall in your classroom or school as reminders of how thankful we should be for these invaluable contributions. ***Jeri Daugherity—Gr. 5, Mother Seton School, Emmitsburg, MD***

Name _____ U.S. geography, spelling

Ghostly Geography

Many of the cities and states listed in the box are haunted—their spellings, that is!
- Ten words have invisible letters—their silent letters have been omitted.
- Ten words have letters that are disguised—a letter has been replaced with one that has a similar sound.
- Ten words are spelled correctly as they are.

Your job? Write each misspelled word correctly on the matching character below. Write each correctly spelled word on "Wylie the Werewolf." Each list has been started for you.

Savanah	Sharlotte	Anapolis	Louisville	Lincon
Navada	Pittsburg	Louisiana	Olimpia	Phenix
Buffalo	Los Angeles	Bismarch	New Havan	New Hamshire
Banger	Minnesoda	Tulsa	Fort Wane	De Moines
Massachusets	Norfolk	Mishigan	Tallahassee	Tucson
Albuquerque	Montpelier	Caspar	Rode Island	San Fransisco

Kount Drakula
(Always uses the wrong letter!)

Gwen the "Gost"
(Thinks invisible is IN!)

Wylie the Werewolf
(What a speller!)

Nevada

Savannah

Buffalo

Bonus Box: Eight of the cities in the list are state capitals. List them with their matching states on the back of this page.

268   ©The Education Center, Inc. • THE MAILBOX® • Intermediate • Oct/Nov 1998 • Key p. 312

Name _____ Addition, guess and check

"To Grandmother's House We Go…"

Sophie traveled from her home in Tramore to her grandmother's house in Dunmore for Thanksgiving. Her family left at 8:00 A.M. and arrived at 12:00 noon. They drove an average speed of 40 miles per hour. How many miles did they drive in all? _____

On the map, use a pencil to lightly trace three different routes that Sophie's family may have taken. After you're sure of each route, trace over it with a crayon. Use a different color crayon for each route.

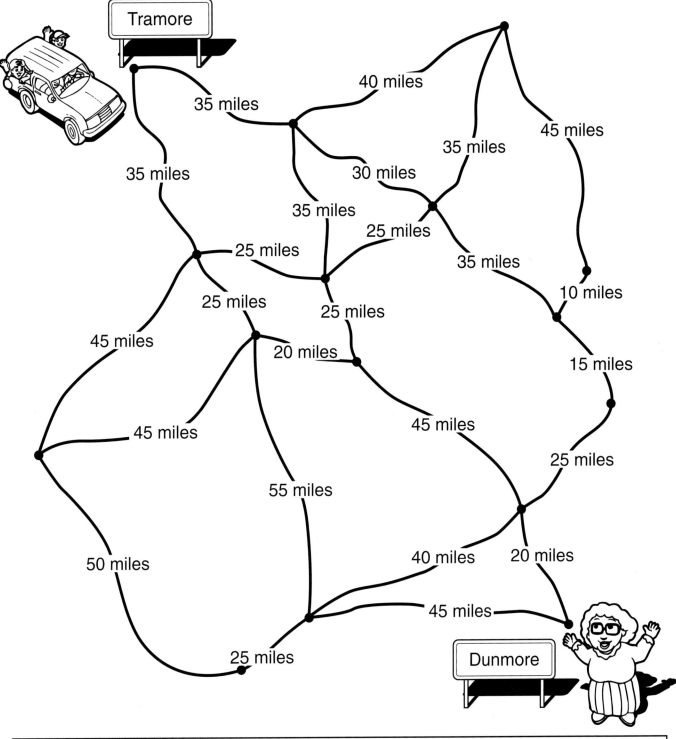

Seasonal
Holiday And Seasonal Activities

Celebrate the special days of December and January with these super seasonal suggestions!

Festive Estimation

Help your students' estimation skills measure up with this fun holiday center! Wrap several boxes of various sizes in colorful gift wrap; then use a marker to number the boxes. Place the boxes on a table along with a supply of ribbon or yarn, scissors, and rulers or tape measures. When visiting the center, each student estimates the amount of ribbon needed to tie around each gift and records it on his paper. The student tests his guess by cutting the estimated length of ribbon and attempting to tie it around the box. Then he calculates how much more (or less) ribbon he needed to adequately wrap the box. For an added challenge, have students estimate the length of ribbon needed to tie two or more boxes together. ***Amy Polcyn—Substitute Teacher, South Lyon Community Schools, South Lyon, MI***

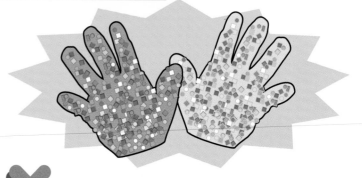

Hanukkah Hopes

Spread the spirit of hope this Hanukkah with a lovely holiday display. Have each student trace his hands on construction paper and cut out the tracings. After he paints his cutouts with thinned glue, have the student place them in a cardboard box and sprinkle construction-paper confetti onto them. Then direct the student to lift the cutouts from the box, tap off any loose confetti, and set them aside to dry. Meanwhile discuss the history of Hanukkah with the class, focusing on the hope that the Jewish people must have felt after the miracle of the lamp that stayed lit for eight days. Give each student an index card and have him write a narrative paragraph describing a time in his life when he was given hope, felt very hopeful, or saw a hope come true. Staple the hand cutouts on a bulletin board in a large circle, making sure that the hands touch each other slightly. Above the circle add the title "Joining Hands For Hanukkah!" Then staple the students' paragraphs inside the circle of hands.

Sock Snowman

Help students trim their holiday trees with "snow-dorable" ornaments fashioned from white socks! Stuff a toddler-sized white tube sock with Poly-Fil® stuffing all the way up to the ribbing. Wrap a rubber band around the sock to make a snowman. Fold the ribbing down, then up, to form a cap; then use a hot glue gun to glue a pom-pom atop the cap. Next tie a strip of plaid flannel fabric around the rubber band for a scarf. Poke a round wooden toothpick that's been painted orange and cut to a one-inch length into the snowman's head to make a nose; then secure the toothpick with a little hot glue. Finally, use a black fine-tipped marker to add eyes, a mouth, and buttons to the snowman. To turn the project into a snowy ornament, hot-glue a loop of narrow ribbon to the back of the snowman. ***Marilyn Davison—Grs. 4 & 5, River Oaks School, Monroe, LA***

Jingle-Bell Wreath

Just jingle down to your local craft store for the inexpensive supplies that result in this one-of-a-kind ornament.

Materials for each student:
1 green and 1 red pipe cleaner, 10 red beads, 41 green beads (number of beads will vary depending on length of pipe cleaner), 1 small jingle bell

Steps:
1. Bend the end of the green pipe cleaner upwards about one inch as shown.
2. String 1 red bead, 2 green beads, 1 red bead, and 5 green beads on the pipe cleaner.
3. Repeat the stringing of 1 red bead and 5 green beads six more times.
4. End by stringing 1 red bead, 2 green beads, and 1 red bead.
5. Twist the ends of the pipe cleaner together.
6. String the bell on the center of the red pipe cleaner; then twist the pipe cleaner into a bow around the top of the wreath.
7. String one green bead on each end of the red pipe cleaner; then twist the ends.

Marlys Cole—Gr. 4, Roy Gomm School, Reno, NV

Pillow Project

For a lasting holiday gift that any parent will cherish, try this pretty pillow project! If you don't have a sewing machine, just enlist the help of a friend or parent volunteer who does.

Materials for each student:
fabric crayons (one set for each group of four or five students)
1 sheet tracing paper
12-inch square of white fabric
12-inch square of holiday or other printed fabric
straight pins
needle and thread
Poly-Fil® stuffing
pencil
iron (for teacher use only)
optional: simple holiday picture from a coloring book

Steps:
1. Draw or trace a picture on the tracing paper. Add a greeting and your name if desired.
2. Use the fabric crayons to color only one side of your tracing. If there are any numbers or lettering, turn the tracing over and color the *back* side.
3. Place the design on the white fabric square, colored side down; then use a warm iron to transfer the design onto the fabric.
4. Pin the white square and the other fabric square back-to-back.
5. Machine-sew the sides of the pillow, leaving an opening for stuffing.
6. Stuff the pillow with Poly-Fil®; then sew up the opening with a needle and thread.

Marilyn Davison—Grs. 4 & 5, River Oaks School, Monroe, LA

The Gift Of Me

Here's a gift idea that sharpens writing skills while providing parents with a present they'll never forget! After reading various books about famous people, my students decided to write their own autobiographies. First we discussed how to gather information about ourselves: interviewing parents and other loved ones, looking at photo albums and past school annuals, etc. Students also began to discreetly bring baby pictures to class to be used in their books. Next I sent a letter home to parents asking for a $2.00 donation to be used for a surprise. I used the money to purchase a blank book for each student. After writing and editing her rough draft, each child recopied her autobiography in a blank book, adding a cover, title page, dedication page, publisher's page, and copyright page. Photos and pictures were also added. Not only did parents love the finished books, but my students also practiced their writing skills in a way that didn't seem like work! *Marilyn Gill—Gr. 6, Noble, OK*

New Year's Day

Betcha Can't Read Just One!

Start the new year with a resolution to read! When students return from the holiday break, ask them to donate emptied potato-chip bags. Staple the bags around the perimeter of a bulletin board titled "Betcha Can't Read Just One!" Then have each child cut a potato-chip shape from yellow construction paper. On his chip cutout, have the student write a brief book recommendation, including the title and author of his recommended book. Staple the chip cutouts to the board. Finally challenge each student to resolve to read at least one book from the display by the end of February. When a student turns in a brief review of the book he read, let him tear a "bite" off of the chip that recommends that book. Betcha can't read just one!

Stepping On
The Cracks
by Mary Downing Hahn

by
Ali

Birthday Of Dr. Martin Luther King, Jr.

Birthday Banners

Celebrate the birth of a great American this January with an activity that invites the entire school to join the party! Divide your class into several groups (one per grade level in your school). Have each group decorate a large sheet of butcher paper to resemble a giant birthday banner in honor of Dr. Martin Luther King, Jr. Challenge each group to title its banner with a birthday greeting, such as "Happy Birthday, Dr. King—A Powerful Peacemaker!" Then post

HAPPY BIRTHDAY, DR. KING!

each banner in your hallway. Invite each class in your school to come by and write their birthday wishes to this great man. If desired, have your students serve birthday cookies and punch when each class comes to add to its grade-level banner. *adapted from an idea by Benita Mudd—Grs. 4–5, Losantiville School, Cincinnati, OH*

National Soup Month

Super Soup

What goes together like soup and a sandwich? This "soup-er" creative-thinking activity and January, which is National Soup Month! Tell students that the country's leading maker of tasty, nutritious soups has just asked each of them to invent a new recipe. This soup must appeal to a lot of people, yet be different from anything that's already sitting on grocery-store shelves. Display a variety of canned soups for students to examine. Then give each child a 4" x 7" piece of white paper on which to design a label that will go on his soup can (looking at the sample cans for ideas). Be sure the student includes:

- the name of his soup
- the ingredients listed in order of quantity
- any catchy phrase or slogan that will help sell the soup
- the net weight of the contents
- the name and address of the manufacturer
- directions for preparing the soup
- any recipes or special tips on using the soup so that people will buy more of it

After students write and color their labels, post the projects on a bulletin board titled "Mmmm, Good!" ***Ann Fisher, Constantine, MI***

NEW!

SUPER
Sesame Seed &
Sweet Potato
SOUP
12 oz.

Hanukkah Happenings

Hanukkah is a joyous celebration of an important event in Jewish history. More than 2,000 years ago, the temple of Jerusalem was recaptured from the Syrians. Work with a partner to discover the exact year of this event. Fill in the blanks below after working the problems. Then write the answer to each problem in the matching star. (If a problem has more than one blank, write the answer in the *last* blank in the star.)

1. A great miracle happened during the battle for the temple. A single day's worth of oil lasted for eight days! List all the factors of 8: _____ Find their sum. _____

2. Hanukkah can occur in December, the 12th month of the year. List the first two multiples of 12, after 12: _____ Find their sum: _____ Add this sum to answer 1. _____

3. Hanukkah can also occur in November, the 11th month. Write the first multiple of 11: _____ Subtract it from answer 2. _____

4. Write the largest multiple of 8 that is less than 100: _____ Now subtract answer 3 from this multiple. _____

5. The Star of David is an important Jewish symbol. It has six points. List all the factors of 6: _____ Find the sum of these factors: _____ Subtract this sum from answer 4. _____

6. List all the factors of 11: _____ Multiply them by each other: _____ Multiply this product by answer 5. _____

7. List all the factors of 12: _____. Find their sum: _____ Subtract this total from answer 6. _____

8. Write the largest multiple of 11 that is less than 100: _____ Write the largest multiple of 12 that is less than 50: _____ Find the difference between these two numbers: _____ Subtract this difference from answer 7. _____

9. List all the multiples of 6 that are between 40 and 70: _____ Add the smallest of these multiples to answer 8: _____ Now subtract the largest of these multiples from that sum. _____

10. Write the fifth multiple of 11 (11 is the first one): _____ Add this number to answer 9. _____

11. Subtract the number of points in the Star of David from answer 10. _____

12. Write the smallest factor of 12: _____ Now subtract that factor from answer 11. Congratulations! You're finished! The year of the temple battle was _____ B.C.

Bonus Box: On the back of this sheet, list all the multiples of 12 between 100 and 300. Then list all the multiples of 11 between 100 and 300. What two numbers are multiples of *both* 11 and 12? Circle them.

Christmas Hideaways

Can you find the hidden Christmas words? Each word on a gift contains a four-letter word related to Christmas. The four letters are in the correct left-to-right order. Your job? Read the clue below for each word. Decide what the word is and find it in the corresponding word on a gift. Circle the letters of the hidden word; then write it on the gift and beside its clue. The first one is done for you.

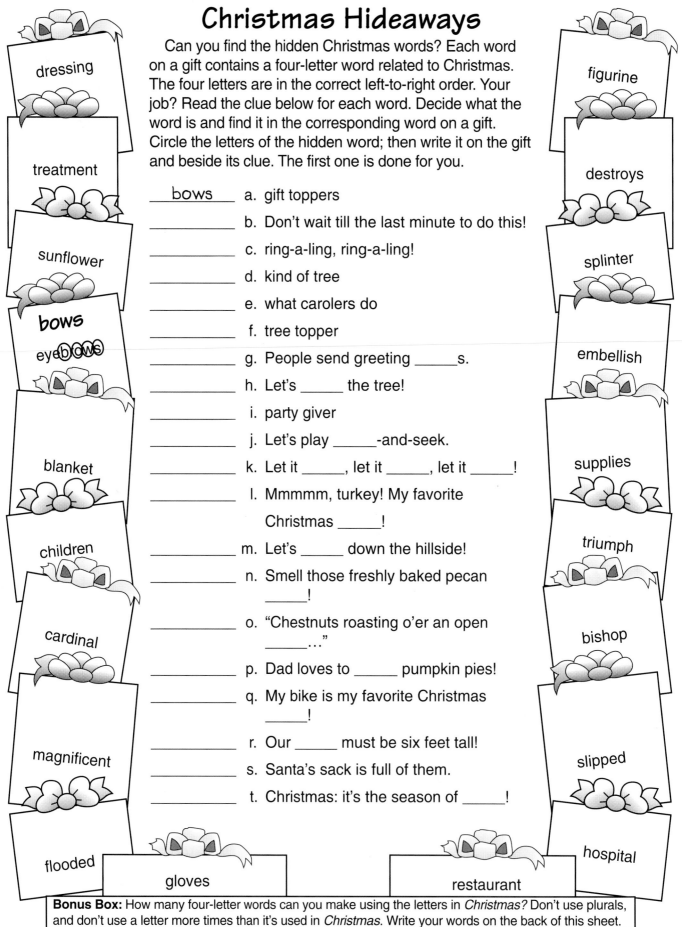

dressing

treatment

sunflower

bows

eyebrows

blanket

children

cardinal

magnificent

flooded

gloves

figurine

destroys

splinter

embellish

supplies

triumph

bishop

slipped

hospital

restaurant

__bows__   a. gift toppers

_____   b. Don't wait till the last minute to do this!

_____   c. ring-a-ling, ring-a-ling!

_____   d. kind of tree

_____   e. what carolers do

_____   f. tree topper

_____   g. People send greeting _____s.

_____   h. Let's _____ the tree!

_____   i. party giver

_____   j. Let's play _____-and-seek.

_____   k. Let it _____, let it _____, let it _____!

_____   l. Mmmmm, turkey! My favorite Christmas _____!

_____   m. Let's _____ down the hillside!

_____   n. Smell those freshly baked pecan _____!

_____   o. "Chestnuts roasting o'er an open _____…"

_____   p. Dad loves to _____ pumpkin pies!

_____   q. My bike is my favorite Christmas _____!

_____   r. Our _____ must be six feet tall!

_____   s. Santa's sack is full of them.

_____   t. Christmas: it's the season of _____!

Bonus Box: How many four-letter words can you make using the letters in *Christmas?* Don't use plurals, and don't use a letter more times than it's used in *Christmas*. Write your words on the back of this sheet.

In Other Words

Writers often look in a thesaurus to find a more exact synonym for a word. A thesaurus alphabetically lists words and their synonyms. Look at the sample page of synonyms for **good.**

Notice that the synonyms of a word may not all be synonyms of each other.

For example:

- good means "beneficial" in: Carrots are *good* for you.
- good means "profitable" in: We made a *good* deal on the sale.
- good means "adequate" in: Jody received *good* care in the hospital.

```
beneficial    caring
         fitting
    nice
profitable    wonderful
    adequate    smart
```

A. Read the following story about Dr. Martin Luther King, Jr.

As a young man, Martin Luther King was a **good (1)** student. He was so **smart (2)** that he **bypassed (3)** the 9th and 12th grades in school! He **began (4)** college when he was 15 years old. Martin later **obtained (5)** a doctorate degree and became a minister.

Dr. King was a **good (6)** speaker. He became the **foremost (7)** leader of the civil rights movement in the United States during the 1950s and 1960s. Even after his home was bombed, he **maintained (8)** that nonviolence was the way to end discrimination. He **directed (9)** more than 200,000 Americans in the March on Washington. During this march, Dr. King gave his **acclaimed (10)** "I Have a Dream" speech.

Dr. King **worked (11)** to get the Voting Rights Act of 1965 passed. He also worked to increase job opportunities for blacks. He wanted to **better (12) bad (13)** housing and poor schools. Dr. King was arrested many times. He was jailed for protesting unfairness and discrimination.

In 1964, Dr. King **earned (14)** the Nobel Peace Prize. Sadly, he was assassinated at the age of 39. After his death Congress passed the Civil Rights Act of 1968. This act **bars (15)** racial discrimination when persons buy or rent most homes. Dr. King's birthday is now a federal holiday celebrated on the third Monday in January.

B. In each group of words below, circle the best synonym for the boldfaced word in the story. To help you decide, reread the sentence in the story that has that word.

1. **good:** nice, useful, excellent
2. **smart:** stylish, intelligent, witty
3. **bypassed:** detoured, skipped, jumped
4. **began:** initiated, started, created
5. **obtained:** caught, earned, acquired
6. **good:** pleasant, helpful, superb
7. **foremost:** good, main, star
8. **maintained:** believed, conserved, serviced
9. **directed:** led, commanded, managed
10. **acclaimed:** famous, great, primary
11. **worked:** performed, strived, satisfied
12. **better:** improve, enhance, exceed
13. **bad:** evil, ill-behaved, inferior
14. **earned:** gained, won, profited
15. **bars:** excludes, slows, prevents

Bonus Box: Some synonyms of *bad* include: *tough, naughty, evil, rotten, defective, wrong,* and *unpleasant.* Choose five of these synonyms and write a sentence for each one on the back of this page.

Gear up for the dandy days of February and March with this simply splendid collection of seasonal ideas and reproducibles.

Valentine's Day

Straight-From-The-Heart Stories

Sweeten your lesson plans this Valentine's Day with a guessing game that combines writing practice with candy hearts! Give each child a candy heart and ask him not to share its message with classmates. Then have the student write a brief story using the words on his candy somewhere in the tale's text (see the example). After all the stories have been written, ask each student to share his tale with the class. Direct him to then call on three classmates to guess the message on his candy heart. Reward the correct guesser with an additional candy heart. If no one guesses correctly, give another candy heart to the story's author. How's that for a sweetheart of an idea? *Judy Holt— Gr. 4, Madison Simis School, Phoenix, AZ*

Excited About Valentine's Day

I was so excited about Valentine's Day that I woke up an hour early! The radio announcer said we'd have a cool day, so I dressed warmly. I was the first one in my class to arrive. Mrs. Cox told me I could stuff the valentines I'd brought into our decorated box. What fun we were going to have!

A Heart-For-A-Heart Frame

Here's a Valentine's Day project that will have students putting a little heart into their work! In advance have each child write and illustrate a Valentine's Day poem. Have him copy his poem onto a paper heart cutout. Laminate the cutouts; then gather the materials listed and have students follow the steps below. The resulting projects can be displayed or serve as great gifts! *Susan Phillips—Gr. 5, Harwood, ND*

Materials for each child: newspaper; a supply of puzzle pieces; red, pink, and white paint; paintbrush; glue; various art materials (sequins, small beads, glitter, permanent markers, etc.); ribbon (optional)

There's nobody else in the world like you— My brown, furry puppy friend who's always true-blue!

Steps:
1. Place the puzzle pieces on newspaper; then paint them with red, pink, and white paint. Allow to dry.
2. Arrange the puzzle pieces around the outer edge of the heart cutout, making sure that the pieced heart shape is slightly larger than your poem's heart.
3. Glue the puzzle pieces together, overlapping them slightly, to make a heart-shaped frame. Allow to dry.
4. Decorate the frame with a variety of art materials.
5. Glue the heart cutout to the back of your frame.
6. To hang the frame, glue a loop of ribbon to the back.

Presidents' Day

Hail To The Chief!

Celebrate Presidents' Day all February long with a display that should make Uncle Sam proud! Enlist a parent volunteer to trace each student's silhouette onto a 12" x 18" sheet of blue paper. Have each child cut out his silhouette and glue it onto a 12" x 18" sheet of white paper. Give the student two precut red paper banners (see the illustration). Have him write "President [student's last name]" on one banner. On the other banner, have him write a sentence about a worthy contribution he'd make if he were president of the United States. These projects will do more than help your students think about patriotism—they'll create a colorful display as well! *Martha Freese—Gr. 5, Regency Park Elementary, Pittsburgh, PA*

President Lopez

I would buy computers for each class.

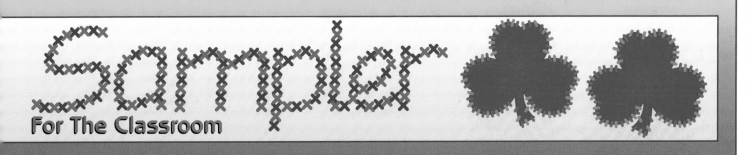

Sampler

For The Classroom

Guess Who?

Combine art and famous African-Americans for a game that's both informational *and* fun! First assign each student a different African-American. Require the student to research to find ten facts about his person. Next have the student illustrate one of his facts on a 12" x 18" sheet of drawing paper. On the back of the drawing, have the student list all ten facts he researched—without mentioning the famous person's name in any of the facts. To play, divide students into two teams. Have a member of Team One come to the front of the room, hold up his drawing, and read the list of facts on the back. Give one point to Team Two if it guesses the person's identity in three tries or less. If Team Two guesses incorrectly, give Team One the point. Alternate teams until all students have shared.

St. Patrick's Day

booklet page

Lucky Shamrocks

You won't need a leprechaun around to benefit from the good luck in this St. Patrick's Day activity! Duplicate a supply of the booklet page shown. Label the shamrock on each page with a different letter of the alphabet; then give one to each student. Ask each child to think of something she's lucky to have that begins with her shamrock's letter. On the shamrock, have her write a paragraph describing her item and add illustrations. Bind students' completed pages into a booklet titled "Not Just The Luck Of The Irish!" Or tape the papers together end-to-end to form a long mural. ***Theresa Roh Hickey—Gr. 5, Corpus Christi School, Mobile, AL***

Mapping The Emerald Isle

Celebrate St. Patrick's Day with this good-as-gold geography activity that explores the Emerald Isle! Give each student a copy of page 280. Divide the class into groups and supply each team with an atlas. Review with students the different purposes of a *political map;* then have groups find a political map of Ireland in their atlases. As students share, list on the board the provinces, counties, major cities, bodies of water, and other items they find on the maps. Finally have each student use colored pencils and the atlas to illustrate the small, blank political map on his copy of page 280. After completing this step, have the student choose another kind of map (*population density, products, physical features,* etc.) and illustrate it on the other blank map on her sheet. Lastly have the student draw and color the Irish flag on the page. Display the completed sheets on a bulletin board backed with three equal-sized rectangles of green, white, and orange paper arranged to represent Ireland's flag. You'll make St. Patrick proud! ***Beth Gress, Granville, OH***

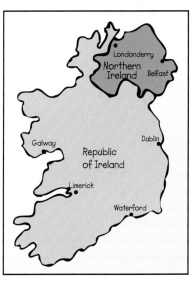

Colorful Poetry

Roses are red.
Violets are blue.
Sugar is sweet
And so are you.

You've probably heard this well-known Valentine's Day verse hundreds of times! Try writing some new Valentine's Day poems by following the same pattern—but with some new twists. For example, switch the first two lines; then add two new lines in the blanks below. The second line must now end in a word that rhymes with *red:*

Violets are blue.
Roses are red.

_____

_____

Here are two possible endings:

When I see you,   *You are the one*
I lose my head!   *I wish to wed.*

Now create five more short rhymes using this pattern. They may be romantic, serious, or just plain silly! Write each four-line poem in the blanks below. Use the back of this sheet if you need more room. Here are some sample lines to choose from:

Carnations are pink...   *Grass is green...*   *Irises are purple...*   *Chocolate is brown...*
Daffodils are yellow...   *Lilies are white...*   *Cherries are red...*   *The sky is blue...*

_____   _____   _____

_____   _____   _____

_____   _____   _____

_____   _____

_____   _____

_____   _____

_____   _____

Bonus Box: Write the name of a famous person you really admire on the back of this sheet. Then write a four-line poem like the ones above to this person.

©The Education Center, Inc. • THE MAILBOX® • Intermediate • Feb/Mar 1999 • written by Ann Fisher

Name(s)_____ Research skills

A Black History Mystery

In celebration of Black History Month in February, test your knowledge of famous Black Americans with this riddle. First decide whether each statement is true or false. Use encyclopedias and other resources to help you. Then circle the letter in either the **true** or **false** column. Write the circled letter in the blank above the matching number at the bottom of the page.

		true	false
1.	Jackie Robinson played baseball for the Cincinnati Reds.	A	E
2.	Dr. Martin Luther King, Jr., was a famous surgeon.	I	O
3.	Matthew Henson was the first man to set foot on the North Pole.	A	S
4.	Althea Gibson was one of the world's greatest skiers.	T	R
5.	George Washington Carver developed over 300 uses for the peanut plant.	M	B
6.	Langston Hughes wrote plays, stories, and poetry about Black life.	H	G
7.	Shirley Chisholm was the first Black woman to serve in the U.S. Congress.	R	N
8.	Rosa Parks was an attorney who fought for civil rights.	K	F
9.	Colin Powell earned the Bronze Star For Valor in the Vietnam War.	E	L
10.	Jesse Jackson won four gold medals in swimming in the 1936 Olympics.	W	D
11.	Dr. Ronald McNair was the first Black U.S. Supreme Court Justice.	J	O
12.	Thurgood Marshall was a Baptist minister who ran for president in 1984.	C	T
13.	Duke Ellington was a great jazz musician and composer.	T	P
14.	Mary McLeod Bethune wrote the famous book *Roots.*	Y	O
15.	Marian Anderson was the first Black soloist with the Metropolitan Opera of New York City.	D	T
16.	In 1753, Benjamin Banneker built a clock made entirely of wood.	E	C

Harriet Tubman helped slaves escape on

" __ __ __   __ __ __ __   __ __   __ __ __ __ __ __ __ __ "
　 12 6 9 　 7 14 3 10 　13 2 　 8 4 16 1 15 11 5

Bonus Box: Rewrite each false statement above to make it true. Write your statements on the back of this sheet.

©The Education Center, Inc. • *THE MAILBOX*® • *Intermediate* • Feb/Mar 1999 • Key p. 313 • written by Beth Gress

Note To The Teacher: You may wish to divide students into pairs to complete this activity.

279

Name

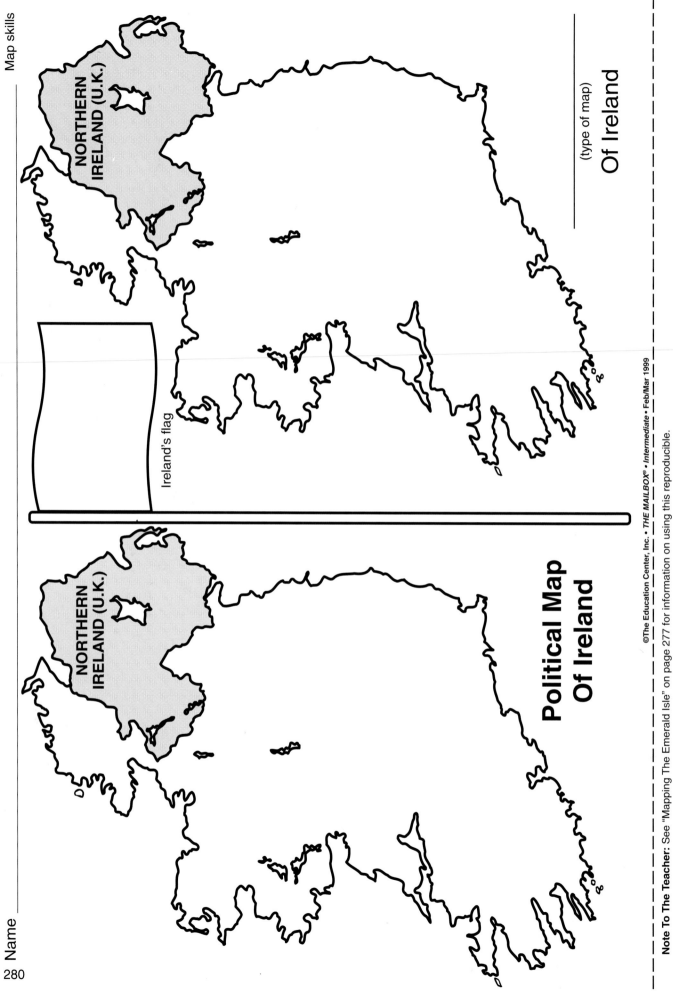

NORTHERN
IRELAND (U.K.)

_____
(type of map)

Of Ireland

Ireland's flag

NORTHERN
IRELAND (U.K.)

**Political Map
Of Ireland**

Note To The Teacher: See "Mapping The Emerald Isle" on page 277 for information on using this reproducible.

A Sip Of Spring

Looking for a cool way to celebrate the first day of spring this March? Then complete the following math puzzle for a refreshing surprise! You'll need four colored pencils: green, yellow, blue, and red. First look at the *circled number* on each puzzle piece. Then follow one of these steps:

- If the number is closest to 0, make a green check mark on the puzzle piece.
- If the number is closest to 1/2, make a yellow check mark on the piece.
- If the number is closest to 1, make a blue check mark on the piece.
- If the number is greater than 1, make a red check mark on the piece.

When finished, check your work. (Your teacher will share the correct answers.) Next color each puzzle piece the same color as its check mark. Then cut out the pieces. On a sheet of construction paper, place the pieces so that each fraction is beside its equivalent decimal. If you've done this step correctly, a sweet treat will be revealed. Finally glue all of the pieces on the construction paper.

©The Education Center, Inc. • THE MAILBOX® • Intermediate • Feb/Mar 1999 • Key p. 313 • written by Beth Gress

Note To The Teacher: Before students color their puzzle pieces, check their work by the answer key on page 313. Then provide each student with a 9" x 12" sheet of black construction paper, scissors, and glue. Display students' completed projects on a bulletin board with a giant lemon slice cutout in the corner. 281

Spring into the months of April and May with the following creative activities that are seasoned just right!

Easter

"Some-bunny" Loves You!

Celebrate Easter with an art project that "hippitty-hops" into a writing activity! Have each student make a bunny pin as a gift for someone special. Then encourage him to write a story about the adventurous trail his bunny will take to get to its new owner.

Materials for each pin:

one 3 3/4" (95 mm) no-roll wooden clothespin
2 small wiggly eyes
tiny pink pom-pom (5 mm)

white glue
pink paint
paintbrush
small pin back

8" length of pink yarn
fine-tipped black marker
3" x 5" unlined index card
markers, crayons, or colored pencils

Steps:
1. Position the clothespin as shown. Then glue the wiggly eyes and pom-pom in place.
2. Use the marker to draw a mouth on the bunny.
3. Tie the yarn into a bow around the bunny's neck.
4. Paint a pink vertical line down each prong of the clothespin. Allow to dry.
5. Glue the pin back to the back of the clothespin. Allow to dry.
6. Write "Some-bunny Loves You!" on the index card. Add other illustrations if desired. Then pin the bunny on the card. ***Ann Scheiblin, Oak View School, Bloomfield, NJ***

Some-bunny Loves You!

Earth Day

Newsworthy Graph

Reduce paper waste in your community with this schoolwide Earth Day project! Assign each participating class a spot along a wall of a large area, such as a multipurpose room. Over a two-week period, share a recycling fact (see the example) during the morning announcements; then challenge students to bring in old newspapers to recycle. As the newspapers come in, have students stack them under their homerooms' assigned spots to create a three-dimensional bar graph. At the end of the two weeks, help students evaluate the impact this waste would have on your community. Afterward sell the accumulated papers to a local recycling company. Use the money to purchase trees that will beautify your school grounds and serve as reminders of this "tree-rific" project! ***Alicia Anton & Judy Bosack, Peebles Elementary, Pittsburgh, PA***

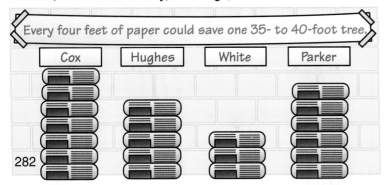

Every four feet of paper could save one 35- to 40-foot tree.

Cox	Hughes	White	Parker

"Trash-y" Poetry

Change the way your students feel about a key environmental issue—taking out the trash—with Shel Silverstein's humorous poem, "Sarah Cynthia Sylvia Stout Would Not Take The Garbage Out," from *Where The Sidewalk Ends* (HarperCollins Children's Books, 1974). Share this poem aloud with students. Then direct each student to copy the line "Poor Sarah met an awful fate…" on paper and finish the poem with an ending of her own. Have students illustrate their poems; then display the projects on a bulletin board decorated with a brown grocery bag and samples of cleaned trash as shown. Follow up by challenging groups of students to research environmental problems that stem from improper trash disposal. ***Kimberly J. Branham—Gr. 5, Wateree Elementary, Lugoff, SC***

Sampler
For The Classroom

Flower Flip Book

Students will flip over these books that make reviewing the parts of beautiful May flowers a breeze!

Materials for each student:
two 8-inch squares of white duplicating paper
scissors   colored pencils
pencil   stapler

Steps:
1. Stack the two squares atop each other. Fold the stack in half; then fold it in half again.
2. Cut along the folds to make eight squares. Stack the sheets and staple them together at the top corners.
3. Starting with the bottom sheet, draw the outline of a simple flower. Flip down the next sheet and trace the flower on it. Repeat for the remaining sheets.
4. Turn back to the bottom sheet. On the flower outline, draw and label the *sepal*. Then color the drawing.
5. Flip down the next sheet. On it, draw both the sepal and the *pistil*, but label only the pistil. Then color the drawing.
6. Continue drawing, labeling, and coloring one new part at a time until the top drawing contains all the parts (with no labels). The seven remaining pages from bottom to top should show these parts labeled in order: *sepal, pistil, ovary, eggs, stamen, anther, pollen.*

Amy Heuer—Gr. 5, West Lane Elementary, Jackson, MO

Step 3

Step 5

My Flower Flip Book

Nicole

Pictographs, Olé!

Celebrate Cinco de Mayo (May 5) with a graphing activity that will put everyone in a festive mood! Pose each of the following questions one at a time to students; then have students raise their hands to respond as you tally their responses on the board.

1. Have you ever held a *peso*?
2. Who has visited Mexico?
3. Who has eaten a *tortilla*?
4. Who has worn a *serape*?
5. Who has read a book about Mexico?

Afterward have students choose a symbol—such as a *sombrero* or *maraca*—to use in a pictograph. Based on the tallies, help students determine how many pupils the symbol should represent. Then have each student create his own pictograph using the class data. Graphing skills will be sharpened before you can say, "Olé!"

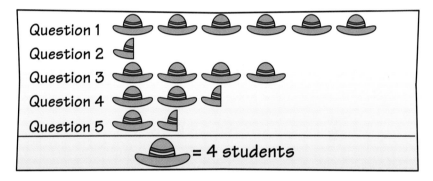

Question 1
Question 2
Question 3
Question 4
Question 5

= 4 students

Three Cheers For Mom!

Remember Mom (or someone who's like a mom to you) this Mother's Day with a gift that's sure to cheer her! Place two lengths of curled curling ribbon in the bottom of a clean, plastic fluted glass. Fill the glass with colorful wrapped candies; then insert two straws into the glass. Next dangle four additional pieces of curling ribbon around the outside of the glass. Punch a hole in the top right corner of a small index card; then label the card with a three-sentence toast to your mom to let her know how great she is. Tie the card to one of the ribbons. Here's to you, Mom! *Colleen Dabney, Williamsburg-JCC Public Schools, Williamsburg, VA*

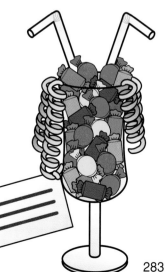

One Stuffed Bunny!

All that candy! This stuffed bunny needs to do some serious exercising to get rid of all those calories. Follow these steps to complete each problem:

1. Use the information in the first chart to find the total number of calories in the candies listed on each egg.
2. Find out how many minutes of each activity the bunny needs to do to get rid of those calories. (Hint: If a quotient has a remainder, *round up* to the next whole number.)
3. Complete your work on another sheet of paper.
4. Write your answers in the blanks provided.

Candy	Calories
10 malted-milk eggs	230
1 chocolate bunny	900
5 Gummy Worm® candies	215
10 jelly beans	410
1 bag of candy-coated chocolates	236
1 peanut-butter egg	220

Activity	Calories Burned Per Minute
dancing	6
cycling	3
golf	5
horseback riding	2
running	12
swimming	9
tennis	7
walking	4

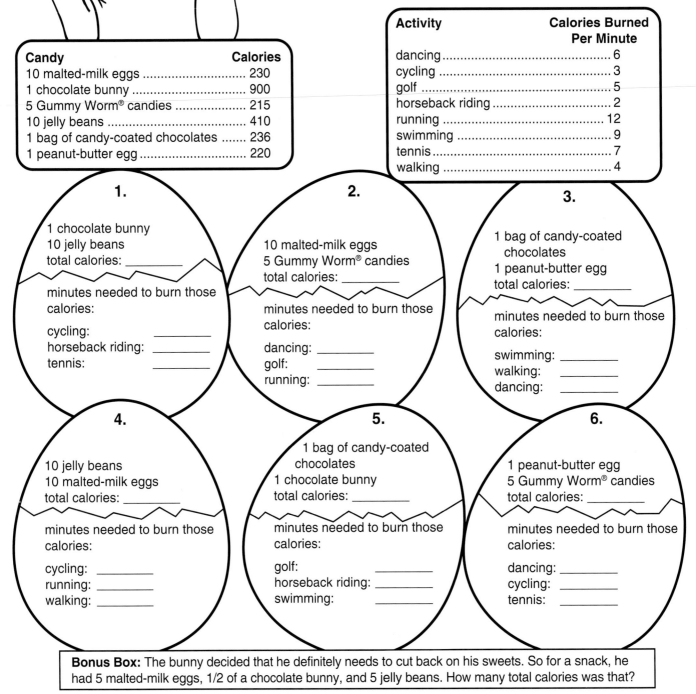

1.
1 chocolate bunny
10 jelly beans
total calories: _____

minutes needed to burn those calories:

cycling: _____
horseback riding: _____
tennis: _____

2.
10 malted-milk eggs
5 Gummy Worm® candies
total calories: _____

minutes needed to burn those calories:

dancing: _____
golf: _____
running: _____

3.
1 bag of candy-coated chocolates
1 peanut-butter egg
total calories: _____

minutes needed to burn those calories:

swimming: _____
walking: _____
dancing: _____

4.
10 jelly beans
10 malted-milk eggs
total calories: _____

minutes needed to burn those calories:

cycling: _____
running: _____
walking: _____

5.
1 bag of candy-coated chocolates
1 chocolate bunny
total calories: _____

minutes needed to burn those calories:

golf: _____
horseback riding: _____
swimming: _____

6.
1 peanut-butter egg
5 Gummy Worm® candies
total calories: _____

minutes needed to burn those calories:

dancing: _____
cycling: _____
tennis: _____

Bonus Box: The bunny decided that he definitely needs to cut back on his sweets. So for a snack, he had 5 malted-milk eggs, 1/2 of a chocolate bunny, and 5 jelly beans. How many total calories was that?

This Is *Your* Classroom!

What's it like to be a teacher? Below are just a few of the many things teachers do and think about...sometimes every day! To celebrate National Teacher Appreciation Week (May 2–8), put yourself in your teacher's shoes for a while. Complete _____ of the following activities by _____.

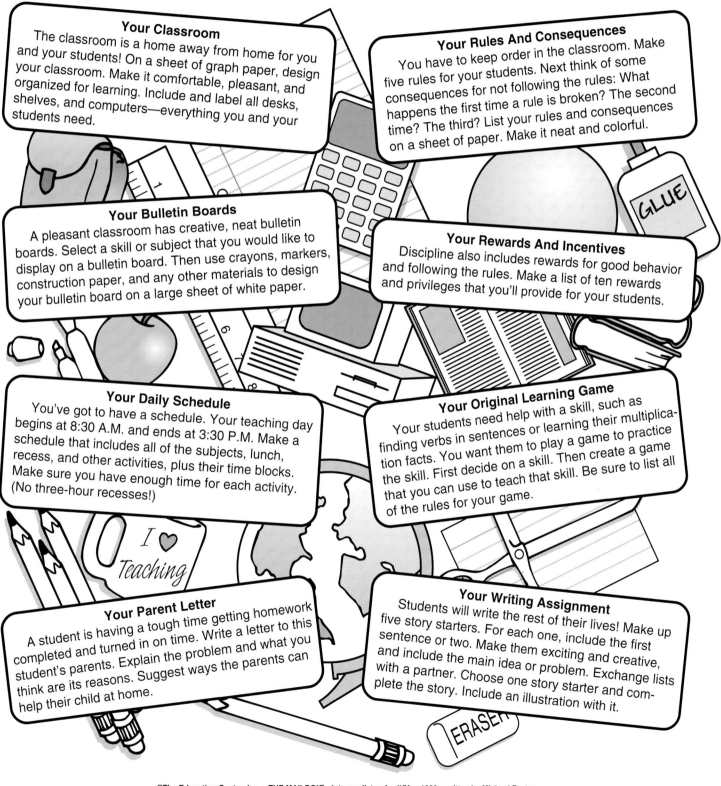

Your Classroom
The classroom is a home away from home for you and your students! On a sheet of graph paper, design your classroom. Make it comfortable, pleasant, and organized for learning. Include and label all desks, shelves, and computers—everything you and your students need.

Your Rules And Consequences
You have to keep order in the classroom. Make five rules for your students. Next think of some consequences for not following the rules: What happens the first time a rule is broken? The second time? The third? List your rules and consequences on a sheet of paper. Make it neat and colorful.

Your Bulletin Boards
A pleasant classroom has creative, neat bulletin boards. Select a skill or subject that you would like to display on a bulletin board. Then use crayons, markers, construction paper, and any other materials to design your bulletin board on a large sheet of white paper.

Your Rewards And Incentives
Discipline also includes rewards for good behavior and following the rules. Make a list of ten rewards and privileges that you'll provide for your students.

Your Daily Schedule
You've got to have a schedule. Your teaching day begins at 8:30 A.M. and ends at 3:30 P.M. Make a schedule that includes all of the subjects, lunch, recess, and other activities, plus their time blocks. Make sure you have enough time for each activity. (No three-hour recesses!)

Your Original Learning Game
Your students need help with a skill, such as finding verbs in sentences or learning their multiplication facts. You want them to play a game to practice the skill. First decide on a skill. Then create a game that you can use to teach that skill. Be sure to list all of the rules for your game.

Your Parent Letter
A student is having a tough time getting homework completed and turned in on time. Write a letter to this student's parents. Explain the problem and what you think are its reasons. Suggest ways the parents can help their child at home.

Your Writing Assignment
Students will write the rest of their lives! Make up five story starters. For each one, include the first sentence or two. Make them exciting and creative, and include the main idea or problem. Exchange lists with a partner. Choose one story starter and complete the story. Include an illustration with it.

Note To The Teacher: Before duplicating this page, fill in the number of activities that you would like for your students to complete and a due date.

Get ready for June's end-of-school frenzy and the summery days of July with this sizzling collection of seasonal ideas and reproducibles.

End Of The Year: "Sun-sational" Shades

Spend a fun Friday afternoon making "sun-sational" shades! First brainstorm with students different themes that could be used for their designs, such as sports, hobbies, animals, cars, etc. Then give each student scissors, clear tape, markers, glue, glitter, a 9" x 12" piece of oaktag, and a 9" x 12" piece of colored cellophane. Have the student draw and color his design on the oaktag, then cut out the glasses and the openings for the eyes. Finally, have him tape the cellophane to the back and trim off the excess. After students add details with markers and glitter, display the decorative sunglasses on a bulletin board titled "'Sun-sational' Shades!" *Joan M. Macey, Binghamton, NY*

End Of The Year: Signs Of Success

Get a jump on August by having your students pre-pare a display that will head next year's class in the right direction! First discuss with students different types of road signs (stop, yield, railroad crossing, speed limit, road work, etc.). Point out how such signs help people move about more safely and successfully. Together, brainstorm words of wisdom that this year's students could give your next class; then assign each student a different letter of the alphabet and give him a sheet of oaktag, scissors, and colored markers. Direct the student to design a road sign and label it with a piece of advice that begins with his assigned letter. Post the signs; then save them to display at the beginning of the next school year. *Margaret Zogg—K–6 Substitute, Liverpool School District, Liverpool, NY*

End Of The Year: Lunch Bag Publishing

Turn plain paper lunch bags into memory books that help students reminisce about their super school year. Have each child fold a lunch bag in half; then have her reinforce the unfolded edges by covering them with clear tape. Direct the student to fold four sheets of plain white paper in half two times, then cut out the resulting sections to make 16 pages for her book. Next have the student staple the pages inside the cover at the fold and glue the first and last pages to the covers. Finally have her title her book "Food For Thought About A Fun Year" and decorate the cover. Direct students to use the suggestions below for writing and illustrating the first few pages of their books, leaving the remaining pages for classmates' auto-graphs. What a treasured keepsake this will become! *Ingrid Wolf—Gr. 5, Catholic Central School, Appleton, WI*

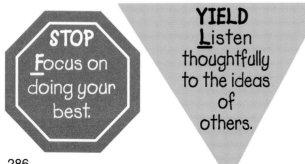

STOP
<u>F</u>ocus on doing your best.

YIELD
<u>L</u>isten thoughtfully to the ideas of others.

Suggestions:

My favorite memory about this school
   year is…
The funniest thing that happened this
   year was…
How could I forget…
The best field trip this year was…

Food For Thought About A Fun Year

End Of The Year:
And The Days Go
Marching On...

"Ant-ticipate" a fun ending to a terrific year with a display that counts down the days 'til school's out! Cover a bulletin board with an inexpensive, red-checkered plastic tablecloth. Staple on paper plates and napkins, empty drink boxes, and other picnic items. Enlarge the ant pattern shown; then duplicate one ant for each remaining school day. Have students color and cut out the ant cutouts; then post them among the picnic items. Each day let a student remove an ant from the board. Before you know it, summer vacation will be here! *Teena Andersen, Hadar Public School, Hadar, NE*

Father's Day:
Magnetic Frame

Want a gift idea that's sure to attract a lot of attention? Then this magnetic frame should do the trick! Give each student four craft sticks and several different shapes of dried pasta. Direct the student to glue the sticks together to make a square. When the glue has dried, have him paint the square and pasta pieces  with paint. After the sticks and pasta have dried, have the student glue the pasta onto the sticks in an attractive arrangement, adding glitter if desired. Finally have the student attach two pieces of self-sticking magnetic tape to the back of the frame. Let students take their frames home to surprise their dads. Or present them at the end of the year to your parent volunteers. *Sherri Kaiser—Gr. 4, Walnut Grove Elementary, Suwanee, GA*

©The Education Center, Inc. • *THE MAILBOX®* • Intermediate • June/July 1999

Flag Day/Independence Day:
Life, Liberty, And Happiness

Create an eye-popping patriotic display with this easy-to-do activity. Together discuss the Declaration of Rights found in the Declaration of Independence (see the illustration); then have students share their interpretations of "life, liberty, and the pursuit of happiness." Next give each student old magazines, scissors, glue, and a 9" x 12" sheet of red construction paper. Guide students through the steps below to make a large American flag. *Jan Kneessi—Gr. 5, Trinity Christian School, Northridge, CA*

Steps:
1. On his red paper, have each student create a collage of pictures representing his thoughts about "life, liberty, and the pursuit of happiness."
2. Tape the collages together side by side as shown to form five red horizontal stripes.
3. Write each part of the Declaration of Rights on a separate 4-inch-wide banner of white paper as shown.
4. Have students cut out and glue 50 white stars to a 26" x 36" blue rectangle.
5. Tape the field of stars and the stripes together to make a giant flag as shown.

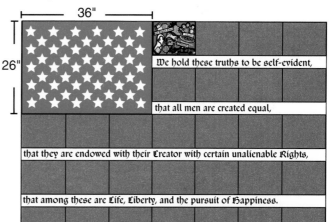

287

288

The "Purr-fect" School

As the school year comes to an end, think about each of the items listed on the sign below. What were they like for you this past year? Now think about this question: What would they be like in a *perfect* school?

Choose one topic from the list. Write a descriptive paragraph about that topic, giving plenty of details about your ideas of "purr-fection." First write your rough draft on another sheet of paper. After a partner edits your rough draft, write your final draft on the cat pattern.

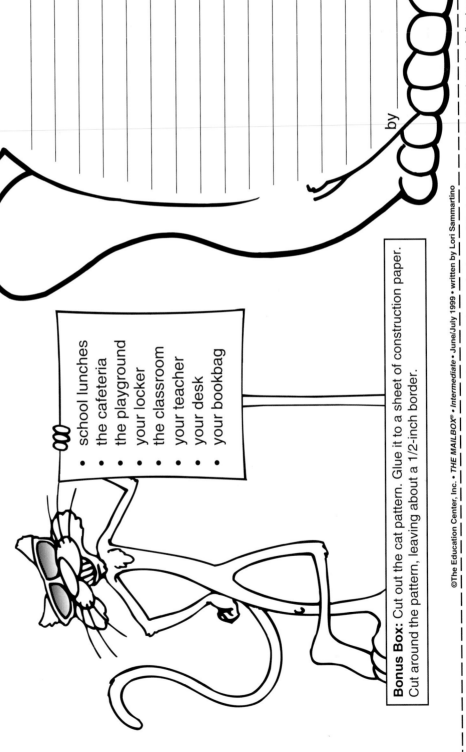

by _____

- school lunches
- the cafeteria
- the playground
- your locker
- the classroom
- your teacher
- your desk
- your bookbag

Bonus Box: Cut out the cat pattern. Glue it to a sheet of construction paper. Cut around the pattern, leaving about a 1/2-inch border.

©The Education Center, Inc. • *THE MAILBOX®* • *Intermediate* • June/July 1999 • written by Lori Sammartino

Note To The Teacher: Provide each student with a 9" x 6" piece of construction paper, glue, and scissors. Attach a length of string to each student's final project and suspend it from the ceiling.

A Trip Down Memory Lane

1. homework

2. turning in work

3. rules & rewards

4. recess

5. morning routine

6. field trips

You've spent the past year learning the rules of the road in your classroom, so now you're an expert driver! Take a trip down Memory Lane to help prepare next year's students for what lies ahead.

First think about the topics on the signs. On the lines, write a sentence about each topic telling upcoming students what they'll need to know in order to stay on the road to success in your teacher's classroom.

Ready? Start your engines!

Rules Of The Road

1. _____
2. _____
3. _____
4. _____
5. _____
6. _____

I ♥ School!

by _____

©The Education Center, Inc. • *THE MAILBOX® • Intermediate* • June/July 1999 • written by Lori Sammartino

Note To The Teacher: When students are finished, have them cut out their patterns on the bold lines. Collect the patterns and save them for a back-to-school bulletin board to welcome next year's group of students.

☆ Fractional Flags ☆

On June 14, 1777, the Continental Congress agreed on a design for our country's flag. We celebrate June 14 as Flag Day to remember this event. To honor this day, you have been asked to design four different flags. Shade each of the rectangles below according to its given fractions and colors. Then, on the lines below the designs, explain how you figured out the fractional parts for each color.

Design 1
1/3 red, 2/3 blue

Design 2
1/2 red, 1/4 blue, 1/4 white

Design 3
1/2 red, 1/4 blue,
1/8 white, 1/8 green

Design 4
1/3 red, 1/4 blue,
1/4 white, 1/6 green

_____
_____
_____
_____
_____
_____
_____

Bonus Box: John Adams stated "...that the flag of the thirteen United States shall be thirteen stripes, alternate red and white; that the 'Union' be thirteen stars, white in a blue field, representing a new constellation." On the back of this sheet, draw the flag Adams described.

OUR READERS WRITE

Our Readers Write

Open House Bulletin Board

Combine an art project with a bulletin board to make a warm, inviting welcome for back-to-school night. Provide each student with a small brown lunch bag. Have the student decorate his bag to look like his house, apartment building, etc. Supply markers and scraps of construction paper for the finishing touches. Then have each student stuff his house with newspaper and staple on a construction-paper roof. Attach the houses to a bulletin board titled "Welcome To Our Open House!"

Colleen Dabney—Grs. 6–7
Williamsburg Christian Academy
Williamsburg, VA

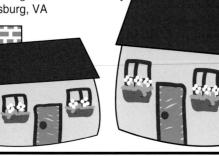

Common Bonds

Searching for a first-day-of-school activity that's uncommonly fun? Label a sheet of paper with a simple sentence that states a topic of interest, such as "My favorite subject is reading" or "I enjoy playing football." Place a sheet on each student's desk. Direct students to move about the room and read the sentence at the top of each sheet. Then have each child sign every sheet with which he agrees. After all signing is completed, share the lists with students. They'll be amazed to see all the common bonds they share with their new classmates!

Nellie Mullins—Gr. 4, Belle Reynolds Elementary, Oakfield, WI

I enjoy playing football:	My favorite subject is reading:
Josh	Ashley
Dylan	Emily
Megan	Katherine
Lauren	Hollis
Garrett	Joseph

Antique Maps

For a fun introduction to map skills, provide each student with a brown grocery bag. Have the student cut the bag to make a large, flat piece of paper; then have her draw a map of the United States on the bag, including symbols for special locations she would like to visit, a scale, and a key. Next have her crinkle the bag so that it looks old and wrinkled. That night, burn the edges of the maps to give them an antiqued look. Display each child's antique map. Then don't be surprised if your students are more than ready and willing to tackle map skills!

Lucretta Kinder—Gr. 4
Licking Elementary
Licking, MO

First-Day Quiz

Believe it or not, my students take a quiz on the first day of school. The topic? Me! I compose a quiz that lists 20 statements about me. Each student completes the quiz by answering true or false for each statement. After learning about me, the student is instructed to write a five-statement quiz about herself to share with her classmates. We read several quizzes a day during the first week of school. What a fun way to learn some interesting information about each other!

Laurette D. O'Donnell—Gr. 5
Brecknock Elementary
Bowmansville, PA

First-Day Quiz

Name_____

Answer **true** or **false** for each statement below:

1. Mrs. O'Donnell has two dogs. _____
2. Her daughter's name is Kelly. _____
3. She has been a teacher for eight years. _____
4. Her favorite food is liver. _____

Graffiti Board

Don't let busy schedules keep you from hearing what students have to say! Create a graffiti board for students to share their thoughts with you. Tape a large sheet of chart paper on the wall. Write a sentence starter across the top, such as "My goal for this school year is…" or "The best part of our class trip was…." Keep a bucket of colorful markers nearby and explain the following rules to students:
- You may visit the graffiti board when all your work is complete.
- One or two students may be at the board at one time.
- If you write inappropriate messages, you will lose your board privilege.
Be sure to change the sentence starter every two weeks.

Terry Castoria—Gr. 5, Frank Defino Central School, Marlboro, NJ

My goal for this school year is...

to make straight A's! Michael

to make the A/B Honor Roll! Holly

to be the fastest runner. Josh H.

A "Scooper-Dooper" Class

Here's a "scooper" sweet idea for a back-to-school bulletin board! Use a knife to carefully cut ice-cream cones in half. Write each student's name on a cone half with a marker; then use rubber cement to attach the cones to the board. Next rubber-cement Poly-Fil® above each cone to create the ice cream. To finish, sprinkle glitter on each cone filling. Title the board "[teacher's name]'s Scooper-Dooper Class!"

Cathy Butler , Shawnee Maplewood School
Lima, OH

First-Of-The-Year Contracts

Start the year on a positive note by providing each student with a copy of an "I Plan To Do My Best This Year" contract. (See the illustration.) Discuss ways that students can do their best throughout the year. Then direct each student to sign and date his contract and place it in the front of his notebook. Encourage each student to look back at his contract whenever he needs a dose of inspiration!

Chana Rochel Zucker—Gr. 5
Be'er Hagolah Institute
Brooklyn, NY

Silhouette Sleuths

Create a little mystery on the night of Open House with the following idea. Begin by using an overhead projector to trace each student's silhouette two times onto black construction paper. Carefully cut out the silhouettes; then secure a ruler between the two profiles with tape. Attach the ruler-supported silhouette to the back of the student's chair. Then challenge each parent to identify his child's silhouette when he visits the classroom during Open House.

Nancy Grow—Gr. 5, Westchester School, Kirkwood, MO

Paper-Plate Preview

When introducing a new unit, I just pass the plate! I provide each group with a large white paper plate labeled with a key term from the unit. For example, before reading *Number The Stars* by Lois Lowry, I might write "Holocaust" or "World War II" on the plate. I provide each group with colorful markers to use to write words and phrases describing what they already know about the topic on the plate. After discussing the topic, I am better able to adjust the unit to meet the needs of my students. I then use the completed plates to make a colorful bulletin-board display.

Martha Ennis
Blackmon Road Middle School
Columbus, GA

Part Of The Puzzle

Use this simple activity to piece together a cooperative class of students! Purchase a blank, precut puzzle; then give each student one puzzle piece. Using an ink pad, have the student place his thumbprint on his puzzle piece, adding his name and details to his print with felt-tipped markers. After all pieces have dried, reassemble the puzzle. Point out that although every student is an individual (represented by his thumbprint), every student is also an important part of the whole class. Finally have each student write a paragraph describing how his individual strengths will add to the class as a whole.

Colleen Dabney—Grs. 6–7
Williamsburg Christian Academy
Williamsburg, VA

Picture-Perfect Displays

Showcase students' writing in the following picture-perfect way! Purchase several 8" x 10" acrylic, self-standing frames. Display students' work in the frames in the media center, school lobby, or office. Change the writings periodically so that each student has the opportunity to showcase his work!

Patricia E. Dancho—Gr. 6
Apollo-Ridge Middle School
Spring Church, PA

Place-Value Necklaces

Use the following hands-on activity to teach place value to students. Provide each student or group with food coloring, uncooked pasta noodles, and string. Have students color the pasta with the food coloring. Allow time for the pasta to dry. Then assign values to the different colors of pasta (for example: blue = 1, red = 10, yellow = 100, and so on). Direct each student to string the pasta, then calculate the value of her necklace. How's that for using the ol' noodle?

David Reitz—Gr. 4
Glenwood Elementary
Virginia Beach, VA

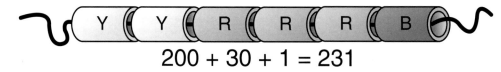

$$200 + 30 + 1 = 231$$

Tabletop Treasure

Have students create a keepsake for the year with this simple idea. Place a vinyl tablecloth on a classroom table. Have each student autograph the tablecloth with a permanent marker on the first day of school. Each time the class does something special throughout the year, have a student record the event on the tablecloth with a small picture and caption.

Julie Eick Granchelli—Gr. 4
Towne Elementary, Medina, NY

The Perfect 10!

Turn your class's behavior in line into a "perfect 10" with the following idea. Explain to students that a perfect 10 means "1 line with 0 noise." After arriving at your destination, decide as a class whether a perfect 10 was maintained throughout the journey. Add a plastic dime to a jar every time the class maintains a perfect 10. When the class earns $1.00, reward students with ten extra minutes of recess or free time. When the class earns $10.00 (100 perfect 10s), reward students with a Perfect 10 Party. You'll find that students will love the rewards as well as the rave reviews from other teachers, parents, and administrators!

Chuck Yeager—Gr. 5, Priceville School, Decatur, AL

Nouns To Know

Create a back-to-school bulletin board that also reviews nouns. Cover a board with inexpensive back-to-school fabric. Make three columns on the board with the headings "People," "Places," and "Things." Under each heading, list actual people, places, and things that relate to your school. What a great way to review nouns *and* help students become more familiar with their new environment!

Marilyn Davison—Grs. 4–5, River Oaks School, Monroe, LA

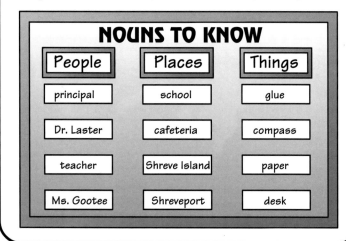

Hospitality Hosts

Let your students take charge of Open House! Have each child place his books, folders, and portfolio on his desk at the end of the school day. Provide each student with a copy of a hospitality checklist (see the illustration) to use as an outline when his family arrives. On the night of Open House, have students greet parents, describe important aspects of the classroom, and answer questions. You can sit in the background with parents and help when the need arises.

Phyllis Ellett—Grs. 3–4
Earl Hanson Elementary
Rock Island, IL

Recycled Timeline

Don't junk those preprinted envelopes from junk mail! Use them to create a timeline in your classroom. Simply have students donate unused envelopes from junk mail. Next have them write important facts and dates on the backs of the envelopes. Then hang the envelopes over a piece of string and seal tightly.

Sr. Margaret Xavier, Mother Seton Academy, Baltimore, MD

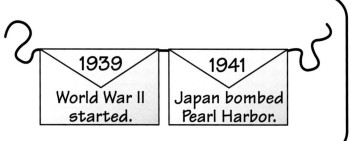

Why Was It Invented?

Begin a unit on inventions with the following ingenious idea! Bring in several different household inventions, such as a peeler, a fitted sheet, or a screwdriver. Have students identify the problem solved by one of the inventions and suggest ways that the invention might be improved. Next display a transparency of the form shown. As a class, evaluate another invention using the form's questions. Then give each pair of students a copy of the form and have them evaluate another invention. For an inventive homework assignment, send a form home for each child's family to complete together.

Jan Drehmel—Gr. 4
Parkview Elementary, Chippewa Falls, WI

Why Was It Invented?

Invention: _____

1. Why was this invention invented? What problems does it solve? _____
2. How have people benefited from this invention? _____
3. How might this invention be improved? _____

Draw a diagram of your improvements on the back of this form.

4. How would you rate this invention?
   Useful _____ Not important _____
   Why did you rate it as you did? _____

Adjective Family Portraits

Promote teamwork, review adjectives, and have lots of fun with this quick-and-easy activity. Divide the class into small groups. Have each group decide on an adjective that describes its "family" (for example, *gloomy, nervous, joyful,* etc.). Then have each group pose for a make-believe family portrait in their stage faces. Challenge the class to guess the type of family (adjective) each group is portraying. Change groups and repeat the activity with different adjectives. Say cheese!

Marsha Schmus—Gr. 4, Ypsilanti, MI

"Tee-rrific" Books

Line up a "tee-rrific" bulletin board this November to celebrate National Children's Book Week! For each student, fold a large sheet of white construction paper in half widthwise. Place a T-shirt pattern on the fold as shown; then trace and cut out the shirt, leaving the shoulder seams uncut. Have each student write his book report inside one of the T-shirts. Next have him decorate the shirt's front with his book's title and author, and an illustration. Hang the shirts over a clothesline that's been strung across a bulletin board. Title the board "Line Up For A 'Tee-riffic' Book!"

Terry Healy—Gifted K–6
Eugene Field Elementary
Manhattan, KS

Don't cut

Pattern

Shiloh
by _____

Math Bumper Stickers

Celebrate math with this easy-to-do art activity! Give each student a white sentence strip (or "bumper sticker"). Have the student create an original slogan promoting math. Next have him use markers to write his slogan on his bumper sticker and add colorful illustrations. Attach the completed bumper stickers to a bulletin board titled "Stick With Math!"

David Reitz—Gr. 4
Glenwood Elementary
Virginia Beach, VA

Don't be a fool—Math is cool!

Pencil Dice

Turn broken pencil stubs into dynamite dice with this nifty recycling idea! Use a black permanent marker to draw a dot on one side of a short, hexagonal pencil. Rotate the pencil and draw two dots on the next side. Continue increasing the number of dots until you have six dots on the last side. Demonstrate for students how to gently roll the pencil on a table or desk. You'll have no more games with missing dice!

Shirlee Angerame
Roxboro Road Middle School
Brewerton, NY

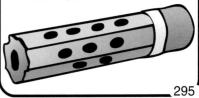

Math Points

Help students see the point to math homework with this easy-to-play game! Divide the class into two teams. Call on a student from Team 1 to answer the first problem from the homework assignment. If she answers correctly, award Team 1 a point. Continue asking Team 1 questions until a student answers incorrectly. Then call on a student from Team 2. Keep awarding points for correct answers until all homework problems have been answered. The team with the most points wins!

Shannon Popkin—Gr. 4, Heritage Christian School, Brookfield, WI

Film Canister First Aid

Involve students in a unique community-service project with the following first-rate idea. Collect empty film canisters from local photo shops. Have students fill each canister with first-aid items such as a bandage, a packaged wet wipe, a plastic glove, etc. Then have them label the outside of each canister "First Aid Kit." Donate the completed kits to community homeless shelters.

Janet Moody
J. W. Faulk Elementary
Lafayette, LA

Peace Cookies

Celebrate United Nations Day (October 24) with this tasty activity. Mix a basic chocolate-chip cookie recipe, leaving out the chocolate chips. Flatten the dough into three-inch circles. Use light brown, dark brown, red, and yellow M&M's® (symbolic of the world's diverse ethnic groups) to create a peace sign on each cookie. Bake the cookies a few at a time in a toaster oven. Then invite another class to join your students as they share original poems and stories about peace. End the celebration by sharing your peace cookies.

Kim Helgeson—Gr. 5
Pecatonica Elementary
Hollandale, WI

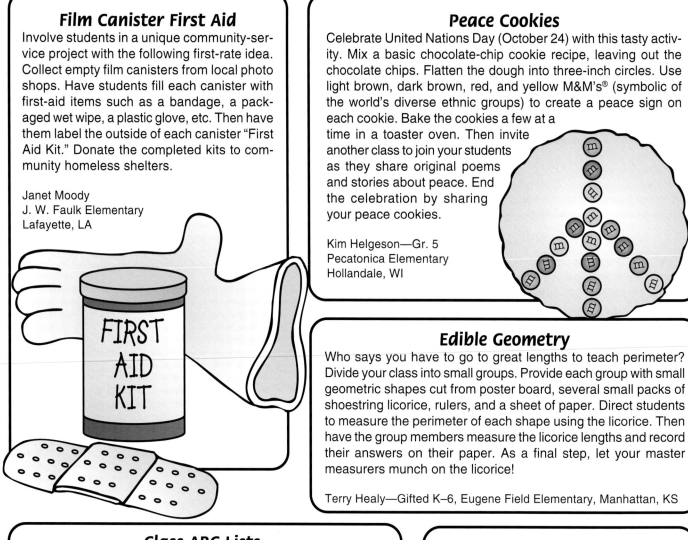

Edible Geometry

Who says you have to go to great lengths to teach perimeter? Divide your class into small groups. Provide each group with small geometric shapes cut from poster board, several small packs of shoestring licorice, rulers, and a sheet of paper. Direct students to measure the perimeter of each shape using the licorice. Then have the group members measure the licorice lengths and record their answers on their paper. As a final step, let your master measurers munch on the licorice!

Terry Healy—Gifted K–6, Eugene Field Elementary, Manhattan, KS

Class ABC Lists

Make review as easy as ABC with this fun class challenge! Each Monday tape a long piece of bulletin-board paper on the back of your door. Write the alphabet in large print down the left side of the paper. Then write a recently studied topic (such as "Trees") at the top of the paper. Encourage students to list one word that fits the topic and begins with each letter by Friday (see the example). Save the weekly lists so students can see how much they've learned at the end of the year!

Traci Baker—Gr. 4
Brassfield Elementary, Bixby, OK

> Trees
>
> A – apple
>
> B – birch
>
> C – cottonwood
>
> D – dogwood

Fruit And Veggie Commercials

At the end of a unit on nutrition, turn your kids into nutritional ad execs! Divide the class into groups. Have each group choose one fruit or vegetable to research. Direct each group to use its information to write a commercial that promotes the nutritional value of its fruit or veggie; then let each group perform its commercial for the class. Did somebody say "nutrition"?

Janet Lantz—Gr. 5
Churubusco Elementary, Churubusco, IN

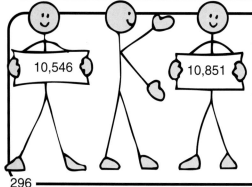

Greater Than/Less Than Aerobics

Treat students to a math workout they'll never forget with this activity on comparing large numbers. Give a 4" x 6" index card to each student. Have her use a marker to write a large, multidigit number on the card. Call two students to the front of the class to display their numbers, side by side. Select another child to stand between them and form a "greater than" or "less than" symbol by extending her arms as shown. Have the rest of the class check the work; then select three new students for the next problem.

Michelle Bauml, Gladys Polk Elementary, Richwood, TX

Spelling In A Puff!

For a spelling activity that's perfect for kinesthetic learners, try this hands-on idea. Provide each student with an index card for each spelling word and access to several colors of fabric puff paint. Direct the student to use the paint to write one spelling word on each card (consonants with one color and vowels with another). After the cards dry, have the student practice her words by tracing the raised letters with her finger. What a "puff-ectly" marvelous way to improve spelling!

because

PUFF PAINT

Julie Fellhauer—Gr. 4
Southeast Elementary
Clinton, MO

Touchdown Tips

Help your students score points for good behavior with the following idea. List your classroom rules on a bulletin board titled "Touchdown Tips." Add a border of laminated football patterns. At the end of each day, choose one student who has exhibited good behavior by following a class rule. Write that child's name on a football with a wipe-off marker, along with a description of the rule he followed. Recognize your touchdown runners each week in a parent newsletter.

Shannon Berry—Gr. 4
Heritage Christian School
Brookfield, WI

Ricky

Ricky waited until I finished talking before asking his question.

Halloween Costume Art

Looking for a fun Halloween art activity? Ask each student to bring in a photo of himself. Have him look through old magazines and cut out a body to use as his costume. Direct the child to glue the cut-out body to a large piece of white construction paper. Then have him cut out the head from his photo and glue it onto the body. Finally have the student decorate the background of the paper with a Halloween scene. Simply "boo-tiful"!

Jane Krier—Gr. 6
Byron Intermediate School
Byron, MN

Not Just The Facts

When creating an essay test, I always ask a question directly related to the content. Then I ask an opinion question to supplement the factual question. With this method I can check for content comprehension on two different levels. It's an easy way to see if my students can do more than just memorize the facts!

Andrea Wohl—Gr. 5
Washington School
Westfield, NJ

States Scrapbook

Wondering how to squeeze a study of the United States into your packed curriculum? Have each student use a three-ring binder, photo album, or scrapbook to create an ABC book of the United States. Direct him to include something related to the United States for each letter of the alphabet (for example, *A* is for *Alabama*, *B* is for *Bunker Hill*, *C* is for *Chelsea Clinton*, etc.). Require each student to include the following in his book:

- five states
- five famous Americans
- five famous events
- five important places
- six other topics relating to any aspect of the United States

Break the assignment up by having due dates for the letters A–G, H–N, O–U, and V–Z. At the end of the assignment, hold a scrapbook party so students can share their books.

Kimberly Conway—Gr. 5
South Graham Elementary, Graham, NC

Sandwich Day Smorgasbord

Celebrate Sandwich Day (November 3) with an activity students can really sink their teeth into! Have students volunteer to bring in various sandwich fixings, such as meat, cheese, bread, and condiments. For lunch on the designated day, let everyone build his own one-of-a-kind sandwich. Later have each child write a descriptive paragraph about his special sandwich. Consider other class "food bars" to build pizzas, tacos, baked potatoes, or hot dogs!

Teena Andersen—Grs. K–6, Wayne County District 25, Pender, NE

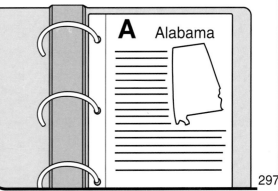

A   Alabama

Santa Claus Pins

Recycle those old pencil stubs into these clever Santa Claus pins! You'll need red, black, and flesh-colored acrylic paints; white fabric paint; paintbrushes; pin backs; glue; and toothpicks. Have students follow these steps.

1. Hold the pencil stub by its eraser and paint the wood part red. Allow to dry.
2. Paint the sharpened end of the pencil black (Santa's boots). Allow to dry.
3. Add a blotch of flesh-colored paint below the metal part of the pencil (the face). Allow to dry.
4. Add white fabric paint around the top of the boots and below the metal part of the pencil. Also use this paint to give Santa a beard and mustache.
5. Put a glob of white paint on top of the eraser (the fur on his cap).
6. After all of the fabric paint has dried, use the tip of a toothpick to add black eyes and buttons. Then add a red nose. Allow to dry.
7. Glue a pin back on the side opposite the face. Allow to dry.

Shirlee Angerame
Roxboro Road Middle School
Brewerton, NY

The "Good Books Gazette"

Extra! Extra! Read all about this idea that combines literature with writing! Have each student choose one important event from a book he has read. Tell him to pretend that the event has actually happened. Direct him to use the five *W*s of writing newspaper articles *(who, what, when, where, why)* to write an article describing this event. Compile the completed articles to make a classroom "Good Books Gazette."

Denise Amos—Gr. 4, Crestwood Elementary
Crestwood, KY

Seasonal Classroom Cheer

To spread a little holiday cheer around your classroom, cover a table with an inexpensive, plastic seasonal tablecloth. A couple of dollars go a long way to brighten a classroom—and everyone's attitude!

Julie Eick Granchelli—Gr. 4
Towne Elementary
Medina, NY

Koosh® Ball Sharing

Intermediate kids are at the age when they begin to feel self-conscious about getting up in front of the class. I've discovered a great way to get students to volunteer. When a student wants to share, I toss him a Koosh® Ball. He shares his work, then throws the ball back to me. I then toss the ball to the next volunteer. Now when I ask for volunteers to share with the class, almost every hand goes up!

Marilyn Kahl—Gr. 4, Highland School, Cheshire, CT

Latitude And Longitude Bingo

Play this fun bingo game after your students have studied latitude and longitude. Make a set of bingo cards with 4 x 4 grids. Write the name of a different country or state in each square on a card, depending on what you're studying. Be sure to label each card differently. Next write each country and state included on a bingo card on a wooden chip, along with its latitude and longitude coordinates. Put all of these chips in a bag. Provide each student with a bingo card, a world (or U.S.) map, and about 15 game markers. To play, draw a chip from the bag and read only its coordinates. Using those coordinates, students locate the country or state on their maps and look to see if it is on their cards. The first student to get bingo gets to call out the next game.

Maria Gonzalez—Gr. 4
Coral Reef Elementary
Miami, FL

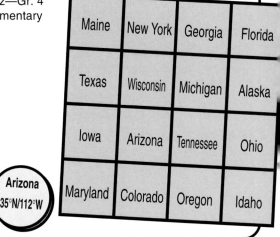

Maine	New York	Georgia	Florida
Texas	Wisconsin	Michigan	Alaska
Iowa	Arizona	Tennessee	Ohio
Maryland	Colorado	Oregon	Idaho

Maine
45°N/70°W

Arizona
35°N/112°W

Take-out Homework

The next time you visit your favorite fast-food restaurant, be sure to save the kids' meal boxes. After you have taught a skill, put an activity that reinforces that skill inside a box. Or include flash cards, fun pages, or an activity with which students need extra practice. Watch as your students beg to "take out" these handy homework boxes!

Sonja Stoll
Frankfort Grade School
Frankfort, KS

Quotable Quotes

Try this fun writing activity to give your students practice in punctuating quotations. Begin by asking students to tell you a quote they hear you say regularly. Write this quote on the board. Ask for more examples of quotes and add them to the board. Then direct each student to choose a person to be the subject of her own "Quotable Quotes" booklet. Have the student first make a list of her person's quotes. Once she has her list, provide her with several 5" x 7" sheets of drawing paper. Instruct the student to write each quote in a sentence—punctuating it correctly—on a sheet of the paper and illustrate it. When all the pages have been completed, instruct the student to bind them into a booklet. Have each student share her booklet with the person it's based on. "Do I *really* say that?"

Geri Harris—Gr. 5, Castlio Elementary, St. Charles, MO

Caught In A Web

For our food chain and food web unit, I cover an entire bulletin board with a web of black yarn. I start the web from the center and proceed outward so that it maintains its shape. Each student then illustrates each part of a food chain on a different paper circle. After coloring his circles, the student punches a hole in each one and links them together with yarn. We then hang all of these chains over the bulletin-board web. You're sure to catch everyone eyeing this wonderful web!

Rifky Amsel—Gr. 4, Yeshiva Shaarei Tzion, Piscataway, NJ

Recycled Wreaths

An easy and inexpensive Christmas craft is in the bag with this idea! Ask each student to bring in one paper grocery bag. Have the student cut off the sides of the bag and lay it out flat. Then have the student roll and twist the paper to form a "rope." Next have him connect the ends with transparent tape to make a wreath. Supply each student with five red pipe cleaners and five candy canes. Have him wrap the pipe cleaners around the wreath, twisting them in any way. Instruct the student to complete the wreath by slipping the candy canes in the pipe cleaners. The finished wreath has a nice, homemade country look and makes a great gift!

Robin Combs—Gr. 4
Cahill Elementary
Saugerties, NY

Learning Geography With Labels

For practice with geography skills, have students bring to school labels from canned foods, empty cereal and soap boxes, and other products. Guide students to find out where each product was manufactured and/or distributed. As each product and its place of manufacture are discussed, have students find these locations on a map or globe. As an extension, encourage students to use encyclopedias, library books, and their social studies textbooks to find out why a product is made in its particular place.

Dr. Marlow Ediger
Truman State University
Kirksville, MO

Build A (Cheap!) Classroom Library

To build an almost-no-cost classroom library, request that your students bring in any kinds of unwanted paperback books from home (with their parents' permission). Take these books to a used-books dealer for in-store credit. With this credit, purchase children's books for your classroom. You can bet you'll love these twice-loved books!

Deborah Sloan—Gr. 4
Parkway Elementary
Crowley, TX

Holiday Postcards

At the beginning of December, I give each student a piece of poster board precut to postcard size. I instruct the student to draw and color a winter or holiday scene on one side. (I don't reveal that they're making postcards.) Then, a few days before Christmas vacation, I write a short message on the blank side of each card, address it to the student who made it, add a stamp, and mail it. Students love opening their mailboxes and discovering their postcards inside!

Patty J. Vermeer—Gr. 4
Galva-Holstein Elementary
Holstein, IA

299

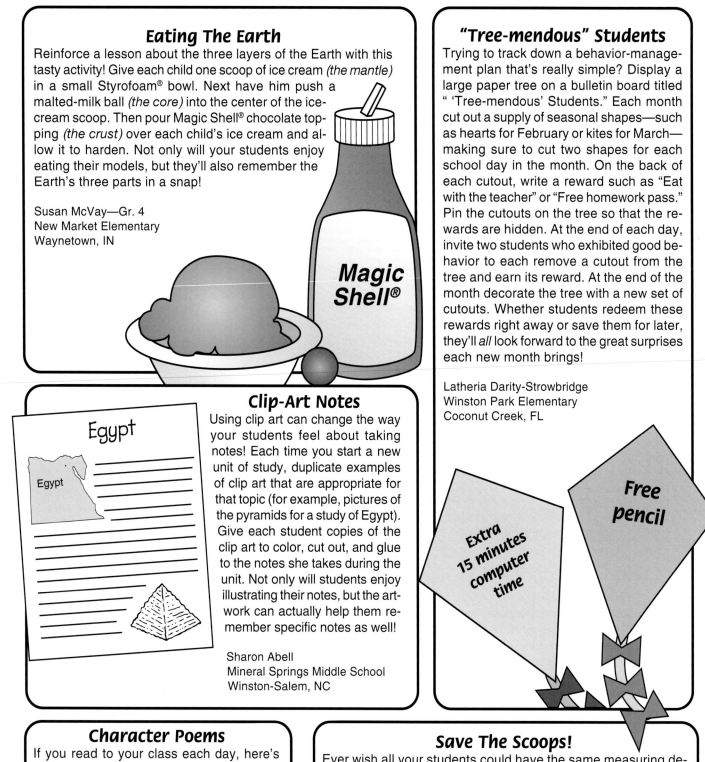

Eating The Earth

Reinforce a lesson about the three layers of the Earth with this tasty activity! Give each child one scoop of ice cream *(the mantle)* in a small Styrofoam® bowl. Next have him push a malted-milk ball *(the core)* into the center of the ice-cream scoop. Then pour Magic Shell® chocolate topping *(the crust)* over each child's ice cream and allow it to harden. Not only will your students enjoy eating their models, but they'll also remember the Earth's three parts in a snap!

Susan McVay—Gr. 4
New Market Elementary
Waynetown, IN

Magic Shell®

"Tree-mendous" Students

Trying to track down a behavior-management plan that's really simple? Display a large paper tree on a bulletin board titled " 'Tree-mendous' Students." Each month cut out a supply of seasonal shapes—such as hearts for February or kites for March—making sure to cut two shapes for each school day in the month. On the back of each cutout, write a reward such as "Eat with the teacher" or "Free homework pass." Pin the cutouts on the tree so that the rewards are hidden. At the end of each day, invite two students who exhibited good behavior to each remove a cutout from the tree and earn its reward. At the end of the month decorate the tree with a new set of cutouts. Whether students redeem these rewards right away or save them for later, they'll *all* look forward to the great surprises each new month brings!

Latheria Darity-Strowbridge
Winston Park Elementary
Coconut Creek, FL

Clip-Art Notes

Egypt

Using clip art can change the way your students feel about taking notes! Each time you start a new unit of study, duplicate examples of clip art that are appropriate for that topic (for example, pictures of the pyramids for a study of Egypt). Give each student copies of the clip art to color, cut out, and glue to the notes she takes during the unit. Not only will students enjoy illustrating their notes, but the artwork can actually help them remember specific notes as well!

Sharon Abell
Mineral Springs Middle School
Winston-Salem, NC

Extra 15 minutes computer time

Free pencil

Character Poems

If you read to your class each day, here's how that routine can help you teach poetry writing! One day each month after reading to the class, introduce students to a specific type of poetry. Then have each child write and illustrate a poem of that type based on a character from your current novel. It's an easy way to teach poetry, check comprehension, and practice writing skills all at the same time!

Marlys Cole—Gr. 4
Roy Gomm School, Reno, NV

Save The Scoops!

Ever wish all your students could have the same measuring device for a science or math activity? Get students to save the measuring cups from boxes of powdered detergent and bring them to school. The next time something needs measuring or sorting, everyone will have the same inexpensive measuring tool!

Lisa Stephens
Southwood Middle School
Anderson, SC

Hall Of Fame

Recognize special student achievements with this glitzy bulletin-board idea. Each month select one or more students as a "Student Of The Month" (or select any child who has won a special honor during the month, written a special story, etc.). Photograph each honored child. To frame each photo, glue four tongue depressors together as shown. Add sparkle to the resulting frame with glue and gold glitter. After the frame has dried, glue the photo behind it. Display the frames on a bulletin board titled "[teacher's name]'s Hall Of Fame." At the end of the year, let students take their frames home as souvenirs.

Maria Gonzalez—Gr. 4
Coral Reef Elementary, Miami, FL

Placemat Review

Discussing school topics at the dinner table? It can actually happen with this cool idea! After any unit of study, give each student an 11" x 14" sheet of paper. On one side of the paper, have the student creatively list several facts that she learned. On the other side, have her design a word search or other types of puzzles about the topic, complete with an answer key. Laminate these special placemats; then ask each student to trade her placemat with a classmate. Direct students to take these placemats home to share with their families at dinner. Just watch your class's appetite for learning increase!

Marsha Schmus
Ypsilanti, MI

Molecule Ball

Wrap up a study of weather with this game that will have students bouncing around like molecules! Take your students to a playground area. Have them stand close together to represent molecules in cold air. Toss a beach ball into the group, challenging students to keep it moving without letting it touch the ground. Then announce a rise in the air temperature—the signal that students should move farther apart because the molecules are heating up. If the ball touches the ground, have students return to the cold-molecule position and begin the game again.

Marlys Cole—Gr. 4, Roy Gomm School, Reno, NV

Math-Practice Strips

Be prepared when parents request extra math practice for their children to do at home. Duplicate a batch of practice worksheets in advance; then cut each sheet into strips of about 20 problems each. Keep the strips in a basket or manila envelope on your desk. With these strips on hand, you'll be more than ready when parents ask for "More practice, please!"

Melissa Goldenberg—Gr. 4
Oak Hill Elementary, Overland Park, KS

Learning-Center Solution

Eliminate the need to check students' learning-center work by making all your centers self-checking! Write each question or math problem on one side of an index card and its answer on the other. Laminate the cards. Then cover each answer with a piece of electrical tape, making sure to fold down one corner of the tape for easy removal. All students have to do to check their answers is pull back the tape! To turn a worksheet into an instant center, tape two copies back-to-back; then write the answers on one copy and cover them with tape.

Patricia Wisniewski—
    Substitute Grs. K–6
Akron, NY

What is the capital of North Carolina?

Raleigh

Teacher's Special Art Book

If you frequently get drawings and other special artwork from your students and don't know where to display them, try this simple solution. Bind the artwork pieces into a special art book. Appoint one child to create a cover, and presto—a great class book!

Sue Mechura—Gr. 4
Ebenezer Elementary
Lebanon, PA

Art
from Mrs. Walker's Class

Journal Log

Help late-arriving or absent students catch up on journal-writing assignments with this simple tip. Each day choose one student to copy the day's writing prompt in a special notebook and date it. Then you have a record of all journal prompts *and* the dates on which they were assigned. When Johnny arrives from a dental appointment, just send him to the journal log!

Kathy Kayiran—Gr. 4
Westwood Basics Plus Elementary, Irvine, CA

Frequently Asked Questions

If you surf the Internet, then you know that many Web sites include a FAQ section to answer the most "frequently asked questions." Familiarize new students and visitors to your classroom with a handy FAQ booklet of your own. With students, brainstorm questions that they would want answered about your room and school if they were new to the school (for example, questions on the locations of rooms and supplies, procedures such as discipline and lunch count, etc.). List these questions on the board. Next pair students; then direct each twosome to select a question and write a practical answer together. After compiling your FAQ pages, publish several copies to share with new students, visiting parents, and community members.

Terry Healy—Gifted K–6
Eugene Field Elementary
Manhattan, KS

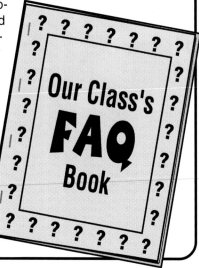

T-R-A-N-S-I-T-I-O-N

Do transitions cut into your precious teaching time? Make each student more aware of the time it takes to switch gears with this quick tip. The next time you notice your students dragging between subjects, have them spell *transition* aloud with you. By the time you reach the second letter *n,* all your students should be ready to begin!

Marsha Schmus, Chambersburg, PA

Honor Roll Celebrations

Encourage student achievement at your school with this award-winning idea! At the end of each semester or grading period, hold an Honor Roll Celebration. Schedule your school's cafeteria in advance for the celebration and send out invitations to the honored students. Also make attractive certificates (one per honoree) on a computer and ask student volunteers to help by decorating the cafeteria. On the day of the celebration, present the certificates to the honorees; then enjoy simple refreshments together. The payoff for all this hard work: the smiles of pride on your students' faces!

Kathy Wolford, Mansfield, OH

Lawn-Chair Webbing

Tired of buying expensive borders for your bulletin boards? Try using lawn-chair webbing as an eye-catching and economical border. It comes in many colors, can be cut to any length, and doesn't need to be laminated. Plus, it won't rip or tear, and lasts forever! Use smaller pieces of webbing to frame posters, pictures, and windows too!

Jackie Maynard—Gr. 5, Pope Elementary, Jackson, TN

It's In The Cards!

Why take a gamble when grouping your students? Use a deck of regular playing cards instead! Simply hand one card to each student; then group the class in one of these ways:

- To form two large groups, divide the class according to students holding red cards and those holding black ones.
- To form groups of four, have each student team up with classmates who have the same number on their cards (for example, the four of clubs, spades, diamonds, and hearts).
- To pair students, have each child partner with a classmate who has the same number *and* color on her card (for example, the eight of diamonds and the eight of hearts).

With this easy idea, grouping students is a sure bet!

Cynthia Wurmnest—Gr. 5, Danvers Elementary, Danvers, IL

Guess My Length

Take linear measurement straight to your students with this weeklong activity! On Monday display a piece of yarn that equals the length or width of some object in the classroom (chalkboard, eraser, desk, etc.). During the week, have each student observe the yarn and guess the object she thinks it measures. On Friday have each student test her guess by measuring that object with the yarn. As a treat, let the winner choose the item to be measured the following week.

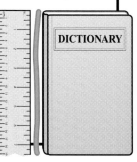

Marsha Schmus

GREAT

Window Wishes

Use your classroom windows to motivate students and smile on the outside world with this eye-catching idea. Cut out large block letters from colored paper, mount them on white construction paper, and laminate them for durability. Next install a horizontal wire that runs across your classroom windows. Clip the letters (facing outside) onto the wire with clothespins anytime you want to wish a student a happy birthday, recognize honor-roll members, welcome a class visitor, or send a positive message to the community.

Phil Forsythe, Northeastern Elementary, Bellefontaine, OH

Check It Out

Check out this tip for a unique way to display students' writing or other work. Purchase an inexpensive plastic or paper checkered tablecloth to use as your bulletin-board background. Staple students' compositions to sheets of red and white construction paper; then mount the papers on the board. Use this same idea to create a display of important class reminders and school news!

Chana Rochel Zucker—Gr. 5
Be'er Hagolah School, Brooklyn, NY

Classroom Consultants

Build a team of helpers in your classroom with this great program. When a student has demonstrated the confidence and knowledge necessary for peer tutoring, issue a "Classroom Consultant" certificate in his name (see the illustration). Post this certificate under a "Help Available" sign on your wall. When a student has a question about a particular topic, direct him to the "Help Available" display to see if there is a classmate who can answer his question. Make the consultant topics specific (for example, "Fractions" instead of "Math"). Also include some generic topics, such as "Note Taker" or "Good Listener," so all children have the opportunity to be consultants.

Millie Richmond—Gr. 4
Coral Springs, FL

Class Lists

Need a classy way to keep students organized and on top of assignments? Laminate several class lists. Use a dry-erase marker to label each list with an assignment; then slip a large paper clip on each list and place it in an assignment folder or basket. In the morning, have each student clip her assignment behind the appropriate list and check her name off with the marker. At a glance you'll see who still needs to turn in an assignment. At the end of the day, simply wipe each list clean and recycle it for the next assignment!

Tammie Boone—Gr. 5, Sheldon Middle School, Sheldon, IA

Comics And Current Events

Make the news a lead-in to learning with this hands-on activity! Collect a class supply of newspapers. Have each student choose a comic strip and a newspaper article. Direct her to trace her comic strip onto tracing paper, leaving the speech balloons blank. Then instruct her to carefully read her article and write dialogue about it in her strip's speech balloons. Have students color their strips before posting the work on a bulletin board. How's that for a newsworthy way to sharpen reading-comprehension, summarizing, and main-idea skills!

Leslie Reeves—Gr. 5
Santa Rita Elementary
Midland, TX

Guess Again!

Increase the math power of a popular estimation activity with this idea. Fill a large, clear jar with a small edible item, such as M&M's® candies, raisins, pretzels, miniature chocolate-chip cookies, etc. Display the jar on Monday morning; then give each student a form as shown. Instruct each student to observe the jar, then write his first guess on his form. The next day write a math clue about the total number of items, such as, "The total is a three-digit even number that is less than 300." Have each student write the clue on his form, and then (if ready) write his second guess. Display a new clue each morning; then collect the forms on Thursday. On Friday, review the clues and reveal the correct total. Give each student a treat from the jar; then award the remaining items to the child who guessed the actual number or came closest to it.

Diane DiPalermo—Grs. 5–6
P. S. 155
South Ozone Park, NY

303

Biosphere Bowl

Tantalize your students' minds *and* taste buds with this refreshing way to wrap up a unit on the biosphere! Place the following in a large glass bowl:

1. **Lithosphere:** To represent **rocks and soil,** spread half a bag of crushed Oreo® cookies on the bottom of the bowl.
2. **Hydrosphere:** Place vanilla pudding colored with blue food coloring on top of your lithosphere to represent **water**.
3. **Atmosphere:** Top your hydrosphere with Cool Whip® topping to represent the **clouds and air** for a tasty way to remember the biosphere long after the test is over!

Melissa Villines—Gr. 4, Krisle Elementary, Springfield, TN

Caution: Great Minds At Work!

Celebrate creativity and hard work in your class with this one-of-a-kind bulletin board! Purchase inexpensive yellow "Caution" tape (used by construction workers to mark off hazardous areas) at a hardware store. Haphazardly place strips of the tape over the background of a bulletin board as shown. Add the title "Caution: Great Minds At Work!" and several cut-out street signs. Also use the tape to frame student projects that you don't want touched or to identify an area to be used exclusively for quiet or small-group work.

Toni Purcell—Grs. 4–6
Sellman School
Cincinnati, OH

" 'Tude" Tool

Are latitude and longitude lines sending your students in circles? Ease their frustration with this simple tool. Give each student a tongue depressor or Popsicle® stick. Direct him to write *Latitude* horizontally and the directions it is measured in (N,S) on one side of his depressor as shown. Then have him flip his depressor and write *Longitude* vertically and the directions it is measured in (E,W). Now all the student has to do when he's confused about latitude and longitude is look at his " 'tude" tool. Plus, it also provides a handy straightedge for plotting points!

Joy Allen—Gr. 4
Sam Houston Elementary
Bryan, TX

Disappearing Dry-Erase Markers

Solve the mystery of disappearing dry-erase markers with this sticky solution. Glue a one-inch strip of Velcro® (hook side) on the top of your dry-erase board. Make a tube out of the matching looped piece and stitch it together so that it can easily be slid onto a dry-erase marker. Attach the marker to your board. When the marker runs out of ink, simply slip off the Velcro® tube and slide it onto a new marker!

Jill Lynn Perry—Gr. 5
Mason Corinth Elementary
Williamstown, KY

Dear Author

Give young authors the feedback they need with this literary tip. Add two or three blank pages to the end of each student-written book that you publish. Label the top of each page "Critical Acclaim"; then place the book on a shelf of your classroom or school library. Keep a tin of pencils nearby so that each reader can write a personal note to the author after reading his book.

Merrill Watrous
Eugene, OR

Plant-Tasting Lab

Culminate your study of the plant kingdom with this great-tasting lab activity. Have each child volunteer bring in an edible plant or plant product for the class to sample. Send home a letter like the one shown asking for parent volunteers to help with the lab. On the day of the lab, have volunteers prepare a plate for each student that contains a sampling of each product. Have students line up outside your classroom; then, as each child enters the room, have him hand you a ticket (an index card labeled with the food he brought and each plant product it contains). As the class samples the foods, discuss with students which part of the plant they are eating. Reward the student who brought in the sample containing the most plant products with a small prize. "Plant-astic"!

Joan K. Wilson—Gr. 5, Mount Vernon Elementary, Gainesville, GA

Dear Parent,
   Your child has been learning about the plant kingdom in science class. We've examined plants, drawn them, and taken notes about them. Now it's time to eat them! We'll be having a special science lab next Friday at 10 A.M. in order to taste as many plants and plant products as possible.
   Would you be willing to join us in this scientific adventure by helping set up our lab at 9 A.M. next Friday? If yes, please sign this letter at the bottom and have your child return it to school tomorrow. Thank you!

Sincerely,
Joan Wilson

Hit The Books!

Use America's national pastime to encourage reading with this home run of an idea! Display a large paper baseball bat labeled "Hit The Books!" over your classroom bookshelves. Each time a student reads a book independently, give her a paper baseball cutout. On the back of the baseball, have her write a brief summary of her book. When she receives four baseballs, let her exchange them for a small prize, such as a baseball-decorated pencil or eraser. Before you know it, your students will be singing, "Take me out to the bookshelves!"

Marianne Hanson—Gr. 6
Lanham Christian School
Lanham, MD

Hatchet

Hatchet tells the story of Brian, who gets stranded when...

Theme Burgers

Searching for a fun Friday afternoon art activity during the final weeks of school? Cook up some theme burgers! Have each student cut a 9" x 12" sheet of brown construction paper into the shape of a hamburger bun; then have him cut the bun into two halves. Direct him to glue these halves to a 12" x 18" sheet of white paper, leaving plenty of room to draw between them. Have the student select a theme, such as sports, insects, animals, birds, or music. Then have him draw and color objects that go with his theme between the buns as shown. Display your students' projects on a bulletin board labeled "You'll Flip For Our Theme Burgers!"

Joan M. Macey
Binghamton, NY

Rashad's Radical
Buggy Burger

Mugs And Kisses

Having difficulty finding a thank-you gift for a special parent volunteer? Kiss that problem good-bye with this nifty idea! Purchase a seasonal mug, colored cellophane, packets of hot chocolate or flavored coffee, and Hershey's® Kisses®. Cut a square of cellophane larger than needed to fit inside the mug. Place the cellophane in the mug and fill it with the hot chocolate or coffee packets and candies. Gather the cellophane at the top and tie it with curling ribbon. What a sweet way to say thanks to those who have helped you throughout the year!

Meshell Kibelkis, Kolmar School
Midlothian, IL

Math Motivation

Motivate a student struggling with math using this simple idea. On an index card have each student write his name, an original math word problem, and the problem's solution. Save the cards in a special folder. Before your next math test, select a struggling child's card from the folder; then have him write his problem on the chalkboard to use as a bonus for earning extra points on the test. Your struggling student will love seeing his work displayed, especially when it earns his classmates extra credit!

Kirsten Sasaki—Gr. 6, Copiague Middle School
Copiague, NY

Ticket To Number Sense

Reinforce number skills with this hot ticket of a math activity! Obtain a roll of numbered ticket stubs, such as those used at fairs or carnivals. (These can be purchased inexpensively at most party supply stores.) Place eight stubs in an envelope labeled with simple directions such as

- List the numbers from the greatest to the least.
- List all of the even numbers.
- Round each number to the nearest thousand.

Use these envelopes as a whole-class activity or place several at a math center for free-time use. Number each envelope and provide an answer key so students can check their work.

Patricia Posen—Gr. 4, Holy Spirit School, Union, NJ

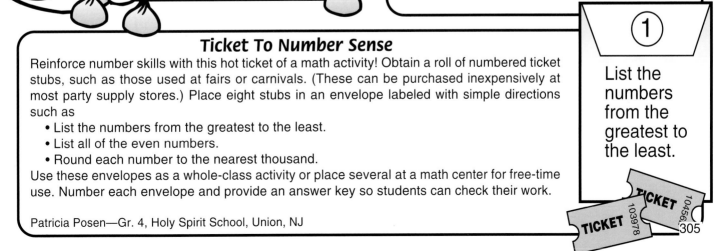

(1)

List the numbers from the greatest to the least.

TICKET
103978
TICKET
10456.
305

Birthday Goodie Bags

Make students feel special on their birthdays with this unbeatable gift idea! During the summer, fill colorful birthday bags with inexpensive dime-store goodies. When school rolls around, place the bags in a large container labeled "Happy Birthday!" On each student's birthday, surprise him with a goodie bag. You'll start a tradition that's guaranteed to make every birthday a happy one!

Heidi Graves—Gr. 4
Wateree Elementary
Lugoff, SC

Student-Teacher Farewell

Tired of making the same old paper banner for your student teacher's good-bye gift? Give her one that lasts with this bright idea! Purchase a large, inexpensive outdoor flag at a discount store. Using fabric markers, have your students write their good-bye messages right on the flag. Now your student teacher has a memorable banner to hang in her very own classroom!

Joy Tweedt
Northwood Elementary, Ames, IA

Onomatopoeia Collage

Turn to the comics page to teach a lesson about onomatopoeia. Gather enough funny pages from your local newspaper for each student to have one. Have the student cut out examples of words that imitate sounds, such as *clattered, buzz,* and *splat;* then have him create a collage from the words as shown. Post your students' collages on a bulletin board labeled "It's As Easy As Onomatopoeia!" Before you can say "Fwip!", your students will be buzzing all around this display!

Brenda Vujaklya—Gr. 6
Beaver Local Middle School
Lisbon, OH

Super Summer Scrapbooks

Encourage students to continue learning through the summer with this end-of-the-year gift idea. Purchase a three-ring binder for each child (or ask parents to donate the notebooks). For each binder, use a computer stationery program to make a cover decorated with the student's name and pictures that represent her personality and interests. Inside each notebook, place a letter from you, stickers, a pencil, a bookmark, fun worksheets, word puzzles, autograph pages, and an envelope labeled with your address. Other items may include a photocopy of the class picture, craft activities, and notebook paper for writing letters. Give students this gift on the last day of school; then let them sign each other's autograph pages. Super!

Linda Flores—Gr. 4
Perrine Baptist Academy, Miami, FL

Remember When...

Start a yearlong scrapbook project with this picture-perfect idea! During the first week of school, have each student bring a disposable camera to school. Throughout the year, give students photography tips as they snap memorable school events. In May send the cameras home to be developed. Include an order form so parents can order scrapbook materials from you, such as a binder, white construction paper, and stickers. During the last week of school, reserve the cafeteria for one morning so students can assemble their scrapbooks. When they arrive, have the students' materials waiting for them in labeled grocery bags and parent volunteers available to help. When finished, let students gather signatures on the last pages of their scrapbooks.

Patti Rogers—Gr. 5, Smithfield Elementary, North Richland Hills, TX

"Pitcher-ing" Good Behavior

Expect good behavior—even at the end of the year—with this idea that really pours on the manners! Obtain a variety of behavior tickets, or make your own labeled with rewards, such as "Sit beside a friend for the day" or "Homework Pass." Place the tickets in a plastic water pitcher labeled "I'm 'Pitcher-ing' Your Good Behavior!" Tape several students' school pictures to the pitcher. Whenever you catch a student behaving, send him to the pitcher to choose a reward. With this idea, your class will be the "pitcher" of good behavior!

Latasha Johnson—Gr. 4, Kittrell School, Readyville, TN

Rain Forest Sounds

End your rain forest unit by letting students sound off about the importance of this ecosystem. Group your class into six equal-sized teams. Assign each team one of the following sounds: insects, birds, snakes, monkeys, chopping wood, or fire. After allowing time to create and practice their sounds, arrange the groups in a semicircle. Make sure everyone is silent; then direct the insect group to start making the sound(s) they've rehearsed. Have them continue as you signal the bird group to add their voices. At ten-second intervals, add each of the remaining groups in the order listed. Once all students are making their noises, start eliminating the groups one at a time until the only sound remaining is fire. Remind your class that if humans continue to destroy the rain forest, the animals' natural habitats will disappear and fire will be the only sound that remains! *(For more rain forest ideas, see the unit on pages 4–13.)*

Therese Durhman, Hickory, NC

Better Bugs Than Drugs!

Combine science and health with an idea your students will go buggy over! After a unit on insects, cover your classroom door with dark green bulletin-board paper and glue on strips of light green paper to resemble grass. Have each student draw, color, and cut out her favorite bug, then tape it on the door. Top off the door with the drug-free slogan "We'd Rather Eat Bugs Than Do Drugs!" You can bet the entire school will be buzzing about your antidrug message!

Brandi Lampl—Gr. 5, W. A. Fountain Elementary, Forest Park, GA

Class Puzzle

Create a memento for your students that's truly unique! Write the name of each student on a slip of paper. Place the slips in a container; then have each child pick a name and write one sentence describing the special qualities of the person he chose. Collect all the clues and type them into a computer program that creates crossword puzzles. Print the puzzles; then staple a photocopy of your class picture to each for a keepsake your students are sure to remember.

Maria Gonzalez—Gr. 4
Coral Reef Elementary
Miami, FL

Descriptive Teachers

Help students get a better grip on adjectives with this easy-to-do idea. Have each student use markers to write the letters of a teacher's name horizontally or vertically on a sheet of unlined paper. For each letter have him write an adjective that describes that teacher. Post these descriptions on a bulletin board titled "T.E.A.C.H.E.R.S. Are Special!" Now that's an activity that can only be described as terrific!

Cathy Ogg—Gr. 4
Happy Valley Elementary
Johnson City, TN

Magestic
Resourceful
Sensible
Smart
Merry
Intelligent
Terrific
Helpful

Healthy Ads

Try this creative art activity during your next drug awareness unit. Give each student a discarded magazine. Have her cut out one ad related to alcohol, smoking, or drugs; then have her glue the ad to a 12" x 18" sheet of white construction paper. With markers or crayons, have the student write a new slogan for the ad that contains a message promoting good health habits. Display the posters and lead a class discussion about the role advertising plays in promoting bad health habits. Then post your class creations in the hall under the title "Take A Second Look!"

Wendy Rodda—Gr. 5
Lawrencetown Elementary
Lawrencetown, Nova Scotia, Canada

A
wine
unique

way to get into a car accident!

Take Flight!

Take vocabulary practice to new heights with this high-flyin' idea! Assign each student a vocabulary word to write at the top of her paper. Then have her fold her paper into a paper airplane. Next give students ground rules for throwing their planes: toss the plane up to avoid hitting anyone, throw only when instructed to, and don't touch the planes once they've landed. After all the planes have been thrown, have each student pick up the one nearest her, unfold it, and write a sentence on that paper using the word at the top. Call out a few words randomly; then have the student with each word read her sentence aloud. Repeat the activity several times so that each student gets to write a variety of sentences.

Leah Titus—Gr. 6
McAuliffe Elementary
Palm Bay, FL

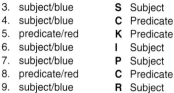

Page 67

1. predicate/red
2. subject/blue
3. subject/blue
4. subject/blue
5. predicate/red
6. subject/blue
7. subject/blue
8. predicate/red
9. subject/blue
10. predicate/red
11. subject/blue
12. predicate/red
13. subject/blue
14. predicate/red
15. predicate/red
16. predicate/red

Answer to the riddle:
COP CAKES

Page 68

L Subject
N Predicate
S Subject
C Predicate
K Predicate
I Subject
P Subject
C Predicate
R Subject
E Predicate
I Predicate
W Subject
U Subject
H Predicate

Correct box: Compound
Predicates
Tonight's special: CHICKEN

Page 74

Correct (tortoise) sentences:

2. Cindy loves chocolate, but Katie prefers vanilla.
4. To help me be less nervous, Mom practiced my speech with me.
6. Shelby asked Mark, Brendan, and Maya to be on her team.
9. Diane, I'm sorry I didn't laugh at your joke.
10. What day will you be here, Caleb?
13. Mr. Yountz, the best coach in the league, spoke to our class.

Incorrect (hare) sentences:

1. My dad loves to cook and, my mom loves to fix cars.
   Corrected: My dad loves to cook, and my mom loves to fix cars.
3. Even though I forgot to remind her Lea still studied for the test.
   Corrected: Even though I forgot to remind her, Lea still studied for the test.
5. I packed a pen a pencil case and two books in my backpack.
   Corrected: I packed a pen, a pencil case, and two books in my backpack.
7. Yes we will be home on Friday, night.
   Corrected: Yes, we will be home on Friday night.
8. Oh did the game start already?
   Corrected: Oh, did the game start already?
11. I've been expecting you Larry since 5:00.
    Corrected: I've been expecting you, Larry, since 5:00.
12. Billy the funniest kid, in our class has read 11 riddle books.
    Corrected: Billy, the funniest kid in our class, has read 11 riddle books.
14. A huge furry animal is at the back fence!
    Corrected: A huge, furry animal is at the back fence!

Page 88

Part 1: Students' answers will vary. Suggested answers:

1. a 1 out of 2 chance
2. 25 times

Part 2: Students' answers will vary.

Page 94

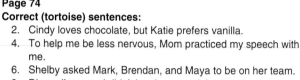

Page 83

The wording of students' answers may vary.

1. Compare the digits in the ones column. Since 7 is less than 8, cross out the 7. Above it write 17, the sum of 10 + 7. Subtract 8 from 17 to get 9. Cross out the 1 in the tens column and write a 0 above it.

2. Compare the digits in the tens column. Since the digits are the same, subtract 0 from 0 to get 0.

3. Compare the digits in the hundreds column. Since 1 is less than 4, cross out the 1. Above it write 11, the sum of 10 + 1. Subtract 4 from 11 to get 7. Change the 5 in the thousands column to 4.

4. Compare the digits in the thousands column. Since 4 is greater than 2, subtract 2 from 4 to get 2. The difference is 2,709.

Page 87

1. 1,320 strides (5,280 feet ÷ 4)
2. 30 minutes

Minutes	5	10	15	20	25	30
Animals	7	4	5	2	3	0

3. 25 farmers raised only Holsteins; 15 farmers raised only Jerseys.

85 raised Holsteins   75 raised Jerseys

4. 2 tables (8 legs) and 2 stools (6 legs)
5. 5 years (One dog is 15 years old; the other is 10 years old.)
6. 11 posts

10-foot sections
1 2 3 4 5 6 7 8 9 10
100 feet

7. 7 dogs, 3 chickens
8. Bessie gets the brush, Bossie gets the bell, Mabel gets the harness, and Matilda gets the hat.

	Bell	Hat	Brush	Harness
Bessie	✗	✗	✓	✗
Bossie	✓	✗	✗	✗
Mabel	✗	✗	✗	✓
Matilda	✗	✓	✗	✗

Farmer Phil has 250 cows on his farm.
150 + 30 + 25 + 15 + 2 + 2 + 5 + 11 + 7 + 3 = 250

Page 95

1.

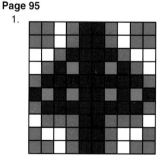

2. R = .22
   Bl = .06
   G = .14
   B = .40
   W = .18

3. .22 + .06 + .14 + .40 + .18 = 1.00
   The sum represents one whole.

4. R + Bl = .28; G + B = .54; R + G + W = .54
   Bl + B = .46; B − W = .22; R − G = .08
   (B + Bl + G) − (R + W) = .60 − .40 = .20

5. B > R
   R > W
   G < W
   G > Bl
   W > Bl

Bonus Box answer: black (.40), red (.22), white (.18), green (.14), blue (.06)

ANSWER KEYS

Page 105

1.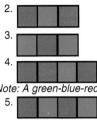

Note: A green-red-blue pattern is the same as a blue-red-green one. Both are correct. This reverse-order rule is also true for numbers 2 and 5–12.

2.
3.
4.

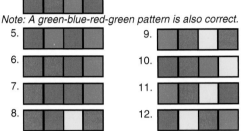

Note: A green-blue-red-green pattern is also correct.

5.   9.
6.   10.
7.   11.
8.   12.

Page 130

Answers will vary depending on the symbols that each student chooses. Features should be drawn in the approximate locations shown.

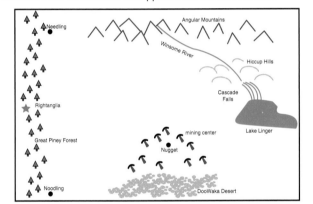

Bonus Box answer: The area should be approximately 21 sq. mi. (Answers will vary depending on each student's map.)

Page 150

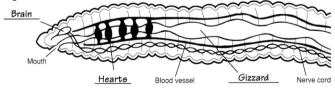

Page 151

If left undisturbed, an invertebrate will choose the environment most like the natural habitat from which it was removed. Roly-polies and earthworms usually prefer dark, damp homes.

Page 111

monthly payment	amount	balance	interest	new balance
—	—	—	—	$100.00
1	$15.00	$85.00	$0.71	$85.71
2	$15.00	$70.71	$0.59	$71.30
3	$15.00	$56.30	$0.47	$56.77
4	$15.00	$41.77	$0.35	$42.12
5	$15.00	$27.12	$0.23	$27.35
6	$15.00	$12.35	$0.11	$12.46
7	$12.46	0		
	$102.46	= total payment		

Bonus Box answer:

monthly payment	amount	balance	interest	new balance
1	$10.00	$90.00	$1.50	$91.50
2	$10.00	$81.50	$1.36	$82.86
3	$10.00	$72.86	$1.22	$74.08
4	$10.00	$64.08	$1.07	$65.15
5	$10.00	$55.15	$0.92	$56.07
6	$10.00	$46.07	$0.77	$46.84
7	$10.00	$36.84	$0.62	$37.46
8	$10.00	$27.46	$0.46	$27.92
9	$10.00	$17.92	$0.30	$18.22
10	$10.00	$8.22	$0.14	$8.36
11	$8.36	0	—	—
	$108.36 = total payment			

Page 140

Maya
Empire centered in southern Mexico and Central America
Worshipped gods and goddesses
Ate cornmeal pancakes
Had no central form of government
Were conquered by the Spanish

Aztec
Empire centered in Mexico
Worshipped gods and goddesses
Ate cornmeal pancakes
Had their capital at the city of Tenochtitlán
Were conquered by the Spanish

Inca
Empire centered in Andes highlands
Worshipped gods and goddesses
Used llamas to carry their goods
Spoke a language called *Quechua*
Were conquered by the Spanish

Page 141

Nouns: boards, Europe, masks, writing, animals, Parcheesi®, lake, fireplace
Verbs: understood, was, carried, raised, built, is
Adjectives: fancy, valuable, married, huge, more
Adverbs: dutifully, patiently, still
Pronouns: their, them, they

Bonus Box answer: Students' answers may vary. Suggested answers are buildings, artwork, tools, bones, and pottery.

Page 155

a. Not all of the substances will absorb the same amount of solar energy. If performed correctly, students should see the following results:
Most efficient: water; Second most efficient: soil; Third most efficient: beans; Least efficient: paper
b. Water would be the best substance to fill the barrels.

Bonus Box answer: Answers will vary. In some places, the sun does not shine enough to make using solar energy worthwhile. Solar energy is expensive to convert.

ANSWER KEYS

Page 156

"Which Waterwheel Works Wonderfully?"

The overshot waterwheel would generate the most power.

"Yesterday And Today"

Answers may vary.

1. horse-drawn carriages   cars and trucks
2. fireplace, wood-burning stove   electric stove
3. horse-drawn plow   tractor and plow
4. broom   vacuum cleaner
5. washtub   washing machine
6. clothesline   clothes dryer
7. candles   lamps
8. mixing spoon   electric mixer
9. abacus, paper and pencil   calculator

Students' answers for 10–12 will vary.

Page 163

1. …it was named *David.*
2. …so we knew it was a cumulonimbus cloud.
3. …we made sure we had blankets and food in the car before driving to town.
4. …I knew that it wasn't located in the United States.
5. …so we evacuated the island.
6. …they are called earth's "air-conditioning system."
7. …my family gathers in the bathroom in the center of our house during a tornado warning.
8. …that name will never be used again.
9. …I know there has been lightning.
10. …so we stopped and took cover in a deep ditch.
11. …we knew houses and cars had been blown away.
12. …so I knew the storm was three miles away.

Page 162

1. **45,000** thunderstorms
2. **54,000** degrees
3. **10,000,000** times a day
4. **60,000** miles per second
5. **79** degrees
6. **74** miles per hour
7. **300** miles per hour
8. **10,000** water droplets
9. **5** to **12** inches of snow
10. **141** tornadoes
11. **3** planes
12. **27** inches of rain
13. **689** people
14. **7,000,000,000** dollars
15. **2 1/5** pounds, **92** people

Page 169

A. One string should be 6 cm long; the other string should be 50 cm long.

B.

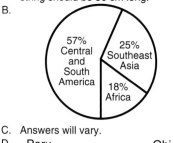

C. Answers will vary.

D.

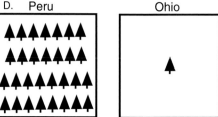

Page 186

page number	phrase
31	met **one** up close
31	ever meet another **one**
31	**one** side of the castle moat
31	towered at least **twenty feet**
31	except **two** bloody ox hides
33	**first** time in my life
33	split **halfway** down the **middle**
33	the **three** knights
33	all **four** fainted
34	**three** fair damsels
34	**two** more knights
34	**one** blow
34	now just a **minute**
34	**three** very powerful magicians
35	**ten** brave knights
35	another **five** knights
36	**two** fish heads
36	**one** rotten apple core
36	wait a **minute**
36	raised **one** foot
36	for a **week**

Page 193

Answers will vary.

Charlie Bucket:
Main personality traits: kind, respectful, polite, good listener
Inside the factory: Charlie listens and minds all the rules. Willy Wonka gives him his factory.
Outside the factory: He and his family get to move to the factory to live. One day he'll own the factory.

Augustus Gloop:
Main personality traits: greedy, gluttonous
Inside the factory: He doesn't listen to Willy's warnings and falls into the chocolate river. He gets sucked up into the tubes and sent to the Fudge Room.
Outside the factory: He is now as thin as a straw.

Veruca Salt:
Main personality traits: spoiled, loud, disrespectful
Inside the factory: She demands that her father get her everything she wants. She doesn't listen and is pushed by squirrels into the garbage chute.
Outside the factory: She's covered with garbage.

Violet Beauregarde:
Main personality traits: chews gum constantly, obnoxious, unhealthy
Inside the factory: She doesn't listen to warnings about trying the magic chewing gum. She turns into a human blueberry.
Outside the factory: She's no longer round, but her face is still blue.

Mike Teavee:
Main personality traits: addicted to television, rude, loud
Inside the factory: He doesn't listen to warnings about Willy's Television Chocolate and gets shrunk.
Outside the factory: He is very tall because he had to be stretched.

Page 203

animals	buildings/shelter	foods/drinks	things made with wood	ways of traveling	things made with flour
tarantula	lean-to	lard	lean-to	steamer	flapjacks
badger	privy	sauerkraut	steamer	oxcart	pies
dragonfly	saloon	chowder	privy		
polecat	tent	flapjacks	oxcart		
bobcat	cabin	broth	saloon		
	outhouse	pies	cabin		
		cactus juice	outhouse		

Bonus Box answer: Students' answers will vary.

ANSWER KEYS

Page 204

1. $12
2. $4
3. $6
4. $2
5. $3
6. $9
7. $18
8. $54
9. $90
10. $81
11. $252
12. $216
13. $540
14. $72
15. $108

Bonus Box answer:
apples = $24
flour = $8
eggs = $12
beans = $4
sugar = $6

Page 227

Page 1:

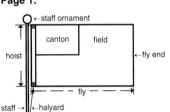

Page 2: Examples will vary.
Page 3: Examples will vary.
Page 4: Examples will vary.
Page 5: A *badge* is an emblem or a design, usually on the fly of a flag.
Page 6: A *battle streamer* is an attachment to the flag of a military unit. It names the battles or campaigns where the unit served with distinction.
Page 7: A *burgee* is a flag or pennant that ends in a swallow-tail of two points.
Page 8: A *canton* is the upper corner of a flag next to the staff where a special design appears.
Page 9: An *ensign* is a national flag flown by a naval ship.
Page 10: A *field* is the background of a flag.
Page 11: The *fly* is the free end of a flag, farthest from the staff. It also refers to the horizontal length of the flag.
Page 12: The *halyard* is a rope used to hoist and lower a flag.
Page 13: The *hoist* is the part of the flag closest to the staff. It also refers to the vertical width of a flag.
Page 14: A *pennant* is a small triangular or tapering flag.
Page 15: The *staff* is the pole a flag hangs on.

Bonus Box answer: A *fimbriation* is a narrow line separating two other colors in a flag. A *guidon* is a small flag carried at the front or right of a military unit to guide the marchers. A *standard* is a flag around which people rally. *Vexillology* is the study of flag history and symbolism.

Page 205

1. Cause (gray): Supplies have to be carted long distances.
   Effect (yellow): Prices for supplies are very high.
2. Effect (yellow): Mrs. Whipple begins to doubt she was right to bring her family west.
   Cause (gray): Butte dies.
3. Cause (gray): Amos Frogge tells the ballad of Rattlesnake Jake.
   Effect (yellow): Lucy becomes suspicious of Mr. Coogan.
4. Cause (gray): Lucy hates California and everything to do with it.
   Effect (yellow): California Morning Whipple changes her name to Lucy.
5. Effect (yellow): Lucy begins teaching school lessons to Butte.
   Cause (gray): Butte is getting too wild, according to his mother.
6. Effect (yellow): Lucy writes an honest letter to Uncle Matt, Aunt Beulah, and Cousin Batty.
   Cause (gray): Lucy's mother told her she won't be allowed to write letters anymore.
7. Cause (gray): Brother Clyde gains Amos Frogge as a church member.
   Effect (yellow): Brother Clyde decides to remain in Lucky Diggins.
8. Effect (yellow): Lucy makes Butte her partner in the pie-making business.
   Cause (gray): Lucy's pies are so popular she can't do the work alone.
9. Effect (yellow): Lucy starts a lending library.
   Cause (gray): Lucy receives a crate of books from her teacher.
10. Cause (gray): Mr. Flagg was mean to his wife and children.
    Effect (yellow): Mr. Flagg was killed, supposedly by Lizzie's mother.

Bonus Box answers: Answers will vary. Some of the effects of the gold rush included:
- People moved to California from all over the world.
- California's population increased greatly.
- Communities such as San Francisco and Sacramento became flourishing towns.
- In 1850, California had so many people that it became the 31st state in the Union.

Page 217

1. Any three of the following: Aberdeen-Angus, Brahman, Charolais, Hereford, Polled Hereford, and Simmental.
   Resource: encyclopedia, "Cattle" entry
2. 114 people
   Resource: almanac
3. Spain
   Resource: atlas (or encyclopedia)
4. Answers will vary.
   Resource: telephone book
5. Answers will vary.
   Resource: newspaper
6. Answers will vary. Possible answers include *identify, label, mark, tag,* and *trademark.*
   Resource: thesaurus
7. New Mexico, Oklahoma, Arkansas, and Louisiana
   Resource: U.S. map (atlas, encyclopedia)
8. Answers will vary.
   Resource: card/computer catalog
9. Spanish
   Resource: dictionary
10. Answers will vary.
    Resource: TV schedule

Bonus Box: Answers will vary. Possible answers include *bovine, calf, heifer, kine,* and *cattle.*

311

ANSWER KEYS

Page 265

Puzzle #1: Starting with the middle B in the top row is Miss Pickwell's advice: Books are the keys to learning. The arrows show the direction through the grid.

```
I → N   (B)  K → S
↑   ↓    ↑   ↑   ↓
N   G   O → O   A
↑   ↓        ↓   ↓
R   T ← S   E ← R
↑   ↓    ↑   ↓
A   O   Y   T → H
↑   ↓    ↑   ↓   ↓
E ← L   E ← K ← E
```

Puzzle #2: The body parts that the zookeeper named were: arm, ear, eye, gum, hip, jaw, leg, lip, rib, and toe.

Puzzle #3:

40	10	30	0	20
30	0	20	40	10
20	40	10	30	0
10	30	0	20	40
0	20	40	10	30

Puzzle #4:
1. T
2. W
3. I
4. O
5. H
6. T
7. U

DON'T LEAVE HOME WITHOUT IT!

Bonus Box answer: 4 ÷ 4 = 1 or 4/4 = 1

Page 269

160 miles

Three possible routes are shown. The return trip is shown with the dashed line.

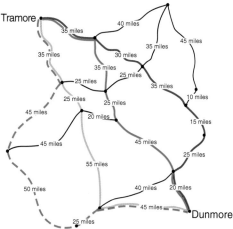

Bonus Box answer: 200 miles

Page 274

bows	a. eye**brows**	snow	k. sun**flower**
shop	b. bi**shop**	food	l. **flooded**
bell	c. em**bell**ish	sled	m. **slipped**
pine	d. s**pline**r	pies	n. sup**plies**
sing	e. dres**sing**	fire	o. **figure**ine
star	f. re**star**ant	bake	p. **blanket**
card	g. **card**inal	gift	q. ma**gnific**ent
trim	h. **triom**ph	tree	r. **treatment**
host	i. **host**al	toys	s. des**troys**
hide	j. c**hild**ren	love	t. g**loves**

Bonus Box answers: Answers will vary. Suggested words include: arch, cart, cash, cast, char, chat, hair, harm, hiss, mach, mart, mash, mass, mast, math, miss, mist, rash, rich, scam, scar, scat, sham, star, stir, this, tram, trim.

Page 268

Kount Drakula (wrong letter)
Nevada
Bangor
Charlotte
Minnesota
Bismarck
Michigan
Casper
Olympia
New Haven
San Francisco

Gwen the Ghost (silent letter)
Savannah
Massachusetts
Pittsburgh
Annapolis
Fort Wayne
Rhode Island
Lincoln
Phoenix
New Hampshire
Des Moines

Wylie the Werewolf (correct words)
Buffalo
Los Angeles
Albuquerque
Norfolk
Montpelier
Louisiana
Tulsa
Louisville
Tallahassee
Tucson

Bonus Box answers:
Montpelier, Vermont
Annapolis, Maryland
Bismarck, North Dakota
Olympia, Washington
Tallahassee, Florida
Lincoln, Nebraska
Phoenix, Arizona
Des Moines, Iowa

Page 273

1. factors of 8 = 1, 2, 4, 8
   1 + 2 + 4 + 8 = **15**

2. first two multiples of 12, after 12 = 24, 36
   24 + 36 = 60
   60 + 15 = **75**

3. first multiple of 11 = 11
   75 − 11 = **64**

4. largest multiple of 8 that is less than 100 = 96
   96 − 64 = **32**

5. factors of 6 = 1, 2, 3, 6
   1 + 2 + 3 + 6 = 12
   32 − 12 = **20**

6. factors of 11 = 1, 11
   1 x 11 = 11
   11 x 20 = **220**

7. factors of 12 = 1, 2, 3, 4, 6, 12
   1 + 2 + 3 + 4 + 6 + 12 = 28
   220 − 28 = **192**

8. largest multiple of 11 that is less than 100 = 99
   largest multiple of 12 that is less than 50 = 48
   99 − 48 = 51
   192 − 51 = **141**

9. multiples of 6 between 40 and 70 = 42, 48, 54, 60, 66
   141 + 42 = 183
   183 − 66 = **117**

10. fifth multiple of 11 = 11, 22, 33, 44, (55)
    117 + 55 = **172**

11. 172 − 6 = **166**

12. smallest factor of 12 = 1
    166 − 1 = **165**

The year of the temple battle was 165 B.C.

Bonus Box answer:
multiples of 12 between 100 and 300 = 108, 120, 132, 144, 156, 168, 180, 192, 204, 216, 228, 240, 252, 264, 276, 288
multiples of 11 between 100 and 300 = 110, 121, 132, 143, 154, 165, 176, 187, 198, 209, 220, 231, 242, 253, 264, 275, 286, 297
multiples of both 11 and 12 that are between 100 and 300 = 132, 264

ANSWER KEYS

Page 275
1. **good:** nice, useful, (excellent)
2. **smart:** stylish, (intelligent) witty
3. **bypassed:** detoured, (skipped) jumped
4. **began:** initiated, (started) created
5. **obtained:** caught, (earned) acquired
6. **good:** pleasant, helpful, (superb)
7. **foremost:** good, (main) star
8. **maintained:** (believed) conserved, serviced
9. **directed:** (led) commanded, managed
10. **acclaimed:** (famous) great, primary
11. **worked:** performed, (strived) satisfied
12. **better:** (improve) enhance, exceed
13. **bad:** evil, ill-behaved, (inferior)
14. **earned:** gained, (won) profited
15. **bars:** excludes, slows, (prevents)

Page 279
1. False—**E**	5. True—**M**	9. True—**E**	13. True—**T**
2. False—**O**	6. True—**H**	10. False—**D**	14. False—**O**
3. True—**A**	7. True—**R**	11. False—**O**	15. True—**D**
4. False—**R**	8. False—**F**	12. False—**T**	16. True—**E**

Answer to the riddle: "THE ROAD TO FREEDOM"

Bonus Box answer: Answers will vary. Suggested responses include the following:
1. Jackie Robinson played for the Brooklyn Dodgers.
2. Dr. Martin Luther King, Jr., was a minister. He led peaceful protests and dedicated his life to ending segregation in America.
4. Althea Gibson was one of the world's greatest tennis players. She was the first Black to play at Wimbledon.
8. Rosa Parks protested the way Blacks were treated on the city buses in Montgomery, Alabama. She is called "the mother of the modern civil rights movement."
10. Jesse Jackson is a civil rights activist, political leader, and Baptist minister.
11. Dr. Ronald McNair was one of seven astronauts who died when the space shuttle *Challenger* blew up in January 1986.
12. Thurgood Marshall was the first Black American to serve on the U.S. Supreme Court.
14. Mary McLeod Bethune started a college for Black teachers that later became known as Bethune-Cookman University.

Page 281
Before students color their puzzle pieces, check to make sure that they have the correct color check mark on each one.

0.5	closest to 1/2 (yellow)
0.9001	closest to 1 (blue)
0.62	closest to 1/2 (yellow)
4/100	closest to 0 (green)
0.99	closest to 1 (blue)
0.409	closest to 1/2 (yellow)
0.496	closest to 1/2 (yellow)
9,001/10,000	closest to 1 (blue)
8/10	closest to 1 (blue)
5/10	closest to 1/2 (yellow)
0.98	closest to 1 (blue)
1/1,000	closest to 0 (green)
1 9/10	greater than 1 (red)

Completed puzzle:

Page 284
1. total calories: 1,310
   minutes needed to burn those calories:
   cycling: 437
   horseback riding: 655
   tennis: 188

2. total calories: 445
   minutes needed to burn those calories:
   dancing: 75
   golf: 89
   running: 38

3. total calories: 456
   minutes needed to burn those calories:
   swimming: 51
   walking: 114
   dancing: 76

4. total calories: 640
   minutes needed to burn those calories:
   cycling: 214
   running: 54
   walking: 160

5. total calories: 1,136
   minutes needed to burn those calories:
   golf: 228
   horseback riding: 568
   swimming: 127

6. total calories: 435
   minutes needed to burn those calories:
   dancing: 73
   cycling: 145
   tennis: 63

Bonus Box answer: 770 calories (5 malted-milk eggs = 115; 1/2 chocolate bunny = 450; 5 jelly beans = 205)

Page 290
Students' designs will vary.
Design 1 has 10 red squares and 20 blue.
Design 2 has 20 red squares, 10 blue, and 10 white.
Design 3 has 24 red squares, 12 blue, 6 white, and 6 green.
Design 4 has 20 red squares, 15 blue, 15 white, and 10 green.

Bonus Box answer:

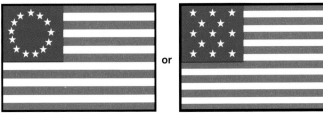

or

Index